# ADVANCES IN SPECIAL EDUCATION

*A Research Annual*

DEVELOPMENTAL PROBLEMS IN INFANCY
AND THE PRESCHOOL YEARS

*Editor:* BARBARA K. KEOGH
*Graduate School of Education*
*University of California,*
*Los Angeles*

VOLUME 5 • 1986

 JAI PRESS INC.

*Greenwich, Connecticut*                    *London, England*

# CONTENTS

# LIST OF CONTRIBUTORS

*Lucinda P. Bernheimer*

Graduate School of Education
University of California
Los Angeles

*Barbara F. Hecht*

Graduate School of Education
University of California
Los Angeles

*Sheila E. Henderson*

Institute of Education
London University

*Jane V. Hunt*

Institute of Human Development
University of California
Berkeley

*Barbara K. Keogh*

Graduate School of Education
University of California
Los Angeles

*Jeanne M. McCarthy*

Department of Special Education
University of Arizona
Tucson

*Sharon Marovitch*

Hospital for Sick Children
Toronto, Canada

*Joyce Nesker Simmons*

Hospital for Sick Children
Toronto, Canada

*Emmy E. Werner*

Department of Human Development
and Applied Behavorial Sciences
University of California
Davis

*Pamela Winton*

Frank Porter Graham Child
Development Center
University of North Carolina

# PREFACE

This is the fifth and final volume of *Advances of Special Education* under my editorship. Beginning with Volume 1 in 1980, my colleagues and I have addressed a number of interesting topics in special education: Basic Constructs, Perspective on Applications, Socialization Influences, and Documenting Program Impact. In Volume 5, we consider Developmental Problems in Infancy and the Preschool Years.

Looking back over my editorial experience, I am struck by two things. The first relates to the complexity of the content we study. It is quite true that we have come a long way in identifying and providing services to handicapped children and their families. It is also true that we have only faint understanding of the causes, developmental dynamics, and long term consequences of many handicapping conditions. Unfortunately, in many cases we are far from understanding what to do about them. This is a somewhat discouraging insight. On the other hand, the second observation which emerged from my editing stint is more positive and leaves me with some optimism about the future. This is the quality of professionals who are concerned about handicapping conditions and about special education. I refer, of course, to the many authors who have contributed to this series. Without exception, the authors have provided substance, breadth, and insight into their topics. As was hoped and expected, their perspectives often differed, but the quality of their products was uniformly high. I thank them all for their willingness to take on this writing task, and I especially thank them for their commitment to the field. It has been a pleasure to work with them all. I have come away feeling a stronger tie to old friends and a sense of having formed new friendships.

I am pleased that the *Advances in Special Education* series will continue under the new editor, Jay Gottlieb. I wish him, and the members of the JAI Press the best of futures.

Barbara K. Keogh
*Series Editor*

# THE CONCEPT OF RISK FROM A
# DEVELOPMENTAL PERSPECTIVE

Emmy E. Werner

What is this stubborn thing in man that keeps him forever picking the lock of time? . . . The odds are against him, the odds have always been against him, and he knows it, but he has never believed it. (Smith, 1954)

In their book *Lucy: The Beginnings of Humankind,* Johanson and Edey (1981) relate the tale of one of the most exciting fossil finds in human history: The discovery of the bones of some 13 hominids, men, women and children, two of them under the age of 5, who walked the earth some three million years ago. They represent a family who lived in what is today the Hadar region of Ethiopia. Speculations about the possible catastrophe that overtook them range from a sudden flash flood to a virulent epidemic.

Other families who lived after this "first" one survived famines and floods, disasters and droughts, and an unending variety of natural and man-made disas-

Advances in Special Education, Volume 5, pages 1–23.
Copyright © 1986 by JAI Press Inc.
All rights of reproduction in any form reserved.
ISBN: 0-89232-313-2

1

ters. They left their East African cradle, crossed oceans and continents, and populated the planet. The concept of risk is closely tied to their journey, and to the chances taken along the way.

The purpose of this chapter is to discuss the concept of risk from a developmental perspective and to illustrate how the definition and expression of risk changes with the social context in which children live, and with their developmental state and gender. I will first provide a brief historical and cross-cultural perspective on the concept of risk, and then present some developmental models that have influenced risk research. I will focus next on some representative studies which have (a) monitored the development of high risk children in different ecological contexts, and (b) explored protective factors which buffer the expression of risk over time. I will conclude with a brief discussion of the implications of a transactional model of human development which focuses on the shifting balance between vulnerability and resiliency that characterizes the range of developmental outcomes in children "at risk."

This chapter is *not* a definitive review of contemporary risk research with infants and young children. For that the reader may turn to the other chapters of this volume, and to a number of excellent reviews in the child development literature. Among them are two chapters in Mussen's (1983) *Manual of Child Psychology,* the chapter on "Risk Factors in Development," by C. Kopp (in Volume 2), and the chapter on "Developmental Psychopathology," by M. Rutter and N. Garmezy (in Volume 4). Both chapters review current research on biological, psychological and social factors that contribute to poor developmental outcomes.

Several special issues of the journal *Child Development* also provide an overview of current risk research that focuses on the early years of children's lives. They range from "Infants at Risk" (edited by Goldberg and Kearsley, 1983), to "Developmental Behavior Genetics," (edited by Plomin, 1983), to "Developmental Psychopathology" (edited by Cicchetti, 1984).

## A HISTORICAL PERSPECTIVE

The idea of measuring risk first took hold centuries ago in the field of maritime insurance (Gruenberg, 1981). Merchants and ship owners, in bargaining sessions, arrived at an agreement on premium payments as a hedge against the possibility of financial loss due to a disaster during dangerous ocean voyages. Such negotiations considered the odds of success or failure of a seagoing mission and the factors that were important in determining the outcome.

From these mercantile origins, the concept and measurement of risk was eventually transferred to epidemiology, the study of health and illness in human populations. In the transition from maritime insurance to epidemiology, elements of the meaning of the term "risk" were transformed:

> The impersonal hazards of financial loss became the personal hazards of loss of health
> through the onset of disease or other debilitating conditions; possibility became the statistics
> of probability . . . and danger became the predisposition for disease that arose out of biolog-
> ical factors, often in combination with adverse circumstances. (Garmezy, in press)

Risk is now defined in epidemiological textbooks as "the probability of an individual's developing a given disease or experiencing a health status change over a specified time period" (Kleinbaum, Kupper, & Morgenstern, 1982).

Epidemiology became the basic science of preventive medicine and public health, and soon after the establishment of the interdisciplinary Society for Research in Child Development (SRCD), psychologists and educators joined their colleagues in obstetrics, pediatrics, psychiatry and public health (in the 1930s) in studies of children exposed to a variety of pre-, peri- and post-natal risk factors (see Table 1).

The systematic examination of the psychological development of infants and young children exposed to such risk factors is a more recent phenomenon, dating back to the late 1950s and 1960s (Kopp & Krakow, 1983). During that period the concept of risk was modified by the adjective "developmental" and has now come to include "a wide range of biological and environmental conditions that are associated with increased probability for cognitive, social, affective and physical problems" (Kopp, 1983).

Recent textbooks in special education and reviews by developmental psychol-

*Table 1.*   Examples of Risk Factors Classified by Three Major Time Periods

| Prenatal[1] | Perinatal[2] | Postnatal[3] |
|---|---|---|
| *Genetic:* | | *Biological:* |
| Chromosomal disorders | Asphyxia | Accidents |
| Inborn errors of metabolism | Cardiopulmonary problems | Chronic disease |
| Neural tube defects | Congenital malformations | Failure to thrive |
| | Disorders of labor and delivery | Infections |
| *Environmental:* | Low birthweight (<2,500 gm) | Protein-energy malnutrition |
| Harmful drugs | Preterm birth (<37 weeks) | (PEM) |
| Maternal infections | Infections | Toxic substances |
| Metabolic disorders | Metabolic disorders | |
| Nutritional deprivation | Neonatal intracranial hemorrhage | *Psychosocial:* |
| Radiation | Neonatal medications | Family dysfunctions |
| Toxic chemicals | | Illiteracy |
| | | Parental psychopathology |
| | | Poverty |

[1]Prenatal: In some studies defined as time from conception to 7th prenatal month; in other contexts the entire prebirth period (Kopp, 1983).

[2]Perinatal: In some studies defined as the period from the 7th month of pregnancy to the 28th day of infant life. Others consider the period lasts only until the 7th day of life (Kopp, 1983).

[3]Postnatal: The period that begins after 28 days of life (Kopp, 1983).

ogists have added qualifiers to the label "developmental risk," a description they find convenient, but not always precise (Kopp & Krakow, 1983). Risk researchers now tend to agree that:

1. Risk is a comparative and relative term used to express the likelihood of current or future developmental hazard or handicap that at present is uncertain (Ramey & Trohanis, 1982, p. 8).
2. In defining the developmental risk associated with any child, the characteristics of the child must be related to the ability of the environment to regulate the development of the child toward social norms (Sameroff & Seifer, 1983, p. 1255).
3. The probability of adverse consequences is not fixed or the same across individuals, and tends to vary as a function of interactions between different (risk) factors or different environmental circumstances in which the child is placed (Pollitt, 1984, p. 13).

These caveats apply to all three types of risk research undertaken with a developmental perspective: that is, research that focuses on *predisposing* factors (e.g., studies of the offspring of mothers suffering from schizophrenia or affective disorders), research that monitors the consequences of *an adverse event* (e.g., preterm birth), and research with infants or young children *with identified problems* (e.g., Down Syndrome; protein-energy malnutrition) that asks what the broader ramifications are of such problems *in addition* to those already predictable (Goldberg & Kearsley, 1983).

## A CROSS-CULTURAL PERSPECTIVE

Four out of five of the world's half billion children under the age of five live in the developing countries of Africa, Asia, Latin America and Oceania, where infant and preschool mortality rates are reminiscent of those of nineteenth century Europe. Nowhere is the relativity of the concept of "risk" more apparent than when we contrast their "lifestyle" with that of most contemporary American children.

Among the major risk factors that affect the development of infants and young children in the developing world are protein-energy malnutrition (PEM), coupled with anemia and Vitamin A deficiency; diarrhea; and infectious diseases such as influenza, measles and whooping cough. Among major risk factors on the community and family level in the Third World are illiteracy rates of more than 30% of the population and low birth weight (LBW) rates of more than 20%; infant mortality rates of more than 120 per 1,000 live births, as well as large family size and high birth order (International Union of Nutritional Sciences, Expert Committee, 1977; Pollitt, 1984).

Below the age of 10, both the *mortality* rates and the *morbidity* rates (i.e., rates of physical and mental handicaps) are higher for girls than for boys in many developing countries because of a traditional preference for male infants. This is the reverse of trends observed in the industrialized countries of Europe and North America (Werner, 1979).

The major risk factors that affect children's physical, cognitive and social develpoment in Third World countries are very similar to those reported in the United States and Europe 100 years ago. For the most part, changes in childhood mortality and morbidity since the turn of the century in the industrialized world were accompanied by a marked decline in *postnatal* causes of central nervous system (CNS) impairments, sensory disorders, paralysis and mental retardation. Since the late 1950s, there has also been a diminuation of *perinatal* mortality and morbidity (Kopp, 1983).

Improvements in sanitation, nutritional status, medical and educational technology, delivery of health care, and family planning have all contributed to these changes. Today the industrialized countries export this technology to the less developed countries, sometimes with unforeseen and "risky" consequences (i.e., the introduction of bottle feeding with contaminated water, which has increased the risk of marasmus among infants of the Third World).

Because of major technological advances in expertise and equipment, risk research in North America and in many European countries is currently paying increased attention to *genetic* and *prenatal* risk factors, and to the LBW survivors of neonatal intensive care (see Chapter 2). Attention to psychosocial *postnatal* risk factors, such as family dysfunctions (i.e., child abuse, divorce) has increased as well, paralleling the rapid rate of social change experienced here and abroad (Garbarino & Ebata, 1983; Wallerstein & Kelly, 1980). Research concerned with the impact of *poverty* on the development of young children—*the* major risk factor around the world (which affects one out of every five children in the United States today) waxes and wanes with the political climate in which behavioral scientists work.

Improvement in technology in the industrialized world has not only led to the survival of many "high risk" children who would have died in infancy, or shortly thereafter, had they been born in the developing world, but also to the creation of new and potent risk factors for young children. Among them are car accidents (the leading cause of death and injury for children between the ages of 1 and 15 in the United States today), harmful drugs, radiation, and toxic poisoning.

The definition and expression of "risk" changes not only with the technology and expertise available to a given culture to ensure the survival of infants and young children, but also with the demands made on each new generation for education and the acquisition of skills for economic maintenance. Less than half of the children in the developing countries (most of them boys) who enter school today will complete the elementary grades. When they leave school, most will be expected to contribute to the subsistence economy of their families, and will work in low-level skill jobs in agriculture. In contrast, most children in the United States today are expected to complete high school (and some additional training), and to compete for jobs that require an ever increasing level of literacy and numeracy as well as the ability to adapt rapidly to changing job markets.

The anthropologist LeVine (1983) argues that parental investment strategies in children will change with the shift from high-fertility agrarian societies to low-fertility, urban-industrial societies. In the former, parental resources are concentrated on maximizing child survival by increasing fertility, reducing mortality, and training children to comply with parental wishes, so that they can begin to contribute to family production in childhood and assist their aged parents in adulthood.

Risk factors recognized and attended to in such a cultural context will be of a different order (and will concern survival and reproduction) than those in low-fertility industrialized societies where parental investment strategies concentrate on the prolonged development and education of fewer children at a cost that is continuously growing. The *qualitative* aspect of development replaces the *number* of offspring as parental goal in industrialized societies. Parental expectations for their offspring's future are greater than in traditional societies and with it the risk of failure (i.e., of not being able to measure up to criteria for economic success).

These differential parental investment strategies which have been observed *across cultures* (e.g., in Africa and Asia), appear to be also at work among various *subcultures* in the United States and may result in differences in parental awareness of, and concern with, risk factors in their young children. Several American investigators have reported such subcultural differences in maternal perceptions of "distress" in the cries of high risk infants, in parental tolerance of young children with "difficult" temperaments, and in incidences of "child maltreatment" (Garbarino & Ebata, 1983; Thomas & Chess, 1977; Zeskind, 1983).

Well meant intervention and special education programs with minority children may not succeed if such subcultural differences in parental investment strategies and expectations are overlooked (Ogbu, 1974).

## A DEVELOPMENTAL PERSPECTIVE

Kopp (1983) has summarized what is presently known about the early developmental course and the trends in developmental outcomes for some 36 major risk factors which have been the focus of extensive research during the past decade (pp. 1088–1094).

Among these risk factors only a few prenatal (genetic) factors with very low incidence rates (ranging from $.5/1000$ to $1/120,000$) have, at present, fairly certain negative developmental outcomes (i.e. they result either in death in early childhood or severe mental retardation). Among these are several inborn errors of metabolism, such as Tay-Sachs disease and the Hurler syndrome, a neural tube defect (anencephaly) and several chromosomal disorders (Trisomy 13, 18, and the "cri du chat" syndrome), all of which lead to severe CNS dysfunctions.

All other risk factors listed, among them the *perinatal* and *postnatal* biological risk factors with the highest incidence rates, such as preterm births (7.4% of liveborn), asphyxia (20% of neonates) and severe nutritional deficiencies, which affect between 20–40% children below the age of five in developing countries, have *variable* developmental outcomes.

Longitudinal studies that have followed infants and young children exposed to such risk factors over extended periods of time have consistently demonstrated that (a) the effects of many biological risk factors (e.g., disorders of labor and delivery, preterm birth) diminish or disappear with the passage of time, and that (b) the developmental outcome of virtually every risk condition ever studied in infants and young children depends on the quality of the caregiving environment (Kopp & Krakow, 1983).

When the first major prospective studies of high risk infants were launched in the mid and late 1950s, many developmental psychologists, child psychiatrists and allied health professionals adhered to a *main effect* model of child development. Its central premise was that constitution and envionment exert influences on development which are independent of each other. Thus, most prospective studies of high risk infants and preschool children focused selectively on either biological risks (such as anoxia or LBW) *or* adverse environmental conditions (such as chronic poverty). As time went by, long range predictions based on such unilateral assessments proved to be disappointing.

For example, in our longitudinal study of the short and long term consequences of pre-perinatal stress in a multi-ethnic birth cohort on the island of Kauai it became soon clear that to predict the probabilities of developmental outcomes in high risk children with any degree of certainty we had to consider *both* the infant's constitutional make up *and* the quality of the caregiving environment (Werner, Bierman, & French, 1971; Werner & Smith, 1977, 1982). As early as 20 months, these effects were seen in several ways: Middle class babies with the most severe perinatal complications had mean scores on (the Cattell) infant tests comparable to those of poor children *without* any complications of labor and delivery. The children with the most severe developmental retardation were those exposed to *both* poverty *and* severe perinatal stress, or to perinatal difficulties *and* family instability.

Perinatal complications were consistently related to later impairment of physical and psychological development (at ages 10 and 18) *only* when combined with persistently poor environmental circumstances (i.e., chronic poverty, family instability or maternal mental health problems). Children who were raised in more affluent homes, with an intact family and a well educated mother, showed few, if any, lasting negative effects from reproductive stress, unless there was severe CNS impairment.

Other investigators, especially those affiliated with the largest of the prospective studies of biological risk factors, the Collaborative Perinatal Project (NCPP), sponsored by the National Institute of Health (Broman, Nicholas, & Kennedy, 1975), and the St. Louis Baby Study (Jordan, 1976), came to similar conclusions. So did investigators in developing countries who studied the impact of nutritional deficiencies on the physical, cognitive and social development of young children (Klein, 1979). Thus risk researchers, both in the United States and abroad, began to turn in the late 1960s and early 1970s to an *interactional* model of human development.

During the past decade, since the mid and late 1970s, there has emerged an added perspective to risk research: A shift from a static linear model of interaction to a dynamic transactional model (Sameroff & Chandler, 1975) that focuses on the reciprocal influences of child and caregiving environment. This model of human development has roots in the Piagetian tradition and in General Systems Theory (Bertalanffy, 1968; Sameroff, 1982).

From this vantage point, children's responses are more than a simple reaction to their environment. Instead, they are actively engaged in an attempt to organize and structure their world, and to seek their niche in it. It is the *transactions* between the constitutional characteristics of the child and the quality of the caregiving environment *across time* that determine the quality of the outcome.

Given the genetically programmed self-organizing and self-righting tendencies of the human organism (Scarr & McCartney, 1983; Waddington, 1966), two possibilities have been suggested that would produce deviant development: The first possibility is an insult to the organism's integrative ability which prevents the functioning of its self-righting ability. The second possibility is that adverse environmental forces present *throughout* the child's *development* prevent the normal integration that would occur in a more favorable setting (Sameroff & Chandler, 1975).

Hence, there is now a growing awareness of the importance of monitoring the development of high risk children within the various social contexts in which they grow up, taking account of the changing demands made on them within a variety of settings, such as the hospital, the home, the neighborhood, the (pre) school and the community at large.

## AN ECOLOGICAL PERSPECTIVE

In practice, only a limited number of these child-setting variations have been studied, but several useful models of human development with an ecological perspective have appeared in the literature since 1975. They offer a more systematic and integrated approach to the study of the development of high risk children than the accumulation of scores on infant and preschool tests (with limited predictive validity) which has characterized much of the ''risk research'' in child development and special education in the past.

Perhaps best known among psychologists and educators is Bronfenbrenner's (1979) model which views the development of the individual child within the context of a series of concentric circles, each embedded within the next, like a set of Russian dolls. The model focuses on the accommodations that occur between the developing individual and the changing properties of the settings in which he or she lives, or with which he or she comes into contact. The settings are described in terms of *microsystems* (such as home or classroom), *mesosystems* (interrelations between two or more settings in which the person participates, such as playground and classroom), *exosystems* (settings that indirectly affect the individual, such as the transportation system between home and school), and *macrosystems* (the institutional patterns and belief systems of which the other systems are concrete manifestations, for example the laws which govern children's access to education).

Another ''systems'' approach that has stimulated much cross-cultural research is the psycho-cultural model proposed by John and Beatrice Whiting, an anthropologist/psychologist team at Harvard University. Their model divides the environmental determinants of psycho-social development into two parts: (1) The *maintenance system* which is the economic, legal, socio-political, family and household structure that assures survival of a group, in a particular ecological niche, at a particular point in human history; and (2) the *child's learning environment* which shapes the child's constitutional dispositions in accordance with the adaptive needs of the group and within the constraints set by the maintenance system.

Among key variables in the child's learning environment on which the Whitings (1975) and their associates have focused attention and which should be of interest to risk researchers are: The relative salience of the mother and father as socializing agents; the role that siblings and elders play as alternate caregivers; the settings occupied by the child; the tasks assigned to him; the disciplinary techniques used; the frequency and consistency of rewards and punishment, and the stresses to which young children are exposed.

John Ogbu (1981), a Nigerian anthropologist, who teaches at the University of California, Berkeley, has developed a cultural/ecological model of the origins of human competence that is particularly useful for the study of minority cultures in the United States (and of subcultures of the handicapped as well). In it he presents a number of key factors that need to be considered in order to obtain an accurate view of the competencies prevalent in such a population, of their origins, and of their relationship to the socialization process. Among them is the population's knowledge of and access to available resources, their subsistence strategies, the dominant adult role models and social organizations, and the ''native'' theories of success and childrearing that influence the socialization process and that result in child competencies which are adaptive survival strategies. Ogbu challenges child development researchers to study minority child development from such a cultural/ecological perspective rather than to automatically consider minority children and their families to be at "high risk."

The empirical and clinical validation of such ecological models in risk research and their application in intervention programs for young children remains a challenge for the future. But already an increasing number of studies of high risk infants and preschoolers are paying attention to "context" variables that influence child/caregiver interactions and developmental outcomes (see Chapters 8 and 9). They range from research on the impact of a macrosystem variable—Public Law 94–152, the Education for All Handicapped Children Act—and the effects of mainstreaming severely handicapped young children (Blacher, in press; Garmezy, Masten, & Tellegren, 1984) to the examination of the cross-cultural and ecological correlates of child abuse (Garbarino, 1976; Garbarino & Ebata, 1983; Giovannoni & Becerra, 1979).

Researchers have also documented behavioral differences in maternal interactions with preterm (and term) infants that vary as a function of social status, parental age and cultural background (Field, 1980; Field & Widmayer, 1981), and have demonstrated the differential impact of social status and parental mental health on the development of the offspring of psychotic mothers (Sameroff & Seifer, 1983).

A number of investigators have found significant differences in the quality of caregiving extended to high risk children (i.e., preterm, perinatally stressed, or with congenital defects) that are related to household structure and composition (i.e., family size, presence or absence of father, sibling, grandparents), and to levels of maternal education and stress (Bee et al., 1982; Cohen & Beckwith, 1977; O'Doughtery, Wright, Garmezy, Loewenson, & Torres, 1983; Weinraub & Wolf, 1983; Werner, 1984; Werner & Smith, 1982).

There has also been an increasing awareness of the importance of socio-cultural context in the design and evaluation of early intervention programs for high risk infants and children. Evaluations of early childhood education programs for the poor and of biological and psycho-social intervention programs for preterm infants have begun to pay attention to cultural differences in settings, expectations and outcomes (Lazar, Darlington, Murray, Royce, & Snipper, 1982; Zeskind & Ramey, 1981). Ramey, Zeskind and Hunter (1981) have provided a generalized model for evaluating such intervention programs in their environmental context.

Prospective studies of young children in the Third World have identified variations in the child's family environment that may substantially increase or reduce the impact of community based intervention programs on high risk infants and preschoolers. Ongoing longitudinal studies of nutritional and educational supplementation programs in Latin America have incorporated such context variables in their design and evaluation, and developmental psychologists and special educators from the Northern Hemisphere can profit from their shared experiences (Balderston, Wilson, Freire, & Simonsen, 1981; Super, Clement, Vuori, Christiansen, Mora, & Herrera, 1981; Townsend, Klein, Irwin, Owens, Yarborough, & Engle, 1982).

So far, risk research with an ecological perspective has tended to focus on *microsystems,* such as the family (see Chapter 8) or school systems (Ogbu, 1974), and hospitals (Bluebond-Langner, 1980). Studies that look at the links between *different* settings that contain or impinge on high risk children and their families are quite rare (Blacher, in press; Zesking & Ramey, 1981), and rarer still are those that take into account the impact of the *macrosystem* on the development of high risk children (Balderston et al., 1981; Greene, 1977).

On balance, the "transactional" or "systems" approach to risk research has proven to be useful, since it has moved investigators and program planners to go beyond a single event or risk factor (such as preterm birth) to explore the multiple factors that mediate developmental outcomes, each enhancing the effects of the other (Kopp, 1983).

What we have learned so far is that the explanatory and predictive power of the constitutional, familial and socio-cultural variables which are the ingredients of a transactional model of human development will *vary* with the setting of the study, the base rate of the risk factors in the population under study, with the developmental outcomes that are under consideration, and with the age and gender of the children exposed to such risk(s).

The task for risk research in the future is to elucidate "the complexity of the relationships between a dynamically organized child and a dynamically organized context" (Sameroff & Seifer, 1983). In that process we need to take a closer look at protective factors in the lives of young children which buffer the expression of risk factors and foster outcomes marked by patterns of adaptation and competence.

# RISK AND RESILIENCY: THE SEARCH FOR PROTECTIVE FACTORS

In the third volume of the series *Primary Prevention of Psychopathology,* the British child psychiatrist Michael Rutter wrote:

> There is a regrettable tendency to focus gloomily on the ills of mankind and on all that can and does go wrong. It is quite exceptional for anyone to study the development of those . . . individuals who overcome adversity, who survive stress and who rise above disadvantage. It

is equally unusual to consider the factors that provide support, protection and amelioration. (1979, p. 49)

As a number of prospective studies of high risk infants and preschool children are "coming of age" in the 1980s, we can begin to examine not only the differential course of young children exposed to a variety of risk factors and of low risk comparison groups, but also the development of high risk children who *did* and *did not* ultimately develop a disorder. The understanding of factors that pull children *toward* or *away* from increased risk at different developmental stages in childhood and adolescence thus gives us valuable information about the resiliency as well as the vulnerability of young children, and should aid our efforts at primary prevention (Sroufe & Rutter, 1984).

Psychiatrists have long noted that even in the most terrible homes, beset with handicaps, and exposed to parental mental illness, some children appear to develop stable, healthy personalities, and to display a remarkable degree of resiliency (Anthony, 1974; Bleuler, 1978; Kauffman, Grunebaum, Cohler, & Gamer, 1979; Rutter, Maughan, Mortimore, & Ouston, 1979). Psychologists and educators have found children with the ability to "recover from or adjust to misfortune or sustained life stresses" in ghettos and barrios and among minority groups who were exposed to poverty, discrimination and political persecution (Clark, 1983; Coles, 1967, 1972, 1973, 1978; Gandara, 1982; Garmezy, 1983; Moskovitz, 1983).

Until recently, most of our knowledge about such resilient individuals had been based on clinical and retrospective accounts, but we now have corroborative evidence from a handful of longitudinal studies which have followed the same group of children from infancy or the preschool years through adolescence to the threshold of adulthood (Block, 1981; Chess & Thomas, 1984; Murphy & Moriarty, 1976; Watt, Anthony, Wynne, & Rolf, 1984; Werner & Smith, 1982).

These studies were conducted in different ecological settings, ranging from metropolitan areas on the East and West Coast to midwestern suburbs, to a small rural island in Hawaii, and included children from different ethnic groups. All have discovered a significant proportion of youngsters who demonstrated unusual psychological strengths, in spite of a history of severe and/or prolonged psychological stress and exposure to a variety of risk factors that ranged from parental psychosis to severe perinatal stress to chronic poverty.

The personal competencies of these children and some (unexpected) sources of support in the caregiving environment either compensated for, challenged or protected them against the effects of risks and stressful life events (Garmezy, Masten, & Tellegen, 1984). Some researchers have called these children "invulnerable" (Anthony, 1974), others consider them to be "stress resistant" (Garmezy et al., 1984), still others refer to them as "superkids" (Kauffman et al., 1979). In our longitudinal study on the island of Kauai, we found them to be "vulnerable, but invincible" (Werner & Smith, 1982).

*A Longitudinal Study of Resilient Children and Youth*

Our study group consisted of 698 children of Oriental and Polynesian descent, most of whom were the descendants of immigrants who had left the poverty of their Asian homelands to work for the sugar and pineapple plantations in Hawaii. The majority of the fathers were semi or unskilled laborers, and most mothers had not graduated from high school.

An interdisciplinary team of local and mainland physicians, public health nurses, social workers and psychologists followed the development of this multi-racial cohort of children from the prenatal period to the threshold of adulthood— at birth, ages 1, 2, 10 and 18 years. Data were collected over the years from medical, educational and social service agencies as well as from the police and family court. We also conducted home observations during pregnancy, the postpartum period and at age 1; pediatric and psychological examinations in early and middle childhood; parent and teacher interviews in middle childhood; and administered a wide range of aptitude, achievement and personality tests in the elementary grades and in high school. We interviewed high risk youth and controls (matched by sex, socioeconomic status and ethnicity) at age 18, and followed two subsamples (the offspring of psychotic parents and teenage mothers) to age 25. A follow-up of the cohort at age 30 began in 1985.

The majority of the children and youth in this cohort were exposed to little risk at birth, grew up in supportive caregiving environments, led lives that were not unusually stressful and coped successfully with the developmental tasks of childhood and adolescence. But approximately one out of three of this cohort were high risk children who grew up in chronic poverty; had been exposed to perinatal complications and/or suffered from congenital defects; were reared by mothers with little formal education ($\leq$ 8 grades), and lived in families characterized by serious instability, discord or parental mental illness.

Where four or more of such risk factors were present *before the age of 2,* three quarters of the children developed either serious learning or behavior problems by age 10, or had delinquency records and/or serious mental health problems by age 18. But one out of four escaped the ill effects of such multiple risks and developed into stable, mature and competent young adults who "worked well, played well, loved well, and expected well."[1]

*Coping Patterns and Sources of Support among Resilient Children and Youth*

Looking back over the lives of these resilient youth ($N = 72$) we contrasted their behavior characteristics and caregiving environment with that of the other high risk children in the cohort who developed either serious coping problems by age 10 ($N = 90$) or by age 18 ($N = 92$).

A number of constitutional, ecological and interpersonal variables contributed over time to the divergent paths taken by the resilient children and their more vulnerable peers. A significantly higher proportion of the resilient children were first-born. Although rates of perinatal stress and low birth weight were above the norm in this group, the resilient children succumbed to fewer childhood illnesses and recuperated more quickly than their high risk peers who developed serious coping problems.

Their mothers perceived them to be "active," "affectionate," "cuddly," "good natured," and "easy to deal with" when they were infants. Because they appeared more energetic and had more attractive features and temperaments, the resilient children were also more successful at eliciting the attention of care-givers, be they parents, grandparents or older siblings.

As toddlers, the resilient children met the world on their own terms. The pediatricians and psychologists, who examined them independently, commented on their pronounced autonomy and positive social orientation, and the develop-mental exams at age 2 showed advanced self-help skills and age-appropriate sensori-motor development for most.

In middle childhood, the resilient boys and girls possessed adequate problem-solving and communication skills, and although not especially gifted, used what-ever skills they had effectively. Throughout childhood and adolescence, they displayed a healthy androgyny, a blend of *both* "masculine" and "feminine" interests, and engaged in activities and hobbies that were not narrowly sex-typed.

In late adolescence, the resilient youth had a more internal locus of control, a more positive self-concept and a more nurturant, responsible and achievement oriented attitude toward life than their high risk peers who had developed serious coping problems. They were satisfied with their past accomplishments in school and their relationships with their friends, optimistic about their future and ex-pressed a desire to improve themselves.

Among key factors in the caregiving environment that appeared to contribute to the resiliency and stress resistance of these high risk children were: the age of the opposite-sex parent (younger mothers for resilient M; older fathers for re-silient F); the number of children in the family (four or less); the spacing between the index child and the next born sibling (more than 2 years); the number and type of alternate caretakers available (father, grandparents, older siblings); the workload of the mother (including steady employment outside of the household); the amount of attention given to the child by the primary caretaker(s) in infancy; the availability of a sibling as caretaker or confidant in childhood; structure and rules in the household in adolescence; and the presence of an informal multi-generational network of kin and friends in adolescence.

The families of these resilient children were poor by material standards, but there was a characteristic strong bond between the infant and a primary caretaker (*not* necessarily the mother) during the first year of life. The physical robustness of the resilient children, their high activity level and their social responsiveness were recognized and responded to by the caregivers, and elicited a great deal of attention. There was little prolonged separation of the infants from their mothers and no prolonged bond disruption during the first year of life. The strong attachment that resulted appears to have been a secure base for the development of the advanced self-help skills and autonomy noted among these children in the second year of life.

Though many of the mothers worked for extended periods of time and were major contributors to family subsistence, they had support from stable alternate caregivers to whom the children became attached. Most resilient children grew up in multi-age households that included members of the grandparent generation.

As older siblings departed from the household, resilient girls took over responsibility for the care of younger siblings. The employment of the mother and the need for sibling caretaking seems to have contributed to the greater autonomy and sense of responsibility of the resilient girls, especially in households where the father was dead or permanently absent. Their competence was enhanced by a strong bond between the daughter and the other females in the family—sometimes across three generations (mothers, grandmothers, older sisters, and aunts).

Resilient boys, in turn, were often first-born sons, lived in smaller families, and did not have to share their parents' attention with many additional children during the first decade of life. There were some males in their family who could serve as models for identification (fathers, grandfathers, or uncles). There was structure and rules in the household, but space to explore and little physical crowding. Last, but not least, there existed an informal multi-age network of kin, peers and elders who shared similar values and beliefs, and to whom the resilient youth turned for counsel and support in times of crises and major role transitions.

### Protective Factors vs. Absence of Risk Factors

In an additional analysis we attempted to separate the factors that led to healthier developmental outcomes, *both* in the presence and absence of risk conditions, from those that *only* had a positive impact in the presence of risk factors, but *no* impact when the risk factors were absent.

We divided the children from the 1955 birth cohort into four groups: Groups 1 and 2 consisted of middle class and lower class children who had experienced one or several risk factors that had been predictive of poor developmental outcomes (e.g., family dysfunctions, handicaps, parental mental illness, etc.). Groups 3 and 4 consisted of middle and lower class children respectively who had not been exposed to such risk factors or serious chronic life stresses. In each of the four groups we examined the variables that differentiated children with positive developmental outcomes from those with negative developmental outcomes at ages 10 and 18.

Both, in the presence and absence of risk conditions, the chances for a positive developmental outcome for children in this birth cohort were greater if they were reared by mothers who had more education (i.e., graduated from high school); if their temperamental characteristics elicited positive responses from their caregivers; if they received plenty of attention from their primary caregivers during the first year of life; and if they had age-appropriate perceptual-motor, communication and reasoning skills at ages 2 and 10 years.

Our data analysis identified additional protective factors that were not found to discriminate between positive and negative developmental outcomes for middle-class children who had not been exposed to major risk factors at birth, and whose lives were relatively free of stress, but that were very important in the lives of children who were growing up in poverty and who were subject to multiple risk factors.

Among such ameliorative factors in the child were: Autonomy and self-help skills, a positive social orientation and a positive self-concept. Among protective factors in the caregiving environment for both sexes were positive parent/child relationships observed during the first 2 years, and emotional support provided by other family members (siblings, grandparents) in early and middle childhood.

For boys, being a first-born son was an important protective factor; for girls, it was the role model of a mother who was gainfully employed. For both sexes, the cumulative number of stressful life events discriminated significantly between positive and negative developmental outcomes.

As the number of risk factors and stressful life events increased, more protective factors in the children and their caregiving environment were needed to counterbalance the negative aspects in their lives and to insure a positive developmental outcome. The largest number of protective factors was found among the resilient boys and girls who grew up in chronic poverty and were exposed to multiple risks, but who managed to cope well in both childhood and adolescence.

Among the key factors that they had in common with the ''stress resistant'' children studied by other investigators (Garmezy, 1983; Pines, 1984) were: (1) An active, evocative approach toward solving their developmental tasks, enabling them to negotiate successfully an abundance of emotionally hazardous experiences; (2) the ability, from infancy on, to gain other people's positive attention, and to recruit ''surrogate parents'' when necessary; (3) a tendency to perceive and interpret their experiences constructively, even if they caused pain and suffering, and (4) a strong ''sense of coherence,'' a belief that their lives had meaning (Antonovsky, 1979; O'Connell-Higgins, 1983).

## The Shifting Balance Between Vulnerability and Resiliency

In Figure 1 we show some of the reciprocal interactions between major risk factors at birth, and some of the most common stressful life events encountered in childhood and adolescence, which *increased* the *vulnerability* of the high risk children we studied, and the protective factors within the youngsters and their caregiving environment which *increased* their *stress resistance*.

It is the balance between risk factors, stressful life events and protective factors within the child and his caregiving environment that appears to account

*Major Risk Factors* (at birth)
Chronic poverty
Mother with little education
Moderate-severe perinatal complications
Developmental delays or irregularities
Genetic abnormalities
Parental psychopathology
↓
VULNERABILITY

*Major Sources of Stress* ← → *Major Sources of Support*

*In Childhood
and Adolescence*

Prolonged separation from pri-
mary caretaker during first
year of life
Birth of younger sib within
two years after child's
Serious or repeated childhood
illnesses
Parental illness
Maternal mental illness
Sib with handicap or learning
or behavior problem
Chronic family discord
Father absent

Loss of job or sporadic em-
ployment of parent(s)
Change of residence
Change of schools
Divorce of parents
Remarriage and entry of step-
parent into household
Departure or death of older
sib or close friend
Foster home placement
(for F: teenage pregnancy)

*Protective Factors
Within the Child*

Birth order (first) CNS
integrity
High activity level
Good-natured: affectionate
disposition
Responsive to people
Free of distressing habits
Positive social orientation
Autonomy
Advanced self-help skills
Age-appropriate sensorimotor
and perceptual skills
Adequate communication
skills
Ability to focus attention and
control impulses
Special interests and hobbies
Positive self-concept
Internal Locus of Control
Desire to improve self

*Caregiving Environment*

Four or fewer children spaced
more than two years apart
Much attention paid to infant
during first year
Positive parent-child relationship in early childhood
Additional caretakers besides
mother
Care by siblings and grandparents
Mother has some steady employment outside the household

Availability of kin and neighbors for emotional support
Structure and rules in household
Shared values—a sense of
coherence
Close peer friends
Availability of counsel by
teachers and/or ministers
Access to special services
(health, education, social
services)

RANGE OF PROBABLE DEVELOPMENTAL OUTCOMES
Adaptive | Maladaptive

| Fewer | Risk Factors<br>Stressful Events | } : { | More | Risk Factors<br>Stressful events |
| More | Protective factors in child<br>in caregiving environment | } : { | Fewer | Protective factors in child<br>in caregiving environment |

*Source:* Werner & Smith, 1982, pp. 134–135. Reprinted by permission of McGraw Hill.

*Figure 1.* Model of Interrelations between Risk, Stress, Sources of Support,
and Coping (based on data from the Kauai Longitudinal Study)

17

for the range of developmental outcomes one observes when one follows high risk infants and preschoolers over extended periods of time.

The relative contribution of risk factors, stressful life events and protective factors within the child and his or her caregiving environment appear to change not only with the stages of the life cycle, but also with the sex of the child and the cultural context in which he or she grows up.

In our study, constitutional factors (the child's temperament and health) appeared to pull their greatest weight in infancy and early childhood; ecological factors (such as household structure and composition) and cognitive skills gained in importance in middle childhood, and intrapersonal factors (self-esteem) in adolescence, judging from the weight assigned to these variables in discriminant function analyses. Boys appeared to be more vulnerable at birth and in the first decade of life; girls were more vulnerable in adolescence.

But to the extent that the boys and girls in this study were able to elicit predominantly positive responses from their environment, they were found to be stress-resistant at each stage of their life cycle, even if they suffered from a congenital handicap, or lived in conditions of chronic poverty, or in a home with a psychotic parent. To the extent that they elicited negative responses from their environment, they were found to be vulnerable.

In sum: Optimal adaptive development appears to be characterized by a balance between the power of the person and the power of the (social and physical) context in which he or she lives (Wertheim, 1978). Intervention on behalf of children may thus be conceived as an attempt to restore this balance, either by *decreasing* a child's exposure to risk factors or stressful life events, or by *increasing* the number of protective factors that one can draw upon within oneself or one's caregiving environment.

# CONCLUSIONS

Risk factors are not black boxes into which one fits children to be neatly labeled and safely stored away. They are probability statements, the odds of a gamble whose stakes change with time and place.

Research has demonstrated that discontinuities in problem development are the rule rather than the exception, unless a child has suffered serious CNS damage or is continuously exposed to adverse caregiving environments.

The predictive validity of early risk indicators will vary with the stage of the life cycle at which the original assessments were made, with the developmental systems that are assessed, and with individual variations in the responses of children to the changing context of their caregiving environments.

Both risk research and intervention programs need to pay more attention to environmental context variables that mediate the expression of potentially harmful biological and psychosocial events over time. The introduction of a transactional perspective to risk research requires also a more careful conceptualization of the relationship between risk factors and protective factors, and of the shifting balance between vulnerability and resiliency that characterizes the range of developmental options in "high risk" children.

Such an approach calls for the application of statistical techniques (both in research and program evaluation) that move away from unidirectional linear assumptions about the relationship between risk and outcome, to design and analyses that capture the reciprocal nature of the interaction between the developing child and the changing context in which he or she lives.

It will also require the merging of two approaches to assessment and intervention that have seldom met (except in recent cross-cultural studies of cognition), that is, the sophistication of the clinician who sensitively monitors the behavior of the child, and that of the ethnographer who carefully observes the world in which the child lives. The last decade has seen great strides in the development of highly refined instruments that capture the behavior of neonates and infants. What we need in the future are more sophisticated assessments of their environments (like those rendered by gifted anthropologists), *and* novel ways to change these environments, so that the impact of risk factors can be attenuated and children's competencies can be enhanced.

For the identification and assessment of risk factors in young children "makes sense" *only* if it plugs into practical intervention programs, and there is a periodic follow-up to determine the efficacy of education, rehabilitation or treatment. Such efforts are ultimately based on the faith that the odds *can* be changed, if not for every vulnerable child, at least for many; if not all the time, at least some of the time; if not everywhere, at least in some places. It is a task that requires *both* interdisciplinary and international cooperation.

## NOTE

1. We are aware that the maximum period for mental breakdown is still ahead of them. This dilemma we share with others who have ventured into prospective studies of the invulnerable offspring of psychotic parents (Anthony, 1974; Watt et al., 1984).

## REFERENCES

Anthony, E. J. (1974). The syndrome of the psychologically invulnerable child. In E. J. Anthony & C. Koupernik (Eds.), *The child in his family*, Vol. III, *Children at psychiatric risk* (pp. 106–109; 529–544). New York: Wiley.

Antonovsky, A. (1979). *Health, stress and coping: New perspectives on mental and physical well-being*. San Francisco: Jossey-Bass.

Balderston, J. B., Wilson, A. B., Freire, M. E., & Simonen, M. S. (1981). *Malnourished children of the rural poor*. Boston: Auburn House.

Bee, H. L., Barnard, K. E., Eyres, S. J., Gray, C. A., Hammond, M. A., Spitz, A. L., Snyder, C., & Clark, B. (1982). Prediction of IQ and language skills from perinatal status, child performance, family characteristics and mother-infant interactions. *Child Development, 53,* 1134–1156.

Bertalanffy, L. von (1968). *General systems theory.* New York: Braziller.

Blacher, J. (1984). A dynamic perspective on the impact of a severely handicapped child on the family. In J. Blacher (Ed.), *Severely handicapped young children and their families.* New York: Academic Press.

Bleuler, M. (1978). *The schizophrenic disorders: Long-term patient and family studies.* New Haven: Yale University Press.

Block, J. (1981). Growing up vulnerable and growing up resistant: Preschool personality, preadolescent personality and intervening family stresses. In C. D. Moore (Ed.), *Adolescence and stress.* (DHHS Publication No. ADM 81-1098, pp. 123–129). Washington, DC: U.S. Government Printing Office.

Bluebond-Langner, M. (1980). *The private world of dying children.* Princeton, NJ: Princeton University Press.

Broman, S. H., Nicholas, P. L., & Kennedy, W. A. (1975). *Preschool IQ: Prenatal and early developmental correlates.* Hillsdale, NJ: Erlbaum.

Bronfenbrenner, U. (1979). *The ecology of human development.* Cambridge, MA: Harvard University Press.

Chess, S., & Thomas, A. (1984). *Origins and evolution of behavior disorders from infancy to early adult life.* New York: Brunner/Mazel.

Cicchetii, D. (Ed.). (1984). Developmental psychopathology. (Special Issue). *Child Development, 55* (1).

Clark, R. M. (1983). *Family life and school achievement: Why poor black children succeed or fail.* Chicago: University of Chicago Press.

Cohen, S. E., & Beckwith, L. (1977). Caregiving behaviors and early cognitive development as related to ordinal position in preterm infants. *Child Development, 48,* 152–157.

Coles, R. (1967). *Children of crisis.* Vol. I: *A study of courage and fear.* Boston: Little, Brown & Co.

Coles, R. (1972). *Children of crisis.* Vol. II: *Migrants, sharecroppers, mountaineers.* Boston: Little, Brown & Co.

Coles, R. (1973). *Children of crisis.* Vol. III: *The South goes North.* Boston: Little, Brown & Co.

Coles, R. (1978). *Children of crisis.* Vol. IV: *Eskimo, Chicanos, Indians.* Boston: Little, Brown & Co.

Field, T. M. (1980). Interaction of preterm and term infants with their lower and middle class teenage and adult mothers. In T. M. Field, S. Goldberg, D. Stern, & A. M. Sostek (Eds.), *High risk infants and children: Adult and peer interactions* (pp. 113–132). New York: Academic Press.

Field, T. M., & Widmayer, S. M. (1981). Mother-infant interactions among lower SES Black, Cuban, Puerto Rican and South American immigrants. In T. M. Field, A. M. Sostek, P. Vietze, & P. H. Leiderman (Eds.), *Culture and early interactions* (pp. 41–62). Hillsdale, NJ: Erlbaum.

Gandara, P. (1982). Passing through the eye of the needle: High achieving Chicanas. *Hispanic Journal of Behavioral Sciences, 4* (2), 167–180.

Garbarino, J. (1976). The preliminary study of some ecological correlates of child abuse: The impact of socioeconomic stress on mothers. *Child Development, 47,* 178–185.

Garbarino, J., & Ebata, A. (1983). The significance of ethnic and cultural differences in child maltreatment. *Journal of Marriage and the Family, 45,* 773–783.

Garmezy, N. (in press). Stress-resistant children: The search for protective factors. In J. E. Stevenson (Ed.), Aspects of current child psychiatry research. *Journal of Child Psychology and Psychiatry.* Book Supplement 4. Oxford: Pergamon.

Garmezy, N. (1983). Stressors of childhood. In N. Garmezy & M. Rutter, (Eds.), *Stress, coping and development in children* (pp. 43–84). New York: McGraw Hill.

Garmezy, N., Masten, A. S., & Tellegen, A. (1984). The study of stress and competence in children: Building blocks for developmental psychopathology. *Child Development, 55,* 97–111.

Giovannoni, J. M., & Becerra, R. M. (1979). *Defining child abuse.* New York: The Free Press.

Goldberg, S., & Kearsley, R. B. (Eds.) (1983). Infants at risk. (Special issue.) *Child Development, 54* (5).

Greene, L. S. (Ed.). (1977). *Malnutrition, behavior and social organization.* New York: Academic Press.

Gruenberg, E. M. (1981). Risk factor research methods. In D. A. Regier & G. Allen (Eds.), *Risk factor research in the major mental disorders.* (DHHS Publication No. ADM 81-1068, pp. 8–19). Washington, DC: U.S. Government Printing Office.

International Union of Nutritional Sciences, Expert Committee (1977). Guidelines on the at risk concept and the health and nutrition of young children. *The American Journal of Clinical Nutrition, 30,* 247–254.

Johanson, D., & Edey, M. (1981). *Lucy: The beginnings of humankind.* New York: Simon and Schuster.

Jordan, T. E. (1976). Developmental factors influencing exceptional status at age six years. *Contemporary Educational Psychology, 1,* 4–19.

Kauffman, C., Grunebaum, H., Cohler, B., & Gamer, E. (1979). Superkids: Competent children of psychotic mothers. *American Journal of Psychiatry, 136* (11), 1398–1402.

Klein, R. (1979). Malnutrition and human behavior: A backward glance at an ongoing nutritional study. In D. A. Levitsky (Ed.), *Malnutrition, environment and behavior* (pp. 219–237). Ithaca, NY: Cornell University Press.

Kleinbaum, D. G., Kupper, L. L., & Morgenstern, H. (1982). *Epidemiologic research: Principles and quantitative methods.* Belmont: CA: Life-time Learning Publications.

Kopp, C. (1983). Risk factors in development. In M. Haith & J. Campos (Eds.), *Infancy and the biology of development* (Vol. 2, pp. 1081–1188). In P. Mussen (Ed.), *Manual of Child Psychology.* New York: Wiley.

Kopp, C. & Krakow, J. B. (1983). The developmentalist and the study of biological risk: A view of the past with an eye toward the future. *Child Development, 54,* 1086–1108.

Lazar, I., Darlington, R. B., Murray, H., Royce, J., & Snipper, A. (1982). Lasting effects of early education. *Monographs of the Society for Research in Child Development, 47,* (2-3, Serial No. 195).

LeVine, R. A. (1983). Fertility and child development: An anthropological approach. In D. A. Wagner (Ed.), *Child development and international development: Research-policy interfaces* (pp. 45–56). San Francisco: Jossey-Bass.

Moskovitz, S. (1983). *Love despite hate: Child survivors of the holocaust and their adult lives.* New York: Schocken Books.

Murphy, L., & Moriarty, A. (1976). *Vulnerability, coping and growth from infancy to adolescence.* New Haven: Yale University Press.

O'Connell-Higgins, R. (1983). Psychological resilience and the capacity for intimacy. Qualifying paper, Graduate School of Education, Harvard University, Cambridge, MA.

O'Doughtery, M. O., Wright, F. S., Garmezy, N., Leowenson, R. B., & Torres, F. (1983). Later competence and adaptation of infants who survive severe heart defects. *Child Development, 54,* 1129–1142.

Ogbu, J. U. (1974). *The next generation: An ethnography of education in an urban neighborhood.* New York: Academic Press.

Ogbu, J. U. (1981). Origins of human competence: A cultural-ecological perspective. *Child Development, 52,* 413–429.

Pines, M. (1984). Resilient children: The search for protective factors. *American Educator*. Fall issue, 34–37.

Plomin, R. (Ed.) (1983). Developmental behavioral genetics. (Special issue). *Child Development, 54*, 253–435.

Pollitt, E. (with S. Jennings) (1984). *Risk factors in the development of young children.* Vol. I: *Risk factors in the development of young children in the developing world.* Houston: University of Texas Health Science Center.

Ramey, C. T., & Trohanis, P. L. (Eds.) (1982). *Finding and educating high risk and handicapped infants.* Baltimore: University Park Press.

Ramey, C. T., Zeskind, P. S., & Hunter, R. (1981). Biomedical and psychosocial interventions for preterm infants. In S. L. Friedman & M. Sigman (Eds.), *Preterm birth and psychological development* (pp. 395–416). New York: Academic Press.

Rutter, M. (1979). Protective factors in children's responses to stress and disadvantage. In M. W. Kent & J. E. Rolf (Eds.), *Primary prevention of psychopathology.* Vol. III: *Social competence in children* (pp. 49–74). Hanover, NH: University Press of New England.

Rutter, M., & Garmezy, N. (1983). Developmental psychopathology. In E. M. Hetherington (Ed.), *Social and Personality Development.* (Vol. 4, pp. 776–911). In P. Mussen (Ed.), *Manual of Child Psychology.* New York: Wiley.

Rutter, M., Maughan, B., Mortimore, P., & Ouston, J. with Smith, A. (1979). *Fifteen thousand hours: Secondary schools and their effects on children.* Cambridge, MA: Harvard University Press.

Sameroff, A. J. (1982). Development and the dialectic: The need for a systems approach. In W. A. Collins (Ed.), *Minnesota symposium on child psychology.* Vol. 15 (pp. 187–244). Chicago: University of Chicago Press.

Sameroff, A. J., & Chandler, M. J. (1975). Reproductive risk and the continuum of caretaking casualty. On F. D. Horowitz (Ed.) *Review of Child Development Research,* Vol. IV (pp. 87–244). Chicago: University of Chicago Press.

Sameroff, A. J., & Seifer, R. (1983). Familial risk and child competence. *Child Development, 54,* 1254–1268.

Scarr, S., & McCartney, R. (1983). How people make their own environments: A theory of genotype-environment effects. *Child Development, 54,* 424–435.

Smith, L. (1954). *The journey.* New York: Norton.

Sroufe, A., & Rutter, M. (1984). The domain of developmental psychopathology. *Child Development, 55,* 17–29.

Super, C. M., Clement, J., Vuori, L., Christiansen, N., Mora, J. O., & Herrera, M. G. (1981). Infant and caretaker behavior as mediators of nutritional and social intervention in the barrios of Bogota. In T. M. Field, A. M. Sostek, P. Vietze & P. H. Leiderman (Eds.), *Culture and early interaction* (pp. 171–182). Hillsdale, NJ: Erlbaum.

Thomas, A., & Chess, S. (1977). *Temperament and development.* New York: Brunner/Mazel.

Townsend, J. W., Klein, R. E., Irwin, M. H., Owens, W., Yarborough, C., & Engle, P. (1982). Nutrition and preschool mental development. In D. A. Wagner & H. W. Stevenson (Eds.), *Cultural perspectives on child development* (pp. 124–145). San Francisco: W. H. Freeman and Co.

Waddington, C. H. (1966). *Principles of development and differentiation.* New York: MacMillan.

Wallerstein, J. S., & Kelley, J. B. (1980). *Surviving the breakup: How children and parents cope with divorce.* New York: Basic Books.

Watt, N., Anthony, E. J., Wynne, L. C., & Rolf, J. E. (Eds.). (1984). *Children at risk for schizophrenia: A longitudinal perspective.* London & New York: Cambridge University Press.

Weinraub, M., & Wolf, B. M. (1983). Effects of stress and social supports on mother-child interactions in single and two parent families. *Child Development, 54,* 1297–1311.

Werner, E. E. (1979). *Cross-cultural child development: A view from the planet earth.* Monterey, CA: Brooks/Cole.

Werner, E. E. (1982). Sources of support for high risk children. In N. J. Anastasiow, W. K. Frankenburg, & A. W. Fandal (Eds.), *Identifying the developmentally delayed child* (pp. 13–30). Baltimore: University Park Press.

Werner, E. E. (1984). *Child care: Kith, kin and hired hands.* Baltimore: University Park Press.

Werner, E. E., Bierman, J. M., & French, F. E. (1971). *The children of Kauai: A longitudinal study from the prenatal period to age ten.* Honolulu: University of Hawaii Press.

Werner, E. E., & Smith, R. S. (1977). *Kauai's children come of age.* Honolulu: University of Hawaii Press.

Werner, E. E., & Smith, R. S. (1982). *Vulnerable, but invincible: A longitudinal study of resilient children and youth.* New York: McGraw Hill.

Wertheim, E. S. (1977). Developmental genesis of human vulnerability: Conceptual re-evaluation. In E. J. Anthony, C. Koupernik, & C. Chiland (Eds.), *The child and his family.* Vol. IV: *Vulnerable children* (pp. 17–36). New York: Wiley.

Whiting, B. B., & Whiting, J. W. M. (1975). *Children of six cultures: A psychocultural analysis.* Cambridge, MA: Harvard University Press.

Zeskind, P. S. (1983). Cross-cultural differences in maternal perceptions of cries of low and high risk infants. *Child Development, 54,* 1119–1128.

Zeskind, P. S., & Ramey, C. T. (1981). Preventing intellectual and interactional sequelae of fetal malnutrition: A longitudinal, transactional, and synergistic approach. *Child Development, 52,* 213–218.

# DEVELOPMENTAL RISK IN INFANTS

Jane V. Hunt

This chapter attempts to bring together different perspectives on the topic of developmental risk in infants. We will consider the major issues in research that are emerging from psychology and medicine, with particular attention to inter-disciplinary studies. We will also examine the theories that underlie research strategies. In addition, we will examine the implications of research findings for education, including the education of the infant and preschool child.

## DEFINING RISK STATUS

Let us begin by defining developmental risk. Research studies that refer to "risk" or "high risk" infants have become increasingly visible over the past decade, lending an air of excitement to the field but also creating some confusion

Advances in Special Education, Volume 5, pages 25–59.
Copyright © 1986 by JAI Press Inc.
All rights of reproduction in any form reserved.
ISBN: 0-89232-313-2

about findings. We need to define who is at risk, and for what. Risk implies probability or chance, and developmental risk implies chance of future events. Therefore, we are considering infants who may or may not develop the forseen outcome, even though the likelihood of doing so is significantly higher than average. (Note that we do not include in this definition those infants who are *certain* to have a specific outcome.) Risk also implies problem outcome. Many problems have been investigated, but for purposes of this discussion we will focus on intellectual disabilities. Our concern is with infants who may develop intellectual disabilities and are at risk for educational problems at school age.

Two major distinctions of risk status come immediately to mind. Some infants are considered at risk because of biological events that threaten the integrity of the developing brain, while others are at risk because of unfavorable social environments that endanger normal development. This discussion will focus on infants with biological risks, but the two major distinctions, biological and social, are rarely disassociated. The biologically at-risk infants are reared in varied environments and the socially disadvantaged infants may be at increased risk for biological problems such as prematurity, malnutrition or disease. High risk infant populations selected for one type of risk will almost certainly include the second to some degree. The distinction in research is often largely heuristic, and many studies have been designed to consider both kinds of risk factors (e.g., Cohen & Parmelee, 1983; Escalona, 1982; Rose, Gottfried, & Bridger, 1978).

## RESEARCH STRATEGIES

We can narrow our topic further by considering the relative advantages of retrospective and prospective research methods. The retrospective study identifies a group in childhood, for example children with learning disabilities, and studies their histories for clues to the development of the problem. Although such studies have helped define major risk categories in infancy for further investigation, retrospective studies are not developmental in the true sense. The histories obtained retrospectively are rarely complete or accurate enough to define infant status with adequate specificity. Also, even when a major risk condition, such as prematurity, is identified with some confidence we still do not know the incidence of infants with that risk who did *not* develop the specific childhood handicap. Without this information, it is difficult to generalize from the results of any one study or to interpret differences between studies.

Prospective research is developmental, isolating specific variables for study in infancy that are of theoretical interest to long-term intellectual development. Because many studies have been restricted to infancy, the implications for school age disabilities remain theoretical. However, such discrete studies are of great importance in formulating developmental constructs and in defining variables of potential relevance. A frequently used method is to examine behavioral differences between a high risk population and a control group of no-risk infants. Results are usually reported as significant differences between the groups. Individual differences *among* high risk infants are not usually reported because individual outcome is unknown. In fact, the possibility exists that the observed group differences between high risk and no-risk infants are of no consequence to future development and reflect only transient conditions. An example is the expected developmental difference in infancy noted between normal preterm and full-term infants that reflects only the maturational lag of the preterm group. A lag of 2 months may be highly significant during the first year of life but is not detectable at school age.

Prospective longitudinal studies complement the discrete studies of infancy by observing the study members at repeated intervals so that associations among observations over time can be investigated. Some studies may be short-term, as when infant intervention programs are evaluated, and may identify specific variables of likely significance. Studies of intellectual development are particularly valuable when they extend into childhood so that educational readiness or progress can be assessed. These assessments provide an external measurement of validity for the behaviors that have been identified as significant.

Long-term studies have some unique disadvantages. They are time-consuming and expensive, requiring great persistence on the part of the investigators. They are plagued by methodologic problems such as the loss of children from the study across successive ages. Nevertheless, when longitudinal studies are organized carefully they provide important developmental information that cannot be obtained in any other way. If, for example, we look at separate groups at each age (the cross-sectional method) in order to shorten the research time and avoid methodologic problems, we cannot examine individual changes across ages nor relate age group differences to intervening developmental events. Also, external events (for example, modifications in neonatal medical care) may prevent meaningful age comparisons among groups of children who were born in different event-related eras. The present discussion will include examples from both longitudinal and discrete prospective studies with particular emphasis on our own long-term follow-up of preterm infants.

# OVERVIEW OF MAJOR ASSUMPTIONS

Infants have been studied from several perspectives, including those of developmental psychology, clinical neurology, pediatrics, psychophysiology, and psychiatry. Discrete studies typically involve a single discipline, whereas longitudinal studies are more likely to be multidisciplinary. The longitudinal studies include or emphasize multidisciplinary interests in varied ways and so different projects tend to compliment one another, each adding new pieces of information to solve the puzzle of the origins of intellectual disabilities.

Despite the variety of disciplines and methods currently represented in studies of high risk infants, we can detect some common assumptions about the genesis of intellectual problems in childhood. These assumptions vary and, although theoretical positions may not always be stated explicitly, they shape the form of each study.

One assumption is concerned with *rates of mental growth*. It is hypothesized that the handicapped child will be identified during infancy by a lag in development. As a result, the risk infant will be less mature than age mates. This construct is exemplified by the use of tests in infancy that yield a mental age or standard score such as the IQ or the DQ. For example, the infant at 12 months with an IQ of 50 will be approximately 6 months delayed; by 24 months the same IQ represents approximately 12 months of delay. To maintain this IQ, the developmental rate must be depressed to one-half the velocity of the normal infant. Successive evaluations across ages are used to plot the rate of development or, more commonly, groups are compared to determine differences in the current level of mental development.

The assumption that the mental growth rate in infancy is associated with intellectual status in childhood is very attractive because we know that the IQ is a powerful predictor of school success by about 4 years of age. However, there are problems in this model when it is applied to infancy, and we will consider those problems in more detail. For the moment it is important to keep in mind that, in general, infant scores are notoriously nonpredictive of childhood IQ, that individual rates of normal infant development tend to vary in a manner indicating spurts and lags in mental growth, and that the construct does not offer a ready explanation for some handicaps, such as learning disabilities, that are found in children with normal IQs. Nevertheless, most longitudinal studies include a standard developmental test in infancy and rely heavily upon the data it generates. The concept of developmental lag in infancy is reinforced by the numerous reports of small but significant score differences in group comparisons between risk and no-risk infants (see reviews by Hunt, 1983; Kopp, 1983) as well as by the observation of developmental lags in infancy for many children with severe mental disabilities (cf. Knobloch & Pasamanick, 1974).

The second general assumption is concerned with *specific functional disabilities,* assuming that specific abilities (and therefore, disabilities) in childhood have their origins in infancy. In this view there is a successive chain of behavioral skills, each dependent upon the one preceeding, that determines the development of each function. Low IQ is a reflection of multiple functional problems. Specific, discrete problems will be identified to explain minor IQ differences noted between risk and control groups in infancy. We can think of this as the ''building blocks'' theory of mental development. In the past, it was assumed that these building blocks would be substantively related. For example, to predict a language disability we would examine the components of infant tests that assess vocalization and responses to speech. When such predictors were not readily identified, a schism grew up within this general construct. Some investigators contend that functional development is discontinuous, meaning that the origins of functional problems may be covert. If the building blocks of infancy are not substantively related to the problem in childhood, then the search for predictors should not be limited by substantive constraints. Other investigators assert that conventional measurements are inadequate and that new ones will reveal a substantive link with infant abilities. One is tempted to label the latter view a "better mousetrap" approach. It is a very active working model for a number of interesting discrete studies being carrier out at present (see as example, Caron & Caron, 1981; Gegoski, Fagen & Pearlman, 1984; Rose, 1983). Longitudinal studies are beginning to incorporate some of these special methods in their research designs and to analyze standard infant test data for predictive items.

A third developmental construct or assumption is concerned with *brain damage.* The thesis maintains that abnormalities of central nervous system (CNS) functioning in infancy predict childhood disabilities; intellectual disabilities in childhood reflect the earlier brain damage and the subsequent disruption of normal brain function; developmental lags in infancy are not necessarily predicted but, when present, are held to be caused by underlying CNS damage. Therefore, CNS abnormalities in infancy are the real predictors. These predictors include behaviors noted in clinical neurological examinations of the infant, such as seizure disorders and neuromotor abnormalities, and aberrant neurophysiological responses such as those determined by EEG or evoked response measurements. By inference, predictors also may be defined as physiological states such as anoxia, or abnormal events such as cerebral hemorrhage that are known to be associated with brain damage. Often these problems are considered together in order to determine an overall risk index for the infant.

Although overt behavioral symptoms of brain damage may disappear during infancy, the theoretical assumption is that the damage remains and can be expected to show its effects on the developing brain. The intellectual expression of CNS abnormality may be delayed until higher-order mental functions mature. Pervasive effects from events in infancy have frequently been postulated in psychology and psychiatry (usually in reference to social or other environmental events) to explain the evidence for associations beyond infancy (cf. Bayley & Schaefer, 1964; Cohen & Beckwith, 1979; Whiting & Child, 1953; Yarrow, Rubenstein, & Pedersen, 1975) although *continuing* interaction effects are generally acknowledged. The CNS hypothesis is even more explicit in suggesting that specific events in infancy are directly predictive of future states of a different order. Many longitudinal studies incorporate neurological assessments and other measurements of CNS function in infancy. The evidence for long-term effects will be considered later in this chapter.

A fourth construct, with major implications for educators, postulates that *the social environment is preeminent in shaping intellectual development,* whether or not CNS problems are postulated in infancy (cf. Sameroff & Chandler, 1975). Except in the most devastating cases of severe brain damage, outcome is largely determined by subsequent events. Those setting forth this position cite the decreased associations between biological events and IQ beyond infancy and point to the increased association with variables such as the socioeconomic or educational level of the child's parents. Although this position does not deny the biological basis of intelligence, the argument is made that the developing infant brain is highly functionally redundant and so has good regenerative potential (Werner & Smith, 1982; Werner, this volume).

Those who argue for the preeminent importance of the social environment for infant development maintain that many aspects of cognitive, language, and emotional development are clearly mediated by the environment with important implications for the ultimate organization and expression of intellect. Transactional social development theory, (Sander, 1976; Thoman, 1976; see review by Osofsky & Connors, 1979) wherein the infant is seen as contributing to reciprocal, chained interactions with the caretaker, is a sophisticated model that attempts to account for the positive or negative direction of subsequent development. According to this model, developmental problems may occur when either partner is unable to participate fully in the reciprocal exchange. The theory would appear to hold out the possibility of reversibility of developmental problems, and so it has considerable relevance for intervention strategies in infancy. We will consider some of the studies that have focused on mother-infant interactions in relation to the development of high risk infants.

Finally, we take note of a point of view that can only be characterized as a "devil's advocate" position. This construct denies that developmental status in infancy can predict intellectual status in childhood. From this position the abilities assessed at each age are seen as conceptually unrelated and, in fact, the abilities that constitute intelligence in childhood are generally unavailable for study in infancy (Lewis & McGurk, 1972; McCall, Eichorn, & Hogarty, 1977). The analogy would be an attempt to predict adult height from the infant's length at birth. Except in the most extreme cases, advocates maintain that information about parent characteristics is a much better predictor of future status than is prediction from measurements in infancy (see McCall, 1979, 1983). Those who hold to this view maintain that we do not find good predictors in infancy because they cannot exist, not because we need better conceptualizations or improved measurement techniques. We will consider this position along with the other major constructs that have been described as we examine specific studies that attempt to predict childhood intelligence.

## PREDICTING OUTCOME FROM DEVELOPMENTAL RATES IN INFANCY

We tend to describe children's intellectual problems in terms that suggest a slowed rate of development ("immature," "slow," "retarded"). The children have not come as far or as fast as their normal peers. If the problems originated from pre- or perinatal events, the assumption that is made for biologically at-risk infants, then the slowing should be detectable in infancy.

Standard infant tests were developed because it was assumed that developmental rates were constant and so the IQ obtained in infancy would be predictive of the IQ in childhood. Longitudinal studies of normal populations disproved this assumption when no correlation was found between infant and childhood IQs. However, we continue to expect that the abnormal child may show developmental lags in infancy, if only because the degree of difference in childhood is greater than that found within the normal range.

We no longer subscribe to the idea that the IQ is immutable and, indeed, many of our educational efforts with infants and young children are directed towards improving developmental rates. A change in IQ from one age to another represents a rate change during that interval. If the new developmental rate is maintained, the IQ will continue to rise. Conversely, adverse events may depress the developmental rate, resulting in a decline in IQ across ages. If we assume that the changes in IQ (positive and negative) can be explained by external events, then we seem to subscribe to a general concept of rate constancy *unless* it is deflected by outside events.

The associations between IQ and developmental rates are presented schematically in Figure 1. The normal rate of development (A) is one where mental age (MA) keeps pace with chronological age (CA), resulting in a constant IQ of 100. The decelerated rate (B) illustrates a case where mental ages are equal to one-half the chronological age at any point (i.e., 2 months at 4 months, or 2 years at 4 years); in this case, the ratio IQ (MA/CA $\times$ 100) will be a constant 50. However, if at time X (Age 4 in Figure 1) the rate is accelerated, for example to match the normal rate ($B_1$), the IQ will improve steadily across subsequent ages. (In our example, $B_1$ will reach an IQ of 80 by age 10). Accelerated developmental rate is illustrated in Figure 1, C. Mental age exceeds chronological age in a proportional way so that, in this example, IQ is a constant 120.

Sudden changes in IQ are not excluded by this model, but are explained by the degree of rate change and by the age and time interval that has elapsed between tests. In general, we expect infant IQ changes to be more precipitous because months are equivalent to years at older ages.

Preterm infant development is a special case that can be considered at this point. If the preterm infant is normal, we expect the developmental *rate* to be normal. However, the developmental *level* will be depressed by a constant increment of months that approximates the months of prematurity (Hunt & Rhodes, 1977). If the infant is born 2 months preterm, mental age will be 2 months at 4 months, 3 months at 5 months, and 10 months at 12 months. By school age the difference of 2 months is trivial. (Normal rate in such a situation is illustrated by $B_1$ in Figure 1).

When preterm infants of varied gestational age are examined together, as is the case in most high-risk studies, the effect of prematurity on test scores is bother-

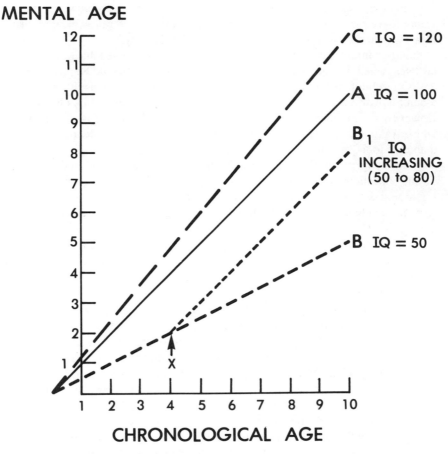

*Figure 1.* Schematic developmental rates for normal (A), delayed (B) and accelerated (C) mental development; rate change from delayed to normal (B₁) also depicted.

some. An IQ of 65 at 6 months would be approximately normal for an infant whose gestational age at birth was 7 months (i.e., 2 months premature) but would represent developmental delay for the infant with a gestational age of 8 months. Also, over time the normal preterm IQ will rise and so the infant's relative IQ position in the group will change. These problems are usually avoided by correcting all preterm IQs according to the infant's adjusted age, allowing for prematurity. Thus, the infant who is 2 months preterm will have an adjusted age of 4 months at the chronological age of 6 months and will be scored on the test according to the standards for 4 months; normal IQ will be 100. By using this correction, infants with true developmental delays can be identified.

There is a degree of controversy over the use of adjusted preterm infant scores as predictors of childhood IQ. Some studies have determined that unadjusted scores are better predictors (Caputo, Goldstein, & Taub, 1981; Siegel, 1983). This is true because, in general, the more premature the infant the greater the likelihood of intellectual problems in childhood. Studies often include infants who are 3 months premature, a decidedly high-risk group. Their unadjusted scores will be very low in infancy, even if the adjusted scores are normal; the predictor in this case is gestational age (maturation level), not developmental *problems* in infancy. Removing the gestational age effect forces an evaluation of infant development with maturational differences controlled. Maturational differences are expected to decrease with age. If other infant predictors are found by using adjusted scores they would be of great interest.

We can examine the evidence for developmental rates by considering longitudinal data for children enrolled in our follow-up study of high risk infants. A brief general description of the study will be presented, followed by an examination of rate data derived from longitudinal assessments.

## The UCSF Follow-up Study

The study was begun in 1965 after the establishment of a neonatal intensive care unit at the University of California in San Francisco. Survivors of this novel approach to newborn care were enrolled in the study if they had very low birth weight or were larger but had serious newborn respiratory problems resulting from prematurity. Smaller groups of other suspect categories also were included, such as infants who had intrauterine transfusions because of incompatibility with their mothers' Rh-negative blood. In general, infants were enrolled in follow-up if there was some serious concern for their subsequent mental or physical development because of perinatal or neonatal events.

Even with the advent of neonatal intensive care, survival was precarious for the smallest and sickest infants, but survival rates improved steadily for very small infants with birth weights below 1500 g. The incidence of severe handicaps in these very low birth weight survivors has been low and comparable to that reported by similar studies (5% to 10%). However, by the time the very low birth weight infants reached 4 to 6 years of age we began to detect additional mild to moderate intellectual problems in approximately 35% (Hunt, 1981). Other categories of high risk infants also showed these problems, although to a lesser extent. The disabilities that we identified in the clinic were expected to cause some educational problems, even when accompanied by normal IQ (Hunt, Tooley, & Harvin, 1982).

We have recently reported the kinds of intellectual outcomes determined at 8 years for 297 children born in 1965 through 1975, including 110 with birth weights at or below 1500 g (Hunt, Tooley, Cooper, & Harvin, in press). The children were tested with the Wechsler Intelligence Scale for Children (WISC-R) and the Bender Gestalt Test of visual-motor integration. Academic achievement also was evaluated with the Wide Range Achievement Test (WRAT). The socioeconomic status of the group was predominantly middle-class. We therefore defined normal IQ by fairly high standards as a Full Scale IQ of 95 or higher and Verbal and Performance IQs of 90 or higher. The Bender score was determined as a quotient, obtained by dividing the earned Age Equivalent by chronological age. Normal Bender score was defined as 85 or higher, equal to no more than 1 year of delay in performance at age 8.

We identified two groups with normal test scores—those who were considered entirely normal (20% of all children) and those who were clinically "suspect" for a variety of reasons related to qualitative performance during the evaluation (30%). In addition to the two normal groups, we identified three groups with specific score deficits: Low Verbal IQ (8%), Low Performance IQ (3%), and Low Bender IQ (9%). The remainder were defined by IQ level: Low Normal (IQ 85–94; 15%), Low (IQ 75–84; 9%) and Very Low (IQ below 75; 5%).

Leaving aside, for the moment, the Normal/Suspect and other special outcome groups, we can examine developmental rates in infancy and early childhood for those in outcome categories defined by IQ status at 8 years: Normal, Low Normal, Low, and Very Low IQ. The standard test administered at 6, 12, and 24 months was the Cattell Test of Infant Intelligence. The Stanford-Binet Intelligence Scale was given at 3 through 6 years of age. Developmental rates were determined by converting average IQs for each group into average mental ages (IQ × age / 100) which could then be plotted according to chronological age. The resulting rates are presented in Figure 2. All IQs used to determine mental ages below 8 years had been adjusted for prematurity, although, in fact, the correlation between IQ and gestational age was no longer significant after 3 years and the IQ adjustment was minor.

The mental age separation of the 4 IQ groups at 8 years was a continuous process across ages. Figure 2 includes the average expected rate (schematic normal), equivalent to an IQ of 100 at each age (i.e., mental age = chronological age). The Normal IQ group showed an accelerated rate of development, particularly after 3 years and reached an average mental age of 9.2 at 8 years (IQ 115). The Very Low IQ group showed a markedly slower rate of development. Mental age at 8 years was 5.2 years (IQ 65). The two intermediate IQ groups showed intermediate developmental rates, with respective mental ages of 7.2 and 6.4 years at age 8 (IQ 90 and IQ 80).

The differences in rates were reflected in progressively greater IQ differences among the four groups across ages. The Very Low IQ group scored significantly lower than the Normal group by 1 year of age, and the Normal group scored higher than all other groups by 2 years. The score difference between the Low and Very Low groups was not significant until 6 years and the difference in scores between Low Normal and Low was not significant at any age below 8 years. Thus, we see a gradual differentiation among the groups across ages.

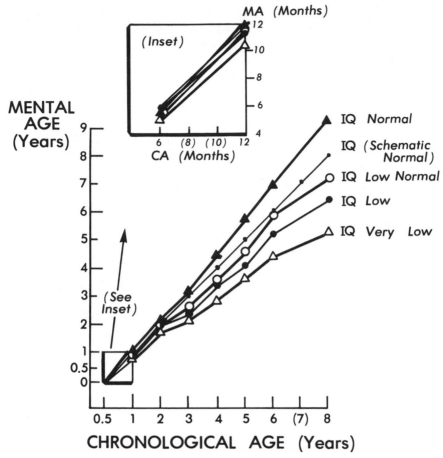

*Figure 2.* Developmental rates for four IQ groups determined at 8 years: Normal (see text), low normal (IQ 85–94), low (IQ 75–84), and very low (IQ <75); schematic normal rate (Figure 1) also depicted.

The actual rates of development depicted in Figure 2 are similar to the schematic rates presented in Figure 1. However, the changes in rates apparent in Figure 2 suggest ages of special importance for mental development. All but the Normal group showed some drift from the expected normal rate between 2 and 3 years. The Very Low IQ group showed a more protracted delay from 2 through 4 years. At the end of that time the group reached an average mental age of 2.8 years, similar to that achieved by the Low Normal group a year earlier. The evidence suggests that developmental delays at 8 years were associated with developmental problems at the chronological and/or mental age of 2 to 3 years. The improved rate noted between 5 and 6 years for the two intermediate IQ groups (Low Normal and Low) corresponds to the usual age of school entry. However, the gains were not maintained and all but the Normal group showed deceleration in developmental rates between 6 and 8 years.

Given the entire perspective of rates across 8 years of development, it is not surprising that the infant scores at 6 months were not predictive nor that only the Very Low IQ group was identified at 1 year of age. IQ differences in infancy are based on months, or even weeks of mental age difference. The insert in Figure 2 shows the group comparisons in months at 6 and 12 months. The very rapid pace of development in infancy does not allow for much mental age variability at any given age. Note that the significant IQ difference at 12 months between the Normal and Very Low IQ outcome groups equalled approximately 1½ months of mental age. Not only is that amount of difference very small absolutely, it is also relatively smaller than the differences noted at older ages. Developmental rates changed and scores drew further apart across ages.

Transient delays or spurts in development drastically alter infant IQ. The scores at 6 months for the Normal outcome group ranged from 59 to 127; in the Very Low IQ group the range of scores at 6 months was 46 to 101. Individual prediction from most test scores was clearly not possible at this age. Errors of classification were noted in both directions (i.e., nonpredictive high and low IQs) but a conspicuous finding was that 19% of the Normal outcome group had scores below 75 at 6 months. These developmental delays were transient, and no scores this low were obtained by the Normal group at subsequent ages. We concluded that prediction from the Cattell IQ was not possible at 6 months for high risk infants, even for those infants with very low scores. This conclusion contradicts conventional assumptions about low-scoring infants and illustrates the importance of prospective studies. The children did not begin to order themselves by IQ in a highly predictive way until age 3 years. However, our data suggested that prediction from infancy may be improved by attention to rate *changes* during the first 2 years.

When we focus on IQ changes within groups rather than IQ differences between groups, we are moving away from an acceptance of the quantitative model of mental development. Rate changes are descriptive rather than explanatory. We cannot assume that they are caused by extrinsic events, an assumption required by the mechanistic model. We may suspect that biological factors such as recovery from illness are influencing changes in infant scores or that intrinsic cognitive differences are expressing themselves at 3 years. We may be concerned that the different standard intelligence tests (Cattell, Stanford-Binet, and WISC-R) are qualitatively dissimilar because IQ changes were noted for some outcome groups at each transition age (3 and 8 years). In short, we become concerned with the qualitative differences that are reflected by variations in IQ. Further, we may be interested in specific behavioral differences in infancy that are not necessarily related to subsequent IQ but have implications for other aspects of intellectual development.

# PREDICTING OUTCOME FROM DISCRETE
# COMPONENTS OF INFANT BEHAVIOR

Our first concern in a discussion of discrete behavioral predictors is to clarify the question of the outcome to be predicted. If outcome is measured only by IQ, then we are predicting to a quantitative measurement of general outcome. As noted, infant IQ is not predictive of later IQ and so the search has persisted for more salient predictors of general IQ status in childhood. Longitudinal studies may include special infant assessments for this purpose or may analyze the standard infant test data for predictive components derived from discrete test items. However, as noted, a comparable IQ level in childhood does not necessarily imply sameness in all mental abilities. If we argue that specific disabilities can be traced back to infancy (the "building blocks" concept described previously), then we will want to predict to the specific outcomes. Longitudinal studies can provide for such analysis retrospectively, once outcomes have been determined. The size of the high risk sample and the frequency of the specific outcome determine the limits for such investigations in longitudinal studies. For example, in our study the incidence of children with specific deficits in non-verbal abilities (the Low PIQ group) was only 3%, or nine children. Because of the small number of cases we are foreclosed from analyzing this interesting group in much detail.

Usually, longitudinal studies have not reported predictors for discrete outcomes (e.g., Low PIQ). Instead, analyses often take advantage of the full range of scores obtained for any measurement in order to examine that measurement as a continuous variable. In the example of the PIQ, we can determine the correlations between PIQ and infant variables for the whole group of high risk children. This method of analysis can be elaborated by a multivariate design. For example, we can determine how PIQ is associated with the infant variables after the correlation of PIQ with IQ has been accounted for. Also, we can determine if there are different infant predictors for PIQ and VIQ. The correlational analyses are often productive and useful. However, it is apparent that, in relying on such analyses, we have returned to a quantitative model of development. We are, for example, no longer focused on the cognitive deficit that is *reflected* in low PIQ but, rather, are examining PIQ directly and across the entire range of scores. High PIQ is now as different from average PIQ as average is from low. We are no longer predicting to a specific deficit. The "best" infant predictors will be those that have corresponding scores or values that match up with the scores of the outcome variable. Infant predictors that are not readily quantified or do not have a linear relationship with the outcome variable may go undetected.

An alternative approach is to compare risk and no-risk infant groups on discrete behavioral variables hypothesized to be relevant to subsequent intellectual outcome. Individual outcomes cannot be specified, but group differences are predicted. This procedure permits us to examine qualitative variables as readily as quantitative measurements. However, the method incurs some problems. First, the risk group must be selected so as to assure that the predicted intellectual problem(s) will occur in a significant proportion of the group. This step is important because we want to predict to two populations with distinctly different intellectual characteristics. Also, the variables studied in infancy must be selected or controlled so that results are not readily explained by transient differences between risk and control groups (e.g., by differences in maturity or health status at the time of observation). The importance of transient effects has been considered in relation to standard infant tests and applies equally when novel variables are used. If the problem is not avoided, then the novel variables selected for study will probably not be the anticipated "better mouse trap," no matter how compelling the theoretical basis for their investigation. Finally, the long-term associations with intellectual status must be confirmed. The infant studies provide hypotheses that influence the selection of variables in longitudinal studies. We can illustrate both the longitudinal and infant comparison methods by examining some specific studies.

## Longitudinal Studies

In our follow-up study we identified two outcome groups with comparable average IQs at 8 years but with distinctly different intellectual characteristics—the Low Normal IQ group and the Low Verbal IQ group. The Verbal, Performance, and Full Scale IQs of the WISC-R were 91, 91 and 90 for the Low Normal group, and 78, 103 and 89 for the Low Verbal group. When average IQs were compared at all younger ages no significant differences were found. The decline in IQ at 3 years was more abrupt for the Low Verbal group, indicating some difficulty with the Binet at that age, but subsequent IQs were higher and not significantly different from those of the Low Normal group. This finding was somewhat surprising, considering the highly verbal content of the Binet at 4 through 6 years. Qualitative differences in Cattell infant test performance at 6, 12, and 24 months are now under investigation for these and other discrete outcome groups and subgroups. However, in this example we do not anticipate that specific test items at preverbal ages will directly predict verbal disability at 8 years. Rather, we expect that group differences in infancy may contribute to prediction in a limited way.

Multiple regression analysis has become an important statistical tool for investigating small but important influences on outcome in longitudinal studies. For example, many studies of both normal and high-risk populations have established the increasing and pervasive association between measurements of intellectual status and familial variables such as socioeconomic status and parent education level. Familial factors emerge as strong predictors of IQ at about 2 years of age and become increasingly important in the next few years. However, using various methods of multiple regression we can explore the enduring importance of variables determined in infancy, even though their direct association with outcome may no longer be obvious. That is, we can determine if they add significantly to the prediction of outcome, over and above the larger effects of the familial variables. For example, we have determined that the level of neonatal illness and birth weight made independent contributions to the prediction of childhood intellectual status in our follow-up study (Hunt et al., in press).

The same methods of multiple regression can be used to investigate infant behavioral variables. A longitudinal study of low birth weight infants is illustrative (Wallace, Escalona, McCarton-Daum, & Vaughan, 1982). Children were assessed at age 6 years with the WISC-R, the Beery test of visual motor integration, the WRAT reading test, and a specially constructed measure of sentence repetition. These outcome measurements were very comparable to those used in our own study at 8 years. The children had been examined at term age (equivalent to 40 weeks gestation) with the Einstein Neonatal Neurobehavioral Assessment Scale. Three summary scores were derived from this neonatal scale for behaviors assessing visual tracking, orientation to acoustic stimuli, and neuromotor status. Acoustic orientation was identified as a significant predictor of Verbal IQ, WRAT reading score and sentence repetition score; prediction was further enhanced by including a measurement of family socioeconomic status. The authors speculated that the association found between neonatal auditory processing and the language-related abilities at 6 years may indicate that audition plays a key role in cognitive development.

In a separate study of preterm infants, Cohen and Parmelee (1983) reported that, after the very significant predictive power of a general familial variable (years of maternal education) had been considered, prediction of Stanford-Binet IQ at age 5 was enhanced by a measurement of visual fixation at term age. The association was negative, so that increased fixation time was associated with lower IQ at 5 years. Visual attention measured at 4 months was not predictive, nor was a measure of exploratory behavior and interest in new objects at 8 months. Many other variables were considered in this study from term age through 2 year assessments, using the multiple regression model. The authors did not speculate on the importance of the visual measurement at term age. However, as longitudinal studies report their varied findings, each contributes to our fund of knowledge about the subtle but significant predictors of later intellectual functioning. The two longitudinal studies cited demonstrate that, with careful analysis, behavioral predictors can be identified even in newborn infants.

## Infant Studies

As noted, studies limited to infancy usually make direct comparisons between risk and no-risk groups. Such studies take advantage of the expected intellectual difference between groups at older ages to explore variables of theoretical interest. Interest has focused on a number of domains including attention, memory, pre-verbal communication, information processing, temperament, and parent-infant interactions.

Researchers tend to view the high risk population from one of two different perspectives. Some investigations have been primarily concerned with the early mental development of the high risk group. In these cases the control group of normal infants was included for purposes of comparison, usually to establish the normal range of values for a novel measurement. Group differences on the experimental variable(s) were interpreted as representing the diminished capacity of the high risk group. Other studies have been primarily focused on normal infant mental development and the investigation of a specific hypothesis, usually generated from studies of older children. In these instances the high risk comparison group was included in order to provide a direct test of the hypothesis. Group differences were interpreted as reflecting the importance of the experimental variable(s) in infancy as constructs in a general model of mental development.

Some recent studies of high risk infants have incorporated both perspectives, that is, testing theories and also searching for better predictors of disability. Studies of cognitive development have been particularly productive in recent years. The infant has become interesting again, following a period in which infant cognition was largely relegated to a Piagetian sensory-motor limbo. Many studies now postulate developmental continuity for specific cognitive abilities, extending back into infancy. Ingenious behavioral measurements have been devised to test this assumption. Studies including high risk groups often are embedded in larger programs of infant studies. We can consider a few recent examples.

Caron and Caron (1981) compared the performance of preterm and full-term infants at 12, 18, 21 and 24 weeks postterm age (i.e., age adjusted for prematurity). Using age-graded stimuli developed in previous studies of healthy term infants they investigated the hypothesis that preterm infants would demonstrate greater difficulty in abstracting relational information from visually presented stimuli. The study produced consistent results that supported the hypothesis. At each age tested, preterm infants responded primarily to changes in the specific elements of the visual array and the full-term infants responded primarily to changes in the relations between elements. The investigators considered these results to be direct evidence for the hypothesis that vulnerability to cognitive deficit is manifest early in life as a difficulty in abstracting relational information (Caron, Caron, & Glass, 1983).

Rose, Gottfried, and Bridger (1979) investigated the effect of bisensory information from vision and touch on visual recognition memory in preterm and full-term infants at 6 and 12 months postterm age. The investigators had previously determined that the manipulatory activities actually interfered with performance on a visual recognition task at these ages for full-term infants. The results replicated the previous findings for full-term infants and demonstrated a developmental lag for preterm infants. Preterm infants at 12 months performed in the same manner as the full-term infants at 6 months, that is, they demonstrated visual memory only when the manipulatory activities were not included. Preterm infants at 6 months showed no evidence of memory in either experimental condition. In a subsequent study (Rose, 1980) evidence was presented that preterm infants took longer to encode visual information than did full-term infants. In reviews of these and other studies (Rose, 1981, 1983) it was concluded that the cognitive abilities demonstrate in infancy suggested a way to detect basic disabilities earlier than ever before.

Another group of investigators has been interested in direct evidence for long-term memory in infants. Using operant conditioning as a model (learning to produce movement in an overhead mobile by kicking), Gekoski, Fagen and Pearlman (1984) extended these studies to include comparisons between preterm and full-term infants at 12 weeks postterm age. The results showed that both preterm and full-term infants were capable of learning the contingency (kicking leads to movement in the mobile) but that preterms were relatively slower in learning this association. Also, once the behavior was acquired only the full-term infants showed evidence that the association was retained after a 1-week interval. The performance of the preterm group at 12 weeks postterm age was comparable to that determined previously for full-term infants at 8 weeks (Rovee-Collier, 1984). The authors concluded that the observed difference between preterm and term infants represented a delay and not a permanent deficiency in the preterms' ability to acquire and retain the contingency. However, they also determined that the delay was associated with the severity of postnatal complications rather than with prematurity per se, suggesting that the significance of the delay for subsequent cognitive development required further investigation.

When longitudinal data are examined for similar cognitive predictors in infancy, the theoretical assumptions can be tested. For example, Kopp and Vaughn (1982) investigated the associations between a measurement of sustained attention at 8 months and performance on test scores at 2 years of age for preterm infants. The attention measurement was derived from data of a study already noted (Cohen & Parmelee, 1983). The measurement of attention contributed to prediction of two standard test scores (Bayley and Gesell) determined at 2 years. However, when gender was considered the effect was found to be associated only with males. Ethnicity was an important predictor for girls and, overall, prediction to scores at 2 years from multiple regression was more powerful for girls. The rationale for examining the sustained attention variable was the known importance of attention deficits in learning disabilities (Keogh & Margolis, 1976). Failure to find an association between attention and the standard test scores at 2 years for girls does not necessarily imply that the infant measurement had no relevance to cognitive development. As noted by the authors, learning disabilities are more common in boys. The distribution of attention scores at 8 months may have varied by sex. In any event, the longitudinal study suggested an important variable, sex, that is not generally considered in cognitive theory.

# PREDICTING OUTCOME FROM NEUROLOGICAL ABNORMALITIES IN INFANCY

The associations between brain development and behavioral change are of special interest to researchers in developmental neurology and developmental neurophysiology. One method of study has been to examine the enduring effects of early brain damage on brain and behavior, using animal models in controlled experiments. In this manner, a number of agents and conditions (e.g., drugs, oxygen deprivation) have been investigated in fetal and infant animals for immediate and long-lasting effects on brain structure and function. Correlaries with human intellectual disabilities have sometimes been suggested from behavioral measurements. Studies of human infants attempt to validate such findings.

Circumstances that are implicated in brain damage are of special concern when we consider infants at risk because of adverse biological events. Risk status may be determined during neonatal life from physical evidence such as the visualization of cerebral hemorrhage, or determined from physiological evidence such as abnormally low blood oxygen level. Further, risk of brain damage may be inferred from adverse events alone, such as fetal malnutrition or fetal exposure to alcohol, when such events are known to cause damage in mammals (see Hunt, 1983 for review).

Very small preterm infants are considered to be at special risk because of their physiological instability at birth and their susceptibility to cerebral hemorrhage. Also, unselected populations of low birth weight infants will include a proportion who are very small for gestational age. Such infants are considered at risk because of the evidence for fetal malnutrition. It is postulated that functional damage to the brain will be manifest in infancy by abnormalities in central nervous system (CNS) functioning and, further, that there will be associations between infant abnormalities and intellectual disabilities noted in childhood.

The neurological status of preterm infants has been studied by clinical assessments and by electrophysiological measurements. Maturational effects are important considerations in both kinds of evaluations. Some clinical signs such as hypotonia (floppy baby) are not necessarily abnormal in preterm neonates. Other signs, such as newborn primitive reflexes, normally wax and wane during early infancy. Still other clinical findings, for example marked laterality differences in muscle tone, are considered abnormal at any age (see Amiel-Tison, 1969; Amiel-Tison & Grenier, 1983). The electrophysiological measurements, such as EEG and evoked response, also have maturational components. As noted for other behavioral measurements, the effects of current status such as illness must be taken into account. Transient disruptions in CNS function may be noted in some neurological measurements during illness and ascribed to specific, correctable medical conditions. The more permanent changes can be differentiated from the transient by evaluating infants after they have recovered from initial illnesses.

## Clinical Evidence

We have examined the clinical neurological status of infants at 3, 9, 15, and 21 months (ages adjusted for prematurity) to determine the developmental course of specific abnormalities and to relate neurological status to Bayley Mental Scale scores at 21 months (Hunt & Davis, unpublished paper). The infants had birth weights at or below 1500 g (very low birth weight). Infants with obvious brain anomalies or chromosomal abnormalities were routinely excluded from the follow-up population. In addition, for this study we excluded 3 other infants with congenital hydrocephalus. The resulting group was considered homogeneous for the purpose of investigating the associations between CNS functioning in early infancy and subsequent mental development.

The neurologic evaluation of Amiel-Tison and Grenier (1983) was administered at each corrected age. The evaluation includes a number of subtle observations of passive and active muscle tone, and is organized to provide a neurological profile at each age. Abnormalities detected at 3 months were almost always mild but were found in 73% of the infants. The percentage of infants with clinical symptoms declined at each subsequent age and was 50% at 21 months. The number of specific kinds of abnormalities also decreased across ages. We found that a diagnosis of mild spastic-like diplegia or quadreplegia (i.e., excessive extensor tone in arms or/and legs), or a diagnosis of mild or marked flexor hypertonia in arms or/and legs at 3 months correctly identified 20 of 21 infants with some neurological abnormalities at 21 months. The diagnoses incorrectly identified 6 of 21 infants (30%) who were neurologically normal at the older age. We also determined that all of the infants who were normal by clinical examination at 3 months were also normal at 21 months.

By 21 months the major neurological abnormalities noted were the diplegias, with severity ranging from mild (most common) to severe. Except for those cases that also included quadreplegia (i.e., involvement of arms *and* legs), mental status at 21 months was varied and not related to the severity of the diplegia. Infants with quadreplegia at 21 months had less favorable mental test results, with a majority scoring in the lower ranges of mental development. Mental test scores for these infants had declined systematically across ages from generally normal scores at 3 months. Delays in language development contributed to the poor test results at 21 months, suggesting that higher mental processes were compromised at that age for children with symptoms of spastic quadreplegia, even when the symptoms were mild. However, the major finding seemed to be that, in general, the mild abnormalities noted at 3 months were better predictors of subsequent neurological abnormalities than of mental test scores.

Although there is no direct evidence from our data that specific clinical neurological abnormalities at 3 months predict mental status at 21 months, we are interested in pursuing this study further. We can soon determine whether or not the abnormalities noted at any of the infant ages contribute to prediction of intellectual status at age 4. By this age we anticipate that the incidence of mild neurological abnormalities noted at 21 months will be further reduced. Also, measurements of intellectual functioning are more definitive at 4 years and less dependent upon motor skills. If predictors are found, the evidence will support the hypothesis that clinical abnormalities are important even though they tend to disappear early in life. Other studies have supported this hypothesis in a general way (Amiel-Tison, 1969; Drillien, 1972).

## Evidence from Electrophysiology

Some aspects of brain activity can be determined by measurements of electrical activity ("brain waves") recorded from the scalp. One of these is the auditory brainstem response (ABR), a wave form generated as various brainstem structures respond to auditory stimulation. The ABR is clinically useful with infants because it does not require cooperation and can be studied during natural sleep. Components of the ABR wave form are associated with specific loci along the auditory pathway. The response has proven to be diagnostic of auditory disabilities and, also, of some diffuse CNS disorders (see Salamy, 1984 for review).

The overall appearance of the ABR wave form undergoes rapid maturational changes in preterm infants. The response is difficult to elicit prior to 35 weeks conceptional age. At term age equivalence (40 weeks conceptional age) a reliable ABR can be obtained and the characteristic wave form of the recorded response assumes adult components by 3 months. Components of the response show further maturational changes in normal infants. We have compared maturational processes in high risk and normal infants across the first year of life (Salamy, 1984; Salamy, Mendelson, Tooley, & Chaplin, 1980). Both latency and amplitude changes were considered. The results suggested that nerve conduction processes (latencies) were delayed in many risk infants but approximated normal values by the end of the first year. In contrast to latency, measurements of amplitude diverged progressively between risk and normal groups during the latter part of the first year. Some children were evaluated to age 4 years. Even in early childhood the risk infants had smaller average ABRs. By 4 years the risk group continued to show amplitude increases, whereas the normal group appeared to be leveling off. Because children with obvious neurological problems or any evidence of hearing loss had been excluded from the long-term comparisons, it was concluded that subtle differences in CNS development were reflected in the ABR amplitude differences.

Future research is planned to examine functioning across the brain, from one hemisphere to the other, by measuring hemispheric differences in latencies of the evoked response to tactile stimulation. Normal intellectual functioning depends upon the cooperation and interaction between the two halves of the brain. The development of hemispheric integration takes place slowly over the first 10 years of life. Disruption of, or delay in, the transfer of information between the hemispheres has been implicated in a variety of learning and language disorders in childhood. Longitudinal measurements will be obtained from chidlren 4 to 11 years of age with documented intellectual disabilities and compared with measurements from a control group of normal children. The evoked response has already become a clinical tool in the assessment of hearing disorders. The extension of the method to study integrated brain functions may lead to further diagnostic uses for infants and children.

## PREDICTING OUTCOME FROM SOCIAL-ENVIRONMENTAL EVENTS IN INFANCY

The environmental milieu, broadly defined, shapes the course of intellectual development for high risk infants. In our study of high risk infants, previously described, the correlation between WISC-R IQ at 8 years and parent education level (averaged for both parents) was highly significant. Moreover, the magnitude of the correlation (.44) was comparable to that reported for parent-child IQ correlations in normal populations. In our previous discussion of other longitudinal studies of risk infants we have noted that similar family variables were the most significant predictors of childhood outcome when multiple predictors were considered and this finding was replicated in our data (Hunt et al., in press).

A measurement such as the parent education level is considered a marker variable, by which we mean that it represents a class of associated variables. The education variable suggests both genetic and environmental components. A consideration of the relative contributions of heredity and environment to intelligence is beyond the scope of this discussion, but we know that both factors influence childhood IQ (cf. Plomin & DeFries, 1985; Plomin, Leohlin, & DeFries, in press). We also have evidence from twin studies that individual patterns of mental development during infancy have a genetic component (Wilson, 1981; Wilson & Harpring, 1972). The environmental component of the parent education variable is conceptualized as an array of parenting styles that determines the physical and social environment of the infant and child. In general, parenting styles are expected to show stability over time (e.g., social class differences) although specific features of parenting may vary according to the age of the child.

The social environment of infants has been of special research interest in recent years. As the social experiences of the infant are largely mediated through the mother (or other consistent caretakers) mother-infant interactions have been the focus of research. An important question to be asked is: How do specific aspects of mother-infant interaction influence the course of mental development? The answer is sure to be inconclusive in infancy because of the lack of correlation between infant and childhood IQ and also because of the low relationship between infant and parent IQ. In fact, the argument has been made that infant development is largely species-specific, that most social environments provide ample opportunities for typical development and therefore that the social influences are relatively nondifferentiating in infancy (Scarr, 1983).

The method often selected to investigate the associations between mother-infant interaction and mental development has been to compare high risk and no-risk infant groups. The rationale is the same as that described for the studies of cognitive development, that is, to compare infant groups that have expected group differences in intellectual outcome. A transactional model of mother-infant interactions has been proposed to account for long-term effects (Sameroff, 1980; Sameroff & Chandler, 1975). According to the model, both mother and infant contribute to the interaction process in a reciprocal manner, and differences in interaction that originate in infancy are elaborated and perpetuated into childhood.

How the mother relates to her infant will be affected by her perceptions of the infant (cf. Broussard, 1980). The assumption is made that risk infants may be perceived differently than are normal infants. For example, small preterm infants may be viewed initially in relatively negative terms as being less attractive, less sociable, or more difficult than normal full-term infants. Such perceptions may be reinforced by anxiety and separation during the preterm infant's neonatal hospitalization. The ability of the preterm infant to respond to social overtures also differs initially from the ability of the full-term, healthy neonate. Immaturity and recuperation from illness influence responses and even govern the neonate's ability to tolerate some kinds of social stimulation (Gorski, Davison, & Brazelton, 1980). Consequently, the earliest reciprocal interactions between mother and newborn are altered. That is, interactions are different than they would have been had the child been born at term. It is hypothesized that such alterations may be mutually reinforced and perpetuated, to the detriment of the preterm infant's development.

Some ways in which mother-infant interactions are thought to mediate intellectual development can be mentioned. The mother is often viewed as the teacher; she is the avenue through which the infant is exposed to the social environment and learns from it, for example in acquiring language (see Bruner, 1977). Also, the mother is seen as providing the emotional support needed to promote attitudes essential for intellectual growth, such as goal orientation in infants (Yarrow, Rubenstein, Pedersen, & Jankowski, 1972) and achievement motivation in children (Kagan & Moss, 1962). A third view of the maternal role in infancy is that the mother is the organizer of the infant. In the case of high risk infants who may have suffered some CNS insult, the ability of the mother to organize the infant and promote normal development is considered crucial (Als, Lester, & Brazelton, 1979). We cannot examine these positions in detail in this discussion, but it is apparent that none is mutually exclusive and all may be important. The complexities of social interaction research are formidable, and particularly in relation to intellectual development.

We can examine some specific studies as examples of current research strategies with high risk infants. One question that has been asked is, how do normal and high risk infants differ in social responsiveness at the time when mothers first begin primary care responsibilities? McGeehee and Eckerman (1983) investigated infant responses to social stimulation at the time of discharge from the hospital, comparing full-term healthy neonates with very low birth weight infants who had no significant neurological or residual medical problems. Behaviors were elicited by adult female investigators under controlled conditions of looking, touching and talking to infants. Preterm infants had more erratic bodily movements, more gasps and grunts, and frequent shifts in state. There were no differences between groups in the ability to orient visually, sustain enface (face-to-face) gaze, or to appear socially available. The authors concluded that the preterm infant was socially responsive but not so "readable" a social partner as the full-term infant of approximately the same conceptional age.

DiVitto and Goldberg (1983) compared preterm and full-term infants and their parents for behaviors during feeding across the first 4 months of life (preterm ages not corrected for prematurity). Although the preterm infants showed less mature feeding behaviors and were more difficult to feed, the behavior of parents during feeding became organized over time in the same manner observed for the parents of full-term infants. This study demonstrated that differences in specific parent behaviors were tied to differences in infant behaviors. The inference can be made that the behavioral differences noted in the parents may have been adaptive and appropriate in facilitating feeding.

The two studies, taken together, strongly suggest that high risk preterm infants are, in fact, different in some characteristics during the early months of home life that make them more difficult to parent. When compared with full-term infants of the same chronological age they are decidedly different, a difference that is not lost on parents. A number of studies have determined that preterm infants are less alert, less active, and less responsive than full-term infants during the first months. There is also evidence that mothers of preterm infants show relatively greater infant-directed activity in the early months, but that such behavior may be counter-productive. Increased maternal activity has been reported to be associated with infant gaze aversion and inattention at 4 months (Field, 1977), responses that suggest the infants were reacting to overstimulation. When the mothers were directed to be less intrusive the infants became more responsive.

The associations between mother-infant interactions and mental development during the first year of life were investigated (Crnic, Ragozin, Greenberg, Robinson, & Basham, 1983). A group of low birth weight preterm infants was compared with a full-term group matched for race, maternal age, sex and other relevant variables. Mothers were interviewed 1 month after the infants were discharged from the hospital. Subsequently, mothers and infants were observed together in structured situations and developmental infant tests were administered at 4, 8, and 12 months corrected age.

The study found that preterm infants were less active and less responsive than full-term infants. They vocalized and smiled less to mothers, averted their gaze and bodies more, and showed less positive affect at 4 months. Many of these differences persisted or even increased across the first year of life. Mothers of preterm infants were more active and stimulating during the early months and this tendency also persisted. Global ratings of affect indicated that mothers and their preterm infants were mutually less positive with each other during interactions than were the full-term mother-infant pairs. Bayley Mental and Motor Scale scores were significantly lower at each test age for the preterm group and the differences increased with increasing age; differences in the amount of vocalization and early language expression favored the full-term group. The authors concluded that the results to 12 months supported the hypothesis that social-environmental factors are important determinants of outcome.

# PREDICTING DISCONTINUITY IN MENTAL DEVELOPMENT

Finally, we can examine the assertion that development in infancy is essentially unrelated to subsequent intellectual abilities. According to this view the infant and child progress through distinct stages of cognitive development, each governed by separate mechanisms. These transformations are so distinctive that no continuities can be predicted from one stage to the next. For example, young infants are developing sensory-motor skills and learning rapidly about the physical and social environment. Although individual differences can be observed in the acquisition of these infant attributes, the most careful scrutiny of individual differences at this stage cannot predict future competencies, such as language development that emerge in subsequent stages of development. New stages of intellectual competence emerge as distinct developmental phenomena. Individual differences may be determined by different genetic and enviromental influences at each stage.

In the case of high risk infants, delayed expression of intellectual disabilities would be predicted. Correlations between infant sensory-motor disabilities and subsequent intellectual disabilities, if found, would indicate that different kinds of disabilities were present in the same individual across development. However, one kind of disability would not necessarily predict the other.

Empirical evidence from longitudinal studies of normal and risk populations can be marshalled to support the argument. Infant IQ is not predictive of subsequent IQ; developmental delay in early infancy may or may not be associated with intellectual problems at older ages; environmental variables (e.g., parent education level) that are important correlates of preschool and childhood IQ are not associated with developmental level in infancy. Many investigators have pointed out that our definition of intelligence in infancy bears no resemblance to the definition that is applied at older ages (cf. Lewis, 1983).

The concept of stages in cognitive development has been largely derived from the seminal theoretical work of Jean Piaget. The concept is now so well established in developmental theory that it requires no elaboration in this discussion. However, the assumption that stage theory precludes behavioral continuity across stages is largely derived from empirical evidence of the kind noted. A more direct test of the hypothesis has been reported (McCall, Eichorn, & Hogarty, 1977). In that study age-to-age correlations were examined from longitudinal data across the first 5 years of life. Principal components were derived from test items of mental tests given frequently across the age span (monthly to 15 months, then every 3 months to 30 months, and every 6 months to 60 months). Component scores were correlated across age and patterns of consistency and change in both developmental function and individual differences were examined. Distinct breaks in the age-to-age correlations were noted (i.e., changes in the order of individual differences) that corresponded to changes in the composition of the principal components (i.e., changes in developmental function). Discontinuities were found at 2, 8, 13, 21, and 30–36 months of age. These results were interpreted as revealing major stages in mental development during the first 3 years of life.

The study demonstrates that stages of mental development can be detected by examining the item content of standard intelligence tests. As noted, however, the content of tests changes across age to reflect our preconceived notions of the behaviors that are "intelligent" as well as the emerging capabilities of the child. For example, items that measure imitative ability are included in the infant test when they appear in the infant repertoire at approximately 12 months and language items are heavily represented in the item pool after 18 months. Such a shift in content will, inevitably, alter the structure of the principal components. The antecedents of imitation and language, if they exist, could not be isolated by the procedure and may not have been included in the test.

# INTEGRATION AND DISCUSSION

The four concepts of intellectual development that have been reviewed are not mutually exclusive but emphasize different aspects of infant behavior. The origins of developmental disabilities were hypothesized to be, (1) delays in the rate of acquisition of normal infant development, (2) differences in the acquisition of specific cognitive abilities, (3) disruption of CNS function, and (4) distortion of social interaction patterns. Illustrations from contemporary research have suggested that all of these hypotheses have some validity in predicting or differentiating the development of high risk infant groups.

Most of the studies cited have focused exclusively on low birth weight preterm infants as the risk group and we will continue to use that example to compare the four conceptualizations of infant intelligence. The emphasis on preterm infant development in research has not been random. The high incidence of poor intellectual outcomes for this class of infants is well established. In the example of our longitudinal study we have determined that nonoptimal outcomes continued to be identified and differentiated to 8 years of age. However, we have also established the broad range of outcomes that can be anticipated. Few problems were severe, most were mild and, indeed, half of the children were functioning at the expected level for our middle-class population. The incidence of major perinatal biological risk factors increased with increasing prematurity. In our discussion we have not cited those studies where mild prematurity was equated with a prediction of poor outcome unless other biological risks had been determined.

Differences in developmental rates in infancy (i.e., IQ differences) discriminated only the most disabled outcome group in our study at 12 months, but outcome groups were increasingly differentiated across subsequent ages. Considerable individual IQ variability in infancy was apparent within each outcome group. Two factors appeared to account for nonpredictive IQs in infancy: infant test scores were associated with neonatal illness even for infants who would later demonstrate normal outcome, and many infants with incipient IQ problems scored in the normal range. In our data very high IQ in infancy tended to be associated with normal outcome, but this finding can probably be attributed to good neonatal health status. Studies of normal infant populations have repeatedly noted that precocity in infancy is not associated with childhood IQ. How, then, can we account for the many studies that have demonstrated IQ differences between high risk and no-risk infant groups? The most parsimonious explanation appears to be that the lower IQs of risk groups during the first year of life reflect incomplete recovery from neonatal stress. The potential resiliency of individual infants cannot be determined from the level of development unless we monitor IQ changes over time. Also, we have noted that IQ differences between high risk and normal groups while significant, were usually not associated with marked delay in the risk populations; average scores for risk groups in infancy were usually within the normal range.

Specific studies of infant cognition demonstrated some discrete behavioral differences between preterm and normal infant groups that were linked conceptually with cognitive abilities in children. Such studies may have important remedial implications and indicate ways in which we can further analyze the group differences in infant IQs. The cognitive studies do not stand in opposition to the construct of developmental rates. When cross-age comparisons were made between preterm and normal groups the performance of preterm infants was found to be delayed rather than qualitatively different. That is, even though the preterms were matched for conceptional age they still were delayed in the acquisition of normal cognitive abilities. Group differences between preterm and normal infants appeared to be of the same magnitude in the cognitive studies as were those noted in the IQ studies. Whether or not the cognitive studies can determine predictors of subsequent status for *individual* infants remains to be determined.

Studies of neurological abnormalities in infancy did establish qualitative differences between preterm and full-term groups. Clinical abnormalities, by definition, are not expected in normal infants but were detected in almost three quarters of our very low birth weight population at 3 months. The association between the early clinical neurological abnormalities and subsequent mental development was highly attenuated. Some specific abnormalities at 3 months were found to be associated with the neurological abnormalities still present at 21 months. Abnormalities at the older age were not associated with concurrent mental status except in the instance of the most functionally generalized (if mild) neurological abnormality. The evidence suggests a correlation rather than cause and effect; the more generalized the clinical neurological signs, the more likely that *other* CNS disruptions have taken place. Such an explanation would account for the prevalence of neurological "soft signs" in learning disabled children.

Neurophysiological studies suggested that subtle deficits in CNS functioning can be determined in infancy. The evoked response measurements are particularly appropriate for studies of risk infants. Other exciting techniques to visualize the "working brain" have been developed in recent years. However, these techniques require procedures that are not, as yet, considered appropriate for research with infants and children who do not have diagnosed, serious conditions. As indicated, the evoked response model can be elaborated to include studies of complex brain functioning.

The longitudinal studies of evoked auditory response have found differences between our high risk preterm infants and normal controls matched for conceptional age. Further, the comparisons have revealed a maturational difference between the groups, with preterms lagging in the development of evoked response measurements. One response difference (latency) decreased during infancy whereas another response (amplitude) was increasingly different until 4 years. As noted, other kinds of brain function mature more slowly than the auditory response, specifically, interhemispheric functioning. Abnormalities in interhemispheric functioning have been identified in children with learning disabilities. The evoked response data from infancy suggests that there may be correlates between these measurements and infant behavioral status. Results are too preliminary for us to infer causality from the neurophysiological data, but the method suggests important possibilities for individual diagnosis and prediction.

The importance of the family milieu in determining childhood status of the high risk preterm infants in our study is unquestionable. The environmental elements that may govern the association are less certain. As indicated, some of the family effects may be genetically determined; infants with better innate capacities for intellectual development may be more resilient in their response to CNS results. However, environmental effects are considered to be of major importance in the ultimate expression of intellect. Studies of mother-infant social interactions were emphasized in this discussion because the topic has generated considerable recent research interest in preterm infants.

The social interaction model has stimulated research efforts to examine the connection between early social experience and the development of intelligence. However, comparisons between high risk preterm infants and normal controls seem to present severe difficulties for interpreting results. If, as the interaction research indicates, high risk neonates are intrinsically different from controls in certain behaviors (and different even when conceptional age is equated for groups) then we cannot interpret differences in social interaction as being either facilitative or detrimental to development. That is, although the "different" preterm infant may evoke different maternal behaviors than those noted in the normal mother-infant dyad, such maternal responses may be contingent and appropriate. Therefore, the expected finding of IQ differences between normal and preterm infants cannot be attributed to differences in social interactions. To establish such an association we would need to manipulate the social interactions (i.e., "normalize" the preterm infant-mother dyad) and study the effects of such manipulation on IQ. The rationale for such a procedure is suggested by the results of Field's study (Field, 1977), where social responses were increased in preterm infants when mothers were instructed to interact less (i.e., only imitate infant behaviors). Pursuing such differences to note changes in mental development would be difficult without consistent and intense intervention studies. Controlled studies are not possible with human infants but some aspects of behavioral change have been studied in mother-substitution research with primates (cf. Soumi & Harlow, 1971).

One possible naturalistic study of human infants would be to examine longitudinal data retrospectively, comparing groups of preterm infants equated for neonatal behavioral status but with different intellectual outcomes. Differences in early mother-infant interaction patterns in such groups would be of great interest. The value of such an approach has been suggested in the study of high risk preterm infants reported by Cohen and Parmelee (1983). The maternal population in that study was very diverse in ethnic and educational background. Caregiver-infant interaction in the first year of life was a better predictor of competence at 9 and 24 months than was maternal education. The normal-vs-risk comparisons of the infant interaction studies need such validation before we can test the hypothesis that intellectual outcomes can be attributed to differences in maternal-infant interactions. Case studies of individuals may be particularly useful in determining essential social interaction characteristics and in separating general environmental effects from mother-infant interaction.

The criticism of those who maintain that infant behavior is not and cannot be predictive of subsequent intellectual status is hard to refute. However, the question is an empirical one and research from all the different conceptual orientations seems to be focused on disproving the criticism. It is reasonable to expect that small predictive effects will be replicated and expanded in longitudinal studies using techniques such as regression analysis. However, such findings have little direct and immediate applicability for individual prediction. The day may come, but it has not yet arrived, when we may be able to construct a predictive battery of observations from the diverse research related to the developmental characteristics of risk infants.

# IMPLICATIONS FOR EDUCATION

We can begin by describing the school performance of the 8-year-olds in our high risk study. As noted, one of the tests given at that age was the WRAT. The three WRAT scores were highly intercorrelated and we derived a composite score that reflected the degree of association among the three tests. When we used regression analysis to predict the WRAT score we found that only IQ and parent education level were significant predictors. Variables from infancy such as the rating of neonatal illness and birth weight did not add to the prediction.

The most surprising finding was that the three WRAT scores (for word recognition, spelling, and arithmetic) did not differ for the groups with special outcomes when compared with groups of similar WISC-R Full Scale IQs. The group with low Bender scores had no special characteristics on the achievement tests that set them apart from normal-scoring children. Also, the group with low Verbal IQs did as well as the group with low-normal IQs. We conclude that the WRAT measurements of rote learning at age 8 were not importantly affected by these specific differences in test scores, although continuing academic success may be questionable for the children with specific deficits. We will reevaluate academic performance in more detail at 11 years of age.

The high correlation of school performance with IQ is hardly surprising and those children who tested below average were having academic problems. Many were repeating second grade and a few had been identified for special remedial help. However, as noted, many of the children were scoring in the expected IQ range and were reported to have no school problems.

The rate data that were presented in Figure 2 suggest that IQ-related problems can be identified with some confidence by 3 years of age and further suggest that children with the most serious problems can be identified even earlier, usually during the second year. However, most infants with future intellectual problems are virtually unpredictable during the first year. We can consider the meaning of these findings for remedial programs in infancy.

Remedial efforts with infants usually include a special emphasis on assisting mothers in their caretaking skills. We recognize the primary role of the mother or other consistent caretaker for infant development. We have suggested three ways in which maternal behavior may mediate infant mental development. The mother was seen as the teacher of culturally-oriented skills, the promoter of social and emotional attitudes relevant to mental development, and the organizer of mental competence. Both the teaching and attitude-promoting roles of the mother are generally accepted and require no special demonstration or discussion. Remedial efforts with infants are typically directed toward assisting the mother in her role as teacher and in helping her to promote an optimal social and emotional climate for the infant. The role of the mother as the organizer of the high risk infant requires further consideration.

Let us once again consider the example of the very premature infant, the group we determined was at highest risk for future problems. At birth the infant is in need of critical hospital care and is subjected to procedures and treatments designed to prevent or treat life-threatening complications. Even so, the infant may sustain some brain damage, as demonstrated by the high incidence of clinical neurological abnormalities evident at 3 months of age in our study. "Brain damage" is a highly emotionally charged description that conjures up the worst possible predictions for intellectual development. However, many of our small preterm infants functioned quite adequately in childhood and only a small proportion suffered serious consequences. How is this possible? Are infant brains different in some important way from the brains of older children and adults? Research with infant animals has established that the mammalian brain is remarkably redundant and resilient in infancy. If a usual functional pathway is destroyed, then an alternative one may be activated (see McKhann, 1981). Such a substitution process may take time, suggesting one possible explanation for the variety of mild developmental delays (both behavioral and electrophysiological) reported for the high risk preterm infants.

After the small preterm infant has recovered from the critical phase of neonatal care, hospitalization may continue for weeks or even months. Infants usually are discharged no earlier than 1 month before term age. Even in the most therapeutic hospital environment there have been stresses and strains associated with premature adaptation to extrauterine life. Disorganized behavior is frequently noted in these infants. Sleep cycles may be erratic, over-responsiveness to stimulation may be noted and, in general, preterm infants may need special assistance in maintaining self-regulation and in organizing their responses to the environment. This is the earliest and most literal example of the mother as "organizer."

Some need for special organizing support may persist throughout infancy and into childhood. We suggest that optimal development depends upon the ability of the mother (or other caretakers) to interpret the infant's special needs. The studies of mother-infant interactions of preterm infants touched upon this topic. The implication for remediation is that the mother must be assisted to recognize and adapt her behavior to the infant's special needs. For example, she must know when and how to help the infant regulate over-responsiveness to stimulation.

Remedial programs that feature "infant stimulation" may do little to promote the risk infant's self-regulation and control, even though such programs may be effective for other infants with more specific mental disabilities.

Preschool and school-age children with hidden handicaps of minimal brain dysfunction are well-known to educators. They may be overdependent upon adults compared with normal peers, erratic in emotional responses, hyperactive or disorganized in their approach to cognitive tasks. Many of our 8-year-olds with normal IQs were considered suspect in outcome because of these behavioral signs. The "dip" in IQ at 3 years in our data was partially attributed to general immaturity in coping with test demands. The progression of subtle signs of disorganized CNS function may be continuous from infancy. For normal infants and children, parents and teachers function as "organizers" in an unstudied way. The function may be highly important, nevertheless, and perhaps is one way that general familial variables are associated with intelligence. In the case of the high risk infant, development may not be smooth and special assistance may be both more crucial and more difficult.

In general, specific remediation with high risk infants should focus on visible problems, just as is the case for handicapped infants. The disorder in self-regulation and social organization is one that can be observed and is likely to be reported by the mother. An exception to this principle of treating the visible problem is suggested by our research on the mild neuromotor disabilities of infancy. The evidence does not suggest that remedial efforts designed to correct these disabilities will influence mental development. The longitudinal evidence indicates otherwise and also demonstrates that most early neuromotor signs are transient. A distinction must be made between mild, transient signs in infancy and severe conditions such as cerebral palsy which do require intervention to maximize the infant's potential for normal neuromotor functioning. Similarly, neuromotor "soft signs" in children such as awkward motor skills and difficulties in speech articulation may respond to remedial efforts designed to improve neuromotor competence. In these instances remedial efforts may improve school performance. However, a functional remedial approach to neuromotor disabilities does not suggest a direct correspondence between neuromotor and intellectual disabilities. There is no evidence that the maturational delay of prematurity should be regarded as abnormal and remedial efforts to "speed up" preterm infant development are not warranted. Many high risk infants may need only monitoring unless a problem is identified. Our data suggest that children should be followed well into the preschool years in order to define intellectual problems as they emerge.

# SUMMARY

The topic of developmental risk in infants, defined as the likelihood of long-term intellectual disabilities, was considered from four major developmental research perspectives: rates of mental growth, specific functional abilities, brain function, and social interaction. We have focused on the determinants of intellectual development in infancy as viewed from each perspective. References to specific studies, including our longitudinal study of mental development in high risk infants, were introduced into the discussion to illustrate the different research conceptualizations and to provide some substantive information from current research with high risk infants. A thorough research review was not attempted but the relative merits of each major research strategy were discussed. Finally, some implications for early education were considered.

## ACKNOWLEDGEMENTS

Support for the preparation of this chapter was provided by the Institute of Human Development, University of California at Berkeley and by SCOR Grant HL-27356 and by HD-17669 to the Cardiovascular Research Institute, University of California at San Francisco.

## REFERENCES

Als, H., Lester, B. M., & Brazelton, T. B. (1979). Dynamics of the behavioral organization of the premature infant: A theoretical perspective. In T. M. Field, A. M. Sostek, S. Goldberg, & H. H. Shuman (Eds.), *Infants born at risk: Behavior and Development*. New York: Spectrum.

Amiel-Tison, C. (1969). Cerebral factors, neonatal status, and long-term followup. *Biological Neonatorum, 14,* 234–250.

Amiel-Tison, C. & Grenier, A. (1983). *Neurologic evaluation of the newborn and the infant.* New York: Masson Publishing USA.

Bayley, N., & Schaefer, E. S. (1964). Correlations of maternal and child behaviors with the development of mental abilities: Data from the Berkeley Growth Study. *Monographs of the Society for Research in Child Development 29* (6, Whole No. 97).

Broussard, E. R. (1980). Assessment of the adaptive potential of the mother-infant system: The neonatal perception inventories. In P. M. Taylor (Ed.), *Parent-Infant Relationships.* New York: Grune and Stratton.

Bruner, J. (1977). Early social interaction and language acquisition. In H. R. Schaffer (Ed.), *Studies in mother-infant interaction.* New York: Academic Press.

Caputo, D. V., Goldstein, K. M., & Taub, H. B. (1981). Neonatal compromise and later psychological development: A 10-year longitudinal study. In L. S. Friedman & M. Sigman (Eds.), *Preterm birth and psychological development.* New York: Academic Press.

Caron, A. J. & Caron, R. F. (1981). Processing of relational information as an index of infant risk. In S. L. Friedman & M. Sigman (Eds.), *Preterm birth and psychological development.* New York: Academic Press.

Caron, A. J., Caron, R. F., & Glass, P. (1983). Responsiveness to relational information as a measure of cognitive functioning in nonsuspect infants. In R. Field & A. Sostek (Eds.), *Infants Born at Risk.* New York. Grune & Stratton.

Cohen, S. E., & Beckwith, L. (1979). Preterm infant interaction with the caregiver in the first year of life and competence at age two. *Child Development, 50,* 767–776.

Cohen, S. E., & Parmelee, A. H. (1983). Prediction of five-year Stanford-Binet scores in preterm infants. *Child Develoment, 54,* 1242–1253.

Crnic, K. A., Ragozin, A. S., Greenberg, M. T., Robinson, N. M., & Basham, R. B. (1983). Social interaction and developmental competence of preterm and full-term infants during the first year of life. *Child Development, 54,* 1199–1210.

DiVitto, B., & Goldberg, S. (1983). Talking and sucking: Infant feeding behavior and parent stimulation in dyads with different medical histories. *Infant Behavior and Development, 6,* 157–165.

Drillien, C. M. (1972). Abnormal neurologic signs in the first year of life in low-birthweight infants: Possible prognostic significance. *Developmental Medicine and Child Neurology, 14,* 575–584.

Escalona, S. K. (1982). Babies at double hazard: Early development of infants at biologic and social risk. *Pediatrics, 70,* 670–676.

Field, T. M. (1977). Effects of early separation, interactive deficits, and experimental manipulations on infant-mother face-to-face interaction. *Child Development, 48,* 763–771.

Gegoski, M. J., Fagen, J. W., & Pearlman, M. A. (1984). Early learning and memory in the preterm infant. *Infant Behavior and Development, 7,* 267–276.

Groski, P. A., Davison, M. F., & Brazelton, T. B. (1979). Stages of behavioral organization in the high-risk neonate: Theoretical and clinical considerations. *Seminars in Perinatology, 3,* 61–72.

Hunt, J. V. (1981). Predicting intellectual disorders in childhood for preterm infants with birth-weights below 1501 gm. In S. L. Friedman & M. Sigman (Eds.), *Preterm birth and psychological development* (pp. 329–351). New York: Academic Press.

Hunt, J. V. (1983). Environmental risks in fetal and neonatal life as biological determinants of infant intelligence. In M. Lewis (Ed.), *Origins of intelligence* (2nd ed.). New York: Plenum Press.

Hunt, J. V., & Rhodes, L. (1977). Mental development of preterm infants during the first year. *Child Development, 48,* 204–210.

Hunt, J. V., Tooley, W. H., Cooper, B. A. B., & Harvin, D. (in press). Intellectual outcomes of high risk infants at 8 years.

Hunt, J. V., Tooley, W. H., & Harvin, D. (1982). Learning disabilities in children with birth weight < 1500 grams. *Seminars in Perinatology, 6,* 280–287.

Kagan, J., & Moss, H. (1962). *Birth to maturity.* New York: Wiley.

Keogh, B. K., & Margolis, J. S. (1976). Learning to labor and to wait: Attentional problems of children with learning disabilities. *Journal of Learning Disabilities, 9,* 276–286.

Knobloch, H., & Pasamanick, B. (1974). *Gesell and Amatruda's developmental diagnosis* (3rd rev. and enlarged ed.) New York: Harper & Row.

Kopp, C. B. (1983). Risk factors in development. In P. H. Mussen (Ed.), Handbook of child psychology, 4th edition. New York: John Wiley & Sons.

Kopp, C. B., & Vaughn, B. E. (1982). Sustained attention during exploratory manipulation as a predictor of cognitive competence in preterm infants. *Child Develpment, 53,* 174–182.

Lewis, M. (1983). On the nature of intelligence. In M. Lewis (Ed.), *Origins of intelligence.* New York: Plenum Press.

Lewis, M., & McGurk, H. (1972). Evaluation of infant intelligence. *Science, 178,* 1174–1177.

McCall, R. B. (1979). The development of intellectual functioning in infancy and the prediction of later IQ. In J. D. Osofsky (Ed.), *Handbook of infant development.* Hillsdale, NJ: Lawrence Erlbaum.

McCall, R. B. (1983). A conceptual approach to early mental development. In M. Lewis (Ed.), *Origins of Intelligence* (2nd ed.) New York: Plenum Press.

McCall, R. B., Eichorn, D. H., & Hogarty, P. S. (1977). Transitions in early mental development. *Monographs,* SRCD, Vol. *42,* No. 3.

McGehee, L. J., & Eckerman, C. O. (1983). The preterm infant as a social partner: Responsive but unreadable. *Infant Behavior and Development, 6,* 461–470.

McKhann, G. M. (1981). Developmental neurology: Endogenous and exogenous brain regulation. In

N. Kretchmer & J. Brasel (Eds.), *Biomedical and social bases of pediatrics*. New York: Masson Publishing USA.

Osofsky, J. D., & Connors, K. (1979). Mother-infant interaction: An integrative view of a complex system. In J. D. Osofsky (Ed.), *Handbook of infant development*. New York: John Wiley & Sons.

Plomin, R., & DeFries, J. C. (1985). *Origins of individual differences in infancy: The Colorado adoption project*. New York: Academic Press.

Plomin, R., Leohlin, J. C., & DeFries, J. C. (in press). Genetic and environmental components of "environmental" influences. *Developmental Psychology*.

Rose, S. A. (1980). Enhancing visual recognition memory in preterm infants. *Developmental Psychology, 16*, 85–92.

Rose, S. A. (1981). Lags in the cognitive competence of prematurely born infants. In L. S. Friedman & M. Sigman (Eds.), *Preterm birth and psychological development*. New York: Academic Press.

Rose, S. A. (1983). Differential rates of visual information processing in full-term and preterm infants. *Child Development, 54*, 1189–1198.

Rose, S. A., Gottfried, A. W., & Bridger, W. H. (1978). Cross-modal transfer in infants: Relationship to prematurity and socioeconomic background. *Developmental Psychology, 14*, 643–652.

Rose, S. A., Gottfried, A. W., & Bridger, W. H. (1979). Effects of hapic cues on visual recognition memory in fullterm and preterm infants. *Infant Behavior and Development, 2*, 55–67.

Rovee-Collier, C. K. (1984). The ontogeny of learning and memory. In R. Kail & N. E. Spear (Eds.), *Comparative perspectives of learning and memory: The Purdue symposium*. Hillsdale, NJ: Erlbaum.

Salamy, A. (1984). Maturation of the auditory brainstem response from birth through early childhood. *Journal of Clinical Neurophysiology, 1*, 293–329.

Salamy, A., Mendelson, T., Tooley, W. H., & Chaplin, E. R. (1980). Differential development of brainstem potentials in healthy and high-risk infants. *Science, 210*, 553–555.

Sameroff, A. J. (1980). Issues in early reproductive and caretaking risk: Review and current status. In D. B. Sawin, R. C. Hawkins, L. O. Walker, & J. H. Penticuff (Eds.), *Exceptional infant* (Vol. 4). Chicago: University of Chicago Press.

Sameroff, A. J., & Chandler, M. J. (1975). Reproductive risk and the continuum of caretaking casualty. In F. D. Horowitz, M. Hetherington, S. Scarr-Salapatek, & G. Siegel (Eds.), *Review of child development research* (Vol. 4). Chicago: University of Chicago Press.

Sander, L. W. (1976). Issues in early mother-child interaction. In E. N. Rexford, L. W. Sander, & T. Shapiro (Eds.), *Infant psychiatry: A new synthesis* (pp. 127–147). New Haven, CT: Yale University.

Scarr, S. (1983). An evolutionary perspective on infant intelligence. In M. Lewis (Ed.), *Origins of intelligence*. New York: Plenum Press.

Siegel, L. S. (1983). Correction for prematurity and its consequences for the assessment of the very low birth weight infant. *Child Development, 54*, 1176–1188.

Suomi, S. J., & Harlow, H. F. (1971). Abnormal social behavior in young monkeys. In J. Hellmuth (Ed.), *Exceptional Infant, Vol. 2: Studies in Abnormalities*. New York: Brunner/Mazel.

Thoman, E. B. (1976). *Development of synchrony in mother-infant interaction in feeding and other situations*. Proceedings of the 58th Annual Meeting of the Federation of American Societies for Experimental Biology.

Wallace, I. F., Escalona, S. K., McCarton-Daum, C., & Vaughan, H. G., Jr. (1982). Neonatal precursors of cognitive development in low birthweight children. *Seminars in Perinatology, 6*, 327–333.

Whiting, J., & Child, I. (1953). *Child training and personality. A cross cultural study*. New Haven, CT: Yale University Press.

Wilson, R. S. (1981). Mental development: Concordance for same-sex and opposite-sex dizygotic twins. *Developmental Psychology, 17,* 626–629.

Wilson, R. S., & Harpring, E. B. (1972). Mental and motor development in infant twins. *Developmental Psychology, 7,* 277–287.

Yarrow, L. J., Rubenstein, J. L., & Pedersen, F. A. (1975). *Infant and environment: Early cognitive and motivational development.* Washington, DC: Hemisphere Publishing Corp.

Yarrow, L. J., Rubenstein, J. L., Pedersen, F. A., & Jankowski, J. J. (1972) Dimensions of early stimulation and their differential effects on infant development. *Merrill-Palmer Quarterly, 18,* 205–218.

# DEVELOPMENTAL DISABILITIES IN PRESCHOOL CHILDREN

Lucinda P. Bernheimer and Barbara K. Keogh

## BACKGROUND

This chapter is focused on developmental disabilities and developmental delays in a preschool population. These terms have appeared with increasing frequency in the clinical and research literature concerned with young handicapped children. It seems appropriate, therefore, to consider their meaning and utility from research and clinical perspectives. In general, the terms serve two broad functions. First, they are frequently used as umbrella categories which signify a continuum of problems (Capute & Palmer, 1980; Kaminer & Jedrysek, 1982). Second, they are used as relatively benign labels for more traditionally pejorative categories, such as mental retardation (Thompson & O'Quinn, 1979). Both terms lack diagnostic precision, yet "developmental disabilities" has some legislative specificity.

Advances in Special Education, Volume 5, pages 61–93.
Copyright © 1986 by JAI Press Inc.
All rights of reproduction in any form reserved.
ISBN: 0-89232-313-2

As defined in the 1978 extension of the Developmental Disabilities Act (PL 95-602), a developmental *disability* is a chronic disability which (a) is attributable to a mental or physical impairment or combination of physical impairments; (b) is manifested before an individual is 22 years of age; (c) is likely to continue indefinitely; and, (d) results in substantial functional limitations in three or more of the following: life activities, self care, receptive and expressive language, mobility, self direction, capacity for independent living, and economic self sufficiency. Summers (1981) notes that the 1978 definition of developmental disabilities replaces traditional categorical labels which had come to connote pejorative stereotypes; it does not, however, reduce the diagnostic or treatment ambiguities which characterize the condition(s). As example, identification as developmentally disabled does not provide information about the nature or the severity of the disability. Summers comments that the new category "contains persons ranging from physically able-bodied severely mentally retarded individuals to quadriplegics with IQs of 150 [which] makes it more difficult to form any kind of homogenized image" (p. 267). The heterogeneity within the diagnostic label has obvious consequences for generalizations about research findings or about treatment or intervention effects, a point to be discussed in more detail later in this chapter. It should be noted, however, that the traditional classification system in which subgroups were delineated (e.g., mental retardation, cerebral palsy, epilepsy), while sometimes providing useful directions for medical treatment, was also limited in terms of psychological description and educational intervention (Lewis & Brooks-Gunn, 1982).

From a practical perspective, the nonspecific term developmental disabilities allows for the delivery of services to children with a range of problems along a continuum of severity. Certainly the term has served as an impetus for special educators to group individuals by functional ability rather than by medical diagnostic category. Unfortunately, however, the functional groupings are often not themselves homogeneous, and the range of problems subsumed within educational groupings is still broad.

The confusion and imprecision of diagnostic terminology is similarly apparent for children diagnosed as *developmentally delayed.* In contrast to developmental disabilities, developmental delay has more clinical than legislative meaning. It has been defined as the "observed disparity between a child's actual development, particularly in language and cognition or motor skills, and the level usually seen in children developing normally" (Grossman, 1983, p. 168). In practice, the two terms are often used interchangeably to describe a single group of children (Hayden, 1982; Izard & Buechler, 1982). Like the developmental disabilities rubric, developmental delay is often used as a substitute for more precise diagnosis. In that sense it lacks diagnostic value. On the other hand, the very breadth of the term may have clinical benefit. Physicians find it a way to describe problem development in the absence of medical diagnosis. Developmental delay may be suggested when a problem is first suspected, thus preparing the parents for a later, more specific, diagnosis (Scherzer & Tscharnuter, 1982). The rationale for avoiding premature diagnosis is two-fold: concern over the predictive power of infant assessment measures (Keele, 1983; Zelazo, 1982), and the physician's hopes for spontaneous improvement, given the wide intra-individual variations in cognitive development during infancy and early childhood (Tjossem, 1976). Keele (1983) advocates the use of the term developmental delay for any child under the age of 6 whose IQ is between 50 and 75. Yet, the lack of specificity may be one of the most troublesome aspects of the term. McCall (1982) considers the term nonspecific and redundant, and notes that it is usually reserved for babies appearing normal, without obvious medical problems, who do poorly on infant tests. In such cases it is often uncertain whether the developmental pattern represents "delay" or "disability." This distinction is reminiscent of the debates about mental retardation (Ellis, 1969; Zigler, 1969). It seems likely that the umbrella term, developmental disability, subsumes subsets of each.

By way of background, then, developmental disabilities may be viewed as a neutral and umbrella term for particular medical diagnostic groups, as well as a comprehensive category for a broad spectrum of nonspecific developmental problems. Recognized subgroups subsumed by the developmental disabilities rubric include Down syndrome, cerebral palsy, autism, and epilepsy. We suggest that nonspecific developmental delays, those children with delayed development of unknown or uncertain etiology, are another subset of the broader category, developmental disabilities. The developmentally delayed group is of particular interest because, with the exception of some specific subtypes, there is little descriptive information available on these children; yet, they comprise a significant proportion of handicapped children. Further, the category maintains a low profile prior to school entry, and treatment and intervention are uncertain. In the following section we summarize information about four types of developmental profiles: cerebral palsy, Down syndrome, autism, and delay of uncertain etiology. Areas to be addressed include identification, assessment, intervention, and prognosis. Because of the voluminous references available for cerebral palsy, Down syndrome, and autism, we review them briefly, reserving most of the chapter for a report on the less well described children with non-specific developmental delay of unknown etiology.

# CEREBRAL PALSY[1]

*Identification*

Definitions of cerebral palsy range from generic summaries (Bax, 1964; Ellison, 1984) to comprehensive discussions of its many complex aspects (Nelson & Ellenberg, 1978; Stanley & Alberman, 1984). Given this broad array of descriptions, Nelson and Ellenberg (1978) have suggested that no single definition meets with general approval, and that no one definition may be considered optimal in different contexts, even by a single clinician. For this overview, cerebral palsy is defined as a nonprogressive, chronic disability resulting from an insult to the central nervous system, characterized by aberrant control of movement and posture and appearing early in life (Ellenberg & Nelson, 1981; Nelson & Ellenberg, 1978, 1979, 1982). The insult may occur in the prenatal, perinatal, or postnatal periods, and may result from genetic and/or environmental causes (Scherzer & Tscharnuter, 1982; Thompson & O'Quinn, 1979).

A recent study of classification in cerebral palsy (O'Reilly & Walentynowicz, 1981) indicated that 38.5% of the cases originated prenatally, 46.3% originated perinatally, and 15.2% originated postnatally. Prenatal factors include maternal infections leading to neurological impairment in the fetus, such as those in the TORCH group (Toxoplasmosis, Rubella, Cytomegalovirus, and Herpes); as well as low birth weight, prenatal hypoxia, and intracranial hemorrhage. Given the complexity of prenatal risk factors in the etiology of cerebral palsy, Stanley (1984a, 1984b) has argued for adoption of a multifactorial etiological approach that considers familial predisposition, early intrauterine influences, and influences during later pregnancy.

Identification of perinatal etiologic factors (e.g., trauma, anoxia, intraventricular hemorrhage, and infection) is complicated by the variable degree of impact at the time of birth. It is difficult to establish a meaningful index of severity regarding asphyxia and intraventricular hemorrage related to later developmental outcomes as they interact and transact with a host of other conditions (Ellenberg & Nelson, 1981; Nelson & Ellenberg, 1978; Sameroff & Chandler, 1975). Postnatal events associated with cerebral palsy include infection and trauma. This latter category, including child abuse and neglect, represents the population of most clearly preventable cases of cerebral palsy and is thus an appealing area for preventive interventions (Stanley & Blair, 1984).

*Assessment and Classification*

Assessment of the motor disability in cerebral palsy is frequently conducted in terms of clinical classification. The reader is referred to the chapter by Henderson (this volume) for a detailed review and discussion of assessment of children with motor problems. In the present section, it is sufficient to note that clinical classification is both topographical and typological (Batshaw, Perret, & Harryman, 1981; Bobath, 1966; Denhoff, 1966; Levitt, 1982). Topographic (e.g., location of the motor impairment) classification is typically employed in clinical classification of spastic cerebral palsy (e.g., hemiplegia, diplegia, quadriplegia, etc.) (Denhoff, 1966). Other clinical classification categories include the state of muscle tone (tonicity) and the severity of the condition (mild, moderate, and severe) (Bobath, 1966; Denhoff, 1966). The most common type of cerebral palsy is spasticity (Glenting, 1982; Haerer, Anderson, & Schoenberg, 1984; Nelson & Ellenberg, 1978; Stanley, 1979b [see Bleck, 1979, for a comprehensive review]). Other types include athetosis, ataxia, rigidity, atonia, tremor, and mixed types (Batshaw et al., 1981; Bobath, 1966; Denhoff, 1966; Levitt, 1982).

Assessment is complicated by the fact that cerebral palsy is often accompanied by other handicapping conditions. Thopmson and O'Quinn (1979) provide the following percentages for the incidence of these conditions: vision problems, 25%; hearing and speech problems, 50%; seizure disorders, 30%–35%; mental retardation, between 50% and 75%.

*Intervention*

Medical management of cerebral palsy often involves ongoing occupational and/or physical therapy. In addition, bracing techniques, medication, orthopedic surgery, neurosurgery, and biofeedback training are medical treatment options (Batshaw et al., 1981; Cruickshank, 1966; Levitt, 1982). The general aim of these therapies and techniques is improvement of motor performance. It should be noted, however, that many treatment methods lack sufficient empirical support to clearly determine their efficacy (DeGangi, Hurley, & Linscheid, 1983; Fetters, 1984; Parette & Hourcade, 1984).

The severity of motoric involvement in children with cerebral palsy is a critical consideration in educational planning as well as in the ongoing intervention process. Educational placement may be determined in large part by the pupil's physical limitations. While some children with cerebral palsy succeed in regular class placements, others require special education programs. Both regular and special education programming is frequently augmented by clinical services from other disciplines within and outside the school (e.g., language and speech therapy, occupational therapy, physical therapy, treatment of visual handicaps and hearing problems, psychological services, medical management, and social services). Other intervention has included training teachers and parents in methods for maintenance of postural tone, positioning techniques, and general relaxation techniques (Finnie, 1975). A number of curricular approaches have been developed for educational interventions with children who have cerebral palsy (Best, 1978; Bigge, 1982; Connor, Williamson, & Siepp, 1978).

*Prognosis*

While adaptations of the standard school curriculum have been developed to accommodate the unique academic and social needs of students with CP (Best, 1978; Bigge, 1982), post school independence and adjustment is often unsuccessful. From the perspective of ongoing development, the prognosis for success in life is unclear. In a follow-up study of 167 physically handicapped high school graduates, Bachmann (1971) found that most were unemployed or underemployed. More recent investigations have suggested that compared to non-CP peers, adolescents with cerebral palsy are at higher risk for social isolation (Anderson & Klarke, 1982; Leichtman & Friedman, 1975), dependence on their parents (Anderson & Klarke, 1982), rejection by peers (Podeanu-Czehofski, 1975), psychiatric disorders (Rutter, Tizard, & Whitmore, 1970), and behavioral difficulties (Minde, 1978). On a positive note, Resnick (1984) found that adolescents with cerebral palsy who have hobbies, friends, and household responsibilities reported higher levels of self-esteem and self-image than those who did not engage in such activities.

# DOWN SYNDROME[2]

*Identification*

Down syndrome is the most common form of chromosomal anomaly associated with developmental retardation (Edgerton, 1979; Kopp, 1983; Menolascino & Egger, 1978; Rynders & Horrobin, 1980; Smith & Wilson, 1973). It occurs in approximately one out of every 700 live births (Donnell, Alfi, Rublee, & Koch, 1975) in the United States, and accounts for approximately 10% of the instance of moderate to severe developmental delay (MacMillan, 1977). Approximately 92% of Down syndrome cases can be classified as trisomy 21 (Donnell et al., 1975; Hamerton, Giannelli, & Polani, 1965; Hook, 1982). Trisomies generally result from a failure of the chromosome to separate during the formation of an ovum or, more rarely, a sperm (Smith & Wilson, 1973). In the case of trisomy 21, one new cell in the division receives an extra 21st chromosome, the other new cell lacks a 21st chromosome. If the cell with the extra chromosome combines with the other parent's normal egg or sperm, Down syndrome results.

Translocations and mosaicism are less common chromosomal problems associated with Down syndrome (Cowie, 1966; Donnell et al., 1975; Hamerton et al., 1965; Lilienfeld, 1969; Penrose & Smith, 1966; Polani, Ford, Briggs, & Clarke, 1960; Richards, 1969; Richards & Stewart, 1962). In translocations, the extra 21st chromosome breaks and fuses to another acrocentric chromosome, generally resulting in Down syndrome. Mosaicism results from a trisomy occurrence after the embryotic cells have begun to multiply, giving some cells the normal 46 chromosomes and others 47. The extent to which the individual has the characteristic features associated with Down syndrome depends on the percentage of body cells with the extra 21st chromosome (Penrose, 1967). The degree of mosaicism does not, however, appear to be predictive of the individual's level of intelligence (Belmont, 1971; Shipe, Reisman, Chung, Darnell, & Kelley, 1968).

The likelihood of a faulty chromosomal distribution appears to increase exponentially with the age of the mother, particularly past the age of 30 (Collmann &

Stoller, 1962; Hook & Chambers, 1977; Penrose & Smith, 1966; Stark & Mantel, 1966; Trimble & Baird, 1978). The possibility of risk associated with paternal age has also been studied, with somewhat unclear results (Mantel & Stark, 1966). While some evidence for a paternal age effect has been reported (Holmes, 1978; Penrose & Smith, 1966), most studies have demonstrated little support for this hypothesis (Milham & Gittelsohn, 1965; Sigler, Lilienfeld, Cohen, & Westlake, 1965). Additional risk factors that have been examined for their potential association with the incidence of Down syndrome include birth order (Matsunaga, 1967; Smith & Record, 1955; Stark & Mantel, 1966), socioeconomic status (Alberman, Creasy, Elliot, & Spicer, 1976; McDonald, 1972), prenatal factors (Buck, Valentine, & Hamilton, 1966; Cowie, 1961; Sigler et al., 1965; Smith & Record, 1966), and recurrence (Stene, 1970; Stevenson & Davison, 1976). Few main effects have been demonstrated, except in interaction with the high risk factor of maternal age.

Early detection and prevention of Down syndrome is accomplished prenatally through a process known as amniocentesis (Kaback & Leisti, 1975; Silverman, 1979). Now routinely performed on high risk pregnant women (e.g., those in the over 35 age range), amniocentesis is an intrauterine procedure in which a needle is inserted into the sac of amniotic fluid surrounding the fetus and a small sample of that fluid is withdrawn. Fetal cells are collected from the fluid and placed in a special nutrient medium for 7 to 10 days. The cultured cells are then karyotyped, allowing determination of the presence or absence of a chromosomal abnormality.

Down syndrome is usually quickly identified in the newborn because of the characteristic physical symptoms associated with the disorder (Smith & Berg, 1976). These include a large fissured tongue (Oster, 1953), a flat broad nose (Hall, 1964; Pueschel, 1983), a small skull (Cronk & Pueschel, 1983; Olson & Shaw, 1969), eyes with prominent epicanthal folds (Solomons, Zellweger, Jahnke, & Opitz, 1965), a short neck (Pueschel, Scola, Perry, & Pezzullo, 1981), and short hands with an abnormal fifth finger (Benda, 1969). These high frequency characteristics do not appear in every child with Down syndrome; a chromosomal analysis is necessary for accurate diagnosis whenever Down syndrome is clinically suspected (Pueschel, Sassaman, Scola, Thuline, Stark, & Horrobin, 1982).

## Assessment

While the diagnosis of Down syndrome can generally be made during the neonatal period, determination of the degree of associated mental retardation is a complex process. The early development of the infant with Down syndrome is similar to that of normal infants (Kopp, 1983). Gradual decreases in rankings on developmental measures have been noted beginning about the sixth month of life and plateauing at age 3 or 4 (Carr, 1975; Cornwell & Birch, 1969; Share, 1975;

Zeaman & House, 1962). At that point, developmental tests appear predictive of later levels of intellectual performance (Koch, Share, Webb, & Graliker, 1963). The use of MA or IQ as a main predictor of ability or potential has been questioned, however (Putnam & Rynders, 1982). In addition to the usual psychometric measures specific to intellectual functioning, new trends in assessment of individuals with Down syndrome include consideration of affective behaviors, temperament, mother-child interactions, and verbal and nonverbal communication within the home environment (Spiker, 1982). Real-life problem solving behaviors (Charlesworth & Spiker, 1975) and functional skills (Brown, Falvey, Baumgart, Pumpian, Schroeder, & Gruenwald, 1979; Sailor & Guess, 1983) are also considered important assessment areas. These alternative approaches provide a description of the individual's functioning which may have greater prognostic and intervention value than do scores on traditional intelligence measures.

*Intervention*

Historically, the standard treatment for individuals with Down syndrome was institutionalization. However, a number of investigators have demonstrated the importance of early experience and the intellectual and social benefits of the home environment on Down syndrome children's development (Carr, 1970, 1975; Francis, 1971; Shotwell & Shipe, 1964; Smith & Wilson, 1973). As a result, early education and services to support home-based care have become an important part of intervention. Participation in infant programs appears to increase the rate at which Down children achieve developmental milestones (Bidder, Bryant, & Gray, 1975; Koch & de la Cruz, 1975; Ludlow & Allen, 1979; Rynders & Horrobin, 1975). Parents are often involved in these early intervention efforts, acting as teachers or assistants (Bricker & Bricker, 1976; Hayden & Haring, 1976; Lance & Koch, 1973), and in many programs an emphasis is placed on facilitating parent-child interactions (Spiker, 1982).

Traditional school programs for children with Down syndrome have focused on the development of language skills (Jeffree, Wheldall, & Mittler, 1973; Rynders & Horrobin, 1980; Tawney, 1974) and simple self-help skills (Smith & Berg, 1976; Smith & Wilson, 1973). In a few programs, the technology of behavior modification has been successfully used to develop basic academic skills (Rynders, 1982). In general, however, academics have received relatively little attention, in part no doubt, due to the commonly held belief that Down syndrome children were not educable (Rynders & Horrobin, 1980). Recent data suggesting that there may be a 30% to 50% chance that an individaul with Down syndrome can function within the educable range of intelligence (Connolly, 1978; Rynders, Spiker, & Horrobin, 1978) support increased educational efforts for this population.

*Prognosis*

Early intervention, home-based care, behavioral technology, and the recent focus on functional skills and related behaviors have increased educational expectations and improved the overall prognosis for individuals born with Down syndrome. While intellectual deficits are common to this population and persist over the lifespan, interventions with children and adults have demonstrated that intellectual and functional abilities can be improved through carefully structured educational efforts (Putman & Rynders, 1982). Today, individuals with Down syndrome are being taught the skills necessary for independent living (Corcoran, 1979) and gainful employment (Clarke & Clarke, 1974; Gold, 1973). With adequate training and support, many Down syndrome adults can function successfully in a wide variety of community settings.

# AUTISM[3]

*Identification*

Autism occurs in 2 to 4 children per 10,000 (DSM-III, 1980). Once regarded as an affective disorder, it is now viewed as a developmental disability (Schopler, Rutler, & Chess, 1979). To a large degree this change in perspective has been the result of experimental research in the areas of cognitive psychology, perception, and language development (Prior, 1984), biomedical research (Cohen & Shaywitz, 1982), and the inability to document the causal role of family dynamics in the etiology of the condition (Cantwell, Baker, & Rutter, 1979; Koegel, Schreibman, O'Neill, & Burke, 1983; McAdoo & De Myer, 1977).

Although some confusion and controversy remain regarding the definition of autism (DSM-III, 1980; Ritvo & Freeman, 1978; Rutter, 1978), four criteria are generally agreed upon as essential for diagnosis. They are (1) early onset (before the age of 3), (2) impairment in social relationships, (3) delayed and deviant language, and (4) bizarre responses to environment, insistence on sameness. The complexity of the disorder and population heterogeneity make diagnosis problematic. Autism coexists with mental retardation (Jacobson & Janicki, 1983; Rutter, 1978), neurological impairments (Blackstock, 1978; Tanguay & Edwards, 1982) and has been linked to genetic factors (August & Lockhart, 1984; Brown, Jenkins, Friedman, Brooks, Wisniewski, Raguthu, & French, 1982; Ritvo, Ritvo, & Brothers, 1982), and rubella (Chess, Korn, & Fernandez, 1971). In addition, the specific behavioral manifestations of autism differ according to mental and chronological age (Freeman, Guthrie, Ritvo, Schroth, Glass, & Frankel, 1979; Freeman, Ritvo, Guthrie, Schroth, & Ball, 1978; Freeman,

Schroth, Ritvo, Guthrie, & Wake, 1980). Such findings have led to theories of multiple causation and to a search for subtypes of the disorder.

## Assessment

Attempts to quantify autistic features generally belong in one of two categories: assessment for the purpose of diagnosis and classification, and assessment for educational planning and therapeutic intervention. Those instruments designed for diagnosis include parent questionnaires (Ornitz, Guthrie, & Farley, 1977; Rimland, 1971; Wing, 1969) and behavioral observation scales (Freeman, Ritvo, Guthrie, Schroth, & Ball, 1978; Krug, Arick, & Almond, 1980; Schopler, Reichler, De Vellis, & Daly, 1980). Unfortunately, questionnaires usually rely on retrospective parental reports (Freeman & Ritvo, 1982), and observation scales for the most part lack discriminant and/or content validity (Parks, 1983). Assessment for treatment purposes may define specific target behaviors (Koegel, Rincover, & Egel, 1982), determine developmental levels of educational functioning (Schopler & Reichler, 1979), or obtain standardized measures of performance (Krug, Arick, & Almond, 1979). A more recent approach to assessment is the consideration of an ecological perspective and methodology. That is, Charlop, Schreibman, Mason, and Vesey (1983) argue that the social features and limited generalization make it imperative to specify settings and their interactions with behavior of autistic children.

## Intervention

Approaches to intervention reflect assumptions about definition and etiology. Some investigators conceptualize autism as primarily an affective disorder (Bettleheim, 1967; Des Lauriers & Carlson, 1969; Tinbergen, 1974). Treatment approaches, thus, are primarily psychotherapeutic, emphasizing interpersonal and intrafamilial dynamics. Other investigators derive their methods from the early work of Hewett (1965), Wolf, Risley, and Mees (1964), and Lovaas, Berberich, Perloff, and Schaeffer (1966), using behavioral techniques to control self-stimulation and self-injury, and to teach speech, educational, and self-help skills. Whichever specific approach is used, most educationally oriented interventions encourage generalization of skills and greater independence. Generalization and independence are more likely to occur when the curriculum emphasizes age-appropriate tasks which can be used in the person's actual environment (Brown, Branston, Baumgart, Vincent, Falvey, & Schroeder, 1979). Ironically, however, "most of the empirical data regarding the characteristics of autism have been generated in highly structured settings, utilizing isolated and nonfunctional tasks" (Donnellan, Anderson, & Mesaros, 1984). Recognition of the limited "real world" impact of many laboratory based treatments has led to two directions in intervention: community based programs, and increased parent involvement. Each deserves a brief statement.

Considering first the community based approaches, autistic persons and their families need specialized services for schooling, housing, support, and respite care; yet, these services are often not available (Janicki, Lubin, & Friedman, 1983), and require conscious and deliberate development. An example of a workable approach is the comprehensive community-based intervention TEACCH program in North Carolina (Schopler, Mesibov, De Vellis, & Short, 1981) which incorporates behavior modification, special education, and parent counseling and involvement.

The important role of the parents in working with the autistic child is emphasized by many. Lovaas, Koegel, Simmons, & Long (1973) demonstrated that parental involvement was an important element of intervention; Harris, Wolchik, and Milch (1982) reported that parents were effective teachers in language training; Moore and Bailey (1973), Norquist and Wahler (1973), and Schopler and Reichler (1971) found parents successful cotherapists in behavior management. In this regard, Harris (1983) emphasizes the need to consider family dynamics before implementing a behavioral program in order to increase the likelihood of continued child progress.

*Prognosis*

Prognosis is influenced by such factors as level of intellectual functioning and language usage. In a review of all follow-up studies, Lotter (1978) reported that only 5%–17% of children studied evidenced satisfactory school or work performance and/or a near normal social life. This is in contrast to a reasonably consistent literature reporting improvement in specific skills during adolescence and adulthood (Ando & Yoshimura, 1979; Ando, Yoshimura, & Nakabayashi, 1980; De Myer, Barton, De Myer, Norton, Allen, & Steele, 1973). An explanation for this discrepancy is that gains do not keep pace with the expectations of the environment; thus, parents report increasing management difficulties and program failures as their autistic child grows older (Schopler & Mesibov, 1983).

# THE ISSUE OF AMBIGUITY

The three subtypes of developmental disabilities, cerebral palsy, Down syndrome, and autism, account for a large proportion of handicapped preschool children and cover a wide spectrum of physical, cognitive, and social-emotional problems. They also represent a spectrum of ambiguity or uncertainty in diagnosis and prognosis. In terms of diagnosis, Down syndrome is clearly the least ambiguous, autism the most ambiguous. As a rule, Down syndrome is identified at birth or during the first weeks or months of life. In contrast, while parents and professionals usually recognize that "something is wrong" by the first or second year of life, it may take several months or even years to establish the diagnosis of autism. Diagnosis of the motor component of cerebral palsy is usually made within the first year of life, unless the degree of impairment is extremely mild. However, diagnosis of associated conditions (visual, hearing and speech problems, mental retardation) is more uncertain, as these deficits are likely to emerge over time.

While the three conditions differ in diagnostic certainty, all are ambiguous in regard to prognosis. As example, while one of the characteristics of Down syndrome is mental retardation, the degree of retardation ranges from mild to severe. The developmental prognosis for the child with cerebral palsy depends in large part upon the presence or absence of associated problems, as well as the degree of motor impairment, which may take years to ascertain. Prognosis for the autistic child is strongly related to intellectual level and language skills.

The concept of ambiguity is an important one, because it has such an impact on availability of services, family stress, and parent-professional interactions over time, a point to be elaborated later. In the following section we present a detailed description of a group of children who, in our view, represent the most ambiguous subset of developmental disabilities: those with developmental delays, etiology unknown or uncertain. We suggest that the level of diagnostic and prognostic ambiguity in this population is a significant variable with implications for parents and professionals.

# DEVELOPMENTAL DELAY

The literature on mental retardation identifies an extensive array of specific syndromes and conditions, many of which have known etiologies (see Carter, 1975; Grossman, 1983; Mittler, 1977 for detailed review). Symptom patterns may differ, but all have in common lowered intellectual functioning, usually evidenced in the early years as slowness in mastering the major developmental milestones, and in significant language delay or deficiency. In addition to the identified syndromes, however, there are a large number of children who show signs of slow development and language problems, but for whom etiologies are unknown. Further, many of these children do not have associated physical or biological impairments, have no history of prior pre- or perinatal trauma, are members of families in which there is no history of retardation, and are in adequate, even advantaged, socioeconomic status homes. In short, such children do not fit the known patterns of retardation, and are considered to be developmentally delayed, unknown etiology. Estimates of their representation in the retarded population range from 50% to 80% (Batshaw & Perret, 1981; Hayden & Beck, 1982; Magrab & Johnston, 1980; Scheiner & McNabb, 1980). Yet, relatively little is known about their early diagnosis, prognosis, or about optimal interventions. Such children were the focus of the REACH longitudinal study.

## Project REACH Study

In 1977 the Graduate School of Education at UCLA was funded for a 5-year period by the then Bureau of Education for the Handicapped as one of four Early Childhood Institutes. The task of these research institutes was to conduct research directed toward improving educational interventions for handicapped children from birth to 5. Project REACH (Keogh & Kopp, 1982) focused on child characteristics and social setting variables that contributed to handicapped children's performance within school and family settings.

The preschool longitudinal study of Project REACH (Bernheimer & Keogh, 1982), a component of the larger research, was designed to document the course of development in a very specific group: young children who exhibited mild to moderate developmental delay(s) in one or more areas (cognitive, language, motor). Subjects were recruited through Regional Centers, early intervention programs, community preschools and pediatricians. The sample was restricted to one ethnic group, Caucasian, in order to avoid the problem of having to tease out complex cultural/linguistic influences from a relatively small sample. In addition, several categories of developmental delay were excluded from the study: drug-related problems, chromosomal abnormalities, and genetic conditions known to be associated with mental retardation, as well as delay that was associated with neglect or abuse, or delay that was secondary to emotional pathology.

The questions posed at the ouset of REACH research were clustered around child characteristics, issues of measurement, and characteristics of the broader environment. The first child question was related to change over time. Fundamental questions about children in the REACH longitudinal study had to do with how much change and what kind of change would be made over a 2-year period? How would change be reflected in the different domains of development? Measurement questions were inextricably involved with questions about child change, as certain standardized measures (Gesell, Bayley, McCarthy, SICD), as well as project-developed techniques, were selected to monitor progress. As most developmental tests have been standardized on a nonhandicapped population, major questions were posed as to their capacity to demonstrate qualitative as well as quantitative change over time. Finally, an effort was made to assess the relationship between the home enviornment and the developmentally delayed (DD) children's development.

Between March 1979 and December 1980 44 children (15 girls, 29 boys) between the ages of 25 and 42 months were entered into the study; mean entry CA was 33.8, *SD* 3.7. The children exhibited identified delay of mild to moderate degree, or were considered at risk because of equivocal signs of delay associated with problems in the perinatal period. The entering Gesell Adaptive

Behavior scores were between 13 and 36 months (mean 24.9, *SD* 6.1). All children were Caucasian from English-speaking homes, and the majority of subjects (89%) were from two-parent families. Parents were well educated (mean maternal education level 13.4 years; mean paternal education level 14.5 years). Most of the children (89%) were in intervention programs, and a number of the children received additional therapies as well (physical, occupational, speech). The sample as a whole, then, could be considered middle class and advantaged.

*Identification*

The majority of families in the longitudinal study had access to private pediatric care, yet identification of the developmental delay was often a lengthy process. Within the group of 44 subjects the mean age at which parents first became concerned about their child's development was 6.5 months. Although 41% of the parents had been concerned since birth, or within the first month of life, the mean age of diagnosis was 13 months. Given the "state of the art" of infant assessment, the tenuous link between early development and ultimate outcome, and the pediatrician's understandable reluctance to label prematurely, 13 months does not seem an unreasonable age for diagnosis. From the parent's point of view, however, this period, from first concerns to official diagnosis, was long and painful. Compounding the problem was the fact that the diagnosis often provided parents with little information about specifics of treatment and/or prognosis. In many cases children were given multiple diagnoses, such as hypotonia, motor planning problem, affective disorder, and neurologically handicapped, to name a few.

Contributing to the diagnostic problem, for the most part these children looked like normal children. Additionally, the delay was often expressed in varying degrees in different areas of development. For example, a 2½-year-old who was not using language may have been close to age level in gross motor abilities. These "islands of normality" (Roskies, 1972) created problems for parents and professionals alike. A final and related child characteristic was the inconsistency exhibited by many of these children from day to day, even from moment to moment. Parents reported a contrast between "on" days and "off" days and described a widely varying range df abilities, depending upon the particular day. In short, professionals as well as parents were confronted with conflicting evidence about the level of these children's abilities; consequently, they had difficulty determining whether development was deviant, or merely uneven.

*Assessment*

In the REACH study, children were assessed on cognitive, affective, and social components of competence. Cognitive measures included the Bayley Mental Scales (Bayley, 1969), the Gesell Developmental Scales (Gesell, 1947), the McCarthy Scales of Children's Abilities (McCarthy, 1972), and the Sequenced Inventory of Communication Development (Hedrick, Prather, & Tobin, 1975), which yields a receptive as well as an expressive communication age. All measures were administered in the homes at 6-month intervals, in the presence of the parents (usually mothers). Affective measures included the revised (Keogh, Pullis, & Cadwell, 1979) Thomas and Chess Parent Temperament Questionnaire (Thomas & Chess, 1977). Measures of the home environment included the Caldwell Home Inventory (Caldwell, 1970) at yearly intervals, and the Resources and Support Systems Interview (Young, 1980) conducted upon entry into the study. The interview was focused on parental responses to developmentally delayed children in terms of the recognition of the handicap, problems surrounding diagnosis, and the use of formal and informal resources and support systems. Finally, at the end of the study all parents participated in an exit interview designed to update information about the child's status and to get some idea about the parents' stresses and their views of the future.

*Status at entry.*    Assessment at entry indicated that the developmental delay was evidence on a number of dimensions. The mean CA was 33.8 months (*SD* = 3.7); mean scores on the developmental measures (Bayley, Gesell, SICD) ranged from 20.4 months (*SD* = 7.3) on the expressive scale of the SICD to 26.3 months (*SD* = 8.9) on the Gesell Gross Motor Subscale. The language scores were consistently the lowest; in addition to the SICD expressive scores, the Gesell language subscale yielded a mean of 21.5 months (*SD* = 6.3), and the mean SICD receptive score was 23.1 months (*SD* = 5.6). Concerns about language were particularly salient for parents, given the mean chronological age of the group. Fifty-nine percent of the parents described speech/language as a presenting problem at entry. Other problems described by parents with high frequency included physical (61%); learning (34%); behavioral (25%); and medical (20%). Of particular interest was the finding that only 14% of these parents described their children as mentally retarded.

*Relationship among tests.*    Children were assessed at 6-month intervals with the developmental and affective measures. Because children entered the study at different times, some had as many as five assessments, some as few as three. Analyses within each assessment period yielded strong relationships among the major scales, especially between the Bayley and Gesell scores. When the two global scales were broken down into subscales, that is, the Gesell dimensions of gross motor, adaptive behavior, and so on, and the Bayley subscales defined by Kohen-Raz (1967) (eye/hand manipulation, imitation-comprehension, etc.), the pattern of subscale interrelationships was logically and statistically consistent. With the exception of the Bayley manipulation and object relation subscales (both of which tap behaviors which emerge in the first year of development), the relationships were all strong and statistically significant (range of *r* .50 to .85). The magnitude of relationships among the language subscales was particularly impressive. For example, for the group at test 1, values of $r$ for the Gesell language subscale and the Bayley imitation-comprehension and vocalization-social and the SICD expressive and receptive language scores were .77, .80, .87, and .71, respectively.

In addition to the overall agreement amongst the various developmental scales, there were high relationships amongst the various subscales of the Gesell and of Bayley (Kohen-Raz dimensions). When the fine motor and gross motor items were excluded, relationships between all other Bayley Kohen-Raz scales were strong; the five subscales of the Gesell were also highly intercorrelated. Several possible interpretations of these interscale relationships have been proposed (Keogh & Bernheimer, 1985). First, it may be that the scales in fact represent one broad ability factor; that is, the constructs (i.e., fine motor, adaptive, personal/social) may not be independent for young developmentally delayed children. Said differently, for DD children, the various ability domains may not be well differentiated and, thus, the tests measure one global ability factor.

A second, related hypothesis is that language is a powerful mediator, and where children have significant delays in language, there is apt to be a consequent negative impact on other developmental dimensions. Finally, another possible interpretation relates to the confounding of measurement and actual ability. It is possible that the developmental tests which were used for assessing these children were not powerful enough to yield differentiated results. Despite their wide use in developmental testing, the techniques still provide rather gross estimates of children's abilities; that is, where there are significant delays in a number of developmental dimensions the tests may not reflect these differences. Clearly, caution must be exercised in the analysis and interpretation of developmental profiles for this group.

*Changes over time.*   The nature and rate of change over time is a major concern for parents and professionals alike. Indeed, the term developmental *delay* implies that the gap between mental age and chronological age may be closed, or at least narrowed, with the passage of time. For the group as a whole, the REACH findings challenge this assumption. Examination of scores on the developmental tests across test sessions documented that all children made progress. There was a great deal of variability, however, in the *amount* of change. As an example, children were given the Gesell either three, four, or five times, depending upon their date of entry into the study. Thus, children seen five times were followed for 24 months. In this group, the average amount of change in a 2-year period was 18 months, but the range of change varied from 6 to 30 months. The average amount of change for children seen four times over an 18-month period was 13 months, with a range from 11 to 18 months. For children followed for 12 months, the average amount of change was 10 months, with a range of 4 to 24 months.

Coefficients of correlation based on the Gesell tests over time illustrate the stability of rate of development. Values of *r* for the DQ were .87, .89, and .99 between tests 1–2, 1–3, and 1–4, respectively. Values for other between-assessment times were comparable. From both the developmentally scaled item scores and from the correlations of scores over time, it is reasonable to conclude that *as a group,* these DD children tended to show stability of rate of development over time: children who were delayed at 2 or 3 years of age were likely to be delayed when they were 4 or 5. However, it was not possible to make predictions for *individual* children with confidence, at least on the basis of single test sessions. Some children made rapid progress, having change scores which were greater than the changes in their chronological ages. Others maintained remarkable stability, and a few showed patterns of declining scores. Analyses of the patterns of growth, especially of the "changers" included the role played by the home environment, behavioral characteristics, and etiologic factors.

*Effects of home environment.* Home environments were examined with data from the Caldwell Home lnventory. In general, the relationships between the Home Environment dimensions and children's developmental status were low and nonsignificant, at least at the beginning of the study. It seems likely that the homogeneity of the sample minimized or washed out within-group variance in home stimulation. These families were middle class, Anglo, English-speaking; the children all had delays in development; and, most children were in some type of intervention program. Given the generally adequate quality of homes, the Caldwell may have not been powerful enough to differentiate within this group, at least in relation to the major tests of developmental status.

The pattern of relationships shifted somewhat by the final test period where the Gesell language and personal-social scales were significantly correlated to the Caldwell Language Stimulation scale (*r* = .58, .69). Two other Caldwell scales were significantly related to developmental scores at this final testing period: the Language Stimulation to the Gesell DA (*r* = .60) and Variety of Stimulation to the SICD expressive score (*r* = .63). As the findings were correlational, it is not possible to infer the direction of effects. On the one hand, maternal behavior can be considered the independent variable. It seems equally likely, however, that mothers who received higher scores on language stimulation had children who were more linguistically competent; that is, mothers who scored higher on the Caldwell Variety of Stimulation Subscale were responding to children with better language skills.

*Temperament.* The temperament framework adopted in this study was that proposed by Thomas and Chess (1977). The REACH data yielded some identifiable relationships between children's temperament patterns and certain dimensions of parent/child interaction, particularly the interactions relating to restrictions and punishment. The pattern evidenced upon entry was generally consistent across the full period of the study. The temperament dimensions of intensity and persistence yielded high relationships to the Caldwell Punishment subscale ($r = -.63, -.70$). This is not surprising given that children's characteristics of intensity and persistence are likely to interact, possibly even conflict, with parents' views on restrictions and on punishment. In addition, the approach/withdrawal temperament characteristic was negatively related ($r = -.52$ and $-.61$) to the Caldwell Punishment and Language Stimulation scales. In this regard, it is interesting to note that approach-withdrawal was the single most stable temperament attribute over time; values of $r$ for assessment periods 1-2, 1-3, and 1-4 were .66, .72, and .80, respectively. As the children grew older, distractibility became more important, being related significantly and negatively to the Caldwell Stimulation, Maturity, and Punishment scales ($r = -.90, -.69, -.71$).

Taken as a whole, the temperament findings suggest that selected patterns of child attributes relate to the amount and kind of interactions children have with their environments. In particular, the intense, withdrawing, negative, and distractible child appears to have negative interactions with those in his environment. Further, at 30 months there was a negative relationship between Language Stimulation on the Caldwell Scale and the temperament characteristics of approach–withdrawal and intensity. Parents apparently made a reasonable and common sense response to their children; that is, there was more interaction with children who tended to be withdrawing and low in response intensity, a finding compatible with the lower limit control notion proposed by Bell (1977).

*Diagnostic subgroups.*   At the time of entry into the REACH study 29 children were considered seriously delayed (mean DQ 62.0). Eight of this group had histories of perinatal stress (prematurity, anoxia, etc.); 21 had no identified perinatal or prenatal problems. Mean DQs for the two groups were 61.6 (12.3) and 63.2 (6.9) at the time of the first assessment. At the end of the project mean DQs for the two groups were 75.7 (19.9) and 57.8 (9.7). The eight suspect children as a group performed better on all subtests of the Gesell and on the language measures. Further, the pattern of development for most of the suspect children reflected continuing improvement or gain over time, whereas many children in the unknown etiology group had relatively flat profiles of change over time. From a clinical perspective it is particularly important to note that pattern or rate of change could not be predicted from entering developmental test scores or profiles at 30 months, the time of first assessment. By three assessment points, however, the patterns were clearly established and maintained. These findings provide convincing evidence for the importance of monitoring DD children over time. A single evaluation, even one which makes use of several measures, should not be considered conclusive or predictive.

## Intervention

While specific programs have been designed to serve children with autism, Down syndrome, and cerebral palsy (Best, 1978; Bigge, 1982; Haydn & Haring,

1976; Lovaas, Koegel, Simmons, & Long, 1973; Rynders & Horrobin, 1975), parents in this study often encountered difficulties in finding programs which were appropriate for their children. For many families diagnosis was not followed by specific suggestions for treatment or intervention. Although the mean age of diagnosis was 13 months, the mean age of entry into intervention was 25 months. Even where referrals were made directly, interventions were not necessarily satisfactory. Early intervention programs, in most cases, tend to serve children with more visible handicaps—children with Down syndrome, orthopedic handicaps, children with severe or profound retardation. These special education programs were also primary interventions for the majority of the delayed children. For many parents the entrance into a world of such obvious abnormality was very difficult. They did not see their children as deviant, but rather as delayed. In addition to seeing their children as different from the others, some parents found it hard to relate to parents of children with clearcut diagnoses. In these cases, the parent groups were likely to create additional stress, as opposed to much-needed support.

In addition, as the children moved from infant intervention to public school programs, parents were faced with a wide range of choices between programs differing in goals, emphases, and instructional modes. While most infant programs are noncategorical and hence not labeled, preschools and public schools present a bewildering array of labels: severe language disorder, severely emotionally disturbed, trainable mentally retarded, educable mentally retarded, orthopedically handicapped, multiply handicapped. Unfortunately, few delayed children had the labels to fit the program. Decisions about schooling and services were especially painful as they forced parents to attempt to make sense out of the marginality and the ambiguity of their delayed child. Should the child appropriately be considered handicapped, or should the goal be "normality"? Some of the parents in the REACH study resolved the dilemma by providing both special and regular school placement for their children. But as one parent noted about her child and her own experience in the regular school:

> I find it a very isolating experience, and it's very painful for me, having nobody there. I have never felt so isolated in a school situation ever before with any of my children. I feel I have not connected with the parents. I feel they sense my child is different. She's just beginning now to be invited to birthday parties—the entire last year she was not invited to any birthday parties. Now that I'm going with her, I'm agonizing at them because I'm always watching her behaviors and wondering if people are going to sense that she's odd. So they're difficult for me, but I think very nice for her.

During the 2-year period of the REACH study, 17 of the children changed programs. Of these, 18% moved to a less restricted setting, and 35% moved to a more restricted setting. The remaining children moved from a handicapped infant program to a handicapped preschool program. At the end of the study period 70% of the children were in special education. While most of these programs offered opportunities for parent involvement (working in classrooms, fundraising, advocacy activities, parent education), few offered support groups which met regularly, and many parents expressed the desire for such a resource.

*Prognosis*

Eighteen months after the end of Project REACH, 35 families were located who agreed to participate in a follow-up study. The sample included 21 males and 14 females; mean CA was 74.4 months ($SD$ = 6.1). Child measures included the short form of the Stanford Binet, and a short word and letter achievement test (Keogh & Wilcoxen, 1980); these data were collected in the homes during a single session. In a separate session, a language sample was collected and the children were given a modified referential communication test. Detailed analyses of the language data have been reported by Briggs (1984).

Data regarding parent perceptions were gathered through the mail and personal interviews. The mailings included the short form of the Thomas and Chess Parent Temperament scale (Keogh, Pullis, & Cadwell, 1979); the Self-help portion of the Alpern-Boll scale (1972), and the Achenbach Child Behavior Problem Checklist (Achenbach, 1981). The parent interview, conducted in the homes, updated information about child and family status.

For these children as a group, the "delay" was still very evident. Mean MA on the Binet was 58.1 ($SD$ = 12.8), with the mean chronological age 74.4 months ($SD$ = 6.1). Self-help skills were also delayed (mean Alpern-Boll age 58.4 months, $SD$ 15.8). Of particular interest was the increase in behavior and emotional problems. Difficulties in these areas had been reported by 36% and 23% of the parents, respectively, at the end of Project REACH. At follow-up 18 months later, corresponding figures were 48% and 42%.

Detailed discussion of behavior and adjustment problems associated with developmental delay may be found in the report by Keogh, Bernheimer, Pelland, and Daley (1985). Based on the findings from the Child Behavior Problem Checklist (CBPC), as a group the children were perceived by their parents as demonstrating serious behavior problems, especially those related to immaturity, dependence, and acting out or aggressive behaviors. For boys, behavior problems were related to hyperactivity, impulsivity, irritability, and aggressiveness. For girls, the immature and inconsistent behavior was associated with socially dependent problem behaviors. Although the range and intensity of behavior problems varied widely, these individual differences were not explained by children's cognitive, language, or self-help competencies. Temperament, however, was a contributor to the CBPC scores; specifically, the factor composed of intensity and sensory threshold, and the factor of approach/withdrawal and distractibility.

At the end of the follow-up, 26 children were in special education, 5 were in regular education, and 3 were in the process of being evaluated for special education. One child was not yet in school, as her parents were unable to decide which setting was more appropriate—regular or special education. Despite the prevalence of special education settings, and the presence of persistent delays, parents continued to express doubts that these children were retarded. Only 29% listed retardation as a presenting problem, with an additional 11% saying they did not know if their child was retarded or not. Fifty-seven percent of the parents, on the other hand, described problems in "learning."

# DISCUSSION

The comprehensiveness of the 1978 developmental disabilities definition has obvious appeal from a legal and political perspective, as it has identified gaps in services and has increased advocacy. It also identifies a range of problems in development which require diagnosis and treatment. However, we suggest that the term is too broad and nonspecific to be useful in clinical decision making or research sampling. Research conducted with developmentally disabled subjects has included children with Down syndrome, organic problems, visual and auditory handicaps, language delays, autism, environmental deprivation, as well as delays of unknown etiology and delays without specific signs of abnormal development (Barna, Bidder, Gray, Clements, & Gardner, 1980; Breiner & Forehand, 1982; Moore, Fredericks, & Baldwin, 1981; Mundy, Siebert, & Hogan, 1984; Wishart, Bidder, & Gray, 1980). Even within identified subgroups (e.g., cerebral palsy, Down syndrome, autism), diagnostic inconsistencies are apparent. This is especially true within groups of children considered developmentally delayed of unknown etiology. The impact of broad within-classification variance is evident in both clinical and research findings.

Considering first some research problems, Kopp and Krakow (1982) have appropriately cautioned against the use of research samples which are heterogeneous in terms of etiology, developmental level, and prognosis. Keogh and MacMillan (1983) note that sample heterogeneity is a threat to one aspect of external validity. If individuals studied are drawn from those classified developmentally disabled, from whom and to whom do we draw inferences? Even within the subcategories of developmental disabilities subject variation presents puzzling problems. How does unknown variation on a variety of subject characteristics affect outcomes of particular studies? Subject heterogeneity within the developmental disabilities category presents serious and continuing problems in research.

From a clinical perspective, within group variance also presents puzzling problems. A particularly important issue relates to child-treatment interactions. Where known medical conditions have known medical treatments (e.g., cleft palate), the issue is resolved. In the case of many children with developmental disabilities, however, both the diagnosis and the treatment are nonspecific. Further, while diagnosed by a physician within a medical setting, the treatment of choice may be primarily educational. Unfortunately, links between particular presenting problems and specific educational interventions are often unknown or at best obscure (Keogh & Kopp, 1978). As a consequence, most special educational programs for developmentally delayed children serve a broad range of problem types and severity. The program is delivered similarly across children, with only minor variations to meet identified individual needs. It should come as no surprise that the same program may work well for one child, yet appear to be ineffective with another. The nature of these program-child interactions and transactions have not been well described to date, and for the most part program evaluation is based on global indices of child change.

This is not to say that educational intervention does not have an impact on at-risk children and their families. The 1982 SRCD monograph by Lazar and Darlington provides ample evidence that educational programs can positively affect the development and performance of risk children as well as having benefits for their families. The interventions described in the Lazar et al. review were not directed specifically at children with developmental disabilities, but nonetheless add to the increasing literature documenting intervention effects. Programs focused specifically on developmentally disabled children have also begun to produce evidence which argues for the importance of early experience and educational intervention (see Bricker & Sheehan, 1981; Colorado State Department of Education, 1982; Hayden & Haring, 1977; Shapiro, Gordon, & Neiditch, 1977). To date, however, this evidence has tended to be global and nonspecific. The nature of the interaction between child and program variables is for the most part undefined and certainly untested. Encouragingly, there are beginning to be efforts to identify and describe the interactional variables within interventions. Research by Marcovitch and Nestor Simmons (this volume) is illustrative, as these authors have identified child temperament variations of importance within groups of Down syndrome, neurologically impaired, and normally developing preschoolers. From a professional perspective, the point to be made is that within and between diagnostic group variations in child characteristics may have important implications for educational treatment. Specification of the program-child links means more refined assessment of children, but it also calls for comprehensive and detailed description of programs. Both of these deserve systematic attention if we are to improve the nature of services for DD children.

Finally, the ambiguity of diagnosis and classification of children with developmental disabilities is a continuing and serious problem for parents. Parental uncertainties are translated into daily management decisions, into the nature of treatment sought, into attitudinal and affective perspectives about their children, and into interactions with professionals.

As example, the ambiguity of developmental delay was evidenced in the number of diagnostic labels used to describe REACH children, as well as the type of label given parents. In their struggle to have their early concerns validated, or to obtain a consensus on the nature of the problem, parents frequently consulted a number of professionals. Not surprisingly, they were likely to be given as many diagnoses and prognoses as the number of professionals consulted. It was not uncommon for any given child to have three or four different diagnoses at various times; one child had received three different labels: hypotonia, cerebral palsy, and autism. Ironically, the very behaviors which were indicative of parent strengths during this period are often viewed in the literature as being maladaptive (Bernheimer, 1981). The persistent parent is likely to be viewed as over-anxious, and the parent seeking a consensus is often considered a "shopper." Parent strengths, thus, became viewed as parent needs: in the first case, the need to be less anxious; in the second case, the need to "accept" the diagnosis offered by the professional. Clearly, the ambiguity which characterized the REACH children during the diagnostic period was still salient for parents at the follow-up when the children were 5–6 years of age. The reluctance of parents to apply a label of retardation to their children may represent their need to maintain hope (Sherman, Austin, & Shapiro, 1981). It may also represent a pragmatic response to the inconsistencies revealed by the children and the number of diagnostic labels used by professionals.

As noted earlier, all four subtypes of developmental disabilities covered in this chapter can be placed along a continuum of ambiguity about diagnosis and prognosis. While the parents of developmentally delayed children are confronted with continuing uncertainty about diagnosis, parents of all developmentally disabled children must live with ambiguity about prognosis; a major concern and a major uncertainty is how self-sufficient the child will be as an adult. As one father commented, "My only anxiety, the one that provokes me the most, is the fear of plateauing. If he always moves like a tortoise, eventually he'll win the race. But if he ever stops. . . ."

The point to be emphasized is that the developmental disabilities rubric, as well as its subtypes, has value as an umbrella classification for purposes of legislation and advocacy. As a result of the 1978 extension of the Developmental Disabilities Act (PL 95–602), children who were previously unserved became eligible for a range of services. In addition, the nonspecific nature of the term developmental disabilities had appeal to parents and professionals who were loathe to use more pejorative labels. However, the term is of questionable value for diagnosis and treatment because it provides so little substantive information about child characteristics or treatment needs. Those who classify—clinicians, researchers, policy makers—would do well to keep the many purposes of classification in mind. The classification, developmental disabilities, has increased the number of services available to children and families. The burden now is on clinicians and reseachers to make the next level of specification, thereby enhancing the quality of those services.

# ACKNOWLEDGMENT

The writing of this chapter was supported in part by Contract #300-66-0306 between the University of California and the Bureau of Education for the Handicapped, U.S. Office of Education, Washington, D.C.

# NOTES

1. We wish to thank Steven Daley for his contribution to this section.
2. We wish to thank Michelle Pelland for her contribution to this section.
3. We wish to thank Sue Sears for her contribution to this section.

# REFERENCES

Achenbach, T. M. (1981). *Child problem behavior checklist*. Burlington, VT: University of Vermont.

Alberman, E., Creasy, M., Elliot, M., & Spicer, C. (1976). Maternal factors associated with fetal chromosomal anomalies in spontaneous abortions. *British Journal of Obstetrics and Gynaecology, 83,* 621–627.

Alpern, G. D., & Boll, T. J. (1972). *The developmental profile*. Aspen, CO: Psychological Development Publications.

Anderson, E. M., & Klarke, L. (1982). *Disability in adolescence*. New York: Methuen.

Ando, H., & Yoshimura, I. (1979). Effects of age on communication skill levels and prevalence of maladaptive behaviors in autistic and mentally retarded children. *Journal of Autism and Developmental Disorders, 9,* 83–93.

Ando, H., Yoshimura, I., & Nakabayashi, A. (1980). Effects of age on adaptive behavior levels and academic skill levels in autistic and mentally retarded children. *Journal of Autism and Developmental Disorders, 10,* 173–184.

August, G. J., & Lockhart, L. H. (1984). Familial autism and the fragile-4 chromosome. *Journal of Autism and Developmental Disorders, 4,* 197–203.

Bachmann, W. H. (1971). *Influence of selected variables upon economic adaption of orthopedically handicapped and other health impaired*. Unpublished doctoral dissertation, University of the Pacific.

Barna, S., Bidder, R. T., Gray, O. P., Clements, J., & Gardner, S. (1980). The progress of developmentally delayed school children in a home-training scheme. *Child: Care, Health and Development, 6,* 157–164.

Batshaw, M. L., & Perret, Y. M. (1981). *Children with handicaps: A medical primer*. Baltimore: Paul H. Brookes Publishing Co.

Batshaw, M. L., Perret, Y. M., & Harryman, S. (1981). Cerebral palsy. In M. L. Batshaw & Y. M. Perret (Eds.), *Children with handicaps: A medical primer*. Baltimore: Brookes Publishing Co.

Box, M. (1964). Terminology and classification of cerebral palsy. *Developmental Medicine and Child Neurology, 6,* 295–297.

Bayley, N. (1969). *Bayley scales of infant development*. New York: Psychological Corp.

Bell, R. (1977). Socialization findings reexamined. In R. Bell & L. Harper (Eds.), *Child effects on adults*. New York: Wiley.

Belmont, J. M. (1971). Medical-behavioral research in retardation. In N. R. Ellis (Ed.), *International Review of Research in Mental Retardation* (Vol. 5). New York: Academic Press.

Benda, C. E. (1969). *Down's syndrome: Mongolism and its management.* New York: Grune & Stratton.

Bernheimer, L. P. (1981, December). *Assessing needs and strengths in families with developmentally delayed children.* Paper presented at HCEEP/DEC Conference, Washington, DC.

Bernheimer, L. P., & Keogh, B. K. (1982). *Project REACH Final Report. Preschool longitudinal study.* Los Angeles: University of California.

Best, G. A. (1978). *Individuals with physical disabilities.* St. Louis: C. V. Mosby Company.

Bettleheim, B. (1967). *The empty fortress: Infantile autism and the birth of self.* New York: Free Press.

Bidder, R. T., Bryant, G., & Gray, O. P. (1975). Benefits to Down's syndrome children through training their mothers. *Archives of Diseases in Childhood, 50,* 383–386.

Bigge, J. L. (1982). *Teaching individuals with physical and multiple disabilities* (2nd ed.). Columbus, OH: Charles E. Merrill Publishing Co.

Blackstock, E. G. (1978). Cerebral asymmetry and the development of early infantile autism. *Journal of Autism and Childhood Schizophrenia, 8,* 339–353.

Bleck, E. E. (1979). *Orthopedic management of cerebral palsy.* Philadelphia: W. B. Saunders Co.

Bobath, K. (1966). The motor deficit in patients with cerebral palsy. *Clinics in Developmental Medicine* (No. 23). London: Heinemann Medical Books, Ltd.

Breiner, J., & Forehand, R. (1982). Mother-child interactions: A comparison of a clinic-referred developmentally delayed group and two non-delayed groups. *Applied Research in Mental Retardation, 3,* 175–183.

Bricker, W. A., & Bricker, D. D. (1976). The infant, toddler, and preschool research and intervention project. In T. J. Tjossem (Ed.), *Intervention strategies for high-risk infants and young children.* Baltimore: University Park Press.

Bricker, D., & Sheehan, R. (1981). Effectiveness of an early intervention program indexed by measures of child change. *Journal of the Division of Early Childhood, 4,* 11–27.

Briggs, M. M. (1984). *Referential communication in developmentally delayed children: A followup at school entry.* Unpublished doctoral dissertation, University of California, Los Angeles.

Brown, L., Branston, M. B., Baumgart, D., Vincent, L., Falvey, M., & Schroeder, J. (1979). Utilizing the characteristics of a variety of current and subsequent least restrictive environments as factors in the development of curricular content for severely handicapped students. *TASH Review, 4,* 407–424.

Brown, L., Falvey, M., Baumgart, D., Pumpian, I., Schroeder, J., & Gruenwald, L. (Eds.) (1979). *Strategies for teaching chronological age-appropriate functional skills to adolescent and young adult severely handicapped students.* Madison, WI: Madison Metropolitan School District.

Brown, W. T., Jenkins, E. C., Friedman, E., Brooks, J., Wisniewski, K., Raguthu, S., & French, J. (1982). Autism associated with the fragile-k syndrome. *Journal of Autism and Developmental Disorders, 12,* 303–308.

Buck, C., Valentine, G. H., & Hamilton, K. (1966). Reproductive performance of mothers of mongols. *American Journal of Mental Deficiency, 70,* 886–894.

Caldwell, B. (1970). *Home observation for measurement of the environment.* Little Rock, AR: University of Arkansas.

Cantwell, D. P., Baker, L., & Rutter, M. (1979). Families of autistic and dysphasic children. *Archives of General Psychiatry, 36,* 682–687.

Capute, A., & Palmer, F. (1980). A pediatric overview of the spectrum of developmental disabilities. *Journal of Developmental and Behavioral Pediatrics, 1,* 66–69.

Carr, J. (1970). Mental and motor development in young mongol children. *Journal of Mental Deficiency Research, 14,* 205–220.

Carr, J. (1975). *Young children with Down's syndrome: Their development, upbringing, and effect on their families.* London & Boston: Butterworth's.

Carter, C. H. (1975). *Handbook of mental retardation syndromes.* Springfield, IL: Charles C. Thomas.

Charlesworth, W. R., & Spiker, D. (1975). An ethological approach to observation in learning settings. In R. A. Weinberg & F. H. Wood (Eds.), *Observation of pupils in mainstream and special education settings: Alternative strategies.* Minneapolis: Leadership Training Institute/Special Education, University of Minnesota.

Charlop, M. H., Schreibman, L., Mason, J., & Vesey, W. (1983). Behavior-setting interactions of autistic children: A behavioral mapping approach to assessing classroom behaviors. *Analysis and Intervention in Developmental Disabilities, 3,* 359–373.

Chess, S., Korn, S. J., & Fernandez, P. B. (1971). *Psychiatric disorders of children with congenital rubella.* New York: Brunner/Mazel.

Clarke, A. M., & Clarke, A. D. B. (1974). Genetic-environmental interactions in cognitive development. In A. M. Clarke & A. D. B. Clarke (Eds.), *Mental deficiency: The changing outlook* (3rd ed.). New York: Free Press.

Cocoran, E. L. (1979). Campus life for retarded children. *Education Unlimited, 1,* 22–24.

Cohen, D. J., & Shaywitz, B. A. (1982). Preface to the special issue on neurobiological research in autism. *Journal of Autism and Developmental Disorders, 12,* 103–107.

Collmann, R. D., & Stoller, A. (1962). A survey of mongoloid births in Victoria, Australia, 1942–1957. *American Journal of Public Health, 52,* 813–829.

Colorado State Department of Education. (1982). *Effectiveness of early special education for handicapped children.* Denver, CO: Author.

Connolly, J. A. (1978). Intelligence levels of young Down's Syndrome children. *American Journal of Mental Deficiency, 83,* 193–196.

Connor, F. P., Williamson, G. G., & Siepp, J. M. (1978). *Program guide for infants and toddlers with neuromotor and other developmental disabilities.* New York: Teachers College Press.

Cornwell, A. C., & Birch, H. G. (1969). Psychological and social development in home-reared children with Down's syndrome (mongolism). *American Journal of Mental Deficiency, 74,* 341–350.

Cowie, V. A. (1961). Maternal constitution and mongolism. *Proceedings of the Second International Conference on Human Genetics, 2,* 1080–1082.

Cowie, V. A. (1966). Genetic counseling. *Proceedings of the Royal Society of Medicine, 59,* 149–150.

Cronk, C. E., & Pueschel, S. M. (1983). Anthropometric studies. In S. M. Pueschel (Ed.), *A study of the young child with Down's Syndrome.* New York: Human Science Press.

Cruickshank, W. M. (Ed.) (1966). *Cerebral palsy: Its individual and community problems* (2nd ed.). Syracuse, NY: Syracuse University Press.

DeGangi, G. A., Hurley, L., & Linscheid, T. R. (1983). Toward a methodology of the short-term effects of neurodevelopmental treatment. *American Journal of Occupational Therapy, 37,* 479–484.

De Myer, M. K., Barton, S., De Myer, W. E., Norton, J. A., Allen, J., & Steele, R. (1973). Prognoses in autism: A follow-up study. *Journal of Autism and Childhood Schizophrenia, 3,* 199–246.

Denhoff, E. (1966). Cerebral palsy: Medical aspects. In W. M. Cruickshank (Ed.), *Cerebral palsy: Its individual and community problems* (2nd ed.). Syracuse, NY: Syracuse University Press.

Des Lauriers, A. M., & Carlson, C. F. (1969). *Your child is asleep.* Homewood, IL: The Dorsey Press.

Donnell, G. N., Alfi, O. S., Rublee, J. C., & Koch, R. (1975). Chromosomal abnormalities. In R. Koch & F. F. de la Cruz (Eds.), *Down's syndrome (mongolism): Research, prevention and management.* New York: Brunner/Mazel.

Donnellan, A., Anderson, J., & Mesaros, R. (1984). An observational study of stereotypic behavior and proximity related to occurrence of autistic child-family member interactions. *Journal of Autism and Developmental Disorders, 14,* 205–210.

*DSM-111. Diagnostic and statistical manual of mental disorders.* (1980). New York: The American Psychiatric Association.

Edgerton, R. B. (1979). *Mental retardation*. Cambridge, MA: Harvard University Press.

Ellenberg, J. H., & Nelson, K. B. (1981). Early recognition of infants at high risk for cerebral palsy: Examination at age four months. *Developmental Medicine and Child Neurology, 23,* 705–716.

Ellis, N. (1969). A behavioral research strategy in mental retardation: Defense and critique. *American Journal of Mental Deficiency, 73,* 557–566.

Ellison, P. H. (1984). Neonatal follow-up studies. The predictive value of neurologic abnormalities in the first year of life. In A. J. Moss (Ed.), *Pediatrics update: Reviews for physicians.* New York: Elsevier Biomedical.

Fetters, L. (1984). Motor development. In M. J. Hanson (Ed.), *Atypical infant development.* Baltimore: University Park Press.

Finnie, N. R. (1975). *Handling the young cerebral palsied child at home.* New York: E. P. Dutton & Co.

Francis, S. H. (1971). The effects of own-home and institutional rearing on the behavioral development of normal and mongol children. *Journal of Child Psychology, 12,* 173–190.

Freeman, B. J., Guthrie, D., Ritvo, E., Schroth, R., Glass, R., & Frankel, F. (1979). Behavior observation scale: Preliminary analysis of the similarities and differences between autistic and mentally retarded children. *Psychological Reports, 44,* 519–524.

Freeman, B. J., & Ritvo, E. R. (1982). The syndrome of autism: A critical review of diagnostic systems, follow-up studies and the theoretical background of the Behavioral Observation Scale. In J. Steffen & P. Karoly (Eds.), *Autism and severe psychopathology* (pp. 1–39). Lexington, MA: D. C. Heath and Company.

Freeman, B. J., Ritvo, E. R., Guthrie, D., Schroth, P., & Ball, J. (1978). The Behavior Observation Scale for Autism: Initial methodology, data analysis, and preliminary findings on 89 children. *Journal of the American Academy of Child Psychiatry, 17,* 576–588.

Freeman, B. J., Schroth, P., Ritvo, E., Guthrie, D., & Wake, L. (1980). The Behavior Observation Scale for Autism (BOS): Initial results of factor analysis. *Journal of Autism and Developmental Disorders, 10,* 343–346.

Gesell, A., & Amatruda, C. (1947). *Developmental diagnosis.* New York: Hoeber.

Glenting, P. (1982). Cerebral palsy in Eastern Denmark 1965–1974. 1. Decreased frequency of congenital cases. Cerebral palsy registry of Denmark (Report No. VII). *Neuropediatrics, 13,* 72–76.

Gold, M. (1973). Research on the vocational habilitation of the retarded: The present, the future. In N. R. Ellis (Ed.), *International Review of Research in Mental Retardation* (Vol. 6). New York: Academic Press.

Grossman, H. J. (Ed.) (1983). *Classification in mental retardation.* Washington, DC: American Association on Mental Deficiency.

Haerer, A. F., Anderson, D. W., & Schoenberg, B. S. (1984). Prevalence of cerebral palsy in the biracial population of Copiah County, Mississippi. *Developmental Medicine & Child Neurology, 26,* 195–199.

Hall, B. (1964). *Mongolism in newborns: A chemical and cytogenetic study. Acta Paediatrica Supplement, 154,* 1–95.

Hamerton, J. L., Gianelli, F., & Polani, P. E. (1965). Cytogenetics of Down's syndrome (mongolism). 1. Data on a consecutive series of patients referred for genetic counseling and diagnosis. *Cytogenetics, 4,* 171–185.

Harris, S. L. (1983). *Families of the developmentally disabled: A guide to behavioral intervention.* New York: Pergamon Press.

Harris, S., Wolchik, S., & Milch, R. (1982). Changing the speech of autistic children and their parents. *Child and Family Behavior Therapy, 4,* 151–173.

Hayden, A. (1982). The effects of educational intervention on cognitive development. In M. Lewis & L. Taft (Eds.), *Developmental disabilities. Theory, assessment, and intervention.* New York: SP Medical & Scientific Books.

Hayden, A. H., & Beck, G. R. (1982). The epidemiology of high-risk and handicapped infants. In

C. T. Ramey & D. L. Trohanis (Eds.), *Finding and educating high-risk and handicapped infants*. Baltimore: University Park Press.

Hayden, A. H., & Haring, N. G. (1976). Early intervention for high-risk infants and young children: Programs for Down's syndrome children. In T. D. Tjossem (Ed.), *Intervention strategies for high-risk infants and young children*. Baltimore: University Park Press.

Hayden, A. H., & Haring, N. G. (1977). The acceleration and maintenance of developmental gains in Down's syndrome school-age children. In P. Mittler (Ed.), *Research and practice in mental retardation* (Vol. 1). Baltimore: University Park Press.

Hedrick, D., Prather, E., & Tobin, A. (1975). *Sequenced inventory of communication development*. Seattle, WA: University of Washington Press.

Henderson, S. (1986). Motor development and motor problems of preschool handicapped children. In B. K. Keogh (Ed.), *Advances in Special Education* (Vol. 5). *Developmental problems in the preschool years*. Greenwich, CT: JAI Press.

Hewett, F. M. (1965). Teaching speech to an autistic child through operant conditioning. *American Journal of Orthopsychiatry, 35,* 927–936.

Holmes, L. B. (1978). Genetic counseling for the older pregnant woman: New data and questions. *New England Journal of Medicine, 298,* 1419–1421.

Hook, E. B. (1982). Epidemiology of Down syndrome. In S. M. Pueschel & J. E. Rynders (Eds.), *Down syndrome: Advances in biomedicine and the behavioral sciences*. Cambridge, MA: The WARE Press.

Hook, E. B., & Chambers, G. M. (1977). Estimated rates of Down's syndrome in live births by one-year maternal age intervals for mothers aged 20 to 49 in a New York State study—Implications of the "risk" figures for genetic counseling and cost-benefit analysis of prenatal diagnosis programs. *Birth Defects Original Article Series, 13,* 123–141.

Izard, C., & Buechler, S. (1982). Theoretical perspectives on emotions in developmental disabilities. In M. Lewis & L. Taft (Eds.), *Developmental disabilities. Theory, assessment and intervention*. New York: SP Medical and Scientific Books.

Jacobson, J. W., & Janicki, M. P. (1983). Observed prevalence of multiple developmental disabilities. *Mental Retardation, 21,* (3), 87–94.

Janicki, M. P., Lubin, R. A., & Friedman, E. (1983). Variations in characteristics and service needs of persons with autism. *Journal of Autism and Developmental Disorders, 13,* 73–85.

Jeffree, D., Wheldall, K., & Mittler, P. (1973). Facilitating two-word utterances in two Down's syndrome boys. *American Journal of Mental Deficiency, 78,* 117–122.

Kaback, M. M., & Leisti, J. (1975). Prenatal detection of Down's syndrome: Technical and ethical considerations. In R. Koch & F. F. de la Cruz (Eds.), *Down's syndrome (mongolism): Research, prevention, and management*. New York: Brunner/Mazel.

Kaminer, R., & Jedrysek, E. (1982). Early identification of developmental disabilities. *Pediatric Annals, 11,* 427–437.

Keele, D. (1983). *The developmentally disabled child: A manual for primary physicians*. Oradell, NJ: Medical Economics Books.

Keogh, B. K., & Bernheimer, L. P. (1985). *Stability and change in the development of young developmentally delayed children*. Unpublished manuscript.

Keogh, B. K., Bernheimer, L. P., Pelland, M., & Daley, S. (1985). *Behavior and adjustment problems of children with developmental delays*. Unpublished manuscript.

Keogh, B. K., & Kopp, C. B. (1978). From assessment to intervention: An elusive bridge. In F. Minifie & L. Lloyd (Eds.), *Communicative and cognitive abilities—Early behavioral assessment*. Baltimore: University Park Press.

Keogh, B. K., & Kopp, C. B. (1982). *Project REACH final report*. Los Angeles: University of California.

Keogh, B. K., & MacMillan, D. L. (1983). The logic of sample selection: Who represents what? *Exceptional Education Quarterly, 4* (3), 84–90.

Keogh, B. K., Pullis, M. E., and Cadwell, J. (1979). *Parent temperament questionnaire.* (Project REACH Technical Report.) Los Angeles: University of California.

Keogh, B. K., & Wilcoxen, A. (1980). *Preschool academic achievement test.* (Unpublished assessment instrument available from senior author.) University of California, Los Angeles.

Koch, R., & de la Cruz, F. F. (1975). *Down's syndrome (mongolism): Research, prevention and management.* New York: Brunner/Mazel.

Koch, R., Share, J., Webb, A., & Graliker, B. V. (1963). The predictability of Gesell developmental scales in mongolism. *Journal of Pediatrics, 62,* 93–97.

Koegel, R. L., Rincover, A., & Egel, A. L. (1982). *Educating and understanding autistic children.* San Diego, CA: College-Hill Press.

Koegel, R. L., Schreibman, L., O'Neill, R. E., & Burke, J. C. (1983). The personality and family-interaction characteristics of parents of autistic children. *Journal of Consulting and Clinical Psychology, 51,* 683–692.

Kohen-Raz, R. (1976). Scalogram analysis of some developmental sequences of infant behavior as measured by the Bayley Infant Scale of Mental Development. *Genetic Psychology Monographs, 76,* 3–21.

Kopp, C. B. (1983). Risk factors in development. In M. M. Harth & J. J. Campos (Eds.), *Handbook of child psychology. Vol. II: Infancy and developmental psychobiology.* New York: John Wiley & Sons.

Kopp, C. B., & Krakow, J. (1982). The issue of sample characteristics: Biologically at risk or developmentally delayed infants. *Journal of Pediatric Psychology, 7,* 361–374.

Krug, D. A., Arick, J. R., & Almond, P. J. (1979). Autism screening instrument for educational planning: Background and development. In J. Gilliam (Ed.), *Autism: Diagnosis, instruction, management, and research.* Austin, TX: University of Texas at Austin Press.

Krug, D. A., Arick, J. R., & Almond, P. J. (1980). Behavior checklist for identifying severely handicapped individuals with high levels of autistic behavior. *Journal of Child Psychology and Psychiatry, 21,* 221–229.

Lance, W. D., & Koch, A. C. (1973). Parents as teachers: Self-help skills for young handicapped children. *Mental Retardation, 11,* 3–4.

Lazar, I., & Darlington, R. (1982). Lasting effects of early education: A report from the consortium for longitudinal studies. *Monographs of the Society for Research in Child Development, 47* (2–3).

Leichtman, S., & Friedman, S. (1975). Social and psychological development of adolescents and the relationship to chronic illness. *Medical Clinics of North America, 59,* 1319–1328.

Levitt, S. (1982). *Treatment of cerebral palsy and motor delay* (2nd ed.). Boston: Blackwell Scientific Publications.

Lewis, M., & Brooks-Gunn, J. (1982). Developmental models and assessment issues. In N. Anastasiow, W. Frankenburg, & A. Fandal (Eds.), *Identifying the developmentally delayed child.* Baltimore: University Park Press.

Lilienfeld, A. M. (1969). *Epidemiology of mongolism.* Baltimore: John Hopkins Press.

Lotter, V. (1978). Follow-up studies. In M. Rutter & E. Schopler (Eds.), *Autism: A reappraisal of concepts and treatment.* New York: Plenum Press.

Lovaas, O. I., Berberich, J. P., Perloff, B. F., & Schaeffer, B. (1966). Acquisition of imitative speech by schizophrenic children. *Science, 151,* 705–707.

Lovaas, O. I., Koegel, R., Simmons, J. Q., & Long, J. S. (1973). Some generalization and follow-up measures on autistic children in behavior therapy. *Journal of Applied Behavior Analysis, 6,* 131–165.

Ludlow, J. R., & Allen, L. M. (1979). The effect of early intervention and preschool stimulus on the development of the Down's syndrome child. *Journal of Mental Deficiency Research, 23,* 29–43.

MacMillan, D. L. (1977). *Mental retardation in school and society.* Boston: Little, Brown and Company.

Magrab, P. R., & Johnston, R. B. (1980). Mental retardation. In S. Gabel & M. T. Erickson (Eds.), *Child development and developmental disabilities*. Boston: Little, Brown and Company.

Mantel, N., & Stark, E. R. (1966). Paternal age in Down's syndrome. *American Journal of Mental Deficiency, 71*, 1025.

Marcovitch, S., & Nestor Simmons, J. (1986). Social and behavioral problems in the preschool years. In B. K. Keogh (Ed.), *Advances in special education (Vol. 5). Developmental problems in the preschool years*. Greenwich, CT: JAI Press.

Matsunaga, E. (1967). Parental age, live birth order, and pregnancy-free interval in Down's syndrome in Japan. *Ciba Foundation study group no. 25: Mongolism*. Boston: Little, Brown and Company.

McAdoo, W. G., & De Myer, M. K. (1977). Research related to family factors in autism. *Journal of Pediatric Psychology, 2*, 162–166.

McCall, R. B. (1982). Issues in the early development of intelligence and its assessment. In M. Lewis & L. Taft (Eds.), *Developmental disabilities: Theory, assessment, and intervention*. New York: SP Medical & Scientific Books.

McCarthy, D. (1972). *McCarthy scales of children's abilities*. New York: Psychological Corp.

McDonald, A. D. (1972). Thyroid disease and other maternal factors in mongolism. *Canadian Medical Association Journal, 106*, 1085–1089.

Menolascino, F. J., & Egger, M. L. (1978). *Medical dimensions of mental retardation*. Lincoln, NE: University of Nebraska Press.

Milham, S., Jr., & Gittelsohn, A. M. (1965). Parental age and malformations. *Human Biology, 37*, 13–22.

Minde, K. K. (1978). Coping styles of 34 adolescents with cerebral palsy. *American Journal of Psychiatry, 135*, 1344–1349.

Mittler, P. (Ed.). (1977). *Research to practice in mental retardation. Vol. III: Biomedical apsects*. Baltimore: University Park Press.

Moore, B. L., & Bailey, J. S. (1973). Social punishment in the modification of a pre-school child's "autistic-like" behavior with a mother as therapist. *Journal of Applied Behavior Analysis, 6*, 497–507.

Moore, M., Fredericks, H. D., & Baldwin, V. (1981). The long-range effects of early childhood education on a trainable mentally retarded population. *Journal of the Division for Early Childhood, 4*, 94–110.

Mundy, P., Seibert, J., & Hogan, A. (1984). Relationship between sensorimotor and early communication abilities in developmentally delayed children. *Merrill-Palmer Quarterly, 30*, 33–48.

Nelson, K. B., & Ellenberg, J. H. (1978). Epidemiology of cerebral palsy. *Advances in Neurology, 19*, 421–434.

Nelson, K. B., & Ellenberg, J. H. (1979). Neonatal signs as predictors of cerebral palsy. *Pediatrics, 64*, 225–232.

Nelson, K. B., & Ellenberg, J. H. (1982). Children who "outgrew" cerebral palsy. *Pediatrics, 69*, 529–536.

Norquist, V. M., & Wahler, R. G. (1973). Naturalistic treatment of an autistic child. *Journal of Applied Behavior Analysis, 6*, 79–87.

Olson, M. I., & Shaw, C. M. (1969). Presenile dementia and Alzheimer's disease in mongolism. *Brain, 92*, 147–156.

O'Reilly, D. E., & Walentynowicz, J. E. (1981). Etiological factors in cerebral palsy. An historical review. *Developmental Medicine and Child Neurology, 23*, 633–642.

Ornitz, E. M., Guthrie, D., & Farley, A. J. (1977). The early development of autistic children. *Journal of Autism and Childhood Schizophrenia, 7*, 207–229.

Oster, J. (1953). *Mongolism*. Copenhagen: Danish Science Press, Ltd.

Parette, H. P., Jr., & Hourcade, J. J. (1984). A review of therapeutic intervention research on gross and fine motor progress in young children with cerebral palsy. *American Journal of Occupational Therapy, 38*, 462–468.

Parks, S. (1983). The assessment of autistic children: A selective review of available instruments. *Journal of Autism and Developmental Disorders, 13,* 255–267.

Penrose, L. S. (1967). Studies of mosaicism in Down's anomaly. In G. A. Jervis (Ed.), *Mental retardation.* Springfield, IL: Charles C. Thomas.

Penrose, L. S., & Smith, G. F. (1966). *Down's anomaly.* Boston: Little, Brown and Company.

Podeanu-Czehofski, I. (1975). Is it only a child's guilt? Aspects of family life of cerebral palsied children. *Rehabilitation Literature, 36* (10), 322–326.

Polani, P. E., Ford, C. E., Briggs, J. H., & Clarke, C. M. (1960). A mongol girl with 46 chromosomes. *Lancet, 1,* 721–724.

Prior, M. (1984). Developing concepts of childhood autism: The influence of experimental cognitive research. *Journal of Counseling and Clinical Psychology, 52,* 4–16.

Pueschel, S. M. (1983). *A study of the young child with Down's syndrome.* New York: Human Science Press.

Pueschel, S. M., Sassaman, E. A., Scola, P. S., Thuline, H. C., Stark, A. M., & Horrobin, M. (1982). Biomedical aspects in Down syndrome. In S. M. Pueschel & J. E. Rynders (Eds.), *Down syndrome: Advances in biomedicine and the behavioral sciences.* Cambridge, MA: The WARE Press.

Pueschel, S. M., Scola, F. H., Perry, C. D., & Pezzullo, J. C. (1981). Atlanto-axial subluxation in children with Down syndrome. *Pediatric Radiology, 10,* 129–132.

Putnam, J. W., & Rynders, J. E. (1982). Advancing the development of independence in adults with Down syndrome. In S. W. Pueschel & J. E. Rynders (Eds.), *Down syndrome: Advances in biomedicine and the behavioral sciences.* Cambridge, MA: The WARE Press.

Resnick, M. D. (1984). The teenager with cerebral palsy. In R. W. Blum (Ed.), *Chronic illness and disabilities in childhood and adolescence.* Orlando, FL: Grune & Stratton.

Richards, B. W. (1969). Mosaic mongolism. *Journal of Mental Deficiency Research, 13,* 66–83.

Richards, B. W., & Stewart, A. (1962). Mosaicism in a mongol. *Lancet, 1,* 275–276.

Rimland, B. (1971). The differentiation of childhood psychosis: An analysis of checklists for 2,218 psychotic children. *Journal of Autism and Childhood Schizophrenia, 1,* 161–174.

Ritvo, E. R., & Freeman, B. J. (1978). National Society for Autistic Children definition of the syndrome of autism. *Journal of Autism and Childhood Schizophrenia, 8,* 162–167.

Ritvo, E. R., Ritvo, E. C., & Brothers, A. M. (1982). Genetic and immunohematologic factors in autism. *Journal of Autism and Developmental Disorders, 12,* 109–114.

Roskies, E. (1972). *Abnormality and normality: The mothering of thalidomide children.* Ithaca, NY: Cornell University Press.

Rutter, M. (1978). Diagnosis and definition of autism. *Journal of Autism and Childhood Schizophrenia, 8,* 139–161.

Rutter, M., Tizard, J., & Whitmore, E. (1970). *Education, health and behavior.* London: Longman.

Rynders, J. E. (1982). Research on promoting learning in children with Down's syndrome. In S. M. Pueschel & J. E. Rynders (Eds.), *Down syndrome: Advances in biomedicine and the behavioral sciences.* Cambridge, MA: The WARE Press.

Rynders, J. E., & Horrobin, J. M. (1975). Project EDGE: The University of Minnesota's communication stimulation program for Down's syndrome infants. In B. E. Frielander (Ed.), *Exceptional infant* (Vol. 3). New York: Brunner/Mazel.

Rynders, J. E., & Horrobin, J. M. (1980). Educational provisions for young children with Down's syndrome. In J. Gottlieb (Ed.), *Educating mentally retarded persons in the mainstream.* Baltimore: University Park Press.

Rynders, J. E., Spiker, D., & Horrobin, J. (1978). Underestimating the educability of Down's Syndrome children: Examination of methodological problems in recent literature. *American Journal of Mental Deficiency, 82,* 440–448.

Sailor, W., & Guess, D. (1983). *Severely handicapped children: An instructional design.* Boston: Houghton Mifflin Company.

Sameroff, A. J., & Chandler, M. J. (1975). Reproductive risk and the continuum of caretaking casualty. In F. D. Horowitz, E. M. Hetherington, S. Scarr-Salapatek, & G. Siegel (Eds.), *Review of child development research* (Vol. 4). Chicago, IL: University of Chicago Press.

Scheiner, A., & McNabb, N. (1980). The child with mental retardation. In A. Scheiner & N. McNabb (Eds.), *The practical management of the developmentally disabled child*. St. Louis, MO: C.V. Mosby Company.

Scherzer, A., & Tscharnuter, I. (1982). *Early diagnosis and therapy with cerebral palsy: A primer on infant developmental problems*. New York & Basel: Marcel Dekker, Inc.

Schopler, E., & Mesibov, G. (1983). *Autism in adolescents and adults*. New York: Plenum Press.

Schopler, E., Mesibov, G., DeVellis, R., & Short, A. (1981). Treatment outcomes for autistic children and their families. In P. Mittler (Ed.), *Frontiers of knowledge in mental health* (Vol. 1). Baltimore: University Park Press.

Schopler, E., & Reichler, R. J. (1971). Parents as cotherapists in the treatment of psychotic children. *Journal of Autism and Childhood Schizophrenia, 1*, 87–102.

Schopler, E., & Reichler, R. J. (1979). *Individualized assessment and treatment for autistic and developmentally delayed children. Vol. I. Psychoeducational profile*. Baltimore: University Park Press.

Schopler, E., Reichler, R. J., DeVellis, R. F., & Daly, K. (1980). Toward objective classification of childhood autism: Childhood Autism Rating Scale (CARS). *Journal of Autism and Developmental Disorders, 10*, 91–103.

Schopler, E., Rutter, M., & Chess, S. (1979). Editorial: Change of journal scope and title. *Journal of Autism and Developmental Disorders, 9*, 1–10.

Shapiro, L. P., Gordon, R., & Neiditch, C. (1977). Documenting change in young multiply handicapped children in a rehabilitation center. *The Journal of Special Education, 11* (2), 243–257.

Share, J. B. (1975). Developmental progress in Down's syndrome. In R. Koch & F. F. de la Cruz (Eds.), *Down's syndrome (mongolism): Research, prevention, and management*. New York: Brunner/Mazel.

Sherman, M., Austrian, R. W., & Shapiro, T. (1981). Labeling and unlabeling: Perceptions of diagnostic terms among mothers and professionals. *Journal of Developmental and Behavioral Pediatrics, 2*, 93–96.

Shipe, D., Reisman, L. E., Chung, C.-Y., Darnell, A., & Kelly, S. (1968). The relationship between cytogenetic constitution, physical stigmata, and intelligence in Down's syndrome. *American Journal of Mental Deficiency, 2*, 789–797.

Shotwell, A. M., & Shipe, D. (1964). Effect of out-of-home care on the intellectual and social development of mongoloid children. *American Journal of Mental Deficiency, 68*, 693–699.

Sigler, A. T., Lilienfeld, A. M., Cohen, B. H., & Westlake, J. E. (1965). Parental age in Down's syndrome (mongolism). *Journal of Pediatrics, 67*, 631–642.

Silverman, B. K. (1979). NIH consensus development conferences. Antenatal diagnosis. Amniocentesis. *Clinical Pediatrics, 18*, 454–462.

Smith, A., & Record, R. G. (1955). Maternal age and birth rank in etiology of mongolism. *British Journal of Preventative Social Medicine, 9*, 51–55.

Smith, D. W., & Wilson, A. A. (1973). *The child with Down's syndrome (mongolism)*. Philadelphia, PA: W. B. Saunders Co.

Smith, G. F., & Berg, J. M. (1976). *Down's anomaly*. London: Churchill Livingstone.

Solomons, G., Zellweger, H., Jahnke, P. G., & Opitz, E. (1965). Four common eye signs in mongolism. *American Journal of Diseases of Children, 110*, 46–50.

Spiker, D. (1982). Early intervention for young children with Down syndrome: New directions in enhancing parent-child synchrony. In S. M. Pueschel & J. E. Rynders (Eds.), *Down syndrome: Advances in biomedicine and the behavioral sciences*. Cambridge, MA: The WARE Press.

Stanley, F. (1984a). *Perinatal risk factors in the cerebral palsies. Clinics in Developmental Medicine, 87*, 98–115.

Stanley, F. (1984b). *Prenatal risk factors in the study of the cerebral palsies. Clinics in developmental medicine, 87*, 87–97.

Stanley, F., & Alberman, E. (Eds.) (1984). *The epidemiology of the cerebral palsies. Clinics in Developmental Medicine, 87*.

Stanley, F., & Blair, E. (1984). *Postnatal risk factors in the cerebral palsies. Clinics in Developmental Medicine, 87*, 135–149.

Stark, C. R., & Mantel, N. (1966). Effects of maternal age and birth order on the risk of mongolism and leukemia. *Journal of the National Cancer Institute, 37*, 681–698.

Stene, J. (1970). Detection of higher recurrence risk for age-dependent chromosome abnormalities with an application to trisomy G (Down's syndrome). *Human Heredity, 20*, 112–122.

Stevenson, A. C., & Davison, B. C. C. (1976). *Genetic counseling*. London: Heinemann.

Summers, J. (1981). The definition of developmental disabilities: A concept in transition. *Mental Retardation, 19* (6), 259–265.

Tanguay, P., & Edwards, R. M. (1982). Electrophysiological studies of autism: The whisper of the bang. *Journal of Autism and Developmental Disorders, 12*, 177–184.

Tawney, J. (1974). Acceleration of vocal behavior in developmentally retarded children. *Education and Training of the Mentally Retarded, 9*, 22–27.

Thomas, A., & Chess, S. (1977). *Temperament and development*. New York: Brunner/Mazel.

Thompson, R., & O'Quinn, A. (1979). *Developmental disabilities*. New York: Oxford University Press.

Tinbergen, N. (1974). Ethology and stress diseases. *Science, 185*, 20–27.

Tjossem, T. J. (1976). Early intervention: Issues and approaches. In T. J. Tjossem (Ed.), *Intervention strategies in high risk infants and young children*. Baltimore: University Park Press.

Trimble, B. K., & Baird, P. A. (1978). Maternal age and Down syndrome: Age-specific incidence rates by single year intervals. *American Journal of Medical Genetics, 2*, 1–5.

Wing, L. (1969). The handicaps of autistic children: A comparative study. *Journal of Child Psychology and Psychiatry, 10*, 1–40.

Wishart, M., Bidder, R., & Gray, O. (1980). Parental responses to their developmentally delayed children and the South Glamorgan Home Advisory Service. *Child: Care, Health, and Development, 6*, 361–376.

Wolf, M. M., Risley, T. R., & Mees, H. (1964). Application of operant conditioning procedures to the behavior problems of an autistic child. *Behavior Research and Therapy, 1*, 305–312.

Young, M. S. (1980). *Factors influencing utilization of resources and support systems by parents of handicapped children*. Unpublished doctoral dissertation, University of California, Los Angeles.

Zeaman, D., & House, B. J. (1962). Approach and avoidance in the discrimination learning of retardates. *Child Development, 33*, 355–372.

Zelazo, P. (1982). An information processing approach to infant cognitive assessment. In M. Lewis & L. Taft (Eds.), *Developmental disabilities: Theory, assessment, and intervention*. New York: SP Medical & Scientific Books.

Zigler, E. (1969). Development vs. difference theories of mental retardation and the problem of motivation. *American Journal of Mental Deficiency, 73*, 536–556.

# LANGUAGE DISORDERS IN PRESCHOOL CHILDREN

Barbara Frant Hecht

## INTRODUCTION

Sometime during the second year of life, children's babbling gradually gives way to recognizable words. Within two or three years, most children progress from a few single-word utterances like "mama," "more," and "no," to complex grammatical constructions like:

> Now let me have some cake so I can eat it all up before Jason comes home from school. (Sarah, aged 3 years, 9 months)

This is a remarkable achievement for a child who can't yet add two numbers together or tie her shoe without assistance, and it's an achievement that most children accomplish without explicit instruction.

Advances in Special Education, Volume 5, pages 95–119.
Copyright © 1986 by JAI Press Inc.
All rights of reproduction in any form reserved.
ISBN: 0-89232-313-2

Unfortunately, there are some children who have difficulty mastering their native language. Their language disorders range from the severe (such as an inability to use and understand a rudimentary vocabulary) to the mild (such as problems in appropriately shifting speech styles for different listeners and varying situations). The sorts of language problems that emerge in the preschool years are extremely diverse. Children may have pronunciation problems, difficulties in learning simple vocabulary, an inability to combine words into phrases and sentences, problems in using their semantic knowledge to aid in the interpretation of sentences, and difficulties in initiating and sustaining conversations. For some children the language problem may be only one symptom of a pervasive handicapping condition, while for others the language disorder is the only (or the most salient) disability.

The research questions that drive the investigation of language disorders are as diverse as the disorders themselves, but one issue has emerged as a recurrent theme: Is language development in language-disordered children *delayed* or *deviant*? Researchers have continually asked whether language development in mentally retarded, autistic, and language impaired children is a slowed down version of normal development or whether it deviates in significant ways. The question of delay versus deviance is complicated by a number of factors, not the least of which is a growing awareness of individual differences in the rate and style of normal language development. It has become increasingly difficult to find patterns of development in atypical children that have not been documented in some children who are seemingly developing language normally. This has led many researchers to reject the notion that deviance is an appropriate characterization of language development in any group of children with language disorders: mentally retarded children, children with specific language impairments, and even autistic children. More recently, some investigators have dismissed the entire delay/deviance dichotomy as an insufficient and misleading paradigm.

This chapter examines the notion of delay and deviance as it applies to the study of language disorders in preschool children. It begins with a brief discussion of methods and findings of research on normal language development, since it is only against this backdrop that issues in language impairment can be clarified. Discussion of studies of mentally retarded, language impaired, and autistic children that address the issue of delay and deviance follows. This discussion demonstrates that the delay/deviance issue is, indeed, an insufficient research paradigm and that some current research practices preclude the possibility of making definitive statements about delay or deviance. Nevertheless, the delay/deviance issue has inspired a considerable body of research that has greatly advanced our understanding of the nature of various language disorders. Tentative hypotheses about the nature of these disorders are proposed, concluding with a discussion of the implications of this research for the identification, assessment and remediation of preschool children with language problems.

# NORMAL LANGUAGE DEVELOPMENT

*Research Methods*

Language development in young children is studied primarily through naturalistic observation and detailed recording of children's exact utterances, their meanings, and the contexts in which they are used. Investigators generally tape record children interacting with familiar adults in their homes. In the longitudinal studies that provide the basis of our understanding of normal development (e.g., Bates, 1976; Bloom, 1970; Brown, 1973) a few children were recorded at regular intervals for a number of years. Verbatim transcripts were made from these recordings, including contextual information that can aid in the interpretation of children's probable meanings. These transcripts were subjected to detailed linguistic analyses in order to uncover patterns of phonological, lexical, syntactic, semantic, and conversational usage. These patterns allowed investigators to make inferences about the child's growing knowledge of the formal properties of the linguistic system.

Longitudinal case studies are often complemented by cross-sectional experiments with larger numbers of children. These experiments are most often used to investigate children's comprehension of particular words or structures, although some experimental techniques have been devised to elicit children's production of specific structures (Clark & Clark, 1977; Clark & Hecht, 1983).

*Major Findings*

Although language development has been studied for centuries, in the past 25 years there has been a virtual explosion of interest in the development of languages spoken all over the world. This surge of interest followed major breakthroughs in linguistic theory, most notably the syntactic theories of Chomsky (1957, 1965), the sociolinguistic analyses of Labov (1970), the analysis of conversational structure of Sacks, Schegloff, and Jefferson (1974), and the speech act theory of Searle (1969). The picture that has emerged from over two decades of extensive research is that normally developing children do not learn language by directly imitating the linguistic forms that they hear, but instead actively construct a grammar by searching for rules and regularities in the language they hear (see Moskowitz, 1978 for an excellent discussion of this process). This view of the child as a "little linguist" has been modified somewhat in recent years with the recognition that caretakers provide a great deal of assistance by modulating and adjusting their language to match their children's abilities (Bruner, 1981; Snow & Ferguson, 1977), and by providing mini language lessons as an incidental consequence of their tendency to repeat, recast, and emphasize parts of their sentences in order to aid children's comprehension. (Clark & Clark, 1977; Snow, 1972).

Most children begin by producing single-word utterances. Their first words typically name familiar animals, people, food, toys, and household objects as well as states (e.g., hot), locations (e.g., down), negatives (e.g., no), and recurrence (e.g., more) (Nelson, 1973). These first words are much more than simple labels. Greenfield and Smith (1976) demonstrated that children use their limited vocabulary to express a wide range of communicative functions. For example, the word "up" can be used to request to be picked up, to comment on their own success in standing up, to call attention to the location of something, or to object to an adult's attempt to sit them down. When children are limited to saying one word at a time, they generally select the most informative element, omitting what the listener can presuppose from the context (Greenfield & Smith, 1976).

Children's first words, especially the nouns, often do not refer to the same range of meanings that exist in the adult lexicon. Children both over-extend and under-extend their first words (Clark & Clark, 1977). For example, the word *doggie* might be over-extended to refer to a number of four-legged creatures including cats and horses, or to refer to other furry things such as stuffed animals and fuzzy sweaters. The word *spoon* might be under-extended if it is used only to refer to the child's cereal spoon, but not to other spoons in the household. Children appear to over-extend their words more often in production than in comprehension (Thomson & Chapman, 1975). Thus, a child who uses *doggie* to refer to a horse, might have no difficulty correctly picking out a picture of a dog from a set of pictures of other four-legged creatures. Over-extensions of well-known words might serve as a useful communication strategy when child has difficulty retrieving newly learned words from memory (Clark & Hecht, 1983).

The next step in normal development is the combination of single words into two-word utterances. Children use their first word combinations to talk about the same sorts of objects and events that they referred to in their single-word utterances, but the combination allows them to express two bits of information in a single unit (Bloom, Lightbown, & Hood, 1975; Bowerman, 1973). These two-word utterances typically occur within 8 to 10 months of the use of the first single words and when children have at least 50 or so words in their vocabularies (Nelson, 1973).

There is no three-word stage. After children have begun to combine two content words, their utterances become more and more elaborated. Grammatical morphemes such as tense and number marking, auxiliary verbs, pronouns, and articles begin to emerge in children's utterances and help to extend and modulate the meanings of the content words (Brown, 1973). Children begin to learn syntactic devices for expressing negative and interrogative meanings. They can use their language to express a wide range of functions. They can exchange information, make requests, give orders, and answer questions (Rees, 1978).

Between 3 and 4 years of age children begin to produce complex sentences, consisting of more than one clause. Coordinate conjunctions and relative clauses appear in children's sentences. Some investigators have claimed that 3-year-olds produce the major varieties of simple sentences in English (Brown & Bellugi, 1964; Limber, 1973), and by 5 or 6 years of age, differences between child and adult grammar are not obvious from their spontaneous language production (Dale, 1976). Between 3 and 5 years of age, children refine their knowledge of certain rules of discourse, such as how to maintain a topic of conversation by adding new and relevant information (Bloom, Rocissano, & Hood, 1976). Thus, if all proceeds normally, children have acquired the basic structures in their language by the time they enter first grade.

## Individual Differences

Although the pattern described thus far is typical, it is not the only one followed by normally developing children. As more longitudinal case studies accumulate in the literature, the range of known normal individual differences has broadened (e.g., R. Clark, 1977; Furrow, Nelson, & Benedict, 1979). Even the three children studied by Roger Brown and his colleagues (Brown, 1973), who provide the cornerstone of our understanding of *similarities* in the language acquisition process, showed vast individual differences in the ages and rates at which they began to talk. As Figure 1 (from Brown, 1973) illustrates, Eve was producing utterances with a mean length of more than four morphemes by 26 months of age—an age when Sarah was just beginning to combine two words. One investigator who followed nearly 1,000 British children found that first words appeared anywhere between 6 and 30 months of age and word combinations appeared anywhere between 10 and 44 months of age (Morley, 1965, cited in Stark, Mellitis, & Tallal, 1983). In this study the eventual language and learning abilities of the early and late talkers were indistinguishable.

Children differ not only in the age and rate of language development, but also in the paths they follow toward eventual mastery of the adult system. Nelson (1973) distinguished two styles of learning the first words. One group of children, whom she called *referential,* use words that primarily name objects and people. Children whom she called *expressive* use words that primarily serve personal-social functions; for example, *more, thankyou, bye-bye,* and *hi.* Different styles are also apparent at the two-word stage (Bloom, Lightbown, & Hood, 1975). Some children typically combine two content words (e.g., Daddy shoe, sit chair) while others combine content words with pronouns and demonstratives (e.g., that doggie, go here). There are even some children who do not appear to begin by using single-word and two-word combinations, but instead launch directly into long, partially unintelligible, utterances that have the intonation of adult sentences (Clark, 1974). These children seem to have more of a *gestalt,* rather than an *analytic* approach to the language-learning process.

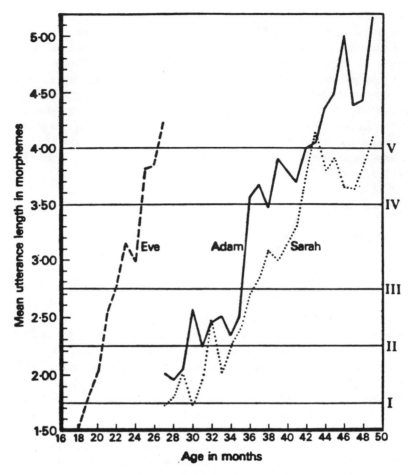

**. Mean Utterance Length and Age in Three Children.**

*Figure 1.*

*From* Brown, R., Cazden, C., & Bellugi, U. (1969). The Child's Grammar from I to II. In John P. Hill (Ed.)
Minnesota Symposia on Child Psychology, Vo. II. Minneapolis: University of Minnesota Press, 28–73.
(Reprinted with permission)

Imitation seems to play a more important role in the acquisition process for
some children than for others. Ruth Clark (1977) has shown that some children
imitate part or all of an adult utterance in order to practice new forms, sustain
discourse, or to communicate messages that are more complicated than they are
capable of formulating on their own. There is increasing evidence from both first
and second language acquisition research that all children produce some "un-

analyzed routines'' (Clark & Hecht, 1983), but some children appear to rely on these memorized forms more than others.

Individual differences in the onset, rate, and style of learning to talk create significant problems when we wish to identify language disorders in the preschool years. The crucial question is, ''When does a difference really make a difference?'' Because so much of our understanding of the normal course of language development is based on in-depth, longitudinal case studies, we are just beginning to accumulate enough data to get a sense of the range of possible paths that lead to mastery of the linguistic system. Our incomplete understanding of individual differences in the course of normal development creates problems for practitioners who would like to identify children at risk for serious language disorders requiring remediation. Individual differences are also of theoretical concern for those researchers who have tried to characterize various types of language disabilities as instances of *delay* or *deviance*.

## DELAY AND DEVIANCE IN LANGUAGE DISORDERS

By 2 years of age most children have begun to use recognizable words and to produce their first word combinations. There are some children, however, who have not begun to talk by this age. For some of these children, this lag is of no serious consequence for later language and academic development, while for others the lack of productive language is an early indicator of a linguistic or more pervasive developmental disability. The degree of individual variation in attainment of early language milestones is so great that many children with normal potential can be misidentified (Stark, Mellits, & Tallal, 1983). One study reported by Stark et al. (Allen & Bliss, 1979) estimated that more than 25% of all preschool children have significant speech and language delays. Estimates of serious speech and language delays among school-aged children are much lower—between 5%–6% (deVilliers & deVilliers, 1978; Marge, 1972). If these figures are accurate, more than three-quarters of preschool children identified as speech or language delayed will have caught up by the time they enter first grade.

Most of the children identified as having significant speech and language problems in the first grade have articulation, voice, or stuttering disorders (deVilliers & deVilliers, 1978). Approximately 12% have more fundamental language disorders. DeVilliers and deVilliers report on one study (Telford & Sawrey, 1967) that found about 40% of these language disordered children to be severely hearing impaired, 25% to be mentally retarded, 1% to be mentally ill or psychotic, and 26% to have specific language impairments without other obvious handicapping conditions. Speech and language disorders are also common among children with cerebral palsy, especially those with serious neuromuscular involvement.

The delay versus deviance issue pervades the literature on the language impairments of three groups of children: children with specific language impairments (e.g., Johnston & Schery, 1976; Leonard, 1972, 1979; Liles & Watt, 1984; Menyuk, 1964), mentally retarded children (e.g., Dooley, 1976; Lackner, 1968; Miller, Chapman, & MacKenzie, 1981), and autistic children (e.g., Bartolucci, Pierce, & Streiner, 1980; Tager-Flusberg, in press). The primary concern has been to provide a characterization of the language development in each of these groups as either a slowed-down version of normal development or as deviating in important ways from the course of normal development.

## Definitions of Delay and Deviance

There are a number of different ways that language development could be delayed or deviant. The *onset* of language can be delayed so that a child is relatively late to begin to talk. If the child rapidly catches up, there would not seem to be cause for concern, although very little is known about these late starters. Some researchers have speculated that temporary delays in language acquisition may be related to interaction or learning styles not compatible with those of the child's caretakers. For example, Stark and her colleagues (1983) suggest that *expressive, referential,* or *imitative* styles (Nelson, 1973) may not mesh with the interaction style of the mother, and may therefore interfere with initial language onset. Another possibility is that late talkers are temporarily delayed in acquiring a skill or ability that is a prerequisite for comprehension or production of speech. Delays in the development of short-term auditory memory, motor sequencing, speech sound discrimination, or certain symbolic or representational abilities have all been suggested as possible causes for late onset, as well as for more long lasting language impairments (Johnston, 1982; Stark et al., 1983; Tallal & Piercy, 1975).

Language delay can also be characterized by a slower *rate* of language development. Recent studies suggest that children whose rate of language development is unusually slow, experience language and learning difficulties throughout the school years (Aram, Ekelman, & Nation, 1984; Stark et al., 1983). Although some of these children eventually catch-up to their normally developing peers, others reach a plateau early on (Lenneberg, 1967; Stark, Mellits, & Tallal, 1983). For these latter children, the end-point may never be the same as that of normal adults (Tager-Flusberg, in press). Their vocabulary might be more limited, they might never be able to use syntactically complex structures (Lenneberg, 1967), and they might never master certain discourse and conversational devices (Kernan & Sabsy, 1985).

Language development may deviate from the norm in either the *what* or the *how* of acquisition—in the product or the process (deVilliers & deVilliers, 1978). For example, the product would be deviant if children's early vocabulary consisted mainly of verbs, or if children used words and sentences only to label and describe objects, but never to make requests or to ask questions. The process would be deviant if children talked about past events before talking about the "here and now," or if they never overextended the reference of their early content words.

Most research on language disorders has focused on the product rather than the process of development (deVilliers & deVilliers, 1978; Tager-Flusberg, in press). This is because, unlike research on normal language development, in-depth longitudinal studies of language impaired children are rare. Most studies of language impaired children have used cross-sectional designs in which impaired and normal children are compared on one aspect of language development at a single point in time. This makes it impossible to examine the interrelationships between, say, the syntactic complexity of the child's language, and the communicative functions the child is able to express. This reliance on cross-sectional research designs has, thus, limited the range of questions that have been addressed and our understanding of the course of development in language impaired children.

One final point must be made about the use of the terms *delay* and *deviance* before turning to some specific research findings. Recently, *quantitative* differences between language impaired and normal children's use of particular linguistic forms have been taken as evidence for *delay,* and *qualitative* differences have been taken as evidence for *deviance* (e.g., Johnston, 1982; Leonard, 1979). Thus, deviance is viewed as a difference in *kind,* not simply *amount.* In cross-sectional comparisons of normal and language-disordered children, a significant difference in the frequency with which one group uses a particular syntactic structure or expresses a communicative function, for instance, is not taken as evidence for deviance. However, in some instances a difference in quantity might itself be deviant. For example, all normal children imitate and use memorized or stock phrases, but a child who relies almost exclusively on stock phrases and persists in using the same set of phrases for more than a few months is clearly using language in a deviant way. This deviance becomes apparent when the memorized phrases are compared to the rest of the child's linguistic system and when the child's language development is followed longitudinally. Thus, the delay/deviance dichotomy is not necessarily synonomous with the distinction between quantitative and qualitative differences.

## Specific Language Impairments

There are some children with serious language impairments who have nonverbal IQs in the normal range and who do not have obvious sensory, motor, or social–emotional problems (Myklebust, 1954). These children are referred to in the literature by a variety of terms, including *language delayed, language disordered, language impaired, aphasic* (more appropriately reserved for disorders due to known brain injury), and *dysphasic.* The term *specific language impair-*

*ment* (SLI) is used here to distinguish this condition from those language impairments that accompany other developmental disabilities.

The lack of agreement on a term reflects a more serious problem of definition and diagnosis. Despite a search for a single term and a single set of diagnostic criteria, recent evidence suggests that children diagnosed as SLI are a very heterogeneous group (Johnston, 1982; Menyuk, 1975). The syndrome is defined in practice by exclusion: When intellectual, social, sensory, and motor deficits can be ruled out, a child with language deficits is classified as SLI. A number of possible causes of SLI have been proposed, but none has been confirmed. Minimal cerebral damage is often suspected, but not revealed by neurological examination (Eisenson, 1972). Recent researchers have suggested that general deficits in symbolic functioning (e.g., Snyder, 1976), information processing (Levy & Menyuk, 1974), and auditory processing (e.g., Tallal, 1976) might account for the language learning problems of SLI children. The search for these underlying deficits remains a major focus of research.

One way that researchers have tried to understand the nature of SLI is to compare groups of children with SLI to other children with developmental disabilities and to normal children. A central theme has been the characterization of children with SLI as either delayed or deviant in language development. Menyuk (1964) was among the first to claim that the language development of SLI children is deviant. She compared spontaneous speech samples from 10 normal children between 3 and 6 years of age to those of 10 children with SLI matched on chronological age. The syntactic structure of the language used in these samples was analyzed, and cross-sectional comparison revealed that SLI children used fewer complex syntactic structures and produced more ungrammatical forms in which obligatory words or grammatical devices were omitted. For example, auxiliary verbs were often omitted, resulting in sentences like ''What he want?'' or ''They running.'' Based on this analysis of children's use of syntax, Menyuk concluded that children with SLI used language in ways that were deviant, ''not simply more infantile than normal for [their] age or delayed in time'' (p. 118).

Menyuk's study was extremely influential, but it had a number of methodological and interpretative limitations. I will discuss four of these in detail—matching criteria, sample size, within-group heterogeneity, and criteria for deviance—because they illustrate problems inherent in using cross-sectional data of this sort to address the issue of delay or deviance. The first limitation of this approach concerns the criteria used for matching the groups. Menyuk matched her groups on the basis of their chronological age; yet, almost by definition, we would expect that SLI children's use of language would differ from that of chronological age matched peers. In order to seriously examine the possibility of language delay, a group of younger normal children would have to be included as a comparison group. Mental age matching, even if based on nonverbal intelligence tests, is similarly problematic, since one of the definitions of specific language impairment is that children have nonverbal IQs in the normal range. Thus, normal and SLI children matched on chronological age would have similar mental ages.

In more recent studies, investigators have recognized the limitations of matching on chronological or mental age and have matched groups on a general index of language development, Mean Utterance Length (MLU) (e.g., Leonard, Steckol, & Schwartz, 1978; Morehead & Ingram, 1973). MLU matching allows investigators to determine whether children use or understand particular linguistic structures in a typical way for their general level of linguistic development. For example, the omission of auxiliary verbs in sentences like those illustrated above is quite typical of young normal children with MLUs of less than 4.0. Thus, what might appear deviant on the basis of chronological age-matching might be quite normal for a given general stage of linguistic development as indexed by MLU. Recent investigators who have carefully matched children on MLU have found far more evidence for delay than deviance in the language development of SLI children. For instance, Morehead and Ingram (1973) examined the syntactic characteristics of the language produced by 15 normal and 15 SLI children matched on MLU. Despite a late onset in the use of the first words and very slow rate of syntactic development, the syntactic constructions used by SLI children were very similar to those used by the normal children.

A second limitation of Menyuk's study is the relatively small sample size (10 children in each group). The small number of children in each of Menyuk's groups is particularly problematic because the children ranged in age from 3 to 6 years. Considerable linguistic development takes place in normal children during the period from 3 to 6 years of age and thus the number of children at any given stage of linguistic development in her sample was very small. Some linguistic constructions that are often used by language impaired children may be much less common among normal children—so much so that they are not observed in studies of small numbers of children. Given what we now know about individual differences in normal language development, it seems quite likely that Menyuk's normal comparison group could not represent the range of normal patterns of language development at each stage. Heterogeneity within the group of SLI children complicates matters further. Some children with SLI may use truly deviant structures or language learning strategies, while others do not. Attempts to characterize the group as a whole as either deviant or delayed can obscure those potentially significant individual differences.

In a later paper, Menyuk (1975) pointed out some individual differences within a group of 13 SLI children between the ages of 4 and 11 years. For example, Menyuk found that not all of the language-impaired children appeared to have equal difficulty with the sound system, or phonology, of their language. In a repetition task, some SLI children made errors and sound substitutions that were similar to those of younger normal children, while others made errors in their repetition of speech sounds that were unlike the errors produced by normally developing children. Menyuk concluded that the linguistic development of SLI children may be either delayed or deviant. Although this conclusion seems quite reasonable, it is important to note that the 13 nursery school children who served as the normal controls were not matched to the SLI children on either chronological age or general language level. As noted above, without such matching, claims about deviance may not be warranted.

A fourth limitation concerns the criteria used as evidence of delay or deviance. Evidence for similarities or differences between the groups in Menyuk's 1964 study was based on the number of children in each group who used a given syntactic structure. As Leonard (1979) has pointed out, Menyuk treated any difference between the two groups that was above chance (.50) as a significant difference. Leonard's reanalysis of her data using the more standard .05 level of confidence, showed that the groups differed on only one of the 33 structures examined.

Even if investigators use more stringent tests of significance, claims of deviance based on the number of children in each group using a particular form must be made with extreme caution. Deviance is a conceptual issue. It is most clear-cut when there is enough understanding of the normal patterns of development that it can be defined a priori with reference to known developmental patterns. Ultimately then, decisions about how much of a difference constitutes a "real" difference cannot be made on statistical grounds alone.

One domain of language development in which such a priori definitions of deviant development can be made is grammatical morphology. Grammatical morphemes in English are the short words and suffixes that indicate grammatical relations, such as prepositions, articles, auxiliary verbs, and tense and number marking on nouns and verbs. Research indicates that normally developing children learn the English grammatical morphemes in a remarkably consistent order (Brown, 1973; deVilliers & deVilliers, 1973). Thus, the development of grammatical morphemes would seem to be an ideal testing ground for evidence of delayed or deviant development. Major deviations from the normal order of acquisition of grammatical morphemes would constitute evidence for deviance, whereas similar patterns of acquisition would suggest delay as the best characterization of the language disorder.

One of the most extensive investigations of the development of grammatical morphemes in SLI children was carried out by Johnston and Schery (1976). They analyzed spontaneous speech samples from 287 SLI children ranging in age from 3;0 to 16;2 (years;months) and noted the lowest MLU level at which each morpheme was used *consistently* (in 90% of all obligatory contexts). This analysis allowed them to derive an overall order of acquisition that was in very close agreement with the order of development in normal children. However, although the *sequence* of development was quite similar in normal and SLI children, Johnston and Schery reported that the SLI children acquired the grammatical morphemes at higher MLU levels than have been reported for normal children. This finding is in accord with other studies of the development of grammatical morphemes in SLI children (Kessler, 1975; Steckol & Leonard, 1979).

These results provide evidence for one type of deviance in the language development of SLI children. Despite a similar order of acquisition of grammatical morphemes, the relationship between MLU and the use of grammatical morphemes deviates from that of normal children. However, this characterization of the SLI children's language as delayed in some respects and deviant in others, does little to illuminate the nature of SLI. What seems crucial is an understanding of why MLU and morphological development might be out of phase. For example, it might be argued that the deviant relationship between MLU and grammatical morpheme acquisition is simply an artifact of severely delayed grammatical development. Children with normal intelligence who have difficulty mastering grammatical structure might try to convey more complicated meanings than their MLU-matched normal peers. It seems plausible that they would do this by adding content words to their messages without necessarily using appropriate grammatical markers. For these children, MLU would be an overestimate of their knowledge of grammatical structure.

Johnston and Kamhi (in press) examined this relationship between semantic complexity and MLU in some detail. Contrary to expectations, they found that SLI children produced *fewer* logical semantic propositions in their sentences than did MLU matched normal children. The factors that lead to greater length without the use of grammatical morphemes are complicated. In general, the content of SLI children's utterances required forms of greater length without greater syntactic or semantic complexity. For example, they used more self-movement action verbs that are often followed by prepositional phrases. The use of these verbs increases sentence length without increasing the number of logical propositions expressed.

The observation that SLI children master linguistic devices in the same order as do normal children, but at higher MLUs, has been made by numerous investigators studying topics from phonological development to pragmatic ability (Johnston, 1982; Leonard, 1979). One such study in the realm of pragmatic development examined children's ability to modify their messages when they were not understood (Gallagher & Darnton, 1978). Gallagher and Darnton used a technique previously used by Gallagher (1977) with normal children who had equivalent MLUs. An adult experimenter conversed with each child for about an hour and periodically pretended not to understand what the child had said. Normal children at the lower MLU levels tended to revise their messages by making phonetic changes. At higher MLU levels, children simplified their utterances by dropping words and phrases, and at the highest MLU level, they began to substitute different words or phrases for the original ones. The SLI children made phonetic changes and omitted words and phrases, but, even at the highest MLU level, substitutions were far less frequent. This finding suggests that the pragmatic ability to adjust one's language to meet the needs of a listener is intact in SLI children, but that they lack the syntactic and semantic facility to substitute new words and phrases for the originals. This is consistent with the observation that SLI children learn syntactic and semantic structure more slowly than their MLU might suggest.

Many of the difficulties that SLI children are reported to experience in the pragmatic domain can be attributed to delays in language onset and to delayed acquisition of syntactic structures. For example, Watson (1977) examined the ability of SLI and normal preschoolers to use conversational devices like turn-taking and maintaining a topic. She found that SLI children were much less likely than normal children to initiate topics or add information to current topics. They took turns appropriately, but often did so with nonverbal nods or head-shakes, or by repeating prior utterances. Watson interpreted these findings to mean that SLI children are not conversationally assertive, but the root of the problem might very well be their insufficient mastery of syntactic structure.

Interestingly, recent evidence suggests that SLI children do not have particular difficulty learning new words. In a study by Leonard, Schwartz, Chapman, Rowan, Prelock, Terrell, Weiss, and Messick (1982), normal and SLI children at the single-word stage were taught 16 new words in the course of informal play with an experimenter. Not only did the SLI children acquire these words in a similar manner to that of the normal comparison group, but they also acquired the same number of new words. This study, one of the few that has explored lexical development in SLI children, provides additional support for the proposal that not all linguistic domains are equally problematic for SLI children.

How, then, can we characterize the language development of SLI children? Cross-sectional comparisons of normal and SLI children have found very little that is unusual about the language development of SLI children. The structures that they use, the order of emergence of those structures, and the ability to use those structures to convey social meanings are similar to younger normal chil-dren. However, the tendency for certain grammatical and pragmatic abilities to show a lag relative to MLU suggests a particular problem with the acquisition of syntactic and semantic structure. To simply characterize this as a type of de-viance does little to illuminate the specific nature of the linguistic deficit. What is clearly needed are longitudinal studies and studies that compare development across a number of linguistic domains. It is only through such studies that we will be able to explore the process of language acquisition in SLI children and the particular sources of difficulty that these children face in learning to speak.

## Language Disorders in Mentally Retarded Children

Language impairments are ubiquitous among mentally retarded children. The more severe the retardation the more likely the child is to have serious language and communication deficits. There is not, however, a simple correlation between

I.Q. or mental age and language ability. In her review of research on nonspeaking mentally retarded individuals, Ryan (1977) found that those individuals who had the lowest I.Q. scores were less likely to develop any useful speech, but there were exceptions to this trend. Some nonspeakers had relatively high I.Q. scores and some individuals with useful speech had relatively low I.Q. scores. There is even more variation in the language abilities of moderately and mildly retarded individuals (Miller et al., 1981). This variation should not be surprising given the heterogeneous nature of the etiologies and of the behavioral, social, emotional, perceptual, and motor abilities within these groups.

Most studies of the language abilities of retarded children have focused on institutionalized children who are at least 6 years old. Detailed studies of the language development of preschool retarded children are rare and usually limited to children with Down's syndrome who are easily identified in the preschool years. One of the earliest such studies to address the issue of delay versus deviance was conducted by Lenneberg and his colleagues (Lenneberg, 1967; Lenneberg, Nichols, & Rosenberger, 1964). These investigators followed more than 50 Down syndrome youngsters, ranging in age from 3 to 22 years, for 3 years. Lenneberg claimed that language development is closely linked to the passage of certain motor milestones. For example, he found a strong relationship between the ability to walk and the emergence of the first words. He argued that, like motor abilities, language emerges as the nervous system matures. Based on some very broad measures of spontaneous speech (such as whether the child babbles, uses words, or uses sentences), Lenneberg concluded that the language development of Down syndrome children is not bizarre or deviant, but a slowed down version of normal language development. Lenneberg's studies were not detailed linguistic analyses, but they did set the stage for in-depth examinations of the language of mentally retarded children.

One of the most detailed analyses of the language development of preschool Down syndrome children is Dooley's (1976) 1 year longitudinal study of two children. Dooley was a student of Roger Brown and his study follows in the tradition of Brown's (1973) detailed longitudinal case studies of the three normally developing children, Adam, Eve, and Sarah. Dooley found that the Down syndrome children progressed very slowly. The mean length of one child's utterances did not increase at all over the course of a year, despite some increases in other domains of development. The other child made a bit more progress, but the rate was markedly slower than that of normally developing children. When Dooley examined the semantic relations expressed in the children's one and two word utterances, he found the same, rather limited range of relational meanings that normal children express at this stage. This finding is supported by Coggins' (1979) study of the two-word utterances of four Down syndrome children between the ages of 3;10 and 6;1. Thus, when compared to normal children with similar mean utterance lengths (MLU), the semantic development of Down syndrome children does not appear to be deviant.

Dooley's longitudinal design allowed him to examine the process as well as the product of language development. He found that both Down syndrome children relied heavily on memorized phrases or unanalyzed routines like *Here they go* and *What a mess*. These phrases give themelves away as unanalyzed routines when they are combined with new words, but are not modified appropriately (e.g., *Here they go* cookies) or when they are used in somewhat inappropriate contexts. For example, one Down syndrome child this author worked with always used the greeting *Nice day out,* no matter how beautiful or dismal the weather. In addition to routines, Dooley found that both children relied heavily on pronouns and demonstratives like *this, here,* and *it* in their two-word constructions.

Dooley suggested that reliance on routines and demonstratives might indicate a type of deviance in the language development of Down syndrome children. However, as noted in the discussion of individual differences in development, the use of routines seems to be a normal variant in children's language learning strategies during the course of development (R. Clark, 1974). Similarly, a preference among some normally developing children for two-word utterances containing pronouns and demonstratives has been well documented (Bloom et al., 1975; Nelson, 1975). It may be that the slower rate of development in Down syndrome children leads to the reliance on routines and demonstratives for a longer period of time than would be typical of normal language development, but present evidence indicates tat this is another example of a delay rather than deviance.

The weight of the recent evidence on retarded children's language development seems to support a delay rather than a deviance characterization of development (Kamhi & Johnston, 1982; Miller & Yoder, 1974; Rondal, 1978). Many researchers have claimed that language development in mentally retarded children is simply a slowed-down version of normal language development. However, recent cross-sectional studies suggest that the picture is more complicated. Miller and his colleagues (Miller et al., 1981) have argued that the slow motion view of language development in retarded children is inadequate "insofar as it predicts a single pattern of language functioning relative to cognitive level" (p. 1). Miller et al. examined data collected on 130 children with mental ages between 7 months and 7 years who were referred to a mental retardation center for interdisciplinary evaluations. They found three major patterns of language functioning relative to cognitive level: A delay in language production only, a delay in both production and comprehension, and no delay relative to cognitive level. Miller et al. conclude that the heterogeneity of language skills relative to nonlinguistic cognitive abilities rules out a unitary view of language development in retarded children as a slowed-down version of normal development. It is important to keep in mind that Miller ct al. do not argue for a deviance model of development. Instead they suggest that the delay versus deviance dichotomy is an inadequate characterization of language development in children with developmental delays, since it does not help to explain discrepancies between cognitive and linguistic abilities.

Research with SLI children suggests discrepancies between sentence length as indicated by MLU and synatactic and semantic complexity. A recent study by Harris (1983) indicates the same sort of asynchrony for Down syndrome children. For example, Down syndrome children use fewer logical operators that refer to recurrence, non-existence, and disappearance in their two word utterances (e.g., more cookie, no truck, all gone juice) and rely more on utterances containing two content words (e.g., Daddy chair). Down syndrome children also tend to have much larger vocabularies at the early stages of language development than do normal children (see also, Rondal, 1976). Thus, Down syndrome children remain at the one-word state far longer than do normal children, but they are not linguistically idle. They are adding to their vocabularies and increasing the range of content that they can express without increasing the syntactic complexity of their utterances. Harris suggests that his research does not support a model of slow, but otherwise normal development in Down syndrome children, but neither is it consistent with linguistic deviance. He concludes that the language development of Down syndrome children is similar to that of normal children, "but with variations in the extent to which the different linguistic subskills are co-ordinated and synchronised over time" (p. 163).

Once again, it is only when we compare abilities across linguistic and cognitive domains that the similarities and differences between normal and atypical language development emerge. Researchers investigating language development in retarded children and SLI children have come to similar conclusions about the possible over-representation of MLU as an estimate of general linguistic abilities. For mentally retarded children, there are also varying degrees of discrepancies between cognitive and linguistic abilities. These asynchronies in development suggest a more complicated picture of development than the delay/deviance dichotomy implies.

## Language Disorders in Autistic Children

If there is one syndrome in which the notion of linguistic deviance would seem to be clear-cut, it is autism. Anyone who has spent any time in the presence of young verbal autistic children comes away with a sense that their language is, at best, peculiar. However, recent studies suggest that there are more similarities than differences between normal and autistic children's development of language.

Autism is a behaviorally defined syndrome characterized by social unresponsiveness, an obsessive interest in sameness, and a seeming preference for inanimate objects over people. Autistic children often exhibit inappropriate repetitive actions such as hand flapping, rocking, or head banging. They typically show significant intellectual impairments, although some autistic children exhibit remarkable feats of memory. Language impairments are a major characteristic of the syndrome, although there are vast individual differences in the degree of linguistic deficit. According to Rutter (1967) only about half of all autistic children develop some productive language by middle childhood. The language impairments are so central to the syndrome and the severity of the language deficits are such useful predictors of eventual improvement in social interaction, that some researchers have suggested that the underlying deficit in autism is linguistic (e.g., Rutter, 1968).

Two characteristic properties of autistic children's language account for the clinical impression of linguistic deviance. First, the intonation and voice quality often sounds peculiarly hollow or flat with poor control of pitch and volume (Ricks & Wing, 1976). Second, autistic children frequently echo back sentences that they have previously heard. Interestingly, the echoed sentences often reproduce the exact intonation of the original (Ricks & Wing, 1976), indicating an ability to perceive and produce some normal intonation patterns. Some of these echoic sentences and phrases are immediate imitations, while others are memorized and used in new and seemingly inappropriate situations. Recent investigators have suggested that the delayed echoic utterances often have a communicative function (e.g., Prizant, 1983), although the communicative intent can often only be understood by knowing the circumstances in which the utterance was originally used. For example, a child described by deVilliers and deVilliers (1978) said "Do you want me to take your shoes off?" whenever he felt that someone was angry with him or was threatening him. His mother reported that she had shouted this sentence to him on an occasion when he had lain on his bed kicking his shoes against the wall. The entire sentence was, from then on, used to express the feeling he had on its first occasion of use.

Echolalia and an odd voice quality make the language of many autistic children sound deviant. However, detailed cross-sectional studies of the perception of speech sounds, the acquisition of grammatical morphemes, and the use of syntactic and semantic structures have uncovered few linguistic characteristics exclusive to autism. For example Cantwell, Baker, and Rutter (1978) studied the syntactic structures used by autistic children and found that their sentences were syntactically complex and rule-governed, and were not unlike the structures produced by normal and mentally retarded children. Bartolucci and Pierce (1977) examined the phonological production and perception of autistic, mentally retarded, and normal children matched on nonverbal IQ. They found no differences in the types of sound substitutions and perceptual errors they made or in the degree of difficulty of the various speech sounds.

The acquisition of grammatical morphemes presents a mixed picture. Two recent studies have examined the percentage of morphemes supplied in obligatory contexts in spontaneous speech samples (Bartolucci, Pierce, & Streiner, 1980; Howlin, 1984). Bartolucci et al. compared 10 autistic children to the same number of normal and mentally retarded children matched on nonverbal IQ scores. They found that almost all of the morphemes examined were used consistently by all three groups of children. A few morphemes, however, were used less frequently by the autistic children and these were not the morphemes that are typically acquired late by normal children. Howlin's (1984) study uncovered essentially the same discrepancy. This would appear to be an example of deviance, since the order of difficulty does not correspond to the order of emergence of the forms in normal language development. However, as Tager-Flusberg (in press) has pointed out, in both studies the overall performance of all children was so high, and the sample sizes were so small, that it is difficult to draw strong conclusions about the relative difficulty of any one morpheme. It is even more difficult to draw conclusions about the order of acquisition of these forms from such limited cross-sectional data.

One area that most investigators agree presents special difficulty for autistic children is language comprehension (Churchill, 1978; Ferrari, 1982; Tager-Flusberg, in press). Tager-Flusberg suggests that this comprehension problem does not reflect a lack of syntactic, semantic, or conceptual knowledge, but an unwillingness to use their knowledge of the world to help interpret difficult sentences. For example, when asked to act out their interpretation of active and passive sentences, normal children use a ''probable event strategy'' (e.g., Chapman, 1977). They interpret a sentence like, ''The horse rides the boy'' as if it were the more probable, ''The boy rides the horse.'' The use of this probable event strategy usually doesn't lead children astray in everyday discourse. It helps them to interpret passive sentences or sentences with unusual word order long before they have the syntactic ability to do so. Tager-Flusberg found that autistic children do *not* make use of probable events to interpret complex sentences. Most importantly, she discovered that although autistic children seem to possess the basic semantic and conceptual knowledge, they simply don't apply it to the task of understanding language.

Another domain of language widely acknowledged to create special difficulties for autistic children is conversational competence (Baltaxe, 1977; Fay & Schuler, 1980). Tager-Flusberg (in press) describes an unpublished study that lends some insight into this problem. One hour spontaneous speech samples from eight autistic children were matched on the basis of MLU to eight similar speech samples from 30-month-old normal children. Tager-Flusberg examined the degree to which the autistic children maintained and expanded on conversational topics. Overall, there were no differences in the amount that autistic and normal children responded to statements or questions. Autistic children clearly understood conversational turn-taking conventions. However, the autistic children differed in the way that they responded. Whereas normal children maintained the conversational topic by expanding on what the previous speaker had said, the autistic children did not tend to expand on a topic. They seemed to have little to contribute to the conversation. These conversational inadequacies do not seem to be specifically linguistic; they are consistent with the well-attested social interactional problems of autistic children.

Tager-Flusberg concludes that her research does not support a view of deviant semantic, pragmatic, or conceptual knowledge among autistic children. What does seem to be atypical is the relationship between social and conceptual knowledge on the one hand, and knowledge of linguistic structure on the other. Although many would argue that autistic children also have problems that are specifically linguistic, Tager-Flusberg's research demonstrates the inadequacies of a simple characteristization of language development in autistic children as delayed or deviant with respect to normal development. Certain aspects of autistic children's language use are quite similar to those of normal children, while others (especially those that can be traced to social-interactional problems) are quite different. This research suggests asynchronies in the development of different linguistic abilities, but an understanding of the exact nature of these asynchronies and the process of linguistic development in autistic children awaits detailed longitudinal studies and studies that compare development across many linguistic domains.

## CONCLUSIONS

Language impairments in young children cannot be neatly characterized as instances of either delay or deviance. The picture is far less clear-cut and far more interesting. Mentally retarded, autistic, and specifically language impaired preschoolers all show instances of significant delays in both the onset and rate of language development. Yet within each group there are discrepancies across linguistic domains. SLI children appear to be particularly weak in syntactic development, leading to a discrepant relationship between sentence length and syntactic complexity. Mentally retarded children also display difficulties in syntactic development relative to their vocabulary size and sentence length. Autistic children who do develop verbal skills appear to be delayed in phonological and syntactic development, but are especially deficient in their ability to draw on their knowledge of the world and to use language for communicative purposes. As Tager-Flusberg (in press) put it, autistic children seem to have little to say. Asynchronies between linguistic and cognitive functioning are also characteristic of all three groups of children, but are surprisingly common among mentally retarded children. Just why language development in mentally retarded children should be even more delayed than other aspects of cognitive functioning is yet to be understood.

Virtually all of the recent research on language disorders has used cross-sectional designs to compare groups of children on a single linguistic domain. We have learned a great deal about what children with language disorders know, but we have learned very little about the developmental process. The few cross-domain comparisons that have been carried out suggest asynchronies in development of linguistic abilities. We clearly need detailed longitudinal studies in order to better understand the developmental processes that lead to these asychronies.

The linguist, Charles Ferguson, is fond of saying that theories and models should not be judged by whether they are ultimately supported by the empirical data, but by the amount of useful research they inspire. In this sense, the delay/deviance dichotomy that has driven much research on language disorders has been an extremely successful paradigm. The fact that, after 20 years of intensive research, delay and deviance seem inadequate characterizations of language disorders, does not diminish the enormous contributions of that research to our understanding of language impairments.

Despite our incomplete understanding of the process of language development among young children with language disorders, the research findings reviewed here have a number of implications for assessment and intervention. First, it is clear that general indices, such as MLU or single test scores, do not characterize the abilities of children with language disorders with enough precision to be useful for determining what language skills to teach. In order to adequately assess the needs of a language disordered child, estimates must be made of proficiency across many linguistic domains and in many contexts of language use. In all likelihood, the wider the range of situations in which linguistic abilities are tapped, the more accurate the assessment will be.

Second, the evidence of discontinuities in the language development of mentally retarded, autistic, and SLI children suggests that clinicians should not necessarily let the order of normal language development determine the order of language skills to be taught. For example, a child may be ready to learn higher level semantic forms while still learning lower level grammatical morphemes. Principled deviations from the normal order of acquisition might be a quite feasible and even desirable teaching practice as long as logical prerequisites are not overlooked.

Discrepancies between linguistic and cognitive development must also be taken into account in the design of language intervention programs. Often the cognitive development of a language disordered child is more advanced in some realms than that of a normal younger child with roughly equivalent language abilities. Language intervention programs might profitably capitalize on these nonverbal strengths.

A final implication concerns the context in which language is assessed and taught. All three groups of language-disordered children reviewed here have difficulties in their use of language for communicative purposes. Autistic children provide the most striking evidence that learning linguistic structure does not insure the appropriate use of that structure in conversational contexts, but the communicative function of language cannot be ignored for any child with language disorders. A great deal of attention has been paid recently to *teaching* language in a communicative context (e.g., Conant, Budoff, & Hecht, 1982; MacDonald, 1982), but far less attention has been paid to *assessing* language in communicatively meaningful situations. Even the recent trend toward using samples of children's conversational speech for assessment purposes does not entirely solve the problem. Language samples must be collected in a *range of communicative situations* and with a range of interlocuters in order to provide an assessment of a child's conversational ability.

In conclusion, we are only beginning to understand the complex nature of language disorders in young children. A fuller understanding of the asynchronies and in development that are suggested by current research awaits comprehensive studies of the *process* of atypical language development.

## REFERENCES

Allen, D. V., & Bliss, L. S. (1979). Evaluation of procedures for screening preschool children for signs of impaired language development. Second Interim Report, Contract NS 6 2533, NINCDS. Bethesda, MD: Department of Health, Education and Welfare.

Aram, D. M., Ekelman, B. L., & Nation, J. E. (1984). Preschool language disorders: Ten years later. *Journal of Speech and Hearing Research, 27,* 232–244.

Baltaxe, C. A. M. (1977). Pragmatic deficits in the language of autistic adolescents. *Journal of Pediatric Psychology, 42,* 376–393.

Bartolucci, G., Pierce, S. J., & Streiner, D. (1980). Cross sectional studies of grammatical morphemes in autistic and mentally retarded children. *Journal of Autism and Developmental Disorders, 10,* 39–50.

Bartolucci, G., & Pierce, S. J. (1977). A preliminary comparison of phonological development in autistic, normal, and mentally retarded subjects. *British Journal of Disorders of Communication, 12,* 137–147.

Bates, E. (1976). *Language and context: The acquisition of pragmatics.* New York: Academic Press.

Bloom, L. M. (1970). *Language development: Form and function in emerging grammars.* Cambridge, MA: M.I.T. Press.

Bloom, L. M., Lightbown, P., & Hood, L. (1975). Structure and variation in child language. *Monograph of the Society for Research in Child Development, 40* (Serial No. 160).

Bloom, L., Rocissano, L., & Hood, L. (1976). Adult-child discourse: Developmental interaction between information processing and linguistic knowledge. *Cognitive Psychology, 8,* 521–552.

Bowerman, M. (1973). *Early syntactic development: A cross-linguistic study with special reference to Finnish.* Cambridge: Cambridge University Press.

Brown, R. (1973). *A first language: The early stages.* Cambridge, MA: Harvard University Press.

Brown, R., & Bellugi, U. (1964). Three processes in the child's acquisition of syntax. *Harvard Education Review, 34,* 133–151.

Bruner, J. S. (1981). Intention in the structure of action and interaction. In L. P. Lipsitt (Ed.), *Advances in Infancy Research* (Vol. 1). Norwood, NJ: Albex.

Cantwell, D., Baker, L., & Rutter, M. (1978). A comparative study of infantile autism and specific developmental receptive language disorder: IV. Analysis of syntax and language function. *Journal of Child Psychology and Child Psychiatry, 19,* 351–362.

Churchill, D. (1978). *Language of autistic children.* Washington, DC: Winston & Sons.

Chomsky, N. (1957). *Syntactic structures.* The Hague: Mouton Publishers.

Chomsky, N. (1965). *Aspects of the theory of syntax.* Cambridge, MA: M.I.T. Press.

Clark, E. V. (1974). Some aspects of the conceptual basis for first language acquisition. In R. L. Schiefelbusch & L. L. Lloyd (Eds.), *Language perspectives: Acquisition, retardation and intervention* (pp. 105–128). Baltimore: University Park Press.

Clark, E. V., & Hecht, B. F. (1983). Comprehension, production, and language acquisition, *Annual Review of Psychology, 34,* 325–349.

Clark, H. H., & Clark, E. V. (1977). *Psychology and language,* New York: Harcourt, Brace, Jovanovich.

Clark, R. (1974). Performing without competence. *Journal of Child Language, 1,* 1–10.

Clark, R. (1977). What's the use of imitation? *Journal of Child Language, 4,* 341–358.

Coggins, R. (1979). Relational meaning encoded in the two-word utterance of stage I Down's syndrome children. *Journal of Speech and Hearing Research, 22,* 166–178.

Conant, S., Budoff, M., & Hecht, B. F. (1983). *Teaching language-disabled children: A communication games intervention.* Cambridge, MA: Brookline Books.

de Villiers, J. G., & de Villiers, P. A. (1973). A cross-sectional study of the acquisition of grammatical morphemes. *Journal of Psycholinguistic Research, 2,* 267–278.

de Villiers, J. G., & de Villiers, P. A. (1978). *Language acquisition,* Cambridge, MA: Harvard University Press.

Dale, P. S. (1976). Language development: Structure and function. New York: Holt, Rinehart, & Winston.

Dooley, J. (1976). *Language acquisition and Down's syndrome: A study of early semantics and syntax.* Unpublished dissertation, Harvard University.

Eisenson, J. (1972). *Aphasia in children.* New York: Harper and Row

Fay, W., & Schuler, A. L. (1980). *Emerging language in autistic children.* Baltimore: University Park Press.

Ferrari, M. (1982). Childhood autism: Deficits of communication and symbolic development I. Distinctions from language disorders. *Journal of Communication Disorders, 15,* 191–208.

Furrow, D., Nelson, K., & Benedict, H. (1979). Mothers' speech to children and syntactic development: Some simple relationships. *Journal of Child Language, 6,* 423–442.

Gallagher, T. (1977). Revision behaviors in the speech of normal children developing language. *Journal of Speech and Hearing Research, 20,* 303–318.

Gallagher, T., & Darnton, B. (1978). Conversational aspects of the speech of language disordered children: Revision behaviors. *Journal of Speech and Hearing Research, 21,* 118–135.

Greenfield, P. M., & Smith, J. H. (1976). *The structure of communication in early language development.* New York: Academic Press.

Harris, J. (1983). Mean length of utterance and Down's syndrome. *British Journal of Disorders of Communication, 18,* 153–169.

Howlin, P. (1984). The acquisition of grammatical morphemes in autistic children: A critique and replication of the findings of Bartolucci, Pierce and Streiner, 1980. *Journal of Autism and Developmental Disorders, 14,* 127–136.

Johnston, J. (1982). The language disordered child. In N. Lass, L. McReynolds, J. Northern, & D. Yoder (Eds.), *Speech, language and hearing* (Vol. II). Philadelphia: W. B. Saunders.

Johnston, J. R., & Kamhi, A. G. (in press). The same can be less: Syntactic and semantic aspects of the utterances of language impaired children. *Merrill-Palmer Quarterly.*

Johnston, J. R., & Schery, T. K. (1976). The use of grammatical morphemes by children with communication disorders. In D. M. Morehead, A. E. Morehead (Eds.), *Normal and deficient child language* (pp. 239–258). Baltimore: University Park Press.

Kernan, K. T., & Sabsy, S. (1985). Referential first mention in narratives by mildly retarded adults. Working Paper #30, Socio-Behavioral Group, Mental Retardation Research Center, School of Medicine, University of California, Los Angeles.

Kessler, C. (1975). Postsemantic processes in delayed child language related to first and second language learning. In D. Dato (Ed.) *Georgetown University Round Table on language and linguistics.* Washington, DC: Georgetown University Press.

Labov, W. (1970). The study of nonstandard English. Urbana, IL: National Council of Teachers of English.

Lackner, J. R. (1968). A developmental study of language behavior in retarded children. *Neuropsychologia, 6,* 301–320.

Lenneberg, E. (1967). *Biological foundations of language.* New York: Wiley.

Lenneberg, E. H., Nichols, I. A., & Rosenberger, E. R. (1964). Primitive stages of language development in mongolism. *Disorders of Communication, 42,* 119–137.

Leonard, L. B. (1972). What is deviant language? *Journal of Speech and Hearing Disorders, 37,* 427–446.

Leonard, L. B. (1979). Language impairment in children. *Merrill-Palmer Quarterly, 25,* 205–232.

Leonard, L. B., Steckol, K., & Schwartz, R. (1978). Semantic relations and utterance length in child language. In F. Peng & W. von Raffler-Engel (Eds.), *Language acquisition and developmental kinesics.* Tokyo; Bunka Hyoron.

Leonard, L. B., Schwartz, R. G., Chapman, K., Rowan, L., Prelock, P., Terrell, B., Weiss, A. L., & Messick, C. (1982). Early lexical acquisition in children with specific language impairment. *Journal of Speech and Hearing Research, 25,* 554–564.

Levy, C., & Menyuk, P. (1974). *Relations between certain cognitive skills and sentence comprehension.* Paper presented at American Speech and Hearing Association.' Las Vegas, Nevada.

Liles, B. Z., & Watt, J. H. (1984). On the meaning of 'language delay.' *Folia Phoniatrica, 36,* 40–48.

Limber, J. (1973). The genesis of complex sentences. In T. E. Moore (Ed.), *Cognitive development and the acquisition of language* (pp. 169–185). New York: Academic Press.

MacDonald, J. D. (1982). Communication strategies for language intervention. In D. P. Mc-Clowerg, A. M. Guilford, & S. O. Richardson (Eds.), *Infant communication: Development, assessment, and intervention.* New York: Grune & Stratton.

Marge, M. (1972). The general problem of language disabilities in children. In J. V. Irwin & M. Marge (Eds.), *Principles of childhood language disabilities.* New York: Appleton-Century-Crofts.

Menyuk, P. (1964). Comparison of grammar of children with functionally deviant and normal speech. *Journal of Speech Hearing Research, 7,* 109–121.

Menyuk, P. (1975). The language-impaired child: Linguistic or cognitive impairment? *Annals of the New York Academy of Sciences, 263,* 54–69.

Miller, J., Chapman, R., & McKenzie, H. (1981). *Individual differences in the language acquisition of mentally retarded children.* Paper presented at the 2nd International Congress for the Study of Child Language, University of British Columbia, Vancouver, B.C., Canada.

Miller, J. F., & Yoder, D. E. (1974). An ontogenetic language teaching strategy for retarded children. In R. L. Schiefelbusch & L. L. Lloyd (Eds.) *Language perspectives: Acquisition, retardation, and intervention.* Baltimore: University Park Press.

Morehead, D., & Ingram, D. (1973). The development of base syntax in normal and linguistically deviant children. *Journal of Speech and Hearing Research, 16,* 330–352.

Morley, M. E. (1965). *The development and disorders of speech in childhood* (2nd ed.) London: Livingston.

Moskowitz, B. A. (1978). The acquisition of language. *Scientific American,* 92–112.

Myklebust, H. (1954). *Auditory disorders in children.* New York: Grune & Stratton.

Nelson, K. (1973). Structure and strategy in learning to talk. *Monographs of the Society for Research in Child Development, 38* (Serial No. 149).

Nelson, K. (1975). The nominal shift in semantic-syntactic development. *Cognitive Psychology, 7,* 461–473.

Prizant, B. M. (1983). Language acquisition and communicative behavior in autism: Toward an understanding of the "whole" of it. *Journal of Speech and Hearing Disorders, 28,* 296–307.

Rees, N. S. (1978). Pragmatics of language: Applications to normal and disordered language development. In R. L. Schiefelbusch (Ed.), *Bases of language intervention* (pp. 191–268). Baltimore: University Park Press.

Ricks, D. M., & Wing, L. (1976). Language communication and the use of symbols in normal and autistic children. In L. Wing (Ed.) *Early Childhood Autism.* Oxford: Pergamon Press.

Rondal, J. (1978). Maternal speech to normal and down's syndrome children matched for mean length of utterance. In C. E. Meyers (Ed.), *Quality of life in severely and profoundly retarded people: Research foundations for improvement.* Washington, DC: American Association on Mental Deficiency.

Rutter, M. (1968). Concepts of autism: A review of research. *Journal of Child Psychology and Psychiatry, 9,* 1–25.

Ryan, J. (1977). The silence of stupidity. In Morton J., Marshal J. (Eds.), *Psycholinguistics: Developmental and Pathological.* (pp. 99–124). Ithaca, NY: Cornell University Press.

Sacks, H., Schegloff, E. A., & Jefferson, G. (1974). A simplest systematics for the organization of turntaking for conversation. *Language, 50,* 696–735.

Searle, J. R. (1969). *Speech acts.* Cambridge: Cambridge University Press.

Snow, C. E. (1972). Mothers' speech to children learning language. *Child Development, 43,* 549–565.

Snow, C. E., & Ferguson, C. A. (1977). *Talking to children: Language input and acquisition.* Cambridge: Cambridge University Press.

Snyder, L. (1976). The early presuppositions and performatives of normal and language disabled children. *Papers and Reports on Child Language Development, 12,* 221–229.

Stark, R. E., Mellits, E. D., & Tallal, P. (1983). Behavioral attributes of speech and language disorders. In C. L. Ludlow, J. A. Cooper (Eds.), *Genetic aspects of speech and language disorders* (pp. 37–52). New York: Academic Press.

Steckol, K., & Leonard, L. (1979). The use of grammatical morphemes by normal and language impaired children. *Journal of Communication Disorders, 12,* 291–301.

Tager-Flusberg, H. (in press). On the nature of a language acquisition disorder: The example of autism. In F. Kessel (Ed.), *The development of language and language researchers: Essays presented to Roger Brown.* Hillsdale, NJ: Lawrence Erlbaum Associates.

Tallal, P. (1976). Rapid auditory processing in normal and disordered language development. *Journal of Speech and Hearing Research, 19,* 561–571.

Tallal, P., & Piercy, M. (1975). Developmental aphasia: The perception of brief vowels and extended stop consonants. *Neuropsychologia, 13,* 69–74.

Telford, C. W., & Sawrey, J. M. (1967). *The exceptional individual: Psychological and educational aspects.* Englewood Cliffs, NJ: Prentice-Hall.

Thomson, J. R., & Chapman, R. S. (1975). Who is "Daddy"? The status of two-year-olds' overextended words in use and comprehension. *Papers and Reports on Child Language Development,* Stanford University, *10,* 59–68.

# SOCIAL AND BEHAVIORAL PROBLEMS IN THE PRESCHOOL YEARS

S. Marcovitch and J. Nesker Simmons

## THE ASSESSMENT OF INAPPROPRIATE BEHAVIOR IN THE PRESCHOOL YEARS: ISSUES AND PROBLEMS

> With respect to the concern that we have for emotionally disturbed children, we should ask why we have built up this level of interest and activity. We should try to be more specific about who these children are and what it is we want to do for them or for ourselves. We should separate out those who are disturbing to us because they do not fit our system and our way of working and those who really need our help. (Rhodes, 1964)

No group are as vulnerable as children who do not behave as demanded. They are not protected by objective measures, or even well-defined criteria (Nesker

Advances in Special Education, Volume 5, pages 121–146.
Copyright © 1986 by JAI Press Inc.
All rights of reproduction in any form reserved.
ISBN: 0-89232-313-2

Simmons, 1981, in press). In fact, of all the labels used to classify children, the term *behaviorally disordered* is both the most subjectively decided and the most context-dependent (Bereiter, 1973; de Lone, 1979; Hobbes, 1974; Nesker Simmons, 1981, in press; Phillips, Draguns, & Bartlett, 1975; Ryan, 1971). For example, behavior of a child in nursery school is judged to be "good" if the child is active in a range of activities, and best if these activities are determined by the child. This same child might find his or her behavior considered "inappropriate" when unable to sit still for most of the day and listen to a Grade 1 teacher. Yet, a child at 6 years of age is expected to learn and behave appropriately in a vast variety of circumstances—reading groups, class lesson, physical education, the school yard (Nesker Simmons, 1981, in press). It is thus no surprise to find that according to a recent survey of Minnesota Elementary School teachers (Rubin & Balow, 1978) over 74% of boys and 54% of girls had been judged as presenting some behavior problems over the period of their primary school years.

Justification for the categorization of children is well-intentioned, namely the recognition of individual differences as access to special programs and funds (Hobbes, 1975; Nesker Simmons, 1981, in press). However, in any distinction of children lies the potential for abuse most pointedly referred to by Ryan (1971) as "blaming the victim" and Braginsky and Braginsky (1974) as "social sanitation." When the child in question is capable of offensive behavior, these possibilities have been found to become even more distinct (Nesker Simmons, 1981, in press).

The potential abuse of labels is complicated by a growing awareness of the vulnerable foundations for categorization and placement decisions. The following areas have been especially criticized:

1. Assessment findings, especially tests, are too influential and accepted too naively (Apple, 1976; Braginsky & Braginsky, 1971; Cottle, 1976; Sarason & Doris, 1979).
2. Minimal attention is addressed to motivations and the social context of the labeling process (Ryan, 1971; Sarason & Doris, 1979; Willis, 1977).
3. The classical circle of poverty remains in motion in all levels of the educational system (Cottle, 1976; de Lone, 1979; Ryan, 1971; Sennett & Cobb, 1973).
4. The interactional nature of deviant behavior is usually ignored (Nesker Simmons, 1981, in press; Rhodes, 1964; Rhodes & Sagor, 1974; Ryan, 1971; Sarason & Doris, 1979).

A child who misbehaves is usually tested and labeled temporarily without context and history. Sarason and Doris (1979) have addressed this issue in the following terms:

> The entire diagnostic process tends to be carried out as if one individual required assessment and help, as if the locus of the problem inhered "in" him or her; whatever the consequences of "his" problem, they are of secondary significance, however upsetting or disruptive to others. (p. 40)

A short case history can best illustrate this point.

## Joey

Joey was referred to the Developmental Evaluation Unit, Hospital for Sick Children in Toronto for assessment. His teacher reported that he presented serious behavior problems in the classroom. Specifically he was not able to focus on required tasks, was disruptive with other children, and not able to work well independently. At the time of the assessment he was in attendance at a highly structured traditional Montessori preschool program. Since this was his second year in the program adjustment problems regarding classroom routines and learning practices were not to be expected.

At the age of 4, Joey was assessed and judged to have problems in the areas of both motor coordination and communication skills. Specifically he was uncomfortable and awkward with demands such as paper and pencil task, cutting with scissors, handling small blocks; his language patterns were somewhat discrepant with age level development. His behavior during the assessment was completely appropriate; he attended well and completed all tasks that were expected of him. As a second stage of assessment, Joey was observed in his nursery placement and the teacher was available to point out her concerns. Classroom observation confirmed that indeed Joey was disruptive, inattentive and unsuccessful in completing tasks. In other words, Joey presents with behavior problems—in certain contexts. The team conference with hospital staff, parents and school personnel focused on the context and circumstances of Joey's inappropriate behavior. Given the nature of his specific disabilities, the majority of his preschool program focused on tasks that highlighted his deficits. As well, little attention was given to accommodating to his individual profile in a developmental manner. His teacher had not considered that an adjustment of program expectation could alleviate the situation. Her natural conclusion was that the problem lies within the child—he had a behavior problem which needed to be identified and managed.

In any case of inappropriate behavior with very young children it is important to consider the context; in the case of a child within a preschool program it is critical. A teacher must consider that inappropriate behavior may stem from inappropriate classroom demands or routine. In situations such as Joey's, we must reflect on whether we should be changing the context of the behavior or changing the child—perhaps the child's behavior problem was created by the context.

Two year old Holly can provide another example of inappropriate behavior that was appropriate, given the context. Unlike Joey, Holly has no developmental problems. She is not yet in a formal education program.

## Holly

Holly's developmental history is unremarkable except to note that she walked independenly at 8 months. She has since both been active and alert. Her activity is extremely organized and focused and her play is well-developed. She is the youngest child in a family with two older brothers. Holly's mother is a journalist. Holly accompanied her mother to an interview of a clinical nutritionist who specializes in dietary control of hyperactivity. Holly and her mother were kept waiting for a half hour. At the point when they entered his office, it was approaching the lunch hour. She entered confidently and willingly lay down on the examining table to serve as a demonstration model for the allergy testing. She lay still for approximately 5 minutes while the nutritionist focused on a background discussion. Holly then began to fidget and explore the apparatus surrounding the examining table. The nutritionist quickly became angered at her behavior yet offered no positive alternatives for her play. His interactions were limited to attempts at control. In response Holly escalated and proceeded to make a mess. The nutritionist continued the interview which focused on the internal causes of hyperactivity. At the end of his discussion he turned to the journalist (and distraught mother) and stated:

"I would seriously suggest that I conduct formal testing on this child. She is undoubtedly hyperactive."

Once again we must reflect on the context of Holly's inappropriate behavior. From the child's perspective, there was no fun to be had so fun must be made. Holly's host activity level, given her age and the expectations, was situationally based. How many other such judgements of child behavior are thus made and unfortunately formalized?

Any parent who has waited in a waiting room for 2 hours with children, stood in the Saturday line-up at the supermarket, or taken long motor trips with young children has witnessed inappropriate behavior. Viewed in isolation, this behavior might trigger serious concern; in context the behavior is highly appropriate.

In the preschool years a social or behavioral problem arises when someone judges a child's behavior and interactions as inappropriate. In considering the identification of social and/or behavioral problems in the preschool years, there is a risk of blurring the distinction between normal and exceptional. Thus a reminder must once again be issued of the importance of a developmental and contextual framework. Rae-Grant, Carr and Berman (1983) state that the identification of a specific symptom as being reflective of an identifiable social or behavior problem is based upon the frequency of the symptom, its severity, the age appropriateness (with respect to whether the normal child would demonstrate that symptom at that particular age), the debilitating aspect of the symptom with respect to daily functioning, and lastly the presence or absence of other associated atypical symptoms. Most preschool children may have occasional temper tantrums. However, frequent tantrums or those that persist into middle childhood may be symptomatic of developmental disorder, possible psychosis or conduct disorder.

Rae-Grant et al. state that:

> In normal children, these symptoms occur frequently but are shortlived. They do not interfere significantly with overall competence or merit concern and intervention. If the parents realize this and avoid overreacting to them, the symptoms resolve, usually without attention or intervention, and do not interfere with ongoing development. Some parents, however, not realizing their innocuous nature, become concerned or upset by the symptoms, particularly in response to exaggerations of their significance by grandparents and physicians. If parents and environment respond to such symptoms with excessive anxiety or by allowing children to use them to manipulate the environment to their advantage, the symptoms are positively reinforced and thus become an increasingly prominent part of the child's behavioral repertoire. At this stage a diagnosis of developmental disorder would be made. For such a diagnosis one would take into account the severity and duration of the symptoms and the degree to which they were interfering with the child's overall functioning. It is the degree of developmental interference that should determine whether or not professional intervention is required. (p. 169)

# VULNERABLE PRE-SCHOOL POPULATIONS

It is now recognized that, from birth, children are social beings and that the quality of parental care is a major factor in social development. While most children are afforded the nurturing to follow a steady path of emotional development, there remain those who for a vareity of reasons are vulnerable to interaction breakdown.

Goldberg and Marcovitch (in press) have examined the mother-child relationship as a major factor in the growth and development of the child at risk. In the case of children who are developmentally delayed, the evidence suggests that atypical appearance, behavior, or temperament may make these children especially difficult to care for (Goldberg, 1982; Sameroff & Chandler, 1975). For example, children who are mentally retarded are over-represented in the child abuse statistics (Frodi, 1981; Schmitt & Kempe, 1977). Thus, children with developmental problems may be doubly disadvantaged, first by virtue of poor skills and second because they are at risk for poor parental care.

Primary prevention of poor developmental outcomes must therefore be directed at ensuring high quality parental care as well as developmental stimulation per se. This requires: (a) identification of families at risk for poor parent-child relationships early in life, and (b) interventions to foster positive parent-child relationships. Both of these strategies require an understanding of the factors that contribute to the development of rewarding mother-child relationships. To date the research on mother-child relationships with at risk children has focused primarily on the preterm infant and the Down's syndrome child with some attention to the blind child and children with wider ranging developmental disabilities. These works deserve brief review.

## The Preterm Infant

The largest group of children with developmental delays that have been studied are those at risk for lasting problems because of premature birth. Although the majority of prematurely born infants are eventually indistinguishable from their post-natal age mates, their initial development is usually consistent with post-conception age and lags behind that of full-term counterparts.

In a review of longitudinal studies of parent-infant interaction comparing full-term and preterm dyads, Goldberg (1978) noted that in the neonatal period, parents of preterm infants were less actively engaged with their babies than those of full-term infants. The preterm babies received less ventral contact (DiVitto & Goldberg, 1979; Liefer, Leiderman, Barnett, & Williams, 1972), touching (DiVitto & Goldberg, 1979; Klaus, Kennel, Plumb, & Zuelke, 1970), vocal stimulation (DiVitto & Goldberg, 1979) and face-to-face positioning (Klaus et al., 1970) than full-term infants. Further evidence suggests that these differences may well be related to behavioral characteristics of the preterm infants including a lowered social responsiveness (Brown & Blakeman, 1979; DiVitto & Goldberg, 1979; Sostek, Quinn & Davitt, 1979), limitations in response to tactile input (Field, Dempsey, Hatch, Ting, & Clifton, 1979; Rose, Schmidt, & Bridger, 1976), and processing of visual information (Parmelee & Sigman, 1976) and a greater likelihood of becoming disorganized in response to multimodal stimulation (Als & Brazelton, in press; McGehee, 1981) relative to full-term neonates. Further evidence for the impact of infants' behavioral limitations on parents' interactive efforts is found in a study by Whitelaw, Minde, Brown, and Fitzhardinge (1981) which showed that preterms who were more seriously ill during their stay in intensive care were less active than healthier infants, and that their parents were not only less interactive during the period of acute illness but continued to show subdued interactions several months after the infants' recovery.

Studies of older preterm infants and their parents indicate that while these babies continue to be less responsive to the task at hand, whether feeding (Brown & Blakeman, 1979), face-to-face play (Field, 1977) or floor play (Brachfeld, Goldberg, & Sloman, 1980; Crawford, in press), their parents are more active and invest more effort in interacting with them than are parents of full-term infants (Brachfeld ct al., 1980; Brown & Bakeman, 1979; Crawford, in press; Field, 1977; Wasserman, Solomon-Schweizer, Spiker, & Stern, 1980). In addition, within a large group of preterm infants, Beckwith and Cohen (1978) found that those who had experienced more medical complications subsequently received more caregiving from parents. This pattern of increased activity has also been reported for parents of blind infants (Fraiberg, 1977), hearing imparied infants (Wedell-Monig & Lumley, 1980), and in some studies of those with Down syndrome (Dunset, 1980; Jones, 1980). There is some evidence that as preterm infants mature, this high level of activity diminishes (Brachfeld et al., 1980; Crawford, in press, Wasserman et al., 1980).

## Down Syndrome Child

Children with Down syndrome have been studied from infancy more intensively than those with other types of developmental delay largely because they are readily identifiable at birth. They also constitute the largest homogeneous subgroup of delayed youngsters. Cicchetti and Sroufe (1976, 1978) found that in addition to delays in development of affective expression (e.g., onset of smiling) responses of Down syndrome infants were qualitatively different from those of normal infants. Both positive and negative expressions were muted and less intense. These reports are corroborated by Emde, Katz, and Thorpe (1978), Sorce and Emde (1980) and Serafica and Cicchetti (1976). Spectrographic analysis of cries of Down syndrome infants reveals that they are characterized by lower pitch, less tonal variation, and longer latencies than those of normal babies (Fisichelli & Karelitz, 1963; Karelitz & Fisichelli, 1962; Lind, Vuorenkoski, Rosberg, Patenen, & Wasz-Hockert, 1970) and are judged less urgent and aversive by adults (Freudenberg, Driscoll, & Stern, 1978). These phenomenon may have contributed to the notion that an "easy" temperament is characteristic of Down syndrome children, a view that is not supported by the empirical evidence (Gunn, Berry, & Andrews, 1981). In addition, Berger and Cunningham (1981) found that social eye contact in Down syndrome babies was not only delayed but differed from that of normal infants in being restricted to gazes of shorter duration. Jones (1980) reports of only minimal amount of referential looking at mother during play sessions of Down syndrome toddlers is consistent with this report as well. Thus the parent of a Down syndrome infant or toddler is responding to a set of social signals that differs from that of normal children; patterns of mother-child interaction might therefore be expected to develop differently.

Reports of mother-infant interaction in this group vary in the extent to which this expectation is confirmed. Jones (1980) found that in comparison to infants and toddlers of the same developmental stage, mothers of Down syndrome children made more initiations without child response, did more structuring of vocal interactions, and had to make more adjustments in expectations of the child's interaction. In contrast to mothers of the normal group who said their goals in the play setting were to "have fun" with their child, those of the Down syndrome group reported that their goal was to "teach" the child. In contrast, two other studies which matched Down syndrome children to a normal group by more specific developmental stages [(one with Piagetian stage assessments (Dunst, 1980) and one with language development assessments (Leifer & Lewis, 1980)], both found that there were few differences in child or mother communicative behavior in the two gorups. Hanson (1980) also reported few differences between mother behaviors in Down syndrome and normal groups. Those that were noted were that mothers of Down syndrome infants initiated more talk and praise, initiated fewer explanations and smiles, and restrained their infants less than mothers of normal infants.

*Other Delays*

Studies of other developmentally delayed children are less numerous because they represent a smaller population and one that is not identifiable with a single criterion. An early study by Kogan, Wimberger, and Bobbit (1969) reported that mothers of 6 retardates (ages 3–7), in comparison with those of 10 normal 4–5 year-olds, displayed extreme positive affect more frequently, and were more often controlling: their children were less actively engaged in interactions. Dyads with a retarded child "did nothing" more often while the normal children and their mothers were more likely to "take turns." More recently Kogan (1980) studied twenty 2–5 year-olds with motor delays and reported more negative and less positive affect for both mothers and children in the delayed group. In contrast, Vietze and his colleagues (Vietze, Abernathy, Ashe, & Faulstich, 1978) reported little difference in interactions of mothers in a mixed group of developmentally delayed children (ages not given but reported to be functioning at infant levels) and those of mothers with normal 12½ month-olds.

Marcovitch (1983) and Marcovitch, Goldberg, and MacGregor (1985) have addressed the issue of individual differences in mother-child interaction with three groups of delayed children, namely neurologically impaired, unknown etiology and Down syndrome children. The report that both the stress which the parent feels at daily handling of the child as well as the type of developmental handicap can be related to differences in the manner of interacting with the child. Both studies yield data indicating that mothers of Down syndrome children report less stress coping with the handicapped child than do mothers of either neurologically impaired or unknown etiology delayed children. Mothers of Down syndrome children as a group had more positive interactions with their children and chose play materials more in keeping with their child's developmental level (Marcovitch, 1983, 1985).

Simmons and Davidson (1984, 1985) have examined the factors influencing the emotional relationships between mothers and blind babies and have observed the blind baby to be less spontaneously receptive to the mother. Without vision, the authors reason, the baby misses a great deal of the basis of the natural bond between mother and child. Since this bond is the basis of the integrated social development, substitution for the visual messages must be established before the mother can be fully available to the child (Davidson & Simmons, 1984).

The social and emotional development of a blind baby is undoubtedly complicated by the medical implications of blindness. Necessarily, the condition causes separations from the mother due to hospitalization that are usually both early and lengthy. Often these separations are repeated several times during the first critical year of development. The mother must, thus, experience difficulty establishing a close relationship with a baby who is often away, and whose health seems so fragile. Furthermore, as important time is lost, and the treatment becomes complicated, it appears harder for the mother to consider the baby's potential and easier to despair over his/her handicap (Nesker, 1974, Simmons & Davidson, 1985).

The above review of the literature on mother-child interaction with exceptional infants and children has highlighted the risk factors evident in early social and emotional development of these vulnerable children. Again, we urge that a label of social or behavioral disorder for these population be interpreted within a context. The disabilities described carry their own context. While it may be socially unacceptable to rock, poke at your eyes, growl, or throw things, the isolation and necessary frustration of being blind in a sighted world, of lacking language in a highly verbal society, or being immobile in a fast paced environment impose a new set of criteria for judging behavior. Furthermore, there is static in the natural attachment of mother and child for these populations that can be attributed to the grieving process, frequent hospitalizations, professional intervention and lack of confidence.

For the exceptional child the relevant history in understanding behavior disorders begins at birth: the type of disability, length of medical intervention, parent reaction to handicapping condition all set the stage immediately for an alternative parent-child environment. As well, factors that would ordinarily be considered relevant to understanding behavior patterns must not be forgotten. Critical to this perspective is a consideration of child temperament.

# THE CONCEPT OF TEMPERAMENT

*Definition and Measurement*

There is evidence that characteristics of temperament are observable soon after birth and are relatively stable into early childhood but influenced by the child's interaction with the environment. By early childhood the temperament of the child is the product of many factors, including the child's constitution, previous experience, and level of development (McDevitt & Carey, 1978). The extent to which constitutional or environmental factors contribute to temperament is a point on which there is less agreement.

"Temperament" has by recent convention been defined as the behavioral style of the child in interaction with his/her environment (Bates, 1980; Thomas & Chess, 1977). Although temperament is considered to be a characteristic of the child, most of the current methods of assessing temperament rely on caregiver reports (e.g., Bates, Freeland, & Lounsbury, 1979; Carey, 1970, 1973; Rothbart, 1981). Since there is evidence that maternal reports on temperament questionnaires are correlated with characteristics of the mother as well as the child (Bates et al., 1979; Vaughn, Deinard, & Egeland, 1980; Vaughn, Taraldson, Chrichton, & Egeland, 1981) these measures should more accurately be described as parent perceptions of temperament. Throughout the following discussion, even where not made explicit, it should be understood that the topic is perceived temperament.

Thomas and Chess (1977) have provided the basic theoretical framework for much of the current research in the field of infant temperament. In their New York Longitudinal Study, which began in 1956 and is still in progress, they attempted to assess the role of temperament factors in the development of normal and deviant behavior. Thomas and Chess' samples included 141 North American children from middle and upper middle class homes; 95 children of working class Puerto Rican parents; a small sample of children on an Israeli kibbutz; 68 premature children (of which 55% of the boys and 36% of the girls showed neurological impairment at 5 years of age); 52 mildly retarded children without motor dysfunction; and 243 children with congenital rubella, resulting from the rubella epidemic of 1964 (many children with multiple handicaps are found within this sample). They have gathered longitudinal data on temperament subscales as well as data from a small number of case histories, on interrelationships between temperament constellations and coping for the particular child over preschool, school and adolescent years.

Factor analyzing the items in their initial protocols, Chess and Thomas evolved definitions for nine separate dimensions of temperament as well as a number of temperament constellations that represent patterns of clustering of the nine subscales for particular types of children. The definitions developed by Chess and Thomas have been applied and operationalized by other researchers including Carey, McDevitt, and Fullard (1978), whose scales have been chosen for this study. They are therefore the definitions to be considered pertinent for the present discussion as well.

The nine dimensions of temperament operationally defined by Chess and Thomas are:

1.  *Activity Level:* The motor component present in a given child's functioning and the diurnal proportion of active and inactive periods. Protocol data on motility during bathing, eating, playing, dressing and handling, as well as information concerning the sleep-wake cycle, reaching, crawling and walking, are used in scoring this category.

2. *Rhythmicity* (Regularity): The predictability and/or unpredictability in time of any function. It can be analyzed in relation to the sleep-wake cycle, hunger, feeding pattern and elimination schedule.
3. *Approach or Withdrawal:* The nature of the initial response to a new stimulus, be it a new food, new toy or new person. Approach responses are positive, whether displayed by mood expression (smiling, verbalizations, etc.) or motor activity (swallowing a new food, reaching for a new toy, active play, etc.). Withdrawal reactions are negative, whether displayed by mood expression (crying, fussing, grimacing, verbalizations, etc.) or motor activity (moving away, spitting new food out, pushing new toy away, etc.).
4. *Adaptability:* Responses to new or altered situations. One is not concerned with the nature of the initial responses, but with the ease with which they are modified in desired directions.
5. *Threshold of Responsiveness:* The intensity of level of stimulation that is necessary to evoke a discernible response, irrespective of the specific form that the response may take, or the sensory modality affected. The behaviors utilized are those concerning reactions to sensory stimuli, environmental objects, and social contacts.
6. *Intensity of Reaction:* The energy level of response, irrespective of its quality or direction.
7. *Quality of Mood:* The amount of pleasant, joyful and friendly behavior, as contrasted with unpleasant, crying and unfriendly behavior.
8. *Distractibility:* The effectiveness of extraneous environmental stimuli in interfering with or in altering the direction of the ongoing behavior.
9. *Attention Span and Persistence:* Two categories which are related. Attention span concerns the length of time a particular activity is pursued by the child. Persistence refers to the continuation of an activity in the face of obstacles to the maintenance of the activity direction.

Three temperamental constellations of functional significance have been defined by qualitative analysis of the data and factor analysis. The first or "Easy" group is characterized by regularity, positive approach responses to new stimuli, high adaptability to change, and mild or moderately intense mood which is preponderantly positive. These children quickly develop regular sleep and feeding schedules, take to most new foods easily, smile at strangers, adapt easily to a new school, accept most frustration with little fuss, and accept the rules.

At the opposite end of the temperamental spectrum is the group with irregularity in biological functions, negative withdrawal responses to new stimuli, nonadaptability or slow adaptability to change, and intense mood expressions which are frequently negative. These children show irregular sleep and feeding schedules, slow acceptance of new foods, prolonged adjustment periods to new routines, people or situations, and relatively frequent and loud periods of crying.

Laughter, also, is characteristically loud. Frustration typically produces a violent tantrum for these children. These are the "difficult" children.

The third noteworthy temperamental constellation is marked by a combination of negative responses of mild intensity to new stimuli with slow adaptability after repeated contact. In contrast to the difficult children, these youngsters are characterized by mild intensity of reactions, whether positive or negative, and by less tendency to show irregularity of biological functions. The negative mild responses to new stimuli can be seen in the first encounter with the bath, a new food, a stranger, a new place or a new school situation. If given the opportunity to re-experience such new situations over time and without pressure, such a child gradually comes to show quiet and positive interest and involvement. This is the "slow to warm up" child (Chess & Thomas, 1977, pp. 12–21).

Thomas and Chess (Thomas & Chess, 1977; Thomas, Chess, & Birch, 1968) noted five variables that defined difficult temperament in their longitudinal sample: irregularity of biological functions, slow adaptation to new situations, high intensity affect, negative mood, and nondistractibility. More recently, Bates and his colleagues (Bates, 1980; Bates et al., 1979) found that the primary component of what parents consider difficult temperament corresponds to the Thomas and Chess dimensions of high intensity affect and negative mood: frequent and intense fussing that is not readily soothed. Items on the Brazelton Neonatal Scales (1973) which involve crying and cluster in what Kaye (1978) called "irritability" have also been used as indicators of difficult temperament (e.g., Crockenberg, 1981).

In the New York Longitudinal Study sample, 40% of the group fell within the Easy Child category, 10% of the group fell within the Difficult Child category, 15% of the sample fell into the Slow to Warm Up category. The three temperament groups comprised 65% of the sample of children studied by Thomas et al. (1963). The remaining 35% of the children showed a variety of behaviors characteristic of each of the temperament categories.

*Temperament and the Exceptional Child*

A child's temperament or behavioral style plays a role in the interaction between the child and his family (Chess & Thomas, 1978). Parents alter their style of interacting in response to the particular temperament constellation of their infant. Behavior problems can result if adaptation to child's temperament does not occur. Thomas and Chess (1977), in examining the relationship between temperament and developmental deviation, again refer to the fact that the child's psychological development was at all times the consequence of the interaction between the child and his individual attributes and parental management and other environmental influences. They stated that developmental disabilities tended to increase the likelihood of maladaptive responding by the child. Buss (1981) examined the effect of a child's activity level on parent interaction with the child and found that parents of active children get into power struggles with their children and that parents of less active children have a more peaceful, harmonious relationship with their child. Again a question arises as to whether or not different levels of activity in children (an aspect of temperament) may pose different socialization requirements for parents. Are the temperaments of developmentally handicapped children perceived as more difficult or easier than temperament of normally developing children?

Although there is some evidence from research on response behavior of Down syndrome infants (Cicchetti & Sroufe, 1976, 1978; Emde, Katz, & Thorpe, 1978) that developmentally delayed infants differ from normal peers in a variety of behaviors that might lead them to be perceived as temperamentally difficult, there is little direct evidence on this point. Field et al. (1978) found that mothers of prematurely born infants were more likely to score their infants as difficult on the Carey Temperament Survey than were mothers of full term infants. Down syndrome children are the group for whom the most data are available and even here the work is limited. Although the stereotype of the Down syndrome child is of one who is temperamentally easy, in comparison to normal children, Gunn et al. (1981) found that among 28 Down syndrome children aged 6–36 months, scores on the Carey Temperament Survey were consistent with Carey's description of the "average infant" in that only 2 children were found to be "easy," and 5 showed signs of being difficult. Eleven of the infants showed more than one sign of Thomas and Chess' difficult child, but none showed more than three. Two earlier studies, one by Baron (1972) using the Carey and one by Chess and Korn (1970) using the Thomas and Chess interview procedures are consistent with this report. There is little evidence to support the stereotype. Down syndrome children appear to show as much variability of temperament as samples of normal subjects.

Bridges and Cicchetti's (1982) work with Down syndrome infants has also yielded results that counter the stereotype of "easy" temperament for this type of handicap. They studied 74 Down syndrome infants, using the Carey Infant Temperament Questionnaire examining stability, as well as interindividual variance over a 6 month period. When the Down syndrome infants were compared with Carey's normative sample, results indicated that a greater percentage of Down syndrome infants would be placed in more difficult temperament categories (including intermediate high and difficult categories). Down syndrome infants were rated as less persistent, less likely to approach and more likely to have a lower threshold for stimulation than normal infants. Whether these results would also be true of other developmentally delayed children is presently being researched.

Marcovitch (1983, 1984) studied parental temperament ratings of 60 developmentally delayed preschoolers (20 Down syndrome children, 20 neurologically impaired children, and 20 children with unknown etiology developmental delay). Results corroborate Gunn et al.'s (1981) and Bridges and Cicchetti's (1982) contribution that the stereotype that all Down syndrome children are "easy" is not totally accurate.

Variability in temperament is reported in all three groups although there were more children in the Down group perceived as "easy" than in the unknown delay group, suggesting one possible reason for the stereotype. With respect to the individual subscales of temperament there were few significant differences between the handicap groups, though the neurologically handicapped children appeared to be rated as less persistent by their mothers. Furthermore, the delayed population as a whole scored their children as generally less persistent than the normative sample.

Greenberg and Field (1982) compared temperament ratings of 55 normal and same developmental age developmentally delayed, cerebral palsied, Down syndrome, and audio-visually handicapped infants by mothers, teachers, and independent observers (using the Carey Infant Temperament Questionnaire). These results indicate that children with audiovisual impairment are perceived as most difficult, with cerebral palsied children rated as somewhat less difficult and Down syndrome infants and normal infants generally found to be the easiest.

Heffernan, Black, and Poche (1982) studied parent ratings (using the Fullard, Carey, & McDevitt, Toddler Temperament Scale) of neurologically impaired toddlers and reports that the temperament characteristics of low activity level and a short attention span, coupled with low persistence were more common in this sample than in normal children. There was, however, no greater incidence of difficult temperament in this sample of neurologically impaired children than in normal children.

Blind infants are frequently termed "good babies" in maternal reports, despite an increased dependency for both care-giving and early learning (Nesker, 1974). Deprived of vital sensory information, the blind infant is necessarily more passive; required to intervene on exaggerated levels, the parent becomes more active (Davidson & Nesker Simmons, 1984; Nesker, 1974; Nesker Simmons & Davidson, 1984). The relevance of temperamental match of mother and child is heighted by this increased interaction, complicated by the necessary cognitive mismatch of a sighted mediator shaping information for a blind child. Hence, results of temperament studies would offer important contributions to an understanding of blind development. However, scales have yet to be developed for this unique population.

Whether the temperament variation in exceptional children follows similar patterns to that of normal children or evolves with a common pattern for each particular disability remains speculative. The prediction usually made is that the infant or child perceived as difficult is likely to be involved in stressful interactions with parents and, therefore may be at risk for later behavior disorders.

*Parent-Child Interaction, Temperament and Behavior Disorders*

Evidence concerning the relationship between perceived difficult temperament and stressful parent-child relationships in the normal population is equivocal.

Thomas and Chess (1977) found a significantly higher incidence of dysfunctional parent and peer relationships among children with difficult temperaments than among children with easy temperaments. They concluded, however, that a given pattern of temperament did not necessarily result in behavioral disturbance and/or disfunctional social relationships, the areas in which symptoms did develop depended on specific features of the parent-child interaction.

Milliones (1978) employed the Carey Infant Questionnaire and a measure of maternal responsiveness in examining the interaction between 24 black children (mean age 11.5 months) and their mothers. Results indicated that the more difficult the child, the less responsive the mother. Campbell (1979) also supported the idea of temperament influencing parent-child interaction in her recent study. Thirty-eight infant mother dyads were observed at home 3 months and 8 months and temperament measures taken (Carey Scale). Infants rated as irregular in biological functioning received less responsive mothering. Mothers of "difficult" temperament infants interacted less and were less responsive to the bids of infants rated difficult, in comparison to matched controls. Patterns were still evident at 8-month follow-up. These findings emphasize the need to further explore the potency of temperament variability as a factor influencing mother-child interaction.

On the other hand, Vaughn, Taraldson, Crichton, and Egeland (1981) reported no significant relationships between child temperament and behavior of mothers of 3- to 6-month-old infants during feeding and play interaction. Using Carey's Infant Questionnaire, Sameroff, Seifer, and Elias (1982) investigated the relationship between temperament and maternal behavior, and found significant relationships between maternal anxiety level, social status, mental health, and temperament ratings. However, findings indicated sporadic and small magnitude relationships between temperament and observed behavior in home and lab settings.

Bates, Olson, Pettit, and Bayles (1981) studied temperament ratings, parent-child interaction, cognitive scores, and subsequent behavior problems in children in a sample of 116 families, with data gathered at 6, 13, and 24 months. They reported no association between perceived difficult temperament and mother-child interaction at 6 and 13 months. They did, however, find that infants perceived as difficult showed signs of behavior problems later. A finding by Lee and Bates (1981) indicated some relationship between perceived difficult temperament and mother-toddler interaction around control issues. Lee concluded that although earlier interactions do not appear affected by temperamental differences, difficult temperament is associated with conflict in interrelationships at 24 months and is correlated with subsequent behavior problems. Bates hypothesized that "one of the interpretations we have put on a perception of infant difficultness is that it reflects the mother's feeling that she is being aversively controlled by her infant. Difficult babies cry and fuss, the mothers have told us, in part because they demand more attention than the average baby and are less able to entertain themselves. By 24 months difficult children are still using aversive forms of control, but these are most apparent when the mother attempts to stop the children from their explorations; and by 36 months, the child who as a toddler gave evidence of difficulties in resolving autonomy issues with the mother has some likelihood of being a child who is having difficulties with impulse management'' (Bates et al. 1981, p. 3). Whether there is at all times a dynamic relationship between difficult temperament and parent-child interaction during various phases in an infant and preschool child's development needs to be explored further. Prediction of whether the same explanations and relationships hold for developmentally delayed populations has yet to be determined. Although some researchers (Campbell, 1979; Milliones, 1978) suspect definite links between early temperament and subsequent parent-infant interaction and later behavioral problems, using a transactional explanation for these relationships, other researchers observe no links between temperament and parent-child interaction at early developmental stages (Bates et al., 1981, Vaughn et al., 1981). Some of the difficulty in arriving at firm conclusions arises from the variety of areas that are focused on as evaluative of the effect of temperament or parent-child interaction: for example, measures include level of maternal responsiveness, mother-child conflict, a diagnosis of childhood behavior problem, to name a few. In summary then, research thus far indicates that there is ample evidence that temperament plays a role in influencing parent-child interaction, but the magnitude of its role, the stages at which it influences the relationship, and the other factors that correlate with temperament to alter relationships are still being researched.

The relationship between difficult temperament and subsequent behavior problems is an issue that has been discussed by Thomas et al. (1968) as well as other researchers. Thomas et al. (1968) concluded that additional information about parent attitudes and practices and amount of family stress was necessary for satisfactory prediction. Those difficult infants whose parents were considered to have poor attitudes and child rearing practices and whose families also experienced repeated stress were most likely to be disturbed as older children.

Cameron (1971) also explored the etiology of childhood behavior problems, using temperament ratings over the first 5 years of life and ratings of parental attitude and treatment. Parental intolerance, inconsistency, and conflict were associated with negative temperament changes over time. Cameron stresses the importance of a transactional approach to parental characteristics and child temperament, given the constant evolution of a subtly changing relationship as parent and child interact over time.

In a population of 2–7-year-olds at risk for psychiatric disorders, Graham, Rutter, and George (1973) found that adverse temperament characteristics of negative mood, low fastidiousness, and low regularity were associated with disturbances at initial and 1-year followup. These characteristics were also found to be associated with indices of family dysharmony. The authors suggest that adverse temperament and family stress can combine in several ways to result in childhood disturbances (Graham, Rutter, & George, 1973).

Chess and Hassibi (1970) found that among a group of 5–12 year old retarded children living at home, a number of behaviors often considered symptomatic of psychiatric disturbance (e.g., high activity level, repetitive behavior) were common in half the children and were judged to be features of the retardation rather than indicators of disturbance. Nevertheless, among this group, Thomas and Chess (1977) found that 31 of 52 were diagnosed as having behavior disorders and that perceived difficult temperament was an associated factor. Of the group with behavior disorders, 19 (61%) were characterized as having three or more signs of difficult temperament. In contrast only 12 of 30 children (40%) with two or fewer signs of difficult temperament had behavior disorders. The authors suggest that mentally retarded children with even mild temperamental difficulties are especially vulnerable to behavior disorders.

A recent study by Crockenberg (1981) explaining the precursors of secure and insecure attachment reported findings that highlight an influential role of temperament characteristics in the development of parent-child relationship. Temperament was assessed objectively by using the irritability cluster from the Brazelton Scales (1973). Irritability alone did not predict secure or insecure attachment. However, when a mother had an irritable infant, her perception of presence or absence of social support was a primary determinant of the quality of mother-child relationship at age 1. Presence of support was associated with maternal responsiveness and secure attachment while absence of support was associated with lack of maternal responsiveness and insecure attachment.

These last four studies together suggest that while difficult temperament may be related to stressful mother-child relationships and behavior disorders, its effect depends upon stresses that impinge on the family and the availability of support to mitigate such stresses. Until recently (Goldberg & Marcovitch, in press; Marcovitch, 1983), there has been little work on this topic among developmentally delayed preschoolers, even though the available literature (e.g., Chess & Hassibi, 1970; Thomas & Chess, 1977) suggests that those with difficult temperament may be highly vulnerable to interactive disturbances and/or behavior disorders.

## Transactional Model: A Key to Understanding Individual Differences

In order to expand the clinical perspective of behavior disorders to include relevant factors in the young child's personal environment, it is necessary to employ a dynamic model.

A transactional framework opens the doors to the idea of developing a model in which variables from both parent and child are presented and investigated as they evolve, to determine those families and children "at risk" for poor outcomes. The child acts and in reaction to his/her behavior is capable of eliciting a continuum of positive to negative responses from his/her environment. Alongside this set of variables, entering into the interaction, is the environment's (e.g., the mother's) set of characteristics (e.g., intellectual, personality, educational) and response styles (from positive to negative) which enter into and evolve somewhat differently as a result of the transaction.

One example of an elaborate and more specific transactional model is provided by Chess and Thomas (1978). Thomas and Chess (1978) refer to their model as the "goodness of fit" model or the consonance-dissonance model. According to the authors "goodness of fit" results when the properties of the environment and its expectations and demands are in accord with the organism's own capacities, motivations, and style of behaving. When this "consonance between organism and environment is present, optimal development in a progressive direction is possible. Conversely, poorness of fit involves discrepancies and dissonances between environmental opportunities and demands and the capacity and characteristics of the organism, so that distorted development and maladaptive functioning occur" (Thomas & Chess, 1977, p. 11).

A number of researchers (Cohen & Beckwith, 1979; Chess & Thomas, 1978, Kogan, 1980; Lerner, 1982) apply a transactional model to their explanations of interrelationships between child and family. This application appears to be conceptual rather than empirical. Thomas and Chess (1977) apply the consonance-dissonance model to their analysis of the impact of temperament on psychosocial development. It is not the temperament per se, but rather the extent to which a child's particular temperament characteristics are consonant with the social milieu's norms for desirable behavior styles. Kogan (1980) studied mother-child interaction within families with developmentally delayed children, employing a transactional framework and noted that: "It is apparent, and readily confirmed, that the mother of the handicapped or slowly developing child participates in transactions that are less rewarding and provide far less positive feedback than received by mothers of normal children" (Kogan, 1980, p. 228).

Lerner, Balermo, Spiro, and Nesselroade (1982) also applied Chess and Thomas' "goodness of fit" model to temperament. They examined the model across a larger age span to address the question: Does the repertoire of temperament characteristics that a person brings to a specific context at a particular age fit the demands of the context? Cohen and Beckwith (1979) reported a study in which a preterm infant's competence at age 2 was examined in respect to possible predictors in early social transactions between mother and child of later competence. Results were interpreted within a goodness of fit model which would state that caregivers who involve in more positive social interactive behaviors in the early months promote consonance between child and environment, thereby promoting higher infant competence at later ages.

The "goodness of fit" model was also applied by Chess, Fernandez, and Korn (1980) to the development of the handicapped child and his family. The developmentally handicapped child is in constant interaction with the environment (in this case parents, siblings and peers, teachers at daycare/nursery school in the early years). Goodness of fit is not a static phenomenon. Through the child's developing years the stresses in the environment change. Family may be a central focus in the early years but school-age peers and demands of adolescence may

create conflicts for the child between peer group norms, demands and expectations and familial ones. Chess, Fernandez and Korn (1980) traced the developmental course of three deaf children and the resultant patterns of consonant and
dissonant interaction with the environment. They highlight the importance of
family influences and the need to evaluate them in the light of the child's
temperament and physical handicap. A highly consonant child environment interaction in the preschool years may become a dissonant interaction at a subsequent stage due to different characteristics becoming more prominent predictors
of success in coping. For example, one young girl was described as academically
successful and extremely verbal (given her handicap) in the elementary school
years. Her success at interacting with her school environment, however, changed
when the sensory handicap became a barrier to social interaction because of the
social demands of an adolescent peer group.

In her study the interactional nature of deviance, Simmons (1982, in press) has
found that emotional disturbance in children is situationally dependent. Simmons
(1982) reports that while over 97% of the sample were considered to be major
problems by the school, over 30% were not considered to be problems at home
even at the point of being excluded from the school system. Moreover, the data
amassed in this study suggest that the problems at school contributed to the
problems within the family since the age of onset of home problems was found to
trail the age of onset of school problems by a noticeable degree.

The focus of a recent study (Marcovitch, 1983, 1985) was on the child's first 5
years and on examining the factors at work in parents, family, child, and outside
support that ultimately lead to consonance in the relationship. The relationships
between characteristics of the child (type of developmental disability and temperament) and factors impinging on the mother (family functioning and support)
were explored as they affected maternal stress levels and ultimately the parent-
child relationship. Of 60 families with developmentally handicapped preschool
children, for whom data were gathered on maternal stress, child temperament,
social support, and family strain, 20 families were chosen on the basis of their
stress scores to be observed in mother-child play sessions. This group included
10 mothers of Down syndrome children and 10 mothers of children with other
developmental disabilities. Videotapes of the interaction were rated for maternal
facial and vocal affect, appropriateness of play materials chosen, and child
activity level of responsiveness.

In dyadic play interaction a relationship was reported between maternal stress
in coping with the child, degree of difficulty of child temperament, type of
handicap, and maternal behavior. Children rated as less adaptable, less persistent
and higher in activity level were treated in a less animated, less positive manner
($p < .05$). Mothers experiencing more frustration with their child exhibited
similar patterns of behavior. Mothers of Down children more often chose play
materials in keeping with their child's developmental level, than did other
mothers.

In summary, then, these findings highlight the importance of applying a transactional model to the understanding of the exceptional child by assessing individual differences in mother-child interaction in conjunction with measurement of maternal stress and child temperament. They suggest that mothers with a developmentally delayed child perceived as more difficult will encounter more difficulty in interacting with that child, experience more stress and should receive more supportive services addressing their individual needs.

## IMPLICATIONS FOR IDENTIFYING SOCIAL AND BEHAVIORAL PROBLEMS IN THE PRESCHOOL YEARS

The authors have thus far offered a perspective on examining social and behavior problems in the preschool years that takes account of a transactional approach and covers factors to consider in identifying disordered behavior in exceptional populations. The behavior problems of a young child with a developmental or sensory impairment should be considered in a different light from the young child for whom no other developmental, physical, or environmental issue impinges on social and emotional development. The label of behavioral problem in the former is in most cases secondary, but for the latter a diagnosis of social or behavioral problem may be the primary diagnosis.

Diagnosis of behavior problems in the preschool years might stem from any of the following: a mother complains to her pediatrician of overactivity in her 18-month-old that is interfering with her daily routines with the child; a preschool teacher refers a 4-year-old child to a mental health clinic because the child constantly hits and bites other children; a public health nurse on a visit notices that a 30-month-old child has minimal attentional skills, poor eye contact, and no obvious language. In all three cases it is possible that inappropriate behavior could be accounted for by undiagnosed developmental problems rather than be the result of a primary emotional problem. Clearly diagnosis and diagnostic labels are in part related to child characteristics and to the diagnostic labeling system employed.

Diagnostic labelling can be approached from a variety of perspectives. Present convention defers to the Diagnostic and Statistical Manual of Mental Disorders (DSM III) categorization of Mental Disorders (Spritzer, 1981). It provides a descriptive approach in the division of the mental disorders to diagnostic classes. All of the disorders without known etiology or pathophysiological process are grouped together on the basis of shared clinical features. A wide range of clinicians have had input into the categorization process. The authors do not wish to replicate this extensive categorization and refer the reader directly to the DSM III (1980).

It is important to note that the DSM III does not actually define the concept of "mental disorder," nor does it assume that mental disorders are well-defined discrete entities. Rather, each mental disorder is described by significant psychological or behavioral patterns, often associated with symptoms of distress or impairment of functioning. On the whole, the DSM III is descriptive of mental disorders with little attention to origins. While the descriptive approach facilitates diagnostic labeling, in the preschool years, origins of emotional disturbance are as relevant to the understanding of the total environment of the child as any other factor.

Analysis of behavior disorders in young children demands attention to a wide panorama of observations which extends beyond the child's behavior into the behaviors and personalities of those individuals central to the child's growth and development from birth. A transactional perspective in the observation and analysis of preschool behavioral and social problems accommodates a total range of critical features including child temperament, mother-child interaction, maternal personality, feature, of handicapping conditions, attitudes or expectations. Intervention based on such a model is equally useful to the aggressive child, the withdrawn child, the deprived child and the hyperactive child, whether disabled or not.

To examine the context of behavior within a transactional framework requires that a clinician go above and beyond the realism of simple chart lists. Such a probing and analytic approach is both demanding and complex. The tester as well as testee is continually involved in problem solving. However, comprehensive diagnostic data gathered in this way, justify the commitment to such an approach. Not only does the identification process result in a better understanding of the social and behavior problems by exposing their context, but as well the stage is set for intervention.

# REFERENCES

Als, H., & Brazelton, T. B. (in press). Assessment of behavioural organization in preterm and full term infants. *Journal of American Academy of Child Psychiatry.*

Apple, M. W. (1976). Commonsense categories and curriculum thought. In R. Dale, G. Esland, & M. MacDonald (Eds.), *Schooling and capitalism: A sociological reader.* London: Routledge and Kegan Paul.

Apple, M. W., & Brady, T. (1975). Toward increasing the potency of student rights claims: Advocacy-oriented policy recommendations. In V. F. Haubrich & M. W. Apple (Eds.), *Schooling and the rights of children.* Berkeley, CA: McCutchan.

Baron, J. (1972). Temperament profile of children with Down Syndrome. *Developmental Medicine and Child Neurology, 14,* 640–643.

Bates, J. E. (1980). The concept of difficult temperament. *Merrill-Palmer Quarterly, 26,* 299–319.

Bates, J. E., Freeland, C. A. B., & Lounsbury, M. L. (1979). Measurement of infant difficultness. *Child Development, 50,* 794–803.

Bates, J. E., Olson, S. L., Pettit, G. S., & Bayles, K. (1981). Dimensions of individuality in the mother-infant relationship at six months of age. *Child Development.*

Beckwith, L., & Cohen, S. E. (1978). Preterm birth: Hazardous obstetrical and postnatal events as related to caregiver-infant behaviour. *Infant Behaviour and Development, 1,* 403–412.

Bereiter, C. (1973). *Must we educate.* Englewood Cliffs, NJ: Prentice Hall.

Berger, J., & Cunningham, C. (1981). The development of eye contact between mothers and normals versus mothers and Down's syndrome infants. *Developmental Psychology, 17,* 678–689.

Brachfeld, S., Goldberg, S., & Sloman, J. (1980). Parent-infant interaction in free play at 8 and 12 months. Effects of prematurity and immaturity. *Infant Behaviour and Development, 3,* 289–305.

Braginsky, & Braginsky (1974). *Mainstream psychology: A critique.* New York: Holt, Rinehart and Winston.

Brazelton, T. B. (1973). *Neonatal behavioural assessment scale.* Philadelphia: J. B. Lippincott.

Bower, E. M. (1969). *Early identification of emotionally disturbed children in school* (2nd. ed.). Springfield, IL: Thomas.

Bridges, F., & Cicchetti, D. (1982). Mothers' ratings of the temperament characteristics of Down's syndrome infants. *Developmental Psychology, 18,* 238–244.

Brown, J. V., & Bakeman, R. (1979). Relationships of human mothers with their infants during the first year of life. In R. W. Bell & W. P. Smotherman (Eds.), *Maternal influence and early Behaviour.* Jamaica, NY: Spectrum.

Buss, D. (1981). Predicting parent-child interaction from children's activity level. *Developmental Psychology, 17,* 59–65.

Cameron, J. R. (1977). Parental treatment, children's temperament and the risk of childhood behavioural problems. I. Relationships between parental characteristics and changes in children's temperament over time. *American Journal of Orthopsychiatry.*

Campbell, S. (1979). Mother-infant interactions as a function of maternal ratings of temperament. *Child Psychiatry and Human Development, 10,* 67–76.

Carey, W. B. (1970). A simplified method for measuring infant temperament. *Journal of Pediatrics, 77,* 188–194.

Chess, S., Fernandez, P., & Korn, S. (1980). The handicapped child and his family: Consonance and dissonance. *Journal of the American Academy of Child Psychiatry, 19,* 56–67.

Chess, D., & Hassibi, M. (1970). Behaviour deviations in mentally retarded children. *Journal of the American Academy of Child Psychiatry, 9,* 282–297.

Chess, D., & Korn, S. (1970). Temperament and behavioural disorders in mentally retarded children. *Archives of General Psychiatry, 23,* 122.

Chiland, C. (1974). Some paradoxes connect with risk and vulnerability. In E. J. Anthony & C. Koupernik (Eds.), *The child in his family: Children at psychiatric risk.* New York: John Wiley & Sons.

Cicchetti, D., & Sroufe, L. A. (1978). An organizational view of affect: Illustration from a study of Down's syndrome infants. In M. Lewis & L. A. Rosenblum (Eds.), *The development of affect.* New York: Plenum Press.

Cohen, S. E., & Beckwith, L. (1979). Preterm infant interaction with the caregiver in the first year of life and competence at age two. *Child Development, 50,* 767–776.

Cottle, T. J. (1976). *Barred from school.* Washington, DC: New Republic Books.

Crawford, J. W. (in press). Mother-infant interaction in preterm and full term infants. *Child Development.*

Crockenberg, S. B. (1981). Infant irritability, mother responsiveness and social support influences on the security of infant-mother attachment. *Child Development, 52,* 857–865.

Davidson, I., & Simmons, J. Nesker. (1984, June). Mediating the environment for young blind children: A conceptualization. *Journal of Visual Impairment and Blindness.*

de Lone, R. H. (1979). *Small futures: Children, inequality and the limits of liberal reform.* New York: Harcourt Brace Jovanovich.

Divitto, B., & Goldberg, S. (1979). The development of parent-infant interactions as a function of newborn medical status. In T. Field, A. Sostak, S. Goldberg, & H. H. Shuman (Eds.), *Infants born at risk*. Jamaica, NY: Spectrum.

Dunn, L. M. (1968). Special education for the mildly retarded—Is much of it justifiable? *Exceptional Children, 35*, 5–22.

Dunst, C. J. (1980, April). *Developmental characteristics of communicative acts among Down's syndrome infants and non-retarded infants*. Paper presented at Southwestern Conference on Human Development, Alexandria, Virginia.

Emde, R., Katz, E., & Thorpe, J. (1978). Emotional expression in infancy. II. Early deviations in Down's syndrome. In M. Lewis & L. A. Rosenblum (Eds.), *The development of affect*. New York: Plenum Press.

Field, T. M. (1977). Effect of early separation, interactive deficits, and experimental manipulations on infant-mother interactions. *Child Development, 48*, 763–771.

Field, T., Goldberg, S., Stern, D., & Sostek, A. (1980). *High risk infants and children: Adult and peer interactions*. New York: Academic Press.

Field, T. H., Dempsey, J. R., Hatch, J., Ting, G., & Clifton, R. K. (1979). Cardiac and behavioural responses to repeated tactile and auditory stimulation by premature and full term infants. *Developmental Psychology, 15*, 406–416.

Fisichelli, V., & Karelitz, S. (1963). The cry latencies of normal infants and those with brain damage. *Journal of Pediatrics, 62*, 724–734.

Frodi, A. (1981). Contribution of infant characteristics to child abuse. *American Journal of Mental Deficiency, 85*, 341–349.

Fruedenberg, R. P., Driscoll, J. W., & Stern, C. S. (1978). Reactions of adult humans to cries of normal and abnormal infants. *Infant Behaviour and Development, 1*, 224–227.

Freedman, D. X., Brazelton, T. B., Comer, J., Cruickshank, W., Crump, E. P., Fish, B., Garrison, G. H., Hewett, F., Hollister, L. E., Kornetsky, C., Ladd, E. T., Levine, R. J., Morisey, P., Schulman, I., & Smith, M. H. (1971). Report of the conference on the use of stimulant drugs in the treatment of behaviourally disturbed young school children. *Journal of Learning Disabilities, 4*, 523–530.

Fullard, W., McDevitt, S. C., & Carey, W. B. (1979). *The toddler temperament scale*. Unpublished manuscript.

Goldberg, S. (1982). Some biological aspects of early parent-infant interaction. In S. G. Moore & C. R. Cooper (Eds.), *Young child: Reviews of research* (Vol. 3). Washington, DC: National Association for the Education of Young Children.

Goldberg, S., & Marcovitch, S. (in press). Nurturing under stress: Infants and preschoolers with developmental problmes. In A. Fogel & B. Melson (Eds.), *Origins of nurturance*. Hillsdale, NJ: Lawrence Erlbaum.

Graham, P., Rutter, M., & George, S. (1973). Temperamental characteristics as predictors of behaviour disorders in children. *American Journal of Orthopsychiatry, 43*, 328–339.

Greenberg, R., & Field, T. (1982). Temperament ratings of handicapped infants during classroom, mother and teacher interactions. *Journal of Pediatric Psychology, 1*,

Gunn, P., Berry, P., & Andrews, R. J. (1981). The temperament of Down's syndrome infants: A research note. *Journal of Child Psychology and Psychiatry, 22*, 189–194.

Hanson, M. J. (1980, April). *The behaviours of Down's syndrome infants in an early intervention project*. Paper presented at the International Conference on Infant Studies, New Haven, Connecticut.

Heffernan, L., Black, F. W., & Poche, P. (1982). Temperament patterns in young neurologically impaired children. *Journal of Pediatric Psychology, 7*.

Hobbes, N. (1975). *The futures of children*. San Francisco: Jossey-Bass.

Illich, I. (1977). Disabling professions. In I. Illich, I. K. Zola, J. McKnight, J. Caplan, & H. Shaiken (Eds.), *Disabling professions*. London: Marion Boyars.

Jensen, R. (1974). The risk of going to school. In E. J. Anthony & C. Koupernik (Eds.), *The child in his family. Children at psychiatric risk*. New York: John Wiley & Sons.

Jones, O. H. M. (1980). Prelinguistic communication skills in Down's syndrome and normal infants. In T. Fields, S. Goldberg, D. Stern, & A. Sostek (Eds.), *High risk infants and children: Interactions with adults and peers*. New York: Academic Press.

Kanner, L. (1965). Emotionally disturbed children: A historical review. In G. S. Lesser (Ed.), *Emotional disturbance and school learning: A book of readings*. Chicago: Science Research Associates.

Karelitz, S., & Fisichelli, V. R. (1962). The cry threshold of normal infants and those with brain damage. *Journal of Pediatrics, 61*, 679–685.

Kaye, K. (1978). Discrimination among normal infants by multivariate analysis of Brazelton scores: Pooling, pumping and smoothing. In A. Sameroff (Ed.), *Organization and stability of newborn behaviour: A commentary on the Brazelton neonatal behavioural assessment scale*. Monographs of the Society for Child Development, 43, 60–80.

Kogan, K. L., Wimberger, H. C., & Bobbitt, R. A. (1969). Analysis of mother-child interaction in young mental retardates. *Child Development, 40*, 799–812.

Kogan, K. (1980). Interaction systems between preschool handicapped or developmentally delayed children and their parents. In T. Fields, S. Goldberg, D. Stern, & A. Sostek (Eds.), *High risk infants and children: Adult and peer interactions*. New York: Academic Press.

Klaus, M. H., Kennel, J. H., Plumb, N., & Zuelke, S. (1970). Human maternal behaviour at first contact with her young. *Pediatrics, 46*, 187–192.

Lebovici, S., & Diatkine, R. (1974). Normality as a concept of limited usefulness in the assessment of psychiatric risk. In E. J. Anthony & C. Koupernik (Eds.), *The child in his family: Children at psychiatric risk*. New York: John Wiley and Sons.

Lee, C., & Bates, J. (1981). *Mother-child interaction at age two years and perceived difficult temperament*. Unpublished manuscript.

Leifer, A. D., Leiderman, P. H., Barnett, C. R., & Williams, J. (1972). Effects of mother-infant separation on maternal attachment behaviour. *Child Development, 43*, 1203–1218.

Leifer, J. A., & Lewis, M. (1980, April). *Maternal speech to normal and handicapped children: A look at question-asking behaviour*. Paper presented at International Conference on Infant Studies, New Haven, Connecticut.

Lerner, R., Palermo, M., Spiro, A., & Nesselroade, J. R. (1982). Assessing the dimensions of temperamental individuality across the life span: The dimensions of temperament survey. *Child Develypment, 53*, 149–159.

Lind, J., Vuorenkoski, V., Rosberg, G., Partanen, T. J., & Wasz-Hockert, O. (1970). Spectrograph analysis of vocal response to pain stimuli in infants with Down's syndrome. *Developmental Medicine and Child Neurology, 12*, 478–486.

Marcovitch, S. (1983, April). *Maternal stress, child temperament and parent-child interaction with developmentally delayed preschoolers*. A paper presented at the Biennial Meeting of the Society for Research in Child Development.

Marcovitch, S. (1983). *Maternal stress and mother-child interaction with the developmentally delayed preschool child*. Unpublished Ph.D. thesis, York University.

Marcovitch, S. (1985). *Individual differences in maternal stress, child temperament and mother-child interaction with developmentally delayed preschoolers*. Manuscript in preparation.

Marcovitch, S., Goldberg, S., MacGregor, D., & Lojkasek, M. (1985). *Family responses to developmentally delayed preschoolers* Manuscript in preparation.

McDevitt, S. C., & Carey, W. B. (1978). Measurement of temperament in 3–7 year old children. *Journal of Child Psychology and Psychiatry and Allied Disciplines, 19*, 245–253.

Milliones, J. (1978). Relationship between perceived child temperament and maternal behaviours. *Child Development, 49*, 1255–1256.

Minde, K. (1977). The role of drugs in the treatment of disturbed children. In P. D. Steinhauer & Q.

Rae-Grant (Eds.), *Psychological problems of the child and his family*. Toronto: MacMillan of Canada.

Nesker, J. (1974). *The importance of the mother as mediator of the environment*. Qualifying Research Paper, University of Toronto.

Parmelee, A. H., & Sigman, M. (1976). Development of visual behaviour and neurological organization in preterm and fullterm infants. In A. D. Pick (Ed.), *Minnesota symposium on child psychology* (Vol. 10). Minneapolis: University of Minnesota Press.

Philips, L., Draguns, J. G., & Bartlett, D. P. (1975). Classification of behaviour disorders. In N. Hobbes (Ed.), *Issues in the clasification of children* (Vol. 1). San Francisco: Jossey Bass.

Prugh, D. G., Engel, M., & Morse, W. C. (1975). Emotional disturbance in children. In N. Hobbes (Ed.), *Issues in the classification of children* (Vol. 1). San Francisco: Jossey-Bass.

Rae-Grant, Q. (1977). The primary care and referral of children with emotional and behavioural disorders. In P. D. Steinhauer & Q. Rae-Grant (Eds.), *Psychological problems of the child and his family*. Toronto: MacMillan of Canada.

Rae-Grant, Q., Carr, R., & Berman, G. (1983). Childhood developmental disorder. In P. Steinhauer & Q. Rae Grant (Eds.), *Psychological problems of the child in the family*. New York: Basic Books.

Rhodes, W. C. (1964). Institutionalized displacement and the disturbing child. In P. Knoblock (Ed.), *Educational programming for emotionally disturbed children: The decade ahead*. Syracuse: Division of Special Education and Rehabilitation, Syracuse University.

Rhodes, W. C., & Sangor, M. (1974). Community perspectives. In N. Hobbes (Ed.), *Issues in the classification of children* (Vol. 1). San Francisco: Jossey-Bass.

Rinder, I. D. (1970). New directions and an old problem: The definition of normality. In B. D. Starr (Ed.), *The psychology of school adjustment*. New York: Random House.

Rose, S. A., Schmidt, K., & Bridger, W. H. (1976). Cardiac and behavioural responsivity to tactile stimulation in premature and fullterm infants. *Developmental Psychology, 12,* 311–320.

Rothbart, M. K. (1981). Measurement of temperament in infancy. *Child Development, 52,* 569–578.

Rubin, R. A., & Balow, B. (1978). Prevalence of teacher identified behaviour problems: A longitudinal study. *Exceptional Children, 45,* 102–111.

Ryan, W. (1971). *Blaming the victim*. New York: Vintage Books.

Sameroff, A. J., & Chandler, M. J. (1975). Reproductive risk and the continuum of caretaking casualty. In F. Horowitz (Ed.), *Reviews of Child Development Research* (Vol. 4). Chicago: University of Chicago Press.

Sameroff, A. J., Seifer, R., & Elias, P. K. (1982). Sociocultural variability in infant temperament ratings. *Child Development, 53,* 164–173.

Sarason, S. B., & Doris, J. (1979). *Educational handicap, public policy and social history: A broadened perspective on mental retardation*. New York: The Free Press.

Serafica, F., & Cicchetti, D. (1976). Down's syndrome children in a strange situation: Attachment and exploration behaviours. *Merrill-Palmer Quarterly of Behaviour and Development, 22,* 137–150.

Simmons, J. Nesker. (1982). After the special setting: A follow-up of students released from treatment. *Special Education in Canada, 56.*

Simmons, J. Nesker. (in press). A study of the interactional nature of deviant behaviour in schools. *The Canadian Journal for Exceptional Children.*

Simmons, J. Nesker & Davidson, I. (1984, April). Mediation for young blind children: An Introduction to the Literature.

Simmons, J. Nesker, & Davidson, I. (1985). *Mediating the environment: A case study approach*. Submitted for publication.

Simmons, J. Nesker, & Davidson, I. (in press). Perspectives on intervention with young blind children. *Child Care, Health and Development.*

Sorce, J. F., & Emde, R. N. (1980). *The meaning of infant emotional expression: Regularities in caregiving responses to normal and Down's syndrome infants*. Submitted for publication.

Sostek, A., Quinn, P., & Davitt, M. (1979). Behaviour, development and neurologic status of preterm and full term infants with varying medical complications. In T. Field, A. Sostek, S. Goldberg, & H. H. Shuman (Eds.), *Infants born at risk*. Jamaica, NY: Spectrum.

Szasz, T. S. (1970). The myth of mental illness. In B. D. Starr (Ed.), *The psychology of school adjustment*. New York: Random House.

Thomas, A., & Chess, S. (1977). *Temperament and development*. New York: Brunner/Mazel.

Thomas, A., Chess, S., & Birch, H. C. (1968). *Temperament and behavior. Disorder in children*. New York: New York University Press.

Vaughan, B., Deinard, A., & Egeland, B. (1980). Measuring temperament in pediatric practice. *Journal of Pediatrics, 96,* 510–518.

Vaughan, B. E., Taraldson, B. J., Crichton, L., & Egeland, B. (1981). The assessment of infant temperament. A critique of the Carey Infant Temperament Questionnaire. *Infant Behaviour and Development, 4,* 1–18.

Vietze, P. M., Abernathy, S. R., Ashe, M. L., & Faulstich, G. (1978). Contingent interactions between mothers and their developmentally delayed infants. In G. P. Sackett (Ed.), *Observing behaviour* (Vol. 1), *Theory and Applications in Mental Retardation*. Baltimore: University Park Press.

Wasserman, G., Solomon-Schweizer, C. R., Spiker, S., & Stern, D. (1980). *Maternal interactive style with normal and at-risk toddlers*. Presented at International Conference on Infant Studies, New Haven, Connecticut.

Wedell-Monig, J., & Lumley, J. M. (1980). Child deafness and mother-child interaction. *Child Development, 51,* 766–774.

Whitelaw, A., Minde, K,. Brown, J., & Fitzhardinge, P. (1981). *The effect of neonatal complications in premature infants on early parent-infant interactions*. Submitted for publication.

Willis, P. (1977). *Learning to labour*. Westmead, Farnborough, Hants, England: Saxon House.

Wolf, T. H. (1973). *Alfred Binet*. Chicago: University of Chicago Press. As quoted in Sarason, S. B., & Doris, J. (1979). *Educational handicap, public policy and social history: A broadened perspective on mental retardation* (p. 34). New York: The Free Press.

Wood, F. H. (1975). Children with social and emotional problems. In J. J. Gallagher (Ed.), *The application of child development research to exceptional children*. The Council for Exceptional Children.

# PROBLEMS OF MOTOR DEVELOPMENT:

## SOME THEORETICAL ISSUES

Sheila E. Henderson

## INTRODUCTION

*Nec Manus, Nisi Intellectus, Sibi Permissus, Multum Valent*

(Bacon)

"Neither hand nor intellect, left each to itself, is worth much."

Movement is a fundamental component of human life. The ability to make precise controlled movements is so much part of daily living that the conduct of countless acts scarcely intrudes upon consciousness. Yet one only has to observe

Advances in Special Education, Volume 5, pages 147–186.
Copyright © 1986 by JAI Press Inc.
All rights of reproduction in any form reserved.
ISBN: 0-89232-313-2

a single handicapped child struggling to make unbiddable limbs execute the most routine of tasks to appreciate the significance of skilled motor behavior. The development of skilled movement is a critical component of developing mastery over the environment.

Children with a wide range of handicapping conditions experience difficulty in acquiring an adequate level of competence in the motor domain. In the long-term, lack of motor competence can be a major obstacle to successful integration into normal society. There is also little doubt that an individual's level of motor competence bears upon aspects of his cognitive and social development. In light of the importance of motor competence, it is distressing to see how little emphasis is placed upon it in the field of special education, in contrast, say, to the tremendous amount of attention paid to language problems or reading difficulties.

There are many reasons why the development of motor competence in children with handicapping conditions is not considered of the highest priority by special educators. One is that adequate competence is less easy to define than in some other domains. In reading, for example, adequate competence is easy to specify. Another reason is that in the motor domain we lack a sound theoretical basis from which to work. It is not that studies of both normal and abnormal motor development do not exist. For almost a century, motor development has attracted the attention of pediatricians, psychologists, neurologists, and specialists in physical education. To a considerable extent, however, the interests of these various groups have been pursued independently. Consequently, the questions posed have varied in conceptual framework as well as in method of investigation.

One dimension on which studies of motor development vary is that of the level of abstraction at which competence is treated. In some studies, the physical pattern of movements is of primary interest. These may be reflex responses (e.g., Touwen, 1976), or they may be voluntary actions (e.g., Roberton, 1982). In other studies, we find that action is of interest as an indication of intelligent planning or social competence. In this case the focus of attention is directed more towards intentions than the physical skills with which they are realized. As Bruner (1970) puts it, "my interest is not in the hands by themselves but in how they both shape and express human instrumental intelligence." Kalverboer and Hopkins (1983) draw a clear distinction between the first as representative of the study of motor behavior in its own right, and the second as the study of the role of motor behavior in general development. This is a useful distinction when we are trying to map out the ways in which motor behavior has been studied.

While it may be convenient when discussing the nature of a disorder to focus on the motor aspect, when considering its consequences, one must consider broader development implications. A profound abnormality in muscle tone, for example, is likely to influence the affective cues that the child can supply when interacting with its mother, as well as influencing its motor development per se. What is required, therefore, is an interactive model which permits us to consider the development of control over the neuromotor system together with the factors which it affects. Given the state of the art, however, that must remain a distant goal and what I propose to do in this chapter is more modest. I shall identify some of the recent advances that have been made in the study of motor development and examine the extent to which our understanding of motor problems in children has progressed or might progress as a result. In the chapter that follows I shall go on to consider the extent to which these advances are reflected in practice.

Broadly speaking, the study of motor development can be discussed under four headings, each of which will be dealt with below. The first section presents the descriptive approach which attempts to chronicle the acquisition of basic skills such as walking or grasping. In the second section, attention shifts to attempts to characterize movement in spatiotemporal terms. The third section focuses on the biological foundations of voluntary motor control. Finally the last section deals with the organization of action in its broadest sense. Here we deal very briefly with how competence in movement affects competence in other domains and is in turn affected by it.

## MILESTONES OR SIGNPOSTS

In the 1940s it was customary to take a view of development which emphasized its systematic nature (Gesell & Armatruda, 1941, 1947). The helpless, passive infant developed in an orderly way into a self-sufficient, active child. Attention was focused on the apparent invariance in the sequence of behavioral change and the relative inflexibility of the timetable. It seemed but a small step, therefore, to consider any deviation from this timetable as indicative of abnormality or pathology, and another small step to assume that early status was useful as a predictor of later status. More recent work has forced upon us a radical reevaluation of this position.

To begin with, our conceptualization of the human infant as a uniformly helpless, passive organism is being continuously eroded. While no one denies that the behavioral repertoire of the infant is limited and immature in some senses, the idea that a baby is no more than a bundle of reflexes receives little support today (Prechtl, 1981). Babies have been shown to begin life as social beings and to socialize others as much as they themselves are socialized (e.g., Rheingold, 1983). They possess much more sophisticated perceptual abilities than was once thought (e.g., Butterworth, 1983) and their motor repertoire includes the ability to make quite accurate aiming movements (e.g., Von Hofsten, 1980, 1982) and to imitate movements made by a caretaker (e.g., Meltzoff & Moore, 1983). Consequently, the picture of development as an orderly transition from passive helpless to active competence has to be rejected.

With regard to normative statements, it is now widely recognised that the neurological and behavioral milestones which have been traditionally used as markers of maturational state exhibit extensive variation within normal populations (e.g., Clarke & Clarke, 1984; Connolly & Prechtl, 1981). There are many causes of variation in motor development. Genetic differences (Freedman, 1965), cultural differences (Hindley, 1968; Super, 1976), social class (e.g., Neligan & Prudham, 1969), and special training (Zelazo, Zelazo, & Kolb, 1972) have all been shown to influence motor development. Of course, no one suggests that the maturational component in development should be disregarded. As Clarke and Clarke (1983) put it "if you seek for constancy you will find it, and if you seek for change you will find that too, because both exist."

Perhaps the most important contribution to our changed view of the determinants of development comes from studies of perinatal complications and their consequences. In the 1960s journals overflowed with studies which attempted to specify the relationship between a particular type of complication (e.g., prematurity) and later development (e.g., educational attainment). In 1975 Sameroff and Chandler produced their influential review of that literature showing that prediction on the basis of reproductive risk alone was singularly ineffective. For example, studies emerged which showed that perinatal complications were more likely to influence later development in children raised in poor environmental conditions than those raised in favorable conditions. As a result of this increasingly complex picture, Sameroff and Chandler proposed their "transactional" model of development which placed considerable emphasis on the dynamic nature of the interaction between the organism and its environment. (It is interesting to note that animal psychologists had for some time been studying the nature of this interaction directly. See Goldman & Lewis, 1978).

Another contribution to our changing view of development comes from the field of assessment. It is now 20 years since Stott and Ball (1965) pointed to the fact that scores on tests of early development were not good predictors of later IQ. Many explanations for why this should be so have been advanced, the title of one analysis being particular acute: "Development Milestones or Conceptual Millstones?" (Gaussen, 1984). A common criticism of the tests is that they contain too many items with a strong motor component. Though the items may be headed personal-social development, the infant often has to possess a considerable amount of motor coordination to be able to pass. Moreover, many of the later items require a verbal response. The fact that speech involves a high level of motor coordination is often forgotten. Further evidence that a child's intellectual status is not *necessarily* dependent on the acquisition of the sorts of perceptuomotor skills measured in these tests has been presented in a number of studies. Decarie's (1969) and Kopp and Shaperman's (1973) work on thalidomide children is often quoted as evidence for the fact that normal cognitive development can occur in the presence of limited motor capacity. That a proportion of cerebral palsied children are of normal intelligence is also testament to the view that the link between early motor development and later cognitive development is not as direct as was once thought.

Finally, Wolfe (1981), argues that insistence on the universality of timing and sequence as criteria of maturation has diverted attention from other theoretically important strategies for studying behavioral development. Regularities of timing or sequence require explanation. Their postulation is not by itself explanatory. They are likely to be produced by the interaction between biological programing and constancies in the environment. Addressing ourselves to the relative proportion of variance in development accounted for by maturation or by experience is not appropriate as a way of studying such an interaction.

Taken together these various lines of enquiry have led to a considerable upheaval in the way development has been conceptualized. Consider, for example, Connolly's (1981) dilation on the term "psychological maturation." He uses the phrase to refer to "various competences and their associated performance which emerge as a result of the growth and development of the central nervous system *in any reasonably normal and natural environment*," i.e., that the organism is programmed to produce a particular outcome over time—provided appropriate environmental conditions are satisfied (p. 218). Interference with either the biological or experiential factors is, therefore, likely to retard or even alter the maturational sequences which would otherwise emerge.

This broader view of maturation has a number of implications. While it remains true that regular relationships exist between structures and actions and that competence gained at one point may be necessary for and may be incorporated into competence at a later point, the processes are more flexible than was previously conceded. The precise contribution of different factors at different points in time will vary, and it is likely that there will be different routes to the same end. What also remains unchallenged is the view that the apparent invariances in order are almost certainly due to genetic mechanisms which have been established during the course of evolution. However, what differs is that there is no necessity to assume closely dependent relationships between all structures or all successive stages. Unfortunately, the extent to which theory in motor development has explicitly embraced these general changes is limited. One reason for this is that the study of motor development is still viewed as the poor cousin of developmental psychology; motor behavior is more often treated as an index of competence in some other domain.

## Documenting Atypical Motor Development

With this orientation serving as a background, we can now turn our attention to the description of children whose motor development does not conform to the normal pattern, considering briefly first, what is normally achieved by age 6 and the broader implications of these achievements. There is no shortage of "what happens when" accounts of early development, some of the most detailed being produced more than 50 years ago (for a comprehensive review see Keogh & Sugden, 1985). The best that can be done within the present confines is to remind the reader of the pervasiveness of skilled movement in the life of a normal healthy 6 year old and emphasize the extent to which motor and other aspects of behavior are inextricably interwoven. Consider, for example, the requirements of independent living. Going to the toilet, dressing, and eating all require considerable degrees of both gross and fine motor control. The 6 year old is competent in all these skills. By 6, the normal child at play exhibits considerable skill both with his hands in constructional play or drawing and with his body in playground games, bicycle riding and so on. Further, the way we move considerably influences the success of social interactions. For example, in the young child, physical independence from caretakers permits play alone or with peers; independence also means that the child is more in control of his own social interactions both in terms of seeking and rejecting meetings. An aspect of motor skill development which is often forgotten is speech. The physical act of speaking requires the coordination of an amazingly complex sequence of movements for it to be clear and understandable. The 6 year old speaks clearly and unhesitatingly. The importance of skilled movement in many different domains of behavior could be documented but suffice it to say that under normal circumstances skilled movement subserves much of our cognitive and social interaction with the environment.

When children's motor development does not conform to the normal pattern, we are faced with two difficulties. The first concerns the nature of the data we have available and the second concerns the heterogeneity of the children exhibiting problems. With regard to data, there is a dearth of studies which deal directly with motor development. There is also an enormous number of reports containing data which are not in useful form. The problem is that studies containing data on motor competence were often done for reasons unrelated to the documentation of motor development. They were concerned, for example, with the relationships between global measures of early development and later IQ, the differences between children brought up at home or in an institution, and so on. Since we know from the content of the tests used that many items require motor skill for their completion, we can conclude that a lower DQ, IQ, or even SQ furnishes presumptive but not direct evidence of a motor lag. Even when motor quotients are given separately, these too often result from a compounding together of quite radically different aspects of motor performance. Although informative to a limited extent, such data conceal the specific content of the competences or deficits being expressed by the child and do not help us to form hypotheses about the precise nature of the problem.

Another difficulty is how to deal with the fact that atypical motor development is common in a wide variety of children with and without other handicapping conditions. Traditionally, discussion of different groups have been conducted separately. Adopting the same strategy, we could take Fraiberg's (1977) work on blind children or Carr's (1970, 1975) work on Down syndrome infants and simply produce a table showing when particular skills are achieved. In the light of the introduction to this section, however, the usefulness of this approach seems limited. Almost by definition a problem of motor development implies that *on average* late acquisition of motor milestones is characteristic of the group. However, nearly every report of such delay is accompanied by a rider which draws attention to the fact that the quoted average values conceal wide variability within the group. Even in populations such as Down syndrome children, which might naively be expected to be homogeneous, wide variability exists. Furthermore, considerable overlap occurs not only between different groups of atypical children but also between atypical and normal children. Separate descriptions of groups defined in terms of medically designated diagnostic categories conceal these facts and distract us from investigating the sources of this variability. What is required is a conceptual framework within which both between and within group variability can be evaluated. Perhaps a consideration of current terms might be a starting point for such a framework.

*Descriptors of Motor Problems*

There are several terms in the literature which appear to denote something specific about the pattern of development in early childhood. These are words like "delayed," "deviant," "step-wise," "dissociated" and "transient." Let us consider the data we have on children with movement problems in the light of these descriptive terms and consider their usefulness. Take first the word "delayed," as at a superficial level it is the starting point for any discussion of children with problems of motor development. Every group of children with developmental problems, however defined, is reported to acquire some of the motor skills expected of them later than normal. Among the many groups reported to be late to acquire skills of locomotion, prehension, or both, are the cerebral palsied (e.g., Donoghue, Kirman, Bullmore, Laban, & Abbas, 1970; Neligan & Prudham, 1969), spina bifida (Anderson & Spain, 1977), mentally retarded of mixed aetiology (e.g., Illingworth, 1968; Molnar, 1978), Down syndrome (Carr, 1970; Cunningham, 1979), blind (Fraiberg, 1977; Parmalee, Fiske, & Wright, 1959), and the deaf (Brunt & Broadhead, 1982). There are obviously substantial differences among these groups which are not captured by the descriptive data on delay. There are, of course, differences in the amount of delay to be expected. Cerebral palsied children are *on average* substantially more delayed than any other group, and Down syndrome children are slower than any other mentally retarded group, and so on, but the variability both between and within groups is so great that by themselves estimates of averages are only of limited value. There are times when data of this kind are useful as a starting point, as in the study of institutionalized vs home-reared handicapped children, but inevitably we begin to ask not only about the causes of the delay in general but also about the source of individual differences. One way to move beyond the more global reports of delay in various groups of children has been to adopt the experimental method, which attempts to identify the processes underlying the delay. However, it is also possible to perform much more detailed analyses of descriptive data which tell us more about the pattern of development than mere "delay."

In the literature on mental retardation, the concept of "slowed down normality" is often invoked, the idea being that mentally retarded children progress normally but at a slower pace. That this is an oversimplification has been argued by numerous authors. Cunningham and Mittler (1981) point to two problems. First there is the question of why normal levels of cognitive competence are not eventually achieved? Second, such a view cannot accommodate evidence of qualitative differences which exist between normal and retarded individuals. The question then becomes whether "*delayed*" is the best word or whether "*deviant*" is more informative. In the motor domain we are faced with the same question. Certainly it can be argued that nearly all mentally retarded children eventually acquire a basic repertoire of motor skills. If one simply adopts a "can do/cannot do" level of analysis, therefore, the use of the word delayed can be justified. Surely this is misleading. A moment's thought should convince the reader that the movement of a mentally retarded child is usually qualitatively different from that of a normal peer. A group of mentally retarded children can usually be recognized from a distance by the way they walk. Furthermore, there are also limits to the kinds of skills which mentally retarded children can learn beyond the basis repertoire of locomotive and manipulative operations. We need to ask questions about what underlies these qualitative differences and what imposes the limitations on the acquisition of more complex skills. In using the word "deviant" rather than "delayed" attention is focused on the qualitative differences.

Usually it is said that the word "deviant" applies only in instances of clear pathology where there is evidence of structural (neurological) damage to the system. There is no doubt that the delayed-deviant distinction based on evidence of pathology is useful and holds for a number of childhood motor disorders. For example, the levels of lesion in spina bifida or polio may be used to determine fairly precisely the extent of motor impairment. In cerebral palsy abnormalities of muscle tone or the presence of involuntary movements accompany the delayed acquisition of skills and allow some tentative conclusions to be drawn about the extent or even location of damage. However, there are also some differences in the *sequence* of development in these children. For example, some do not pass through a crawling stage (Robson, 1970), others can walk but find standing difficult. In addition, their movements look different even when they acquire adequate competence. In this instance we have both pathological and behavioral evidence of "deviance."

If one decides to rest the case for "deviance" wholly on the demonstration of brain pathology, however, then a number of difficulties arise. For example, there is the problematic borderline between cerebral palsy and "clumsiness." Certainly there are children whose motor problems begin to appear in the preschool years and in whom nothing odd was previously noted. They may even have reached some of the normal milestones early. Furthermore, no clear evidence of brain pathology can be demonstrated. Yet detailed observation in later years might imply on the one hand delay—cannot hop, cannot catch a ball, cannot fasten shoes—and on the other deviance—walks in an "odd" way, trembles under stress, associated movements are excessive, balance reactions are diminished. Defined in one way, a child may be described as delayed, in another deviant. Another example of this problem occurs in Down syndrome where there is evidence that such children are even more delayed than other equally intellectually retarded children. The pathological evidence for the existence of a specific motor problem is circumstantial but the behavioral evidence is quite strong. In view of these difficulties there seems to be a good case for developing behavioral criteria for "deviance" in addition to the more limited criteria founded on pathological evidence.

The term "step-wise" generally has led to a clarification of the pattern more loosely described as delayed, and has generated hypotheses about the causes of the particular patterns observed. Two examples are illustrative. In congenitally blind children with no additional problems, motor development seems to proceed in a discontinuous fashion. In early infancy the blind baby supports his head well when held upright. Placed on the stomach, however, the arms are not brought forward to raise the head, even though adequate strength and coordination is present. Sitting develops within the normal timespan but then there is a pause. "Pulling up to standing" and creeping are markedly delayed. Progress in walking, too, is of this start–stop pattern. The blind child may take a few steps with his hand held when a normal infant does but whereas the sighted child walks confidently alone within 3 months it may be 9 months before the blind infant proceeds further. The plateaux have been considered in terms of periods when vision acts as the primary stimulus for new developments and in terms of the social consequences of lack of vision (e.g., Fraiberg, 1977). Another example of step-wise motor development comes from Cunningham's (1979) work on Down syndrome infants, whom he studied at 6-weekly intervals between the ages of 6 weeks and 24 months. Though at quite different times from blind children and, for very different reasons, there were plateaux in the pattern of development which lasted sometimes as long as 6 months. Cunningham's explanation of these plateaux focused on attentional difficulties which affected things like holding on to an object in one hand while receiving another. Though the explanations of step-wise development were quite different in nature, it is important to note that the starting point for both was descriptive data. Both Fraiberg's (1977) work on blind children and Cunningham's (1979) on Down syndrome children employed the Bayley Scales. What these investigations did not do, however, was simply add up the scores to produce a global measure of developmental level.

The next term, *"dissociated,"* is not commonly encountered in the literature. What is meant is that features of motor development which are normally linked in sequence and timing appear to be disconnected (Hagberg & Lundberg, 1969; Haidvogl, 1979; Robson, 1970). The most commonly reported instance is delayed gross motor development accompanied by normal fine motor development. According to Haidvogl (1979), head and trunk control emerges normally as does reaching, grasping, and releasing objects, but sitting develops late, marking the beginning of delays in crawling, standing, and walking. A common characteristic among these children is the posture they adopt when held in ventral suspension. This is described by Robson (1970) as the "sitting on air" posture. Many are also bottom shufflers (Haidvogl, 1979). Other characteristics such as atypical aspects of gait pattern are reported. The later development of children showing dissociated patterns in the first 2 or 3 years seems variable. Of the 32 children described by Hagberg and Lundberg (1969), 15 were reported to "grow out" of their problems, whereas the others continued to experience difficulties. The first 15 might be described as cases of "transient" motor dysfunction.

The question of whether a child can "outgrow" motor impairment is of considerable interest. "Transient" cases of motor dysfunction have been reported quite frequently (e.g., Drillien, 1972; Nelson & Ellenberg, 1982). In the National Collaborative Perinatal Project conducted in the United States by Nelson and Ellenberg (1982), a proportion of children who were clearly classifiable as cerebral-palsied at 1 year were not so classified at age 7. However, among this group described as having "grown out" of cerebral palsy there was an increased frequency of mental retardation, hyperactivity, and febrile seizures, when compared to a control group of infants normal at 1 year. Whether or not such children continue to have minor problems in skill acquisition is not well documented. Given these problems the question of what is really meant by "transient" requires clarification. If the behavioral manifestation of a problem at time one changes to manifest itself in another way at time two, then this is not strictly speaking transience. That is, the problem has not disappeared. Of interest, of course is the question of what produces change in some children but not in others? Ellison, Browning, and Trostmiller (1982) report changes in severely hypotonic infants, linking recovery with competence in personal-social skills.

Although the words "delayed," "deviant," "dissociated," and "transient" turn out not to be as clear-cut as they at first seem, data from the studies which use them force us to consider the interaction between intrinsic and extrinsic factors, as was suggested in the introduction to this section. To increase our understanding of atypical motor development further, however, it is essential to have recourse to other modes of enquiry.

# THE CHARACTERISATION OF MOVEMENT

The movement of babies and young children often appears staccato and halting when compared with the smoothly orchestrated performance of older children and adults. In contrast to normal children, many of those whose motor development is atypical never reach a stage at which their movements look fluent. Even when they do learn to run or catch a ball, the way they do so may still be described as "clumsy" or "awkward." Our problem is to understand why. During the transition from the apparently effortful attention–absorbing state of being a novice, to the effortless state of being skilled, changes of different kinds occur. Some of these changes result directly from the child gaining more control over his neuromotor system; others come indirectly from advances in other aspects of development. In this section we will focus on how movement becomes organized at a physical level.

## Pattern in Movement

There is noticeable regularity in the way human beings perform actions like walking, running, throwing, and manipulating objects. All but the most profoundly impaired acquire the same basic repertoire and in many ways the similarities between us are more remarkable than the individual differences. Rudimentary aspects of this regularity are evident from a very early age but as a child grows older substantial changes do occur. The 2 year old walks rather differently from the 7 year old. Not only is the 7 year old more confident and more efficient in the sense that less attention is required to perform the skill, but also the way he moves can be said to be biomechanically more efficient. We will consider some examples of how children's movement has been depicted and whether the available methods have enabled us to characterize atypical movement adequately.

An obvious question that comes to mind as we note the regularity in how we move is what produces it? How is the neuromotor system organized to emit such regular patterns? It might be revealing to elaborate a little upon the problem to be solved. The baby is already equipped with the full complement of almost 800 muscles which act upon 100 mobile joints to produce the movement we observe. Unfortunately, the way the joints and muscles interact is not straightforward. Joints vary in the kinds of anatomical pieces they link (cartilage or bone) and the numbers of axes over which they change (for example, hinge joints like the elbow only flex and extend and are, therefore, uniaxial; ball and socket joints like the hip move on three axes). The muscles which produce the movement at these joints always work in groups, some taking a primary role in the movement, others acting to stabilize parts which do not move. The same muscle, however, may act differently in different situations. These are but a few examples of the complexity of the machinery. The brain, therefore, would have a mammoth task if it were to control individually all the potential variables in the system, whether we consider them at the level of particular muscles, entire limb segments, or whatever. In one line of enquiry, stemming from the work of Bernstein (1967), this problem has been labelled the "degrees of freedom" problem. Using the language of the physical sciences, the variables to be controlled such as the angle of a joint or the length of the muscle are formally designated "degrees of freedom." Couched in this terminology, the question then becomes how might the nervous system be organised so that the number of degrees of freedom to be controlled by the brain are reduced to the minimum? (See Kelso, 1982, for a review.)

So far we have considered the organization of movement into regular patterns. What is equally striking in the way we move, is our ability to adapt to changes in environmental conditions. Even in the most practised of actions (e.g., walking) the movements never appear stereotyped. Though we are often unaware of it, we are constantly adjusting to slight undulations in the terrain, to objects in our path, and so on. The reason we can perceive both regularity and variation in an action at the same time is that some parameters of the pattern remain fixed, whatever the conditions, whereas others are free to vary according to the demands of the environment. One of the most fundamental processes which contribute to this adaptive capability is that which enables us to automatically adjust our posture in response to changes in sensory input. As far as children with atypical motor development are concerned, two questions arise. First, we might ask whether they lack the means to produce the regular patterns to be observed in normal movement. Second, there is the possibility that they lack the ability to tailor their movements to changing sensory input. Whether both of these faculties are impaired is, of course, a third possibility.

## Describing Pattern

How we move is difficult to describe concisely. We can all distinguish a well coordinated child from a clumsy one, but when we try to characterize the exact nature of the difference between them, we find that our judgements are made on a global basis which defies precise explication. Various attempts have been made to produce methods of capturing as much of the detail in movement as possible. I will describe just two which illustrate the extremes on a continuum of technical sophistication.

*Verbal description.* Some of the most exquisite descriptions of how children move were produced as long ago as the 1930s (Halverson, 1931; McGraw, 1945; Shirley, 1931). Many of the early portrayals were based entirely on what the observer gleaned from watching how the child performed an action. More recent studies use film recordings which permit much more intensive analysis and, therefore, yield more detailed description. For example, one can examine the leg movements frame by frame in one sweep through the film, then proceed to the arm movements, the head movements, and so on. The development of maturity in skills like walking (e.g., Statham & Murray, 1971) running (e.g., Wickstrom, 1977) throwing (e.g., Roberton, 1977) catching (e.g., Gallahue, 1982) and manipulative hand movements (e.g., Elliot & Connolly, 1984) have all been described in varying amounts of detail. These investigations have been carefully summarized by Gallahue (1982) and Keogh and Sugden (1985).

In general terms, what emerges from these studies is that the move towards increased biomechanical efficiency involves two processes. Fewer irrelevant movements occur and variability from trial to trial diminishes; increased control permits larger excursions of movement. For example, in throwing, the older, more mature child shows more trunk rotation, more arm withdrawal and more follow through of both arm and shoulder than the younger less efficient child. Another general observation is that distinct stages or phases seem to be identifiable in the changes which constitute development (e.g., Roberton, 1977, 1982; Seefeldt & Haubenstricker, 1982). Until recently little attempt was made to provide a theoretical framework against which such changes might be interpreted. An obvious possibility was to test the utility of the basic assumptions of stage theories as they have been formulated in other domains. Roberton has done this using Piaget's theory as one of her referents and has run into many of the problems now being encountered in the cognitive domain.

A very different perspective on the origins of these changes has been taken by Kugler, Kelso, and Turvey (1982). Kugler suggests that it may be more fruitful to study alterations in the form of a movement sequence in relation to alterations in the child's body dimensions. Though the baby has the same number of bones, joints, and muscles as the adult these are not physically mature and continue to develop well beyond the period we are discussing here. Thus, adaptation to continuous (but not necessarily linear) changes in height, weight, and so on must be taken into account as well as any other changes which contribute to development. As Kugler's view is that many of the problems to be solved in motor control are best considered in the context of theories of how physical systems operate, he uses an engineering analogy to illustrate his point. If, having built a small durable bridge, the engineer then proceeds to build a bigger one by simply applying a scale factor to the original bridge's linear dimension, the result is unsuccessful. Unfortunately, increasing the size in this way does not result in a corresponding increase in strength or stability. Applying the same logic to the problem of the growing child, it may be argued that within "a stage" the physical system is stable and the movement patterns are correspondingly so. Beyond a certain point, however, the physical changes are such that the system becomes unstable, leading to the emergence of a revised pattern, qualitatively different from the previous one.

This theory remains largely untested but I have outlined it because it draws attention to the fact that to understand motor development and its deviations fully it may not be sufficient to focus only on the neurological and cognitive determinants of change. This point is, of course, entirely consistent with the view taken by bioengineers and therapists who for years have been devising aids for the physically handicapped; however, it may be new to psychologists and educators.

When considering the difficulties faced by children with orthopedic problems it may force us to be more aware of things like the costs that can accrue from not seating a child properly for a writing lesson. Conversely the benefits that a child may gain in terms of being able to attend longer because he is comfortably positioned are obvious to any sensitive teacher.

There are two important points to note before we turn to the description of atypical children. The first is that few of the basic skills we have mentioned are fully mature by age 6, so that in the preschool period comparison between typical and atypical is more difficult than at age 9 or older. The second is that just as there is considerable variation in when children acquire certain skills there is also variation in the rate at which they progress towards consistency in the way they move. Furthermore, such progression may be different for different skills.

## Describing Atypical Movement Patterns

Turning now to descriptive studies of children with problems of motor development, at present our data base remains relatively impoverished, but in the last few years there has been a rapid increase in the number of studies with this orientation (e.g., McClenaghan & Gallahue, 1978). There is, however, a gap separating portrayals of children with mild problems and those whose movement is more severely impaired. There are several reasons for this. In part, it is because the distinction between "deviant" and "delayed" already discussed is assumed to be clearer than it actually is. In practice, clinicians often debate whether a particular child is a case of mild cerebral palsy or not. In borderline cases, the child's movement may look like that of a younger one in some respects but be quite different in others. For example, when bilateral movements are attempted, marked asymmetry may be present or mild but definite tremor may emerge under conditions of stress. Another reason for the gap is that it is often difficult to find tasks which all children can perform, whatever their degree of impairment. What we find in the literature, therefore, are two rather separate sets of papers published by different professionals in different journals and from different perspectives.

On one side of the divide lies the work of physiotherapists. In the main they have concentrated their attention on children with severe problems and tend to focus on the documentation of abnormalities of tonus or reflex reactions. Little attention is paid to looking for signs of intentionality in the movement of severely impaired children or to describing how they move when they do find a way to perform an action. It is true that in the preschool period particularly, severely impaired children may lack control of even their own head movements; yet, voluntary effort must be of primary concern. When skills are acquired, however slowly, we need to be able to document the progression towards success.

On the other side of this apparently clear gap, lies the work of physical educators and psychologists. Their focus is almost exclusively on matching the movement of mildly intellectually impaired or so called "clumsy" children against the descriptions provided for "normal" children. Because these children can register some success on the actions documented for normal children, then it is relatively straightforward to make a comparison. This can mean, however, that factors like tremor, inadequate strength, or abnormally low tone go unnoted because they lie outside the range of observations made on normal children.

There are both practical and theoretical reasons why it is important to avoid perpetuating this dichotomy. From a practical point of view there is a need for better communication between therapists and teachers. A means of describing movement which encompasses the whole range of severity would be valuable in this respect. Not only would it provide common grounds for discussing approaches to intervention but it should also help to make the measurement of progress easier. A common complaint from practitioners working on children with problems of motor development is that the measuring instruments they have available at present are not finely graded enough to record the subtle changes which take place between the child totally failing a task and achieving success. From a theoretical viewpoint, the lack of a means of describing movement on a single continuum (from impaired to normal) deters us from studying the effect of deviation from normal on the outcome of an action (e.g., in terms of its speed or accuracy). We need to know, for example, whether some atypical patterns of movement lead to less efficiency than others or whether some act as barriers to further progress while others do not. Some Down syndrome infants move from a lying position to sitting quite differently from normal children (Lydie & Steele, 1979) but perhaps this is of no consequence. Certain types of sitting or crawling positions are discouraged by therapists treating cerebral palsied children of the spastic type because it seems to have a detrimental effect on their later walking. Sometimes, notions about pattern in movement and its effect on the outcome are proved wrong, however. Recently, Peters (1984) has shown that the hooked position adopted by left-hand writers has no detrimental effect on either speed or quality of output. The relationship between the outcome of an action and the movements which comprise the action is a complex one and is not yet well understood. Knowing more about the interaction between the two would be of some importance to interventionists. At present, decisions to concentrate on trying to improve the pattern in movement or on simply finding a way that the child can achieve functional success, by whatever means, are made arbitrarily.


*Biomechanical analysis.* In parallel to attempts to find ways of increasing the precision of verbal descriptions of movement patterns, there have been attempts to use the "language" of the physical sciences to produce quantitative analysis of its spatial and temporal characteristics. This particular branch of mechanics is called kinematics, and may be applied either to the measurement of the movement of the limbs and/or the entire body. Perhaps the most common of the kinematic methods involves recording the location of the limbs during a movement. Early in the history of biomechanical analysis researchers used cinematography to record movement and the films were studied frame by frame to mark the location of certain critical points (e.g., the hip joint, knee and ankle in walking). The change in location of these points was then plotted against time. Similar data can now be obtained by using light sensing devices which detect the location of tiny light bulbs attached to the limbs and record their location automatically in digital form. Using computer analysis, measures of the velocity of the moving part, the pattern of acceleration and deceleration, the peak velocity and so on, can be derived from these basic data. In addition to spatio-temporal factors, many studies now include measures of the forces exerted during movement. This is done in walking, for example, by having the child walk over a force sensitive plate inserted in the floor of the room.

Various authors have reported the use of biomechanical analysis of movement in young children, the most frequently studied skill being walking (e.g., Burnett & Johnson, 1971). The analysis of gait pattern has proved of clinical value in understanding the problems of cerebral palsied children (e.g., Aptekar, Ford, & Black, 1975; Holt, 1966) and of those with Duchenne Muscular Dystrophy (Sutherland, Olshen, Cooper, Wyatt, Leach, Mubarak, & Schultz, 1981). More recent studies, which we shall review below have proved of considerable theoretical importance (e.g., Nashner, Shumway-Cook, & Marin, 1983).

## What Underlies Regularity in Movement

For a long time it has been considered unlikely that the brain controls the many muscles involved in an action individually. It has been supposed instead that its work is simplified by the existence of low level movement pattern generators whose activities are coordinated by the brain. For theorists committed to this view, it is necessary to explain how variation in movement production occurs. For the moment, however, we will continue to focus on regularity.

The basic units which are thought to exist with some degree of autonomy within the central nervous system have been given different names by different authors. Essentially Turvey's (1977) view of coordinative structures is similar to what Greene (1972) calls function generators and what others call synergies. A synergy consists of a group of muscles activated concomitantly to create an overt movement pattern which has distinct biomechanical properties. Studies which examine the characteristics of synergies employ biomechanical analysis to describe the pattern of movement emitted and electromyography to specify the activity in the muscles which comprise the synergy. Thus, it is possible to determine how the regularity in movement is produced and what changes occur in the transition from immature, variable, patterns to mature, consistent ones.

The existence of synergies have been demonstrated for postural control (e.g., Nashner & Woollacott, 1979) locomotion (Grillner, 1975) and respiration (Gurfinkel, Kots, Paltsev, & Feldman, 1971). A study of locomotion by Shik and Orlovsky (1965) illustrates the synergy notion rather well. Imagine an animal suspended over a treadmill so that only one limb is in contact with the moving surface. What the authors found when the animal walked on the moving surface was that the relative onset times of flexor and extensor muscle action in the ankle, knee, and hip joint was the same regardless of how fast the animal was moving. Since this same pattern of activation was observed in the animal when the spinal cord was sectioned to remove the influence of higher brain centers, the stepping pattern of the limbs must have occurred as a result of relationships between muscles controlled at the level of the spinal cord.

Rather little work on synergies has been done on normal children and even less on children exhibiting atypical development. However, what does exist is of interest. In a discussion of organized sequences of movement which are apparent early in the life of a normal infant, Thelen and Fisher (1983) cite as examples: the constellation of ingestion movements comprising looking, sucking, and swallowing; spontaneous hand to mouth contact; and, the rudimentary aiming movements demonstrated by Von Hofsten (1982). In their own studies of spontaneous leg movements in 2 to 4 week old infants (e.g., Thelen, Bradshaw, & Ward, 1981) some invariant characteristics were already evident, demonstrated in the temporal organization, in the cyclical nature of the repetitions, and in the duration of the episodes. There were, of course, individual differences among infants but, even within the 2 week period studied, an increase in consistency could be discerned.

In young children synergies for postural control (Shumway-Cook, & Woollacott, 1985) and locomotion (Forssberg & Wallbert, 1980) have been studied. There are some nice parallels between the findings of these studies and those relying on verbal description to document progression. Taking postural control as an example, we find that the transition from immature to mature response patterns entails a reduction in variability in parameters like the timing of muscle actions. This, of course, makes the movement look more fluent. Furthermore, the changes do not occur in a linear progression but are stage-like as Roberton (1977) described. What we do not know, of course, is whether the mechanisms which control synergies are built into the system, how they are refined, and finally, how they are endowed with the facility to adapt to environmental demands.

There are several questions we might ask about children with atypical motor development. For example, is it possible that the mechanisms which direct synergies could be completely absent? Do muscles which normally work together do so but in a disorganized fashion? Is the capacity to produce regular patterns of movement present but somehow inhibited by another problem at a different level of the system? Work on questions like these is only in its infancy but already some interesting findings have emerged. These come mainly from the laboratory of Nashner and his colleagues. For example, within the group of children labelled cerebral-palsied there appear to be differences among subgroups. In spastic children the muscles act in a disorganized fashion, whereas ataxic children's movement is normally organized (Nashner, Shumway-Cook, & Marin, 1983). In another study, Shumway-Cook and Woollacott (in press) examined the postural control of Down syndrome children. The differences between the Down syndrome and normal children were sufficiently marked for the authors to suggest that the equilibrium problems found in Down syndrome children are not just the results of delayed, albeit normal, development—but may in fact represent a difference in the evolution of postural control.

## Automatic Adaptation to Environmental Conditions

When a normal person standing in a well balanced position is suddenly disturbed he or she will make rapid alterations of the body so that balance is preserved under the new conditions. In both adults and children this capacity is something which often becomes disturbed as a result of damage to the neuromotor system. Under normal circumstances the muscle activity which occurs in the act of regaining balance shows some interesting characteristics. Whereas the absolute *amount* of activity in the muscles at hip, knee, and ankle varies, the *ratio* of activity among those muscles remains unaltered (Nashner, 1977). Thinking in terms of synergies and how they function, we can consider the ratio of activity as an invariant parameter of the synergy and the amount of activity as a variable parameter. It is the process of "tuning" or regulating the variable parameters in response to sensory input which contributes to our ability to respond adaptively to environmental conditions.

From a developmental viewpoint numerous questions have been asked about the mechanisms which underlie this adaptive capacity. For example, one line of enquiry has focused on the relative importance of visual and nonvisual sources of sensory information in the early stages of learning to maintain balance. For us as adults, shutting our eyes makes little difference to our ability to stay upright. The information we receive internally from our vestibular system, through the soles of our feet and so on, seem to be quite adequate as a means of knowing where we are, and even if someone pushes us we still adapt appropriately. The question is, was this always so for us or does it take time for the visual and nonvisual systems to function interchangably in this way?

In 1974, Lee and Aronson began a series of experiments which pursued this line of enquiry. One way of approaching the problem of establishing the relative importance of visual and nonvisual information is to put the two in conflict. As all of these experiments are similar it might be useful to have a brief outline of how they are done. The task is a simple one—to sit or stand up. The infant's problem, however, is that both the room around him and the floor under him are moveable. The room may move backwards or forwards parallel to the infant's line of vision and the floor tilts so that the toes move upwards or point downwards. This enables the experimenter to manipulate the sensory input available to the infant through somato-sensory receptors in the legs and ankles and through the eyes. What is recorded is the infants' attempts to stay upright. The early experiments simply recorded the amount of sway noticeable to an observer, whereas later studies also include electromyographic recording of muscle action.

What Lee and Aronson (1974) found when they exposed normal infants to the moving room was that those who had just learned to stand or sit could not accommodate to the apparent loss of balance being signaled visually. Even though their internal receptors were signaling that they were stable (the floor did not move) they were apparently "tricked" by the misleading visual information into "feeling" off balance and fell over completely or staggered. In other words, vision seemed to be the dominant sense at this time. As infants gain experience of sitting or standing, however, they become less influenced by the discrepant visual information and can accommodate to it with little trouble. They seem to "know" that the visual information is misleading and may well laugh at the trick. Lee and his colleagues interpret their results as evidence for the fact that infants take time to develop a stable frame of reference which is independent of vision. Using a wider age range of children, Shumway-Cook and Woollacott (1985) examined the effects of varying somatosensory input as well as putting it in conflict with vision. The ability to resolve the kind of intersensory conflict they produced was not present in the youngest group (15–31 months) but emerged in the 4–6 year old group and had reached adult form in the 7–10 year old group.

It has long been known that problems of postural control are characteristic of adults and children with certain kinds of brain damage but it is only recently that psychologists have begun to study young children whose motor development is atypical using these experimental techniques. One of the first studies to focus on this problem was that of Butterworth and Cicchetti (1978). Following on the work of Lee and Aronson (1974) they compared the effects of conflicting visual and nonvisual perceptual input on Down syndrome and normal infants. They found that Down infants who had recently learned to sit were much *less* responsive to the movement of the room than normals whereas those who had just learned to stand unsupported were much *more* so. Since it was not the case that the seated babies failed to perceive the movement of the room, it seems that they differed in the way they responded to it in the two positions. Butterworth and Cicchetti suggest that since postural control depends on congruence between mechanical-vestibular and visual indices of stability, a relatively unstable posture may "tolerate" less of a discrepancy between visual and somato-sensory input before compensation is required. Hence standing is on average more influenced by the surround than sitting. This in turn suggests that the function of vision may be to calibrate or tune the internal system against the stable surround. As the child gains control over his internal system he becomes progressively more independent of visual cues so that eventually he can override the effects of the discrepant visual input.

Though they do not specifically say so, Butterworth and Cicchetti's explanation of their findings seem to suggest that the Down syndrome child's problem is temporary and may disappear with age. Shumway-Cook and Woollacott (in press), on the other hand, present data which show that the performance of Down syndrome children was still deficient at age 6. Furthermore, they examined the underlying organisation of the patterns of movement which resulted from the subjects' attempts to maintain balance either in a completely natural setting (noted above) or when intersensory conflict was produced. At a gross level of analysis the sequencing of muscle responses was similar in Down and normal children, though much more variable from trial to trial in the Down children. When the temporal and force characteristics of the muscle actions were examined, however, many more differences emerged. In particular, slowness in the onset latencies of the muscles comprising the acting synergies was noticeable at all ages. Especially in the very young children between 1 and 3 years, the differences between the Down and normal children were greatly exaggerated. In response to intersensory conflict the Down syndrome children fared much less well than their normal counterparts and at 6 were still unable to respond appropriately.

To conclude we must refer again to the study of cerebral-palsied children mentioned earlier (Nashner, Shumway-Cook, & Marin, 1983). Although the ataxic subjects in the group seemed to have the potential to produce normally organized patterns of movement, they could not do so because their responses to sensory input were inappropriate. The single athetoid child in the sample seemed to be impaired in both ways—his movement was fundamentally disorganised and his responses to sensory input were abnormal. Taking all their findings together Nashner et al. (1983) have provided us with some new insights into the differentiation of the sources of failure in motor control. It is a fruitful line of enquiry and one which deserves intensive investigation.

## THE BIOLOGICAL FOUNDATIONS OF SKILLED MOVEMENT

When discussing what mechanisms might underlie invariances in the pattern of movement, I introduced the crucial notion that the brain exercises control of subunits rather than sending commands directly to every muscle involved in an action. Pursuing this theme in a developmental context we might ask whether these units of movement are "prewired" into the system in some rudimentary form and if so, how voluntary control over them is developed? We do not yet know the answer to this important question and so must be content with a consideration of the issues.

Until recently the movement of the newborn infant was thought to be entirely without purpose. Two classes of movement seemed sufficient to characterise the entire repertoire—reflex movements and spontaneous movements, which were often described as random. Both types of movement have been considered as candidates for the foundations from which voluntary movements emerge, but the former had received much more attention. One reason for the persistent failure to consider the significance of spontaneous movement in infants was that their existence was an embarrassment to those of the behaviorist persuasion—the eliciting stimulus could not be identified. The accumulating evidence that very young infants can, in fact, exert voluntary control over their movements has obvious consequences for arguments concerning both our view of behavioral development and of the developing nervous system which underpins it.

*Reflexes*

We will begin with the case for considering "reflexes" as the precursors of voluntary motor control. It is unnecessary to provide a description of an infant's reflex repertoire as numerous reviews exist (e.g., Fiorentino, 1973; Taft & Cohen, 1967). It is sufficient to make two points: First, some of the patterns of movement which characterize infantile reflexes bear an intuitive resemblance to later aspects of voluntary movement, whereas others do so much less. It tends to be those that resemble voluntary movements which are considered as precursors of their voluntary equivalent. Where no such resemblance is evident an explanation in terms of phylogenetic vestiges or remnants, lacking an adaptive function is often proposed (e.g., McGraw, 1945). Second, and broadly speaking, the whole class of reflexes can be divided into two groups: primitive reflexes present at birth but disappearing in the first few months of life; and, postural adjustment reactions which emerge later and remain present. Commentators on the relationship between early "reflex" responses and the voluntary control of action have adopted such strikingly different positions that it is difficult to believe they were observing the same species. The traditionalist view is epitomised in Wyke's (1975) statement that:

> until it has attained three months of age, a baby cannot be said to *learn* anything of neuromuscular behaviour—for one cannot learn to do anything with one's reflexes; on the contrary, one's reflexes do things to one. (p. 27).

In support of his position Wyke (1975) claims that the motor behavior of a normal infant differs little from that of an anencephalic infant until about 3 months.

This general perspective is now considered quite obsolete. The case against it is irrefutable. In order to illustrate just how much our view has changed, I will focus on two lines of attack which have particular significance for our understanding of abnormalities in motor development. The first concerns the nature of "reflex" movement. By comparing the motor behavior of the normal infant to that of an anencephalic it is implied that the behaviour is totally stimulus-driven and stereotyped in form. This is not so. An infant's response to an eliciting stimulus presented in an identical manner is not consistent from time to time. To a large extent the frequency and the intensity of the response are dependent on the infant's state. Andre-Thomas and Autgaerden (1966) noted for example that the newborn is capricious and does not always walk to order when he is put in the position which normally elicits the stepping reflex. A second and equally important observation is that the extent to which the pattern in "reflex" movement can be described as truly stereotyped is limited. Touwen (1978) found considerable variability in several of the "reflexes" he studied. During repeated attempts to elicit the palmar grasp reflex, the sequence of finger flexion varied in three out of five trials. Thus, Touwen suggests that it is misleading to think of these movement sequences as "reflexive" in the traditional sense. Preferring to call them "reactions," he describes them as "age-specific manifestations of an *active brain*," and emphasises the fact that this variation is what characterizes the motor activity of a normal healthy infant. An important corollary of this position is that obligatory stereotyped responses are one of the hallmarks of abnormality. Several authors have pointed to the fact that reflexes which reappear as a consequence of damage to the adult brain differ from those evident in infancy *because they are so stereotyped* (e.g., Prechtl, 1981). As we shall see below, the same appears to be the case in brain damaged children.

Our second point of departure from the traditional view of the relationship between reflexive and voluntary behavior concerns the sequential order in which they were believed to emerge. Essentially, the traditional position was that "reflexive" behaviors disappeared because their manifestation was inhibited by newly developed cortical structures which had previously been nonfunctional. It was only when these cortical structures had matured that voluntary control over movement could emerge. This view turns out to be simplistic. For example, we now know that there are more variants of the sequence of development than the simple one outlined above. One of the most comprehensive and detailed studies of these progressions was that of Touwen (1976) who documented the onset, the duration of elicitability, and the disappearance of a variety of early behaviors in a group of 50 normal infants between birth and the beginning of walking. Four groups of behaviors emerged: those which showed no substantial change from birth onwards and no differences among subjects; those which developed rapidly and showed only minimal variation among subjects; those which showed a protracted but distinct developmental course and substantial between subject variability; and, a fourth group which contained behaviors showing so many intra and inter individual differences that a definite developmental sequence could not be established. The fact that many of the behaviors occurring in the last group are currently included in tests designed to identify abnormal infants is cause for concern. If the picture is so variable for normal infants, what are we to make of the presence or absence of such behaviors in infants thought to be abnormal?

In the same study, Touwen (1976) also examined the relationships between the variables measured. Perhaps the most interesting findings to emerge were instances where relationships which might have been predicted were not found. For example, there was no relationship between the disappearance of the palmar grasp reflex and the onset of a more mature radial grasp. In fact, the two patterns co-exist for some time and the baby can switch from one type of grasp to the other. Hence, it can hardly be assumed that the neural mechanism subserving the former is simply transformed into the mechanism subserving the latter.

An alternative to the simple maturational model, which assumes little if any substantive relationship between reflexive and voluntary behavior is that reflexes do not disappear at all but maintain their identity as components of a hierarchically organized action system (Easton, 1972, 1979). Some support for this view comes from the work of Zelazo and his collaborators (Zelazo, 1976; Zelazo, Zelazo, & Kolb, 1972) who have shown that the walking "reflex" can be prolonged for a considerable length of time after it would normally disappear, and also that the "practice" the baby gets while performing these supported stepping movements accelerates the onset of voluntary walking. If there were no relationship between the reflexive and voluntary behaviors which bear so much resemblance to each other, it would be difficult to explain such an effect. However, as Zelazo, (1976) points out we are still left with the problem of explaining why these age-related behaviors disappear under normal circumstances.

Even stronger evidence against the view that reflexive behavior exists entirely separately from that which underpins voluntary control comes from work which shows that reflexive behavior is adaptable and can be brought under instrumental control. In one of the most rigorous demonstrations of the modifiability of reflexive behavior in newborns, Lipsitt and Kaye (1965) showed that babies could adapt their reflexive sucking to changes in nipple shape. Having demonstrated the utility of this approach, numerous other studies followed which yielded even more convincing evidence of the fact that the infant could bring his own "reflex" behavior under voluntary control. For example, Lipsitt (1971) showed that young infants will suck to produce movement in a mobile and Siqueland (1969) found that 1 month old babies will suck to control the presentation of colorful slides. Such signs of adaptability and self-control are the hallmarks of voluntary behavior.

As far as the reflexes are concerned, we now seem to have quite strong behavioral evidence for the notion that at least some of those present early in infancy constitute the building blocks of voluntary motor control. However, much remains to be learned. We still do not know why this particular set of behaviors are tied, albeit loosely, to specific eliciting stimuli, why many disappear under normal circumstances, or what exactly determines the way they are incorporated into voluntary action.

## Spontaneous Movements

The other class of behaviors which have recently been explored for their potential as the precursors of voluntary movement are "spontaneous" movements which contrast with reflex movements in that no eliciting stimuli are evident. Often called stereotypies, these include the kicking, waving, and banging movements which babies so frequently and exuberantly indulge in during the first year of life. In the past such movements were described as random (e.g., Peiper, 1963). Recently, however, Thelen and her colleagues (Thelen, 1979; Thelen, Bradshaw & Fisher, 1981) have demonstrated that they are, in fact, highly organized in their spatial and temporal characteristics and might also qualify as the fundamental structures underlying the organization of voluntary movement. These behaviors too, can be brought under instrumental control with no loss of consistency in the movements observed (Thelen & Fisher, 1983). Having considered two apparently distinct candidates for the fundamental structures underlying the coordination of voluntary action, it now seems possible that the two have something in common. Thelen and Fisher (1982) present an intriguing finding which brings together the two alternatives. Using both kinematic and electromyographic recordings of movements, Thelen and Fisher demonstrated that neonatal stepping and spontaneous kicking are identical movement patterns. The spatial and temporal organization is remarkably similar, and so too, is the pattern of electrical activity generating the movement. Thelen and Fisher suggest that the two patterns of movement are produced by the same neural generator. Why then does stepping disappear and spontaneous kicking continue? They propose that the answer lies in the differential effect of gravity on the muscles in the two postures. As the infant matures, the mass of the legs increases dramatically altering the dynamics of the moving limb—in the supine position the movements are aided by gravity, whereas in the upright position, gravity does not facilitate the necessary movements. Thus, instead of their naturally disappearing, it may be that biomechanical factors simply limit the expression of the movements in the upright position.

In sum, we now have a much expanded picture of the motor repertoire of the infant in the first few months of life. Our perspective on its significance has changed considerably but there are still enormous gaps in our understanding of what underlies the transition from the immature forms of movement to later voluntary control.

*Atypical Children*

When we turn to the study of atypical infants we find the focus has been mainly on the reflexive part of the repertoire. Studies of reflex responses in infants suspected of having suffered some perinatal insult have followed a similar pattern to those on normal infants. Much effort has been devoted to documenting the timetable of emergence and dissolution of various reflexes and comparing it to that observed in normal infants. Attempts have been made to identify which particular deviations from normality have most clinical significance. However, apart from one or two (e.g., the obligatory, asymmetric tonic neck reflex) there is still much debate about alternatives. Recall that under normal circumstances the evolution of infantile reflex behavior entails the dissolution of the primitive reflexes which are present at birth and disappear in the first 6 months or so; and, the emergence of postural adjustment reaction which then remain throughout life. Though there are differences among subgroups, generally speaking, abnormality can be described in terms of the form of the responses and their timetable. As far as the so-called primitive reflexes are concerned, these are more stereotyped in form and persist much longer than they normally would. Postural adjustment reactions are often late in developing and in some instances may never develop. Their form too, may vary, either being incomplete or exaggerated in comparison to normal.

The majority of studies on this topic focus on children known to have or suspected of having cerebral palsy. It is essential to include the phrase "suspected of," because it is not always possible to make a firm diagnosis in the first year of life. One of the most difficult problems pediatricians have to deal with is the interpretation of signs of abnormality of tone and reflex responses in the early stages. As noted above, reports of children who show many signs of abnormality in the first few months and are later normal are not uncommon. Relatively speaking, however, the number of transient cases is small.

Abnormalities in reflex responses is one of the cardinal signs of cerebral palsy and detailed clinical descriptions of the various deviations exist (e.g., Bobath, 1980; Capute, 1979; Paine, 1964). Cerebral-palsied children exhibit all of the deviations to a greater or lesser degree depending on the extent of the damage to the central nervous system. Their primitive reflexes are stereotyped in form and dissipate very late. Smith, Gossman, and Canan (1982) report the presence of several primitive reflexes in children up to 6 years old and clinical reports of even older children exist (e.g., Bobath, 1980). One of the most commonly reported signs is an obligatory asymmetric tonic neck reflex. Voluntary control of the upper limbs in children who are "dominated" by this reflex is often severely restricted. In fact, cerebral-palsied children are often described as being dominated by reflexes because they cannot voluntarily break out of the stereotyped patterns of movement which the reflexes impose on them. If one were to use Easton's (1972) terminology, it is almost as if the mechanism which permits the reflexes to be tuned to circumstances is missing.

Among the other groups of children who experience difficulty in gaining adequate motor competence, the intellectually retarded are in many respects similar to cerebral-palsied children. Cowie (1970) documents delayed dissolution of primitive reflexes among Down syndrome infants, and abnormalities of postural adjustment reactions have been noted by several authors. Among other intellectually retarded children the severity of the intellectual handicap seems to relate to the course of reflex development. In less severely retarded children the primitive responses are reported to be appropriate in expression and disappear normally, but the postural reflexes develop late (Molnar, 1978). Perhaps this is not surprising in that the probability of damage so diffuse as to embrace the motor component of the nervous system must increase with increased intellectual retardation. Among profoundly handicapped children it is often difficult to determine which is the major handicap. Tscherzer and Tscharnuter (1982), however, do consider that the condition of the primitive reflexes is a good way to differentiate between a child who will be mentally retarded and one who will suffer cerebral palsy.

When it comes to the detection of milder forms of abnormality, however, the picture is a much cloudier one. Some clinicians believe that standard neurological examinations which are heavily weighted with tests of reflexes are not suitable for the identification of more subtle problems of development; others take the view that the measures we use are simply too crude (e.g., Capute, Palmer, Shapiro, Wachtel, Ross, & Accardo, 1984). As far as those of us intested in motor problems are concerned, the best approach might be to combine the two viewpoints. On the one hand, more sensitive measures of reflex responses are bound to tell us more of their variation and of the limits they place on the emergence of voluntary action. On the other hand, it would be foolish to ignore the move towards exploring what capabilities the child does have to exert control over his environment. The child who uses his ability to smile, sustain eye contact, and vocalize may be the one who can be effective at minimizing the impacts of other problems he might have. To complete the picture, it is important to emphasize that not all children who have problems in motor development exhibit signs of abnormality of the neuromotor system early on. The development of the blind child is quite normal in this regard. So too is that of children who later develop progressive disorders such as childhood Parkinsonism or muscular dystrophy.

As well as being able to identify the existence of damage to the neuromotor system reliably, it is also important to attempt to predict the severity of impairment in later life. After the question "will he be mentally normal?" that most frequently asked by parents is—"will he walk?" In order to consider this issue we will focus on two prospective studies, one on mainly cerebral palsied children, the other on mentally retarded children. In 1975, Bleck reported a study of 73 cerebral palsied children who were not walking when first examined and could be followed up until they were 5 years old. On first examination, the children were tested on seven reflexes. The abnormal reflexes present were summed, a total score of zero was designated as predicting good prognosis, a one point score uncertain, and two or more poor prognosis. The prognosis was accurate in 94.5% of cases. Forty-nine children had zero scores and 46 became ambulatory. Of the 17 who were not walking at the end of the study, 16 had scores of 2 or more. Of the seven children receiving a score of 1 all were walking, but five used crutches. Bleck (1975) is careful to point out, however, that the *way* the children walked was different from normal and that some showed definite problems of maintaining balance.

Molnar and Gordon (1976) have also discussed the prognostic significance of clinical signs in cerebral palsy but in the interest of variety I shall describe instead, Molnar's (1978) study of 53 mentally retarded children who were followed up for an average of 2 years. During the course of the study four primitive reflexes and ten postural adjustment reactions were examined. These responses were then considered in relation to the acquisition of five basic skills—rolling over, sitting, creeping, standing, and walking. Little could be said about the primitive reflexes because most had disappeared when the study was begun. There was a very definite temporal relationship, however, between the emergence of the postural adjustment reactions and the acquisition of each functional skill. Though the appearance of the automatic reactions was considerably delayed in these children, whenever they did emerge they were soon followed by the same functional attainment as would be acquired by a normal child. Interestingly, the time lag between the postural adjustment reaction and the following functional skill was the same as it is in normal children. In demonstrating specific relationships between particular reflex responses and particular functional attainments, this study represents a considerable advance on the more global studies characteristics of earlier attempts at prognosis.

*Postural tonus.* Though it does not fit very comfortably into this section, there is one other aspect of the neuromuscular system which must at least be described as its impairment is a frequent concomitant of many forms of atypical motor development, that is postural tonus. Normal postural tonus is required to enable weight bearing and support against gravity, yet at the same time it must not be too great as to interfere with rapid change in voluntary movement. Virtually all aspects of motor behavior are influenced by the state of tone in the body, even the amount of movement we make. Paucity of movement is a characteristic of many infants who are either too floppy or too stiff. The expression of reflex responses is greatly influenced by abnormal tonus. Tonus is always examined alongside reflex testing. The mechanisms which control the maintenance of tone in infants are not well understood and "normal" tone is difficult to specify, but abnormality of tone in a baby is often the precipitating cause of concern. A sense of abnormality is frequently conveyed intuitively to the caretakers when the child is difficult to handle or does not seem to respond "naturally" in the positions one tends to hold a baby.

Dubowitz (1980) notes that the rag doll mimics most of the clinical features evident in hypotonic infants. These features are: increase in the range of movement of the joints, diminished resistance of the joints to passive movements, and unusual postures such as the frog-like position of the legs adopted in the supine position. To the caretaker, these abnormalities reveal themselves in nearly all interactions with the infant. For example, head and neck control is often poor, so finding a comfortable position for feeding may be difficult; dressing, bathing, and carrying all require that the child be handled differently; and, perhaps most importantly, the child does not seem to convey the same affective signals as the normal child. Normal babies seem to "cuddle into" comfortable positions, and "take part" in bathing and dressing. However, hypotonic children are usually perceived as "good" babies, they move little and seem contented. Excess tonus (hypertonicity) creates handling problems of a very different kind for caretakers. The child is difficult to dress because he does not bend in the right places at the right time and the excessive stiffness may at first be interpreted as obstinacy. The child appears to resist attempts to cuddle or calm him and feeding is often a time of considerable trauma rather than enjoyment.

Abnormality of postural tonus is not a sign which can be easily interpreted by itself. Hypotonia, for example, may or may not be associated with lack of strength, it may or may not be accompanied by abnormal reflexes, it may be accompanied by other physical defects (it is a very common feature of Down syndrome for instance), and it may exist alone (for a review of the medical background see Dubowitz, 1980). Postural tone may change as the infant develops. In cerebral palsy, for example, it is quite common for a hypotonic infant to become spastic and for initial hypertonicity to appear ultimately as athetosis (e.g., Bobath, 1981). It is often the case, too, that abnormality of tone is not evenly distributed in the body. A hypotonic trunk may be associated with stiff upper extremities. Moreover, tone varies considerably with the "state" of the child and unfortunately increased voluntary effort may have an adverse effect, particularly on hypertonicity.

It is unfortunate that our knowledge of the mechanisms governing the maintenance of postural tonus in normal individuals is so limited, as our comprehension of abnormal tone is greatly hampered by it. Lack of understanding of all the variants of abnormality of tone in cerebral palsy, for example, is a major obstacle at all levels. It makes early classification of cases very difficult, limits prediction to probabalistic terms, and most important, means our attempts to treat abnormality of tone remain at an intuitive level.

## ACQUIRING MOTOR COMPETENCE—THE BROADER CONTEXT

Throughout the previous section we moved between theoretical questions concerning the mechanisms which determine the development of voluntary motor control and practical questions relating to the extent to which clinicians can rely on behavioral observations as indices of damage to the nervous system in infancy. There is no doubt that the two are related but it is possible to some extent for the one to advance without the other. For example, though we do not fully understand the significance of the "primitive reflexes," we do know that their long persistance in stereotyped form is a reliable index of abnormality and greatly impedes the progress of children with conditions like cerebral palsy. However, the clinicians job is not just to identify abnormality, it is also to do something about it. Though understanding of deviant development does not automatically ensure successful therapy a sounder conceptual framework might direct our efforts more specifically. A better knowledge of the mechanisms which determine the acquisition of voluntary control of movement would improve our understanding of motor problems in children.

When considering the question of what makes a child competent or incompetent in the motor domain we must look beyond the bounds of the neuromotor system and how it is organised. The crucial question is: How far should we go in our search? Clearly questions relating to the child's ability to see or make perceptual judgements are important but what of other nonmotor factors which contribute to overall success or failure? For example, physical qualities such as healthiness or attractiveness or social qualities such as outgoingness have an affect on how a child is responded to by his peers and adults; this may in turn have an affect on the opportunities afforded to him to acquire motor competence. The overprotected motorically handicapped child is a familiar phenomenon.

To a certain extent, the answer to the question of how far we must look beyond the intactness of the neuromotor machinery depends on the interests of the investigator. A sensible distinction can be drawn between questions of a more theoretical nature and those of more practical import. For the theoretician, the problem is one of understanding exactly what underlies particular deviations from normal and what such information can tell us about normal motor development. For the clinician the same problem must be put in a broader context. Ultimately what is of concern is how well the child is functioning in the environment in which he lives. In practical terms, this means that two related areas of enquiry must be considered together: the analysis of the factors specifically concerned with the acquisition of *motor* skills and the analysis of the child's strategies for dealing with the demands of living in general. Though there are obviously times when it is useful to keep the motor and nonmotor aspects of competence conceptually separate, in the practical setting neither aspect is more important than the other for they are in a mutually interactive relationship.

*Analysing Action*

While the focus of this Section must be on the more limited construct of motor competence, in the ensuing pages we will devote some attention to the broader context. In order to impose some structure on the discussion of what factors might affect motor competence, we will begin with an analysis of a paradigmatic motor act. If we envisage an action as being comprised of a series of events directed at achieving a specified goal, then a basic question concerns the component processes involved in achieving that goal. When a child fails to achieve success we can then adopt a strategy of searching for the specific point (or points) in the chain of events where problems might have arisen. Added to this must then come the questions of a more general nature which might inform us about the child's overall competence.

Consider a task like picking up a cup and drinking from it. What are the specific task demands? Before any plan of action can be formulated for achieving this goal precise information of a perceptual and cognitive nature is essential. For example, the child must be able to establish the location of the cup, estimate its size, its shape, its weight, how much liquid it contains, and so on. As far as his own body is concerned, the child must "know" where his body parts are in relation to the object and to each other. Conceptually, the child must know that a cup is for drinking from, that liquid has certain difficult properties, and that handles are for grasping.

Failure to get even this far in planning the action may result from a number of quite distinct deficits. First, the sensory systems involved may be defective. This could mean that either the receptors located in the muscles, joints, skin, eyes, and ears malfunction or that messages received from the receptors are not efficiently transmitted to the brain. Second, the sensory systems may be intact but the strategies adopted for extracting the available information may be inadequate. This might mean, for example, that although the child "sees" perfectly well, the way he scans a scene still leads to inaccurate perceptual analysis. A third possibility is that failure results from deficits residing squarely in the knowledge domain. The child may not hold the cup upright because he does not understand the properties of liquid. At the most abstract level, the child's inability to plan an appropriate solution to a particular task may result from a failure to accumulate knowledge which permits him to "know" whether the task is within his sphere of competence.

To continue with our analysis of the task demands, we must now turn to the translation of the requisite perceptual and cognitive information into a plan of action. What must be done? The arm must reach forward a specific amount with the hand taking the correct shape for lifting the object as it proceeds. The hand must then grasp the cup with sufficient tension to lift it without spilling the contents. The cup must then be transported to the mouth at the correct orientation, must be tipped to an appropriate angle, and the swallowing action initiated. Even at this simplified level, the complexity of this task must be obvious.

Failure to execute this sequence of movements successfully can also result from a number of distinct problems. Obviously the deficit may lie in the neuromotor system itself (much of this chapter has been devoted to discussing this aspect of motor problems). However accurate the child's judgements, the "machinery" he has available to him to perform the movements may be so defective that the plan of action cannot be executed. Not all children who have problems of motor development have obviously deficient "machinery." An alternative locus for the deficit may be in the mechanism which translates the perceptual input into motor commands. Put another way, the problem might be that the child's spatial representation of the world is not very precisely "mapped on" to the motor system. Consequently, though precise movements are physically possible, there is no means whereby they can be planned.

There are other questions we might ask about what is required to be able to lift a cup to the mouth and drink from it. However, what we have considered so far should be sufficient to illustrate how this kind of approach enables us to form specific hypotheses about particular deficits in the chain of events leading to performance of an action, and their possible consequences. It is also important to note that although a deficiency at any one point may result in failure to achieve the final goal, identification of that deficiency does not allow us to *assume* that a child will fail overall. Compensatory mechanisms can be powerful and deserve careful consideration in the practical setting.

## Compensatory Mechanisms

The ability to compensate for an impairment is something which compels us to move between the narrowly defined sphere of motor competence and the more braodly defined sphere of overall competence. Within the motor domain, we find children with amazing facility to compensate for specific defects. Some blind children do become skilled at using nonvisual sources of information to manipulate objects and get around the world. Children with involuntary movements which are difficult to control find ways of fixing their limbs in such a way that voluntary action is made easier. Others with grossly deformed limbs may nevertheless be able to use unorthodox means of achieving an end state.

Thus far, we have only mentioned compensatory mechanisms which permit the child to remain an active participant in his own existence. There are other ways of compensating for a deficiency which are more difficult to evaluate. For example, one could identify a state of learned helplessness as a compensatory mechanism which meets with success. The child who allows most things to be done for him is free to do other things. One might view positively the obviously bright child who manipulates the world around him in such a way that the effort required to develop his own motor competence is unnecessary. It is fashionable at present to cite instances of adequate cognitive and social competence in the absence of motor competence. This is an understandable consequence of the overemphasis on the role of ''activity'' in development in general. However, there is ample evidence of the costs attached to being totally dependent on someone else for one's every need. In analyzing what we mean by the ability to compensate, therefore, we must be careful to specify what is being compensated for.

## Analysing Atypical Performance

In order to demonstrate the value of this approach as a means of studying atypical development I will now consider a few concrete examples. With regard to the potential effects of sensory defects on the development of motor control, it is clear that the absence of vision has profound consequences. The points at which many blind children come to a temporary halt in their development can be linked to the times when normal children achieve skills which involve vision. For example, although the blind child has the capacity to do so he does not bring his hands together in midline and indulge in the playful finger games that the normal child does. As Fraiberg (1977) puts it, during this activity the normal infant appears to be both the performer and spectator, observing his own prowess. For the blind child this learning experience is not possible. As the world beyond his reach must initially be a near void, it is perhaps not surprising that loss of contact with an object does not lead to normal searching and reaching out in the blind child. The process of forming a schema of the world beyond their own body space is long and laborious for blind infants and one which some never satisfactorily achieve. When loss of vision is incomplete or when other visual defects are present the effect on motor development is much less clear. For example, squints are common in cerebral palsied children but have not been studied with respect to their effect on motor competence.

The other sense which plays an important role in the control of movement is kinaesthesis or proprioception. In comparison to vision, proprioception is a difficult sense to characterise. Whereas visual information is gathered through one set of sensory receptors, proprioceptive information is gathered through a number of quite different receptors located in the muscles, tendons, joints, and the vestibular system. Because it is so multidimensional no unitary measure is possible and existing measures of the component parts (e.g., Laszlo & Bairstow, 1985) are not suitable for very young children. The lack of data on proprioceptive deficits and their consequences in preschool children is unfortunate because it has resulted in an enormous gap between theory and practice. There are a few reports of tactile loss and poor proprioceptive activity in older cerebral palsied children (e.g., Jones, 1976; Laszlo & Bairstow, 1985) but data on other groups are lacking. Yet, in clinical settings assumptions are commonly made about deficiencies in these receptors. Therapists and teachers frequently make observations about a child's dislike of being rotated (vestibular impairment?), inability to differentiate textures (tactile impairment?), or apparent lack of awareness of the location of his own body parts and the relationships between them (kinaesthetic impairment?). Though these observations may be accurate, what is usually lacking is any attempt to systematically separate a purely sensory deficit from a perceptual one, a point we now turn to.

The possibility that critical differences reside not in sensory discrimination but in the activity directed towards the extraction of sensory information from the world, has received a great deal of attention. As far as questions relating to motor competence are concerned, one particularly interesting line of enquiry involves the study of how information gathered by the hand and the eye are integrated (see Pick & Pick, 1981 for review). Throughout the literature on atypical children there are numerous suggestions of particular problems with the analysis of information from nonvisual channels. Brain damaged children in general (e.g., Birch, 1964) cerebral palsied children (e.g., Abercrombie, 1964) mentally retarded children of mixed aetiology (Davidson, Pine, Wiles, & Appelle, 1980) and Down syndrome children (Lewis & Bryant, 1982; O'Connor & Hermelin, 1961) have all been described as having problems of this type. What usually happens in these experiments is that the child is presented with an object or shape which he must feel (without vision) and then is asked to match it to a visual standard or select it from a set of visually presented alternatives. Unfortunately, there are problems of design and interpretation in many of these experiments which make it difficult to draw inferences about movement. One problem is that most studies do not clearly describe what information is available to the subject. Tactile information may or may not supplement proprioception; manipulation of the shape may be active or passive; visual stimuli are usually presented statically whereas haptic information is derived dynamically. At first sight, the last may seem to present no problem as this is how such information is obtained in the real world. Yet, haptic perception may require conceptual processes in a way that vision does not. This raises questions about the strategies the child brings to bear on the task of feeling the object. Davidson, Pine, Wiles, and Appelle (1980) have shown quite clearly that accuracy on shape matching tasks was related to the way the shape was handled. Examination of the literature on haptic perception reveals that different investigators used different techniques. In sum, though a number of studies are available, the meaning of the outcome may not be as simple as some have suggested.

So far we have dealt with the occurrence of deficits which may result in reduced or inaccurate information on which to base a plan of action. When we turn to the question of how accurately movements are executed with respect to a predefined goal, we find there is a dearth of studies on atypical children in the preschool age range. Three are relevant in the present discussion. Cunningham (1970) documented a step-wise progression in the motor development of preschool Down syndrome children. In order to provide an explanation of one of these pauses in development, Cunningham also undertook a more detailed study of the visually directed reaching. When compared with a nonhandicapped control group, the Down syndrome infants not only showed marked deviations in the accuracy of their reaching behavior but also significantly fewer adjustments or corrections. Cunningham suggests it may take longer for the neuromotor system of the Down syndrome child to become visually calibrated than in normal children, a proposal which is consistent with the interpretation of the delays in postural control noted earlier. Another demonstration of the problems that Down syndrome children seem to have in accurately planning their movements comes from the work of Hogg and Moss (1983) who showed that they were much slower at performing a peg insertion task than normal children. A third study involved a group of children described as suffering slight neurological disturbances (Forssrtöm & Von Hofsten, 1982). The focus of interest was the accuracy of the reaching movements towards moving objects. The results indicated that the relative lengths of the approach paths was greater for children in the clinical group than for the controls. The neurologically impaired children were also less able than the controls to improve the efficiency of their reaches, but interestingly, were able to take their lack of proficiency into account by aiming further ahead of the moving target than the controls. Thus, we have an important demonstration of a compensatory mechanism acting to minimise a basic perceptuomotor inefficiency.

Unfortunately, there are few studies of compensatory mechanisms of children with motor impairments, yet powerful clinical examples of children who overcome their difficulties in interesting ways are common. One of my own students recently performed an experiment which highlighted the extent to which children differ in their ability to deal with an impairment in motor functioning (Kilburn, 1981). The study was one of haptic perception in cerebral palsied children. In addition to the obvious measures of recognition accuracy three other measures were taken: an independent observer rated how systematic the child's exploration of the shape was; an assessment was made of how well the hands functioned (e.g., tasks included turning a door handle, moving the fingers independently); and intelligence was measured. The differences among subjects were extensive. There were children who had good control of their hand movements but were totally unsystematic (unintelligent) in their exploration of the shapes and consequently poor at recognizing them. What was the problem? Were they receiving inadequate sensory input or had early motor problems resulted in a dissociation between the agility of the hand and the efficiency of its usage? Conversely, there were children who could do little on the hand function test but found ways of making the most unbiddable limbs seek out and extract the crucial information about the shapes. They could be seen dwelling on corners and "contemplating" the orientation of straight edges. There were also children who had already decided that they were no good at such tasks and showed little motivation. Variations in intelligence did not account for the differences nor did variations in age or degree of mobility.

This experiment presents interesting problems for the theoretician but more importantly it reminds us as practitioners about the importance of seeing each child as an individual. The assessment of cognitive competence is taken for granted but the analysis of social competence is also important. There is no doubt that a child's social "persona" influences his opportunity to achieve adequate motor competence. Some motorically handicapped children are bright, outgoing, interactive, eager companions to adults or peers. Others are withdrawn, timid and isolated. They are neither fun to play with nor fun to teach. It is at our cost that we consider only the perceptuo-motor components of the disability and ignore the broader perspective.

# REFERENCES

Abercrombie, M. J. L. (1964). Perceptual and visuomotor disorders in cerebral palsy. *Clinics in Developmental Medicine, No. 11.* London: S.I.M.P. with Heinemann.

Anderson, E. M., & Spain, B. (1977). *The child with spina bifida.* London: Methuen.

Andre-Thomas, C., & Autgaerden, S. (1966). Locomotion from pre- to post-natal life. *Clinics in Developmental Medicine, No. 24.* London: S.I.M.P. with Heinemann.

Aptekar, R., Ford, F., & Bleck, E. E. (1976). Light patterns as a means of assessing and recording gait II: results in children with cerebral palsy. *Developmental Medicine and Child Neurology, 18,* 37–40.

Bernstein, N. (1967). *The co-ordination and regulation of movements.* New York: Pergamon.

Birch, H. G. (1964). *Brain damage in children, biological and social aspects.* Baltimore: Williams and Wilkins.

Bleck, E. E. (1975). Locomotor prognosis in cerebral palsy. *Developmental Medicine and Child Neurology, 17,* 18–25.

Bobath, K. (1980). A neurophysiological basis for the treatment of cerebral palsy. *Clinics in Developmental Medicine, No. 75.* London: S.I.M.P. with Heinemann; Philadelphia: Lippincott.

Bruner, J. S. (1970). The growth and structure of skill. In K. Connolly (Ed.), *Mechanisms of motor skill development.* New York: Academic Press.

Brunt, D., & Broadhead, G. D. (1982). Motor proficiency traits of deaf children. *Research Quarterly for Exercise Science and Sport, 53,* 236–238.

Burnett, C. N., & Johnson, E. W. (1971). Development of gait in childhood. *Developmental Medicine and Child Neurology, 13,* 196–206.

Butterworth, G. (1983). Structure of the mind in human infancy. In L. P. Lipsitt & C. K. Rovee-Collier (Eds.), *Advances in Infancy Research, Vol. 2.* Borwood: Albex Publishing Co.

Butterworth, G., & Cicchetti, D. (1978). Visual calibration of posture in normal and motor retarded Down's syndrome infants. *Perception, 7,* 513–525.

Capute, A. J. (1979). Identifying cerebral palsy in infancy through study of primitive reflex profiles. *Paediatric Annals, 8,* 589–595.

Capute, A. J., Palmer, F. B., Shapiro, B. K., Wachtel, R. C., Ross, A., & Accardo, P. J. (1984). Primitive reflex profile: A quantitation of primitive reflexes in infancy. *Developmental Medicine and Child Neurology, 26,* 375–383.

Carr, J. (1970). Mental and motor development in young mongol children. *Journal of Mental Deficiency Research, 14,* 205–220.

Carr, J. (1975). Young children with Down's syndrome. *IRMMH Monograph 4,* London: Butterworth.

Clarke, A. D. B., & Clarke, A. M. (1983). Constancy and change in the growth of human characteristics. Jack Tizard Memorial Lecture, Association for Child Psychology and Psychiatry. London. An adapted version was printed in *Journal of Child Psychology and Psychiatry, 25,* 191–210.

Connolly, K. J. (1981). Maturation and ontogeny of motor skills. In K. J. Connolly & H. F. R. Prechtl (Eds.), *Maturation and development: Biological and psychological perspectives. Clinics in developmental medicine, No. 77-78.* London: S.I.M.P. with Heinemann; Philadelphia: Lippincott.

Connolly, K. J., & Prechtl, H. F. R. (Eds.). (1981). *Maturation and development: Biological and psychological perspectives. Clinics in developmental medicine, No. 77/78.* London: S.I.M.P. with Heinemann; Philadelphia: Lippincott.

Cowie, V. A. (1970). *A study of the early development of mongols,* Oxford: Pergamon Press.

Cunningham, C.C. (1979). *Aspects of early development in Down's syndrome infants.* Unpublished doctoral thesis, University of Manchester, England.

Cunningham, C. C., & Mittler, P. J. (1981). Maturation, development and mental handicap. In K. J. Connolly & H. F. R. Prechtl (Eds.), *Maturation and development: Biological and psychological perspectives. Clinics in developmental medicine, No. 77/78.* London: S.I.M.P. with Heinemann; Philadelphia: Lippincott.

Davidson, P. W., Pine, R., Wiles, M. K., & Appelle, S.(1980). Haptic visual shape matching by mentally retarded children: Exploratory activity and complexity effects. *American Journal of Mental Deficiency, 84,* 526–533.

Decarie, T. G. (1969). A study of the mental and emotional development of the thalidomide child. In B. M. Foss (Ed.), *Determinants of infant behaviour* (Vol. 4), London: Methuen and Co.

Drillien, C. M. (1972). Abnormal neurologic signs in the first year of life in low birthweight infants: Possible prognostic significance. *Developmental Medicine and Child Neurology, 14,* 575–584.

Donoghue, E. C., Kirman, B. H., Bullmore, G. H. L., Laban, D., & Abbas, K. A. (1970). Some factors affecting age of walking in a mentally retarded population. *Developmental Medicine and Child Neurology, 12,* 781–792.

Dubowitz, V. (1980). The floppy infant, 2nd edition. *Clinics in Developmental Medicine, No. 76.* London: S.I.M.P. with Heinemann; Philadelphia: Lippincott.

Easton, T. A.(1972). On the normal use of reflexes. *American Scientist, 60,* 591–599.

Easton, T. A. (1978). Co-ordinative structures—the basis for a motor program. In D. M. Landers & R. W. Christina (Eds.), *Psychology of motor behaviour and sport,* Champaign, IL: Human Kinetic Publishers.

Elliott, J. M., & Connolly, K. J. (1984). A classification of manipulative hand movements. *Developmental Medicine and Child Neurology, 26,* 283–296.

Ellison, P., Browning, C., & Trostmiller, T. (1982). Evaluation of neurologic status in infancy: Physical therapist versus paediatric neurologist. *Journal of California Perinatal Association, 2,* 63–66.

Fiorentino, M. R. (1973). *Reflex testing methods for evaluating C.N.S. development* (2nd edition). Springfield, IL: C. C. Thomas.

Forsstrom, A., & Von Hofsten, C. (1982). Visually directed reaching of children with motor impairments. *Developmental Medicine and Child Neurology, 24,* 653–661.

Forssberg, H., & Wallbert, H. (1980). *Infant locomotion: A preliminary movement and electromyographic study.* In K. Berg & B. Erikson (Eds.) *Children and Exercise Vol. IX.* Baltimore: University Park Press.

Fraiberg, S. (1977). *Insights from the blind.* New York: Basic Books.

Freedman, D. (1965). An ethological approach to the general study of human behaviour. In S. G. Vandenberg (Ed.), *Methods and goals in human behaviour genetics.* New York: Academic Press.

Gallahue, D. L. (1982). *Understanding motor development in children.* New York: Wiley.

Gaussen, T. (1984). Developmental milestones or conceptual millstones? Some practical and theoretical limitations in infant assessment procedures. *Child: Care, Health and Development, 10,* 99–115.

Gesell, A., & Armatruda, C. S. (1941). *Developmental diagnosis.* New York: Harper.

Gesell, A., & Armatruda, C. S. (1947). *Developmental diagnosis* (2nd edition). New York: Harper.

Goldman, P. S., & Lewis, M. E. (1978). Developmental biology in brain damage and experience. In C. W. Cotman (Ed.), *Neuronal plasticity.* New York: Raven Press.

Greene, P. H. (1972). Problems of organisation of motor systems. In R. Rosen & F. Snell (Eds.), *Progress in theoretical biology* (Vol. 2). New York: Academic Press.

Grillner, S. (1975). Locomotion in vertebrates. Central mechanisms and reflex interaction. *Physiological Review, 55,* 247–304.

Gurfinkel, V. S., Kots, Ya. M., Pal'Tsev, Yc. I., Fcl'dman, A. G. (1971). The compensation of respiratory disturbances of the organisation of the interarticular interaction. In I. M. Gel'fand,

V. S. Gurfinkel, S. V. Fomin, & M. L. Tsetun (Eds.), *Models of the structural-functional organisation of certain biological systems*. Cambridge: MIT Press.

Hagberg, B., & Lundberg, A. (1969). Dissociated motor development simulating cerebral palsy. *Neuropadiatric, 1,* 187.

Haidvogl, M. (1979). Dissociation of maturation: A distinct syndrome of delayed motor development. *Developmental Medicine and Child Neurology, 21,* 52–57.

Halverson, H. M. (1931). An experimental study of prehension in infants by means of cinema records. *Genetic Psychology Monographs, 10,* 107–286.

Hindley, C. B. (1968). Growing up in five countries: A comparison of data in wearing, elimination training, age of walking and IQ in relation to social class from European longitudinal studies. *Developmental Medicine and Child Neurology, 10,* 715–742.

Hogg, J., & Moss, S. C. (1983). Prehensible development in Down's syndrome and non-handicapped pre-school children. *British Journal of Developmental Psychology, 1,* 189–204.

Holt, K. S. (1966). Some facts and fallacies about neuromuscular function in cerebral palsy as revealed by electromyography. *Developmental Medicine and Child Neurology, 8,* 255–268.

Illingworth, R. S. (1968). Delayed motor development. *Paediatric Clinics of North America, 15,* 569–580.

Jones, B. (1976). The perception of passive joint-movements by cerebral palsied children. *Developmental Medicine and Child Neurology, 18,* 25–30.

Kalverboer, A. F., & Hopkins, B. (1983). Motor behaviour. *Journal of Child Psychology and Psychiatry, 24,* 61–63.

Kelso, J. A. S. (1982). *Human motor behaviour: An introduction.* Hillsdale, NJ: Elrbaum.

Keogh, J., & Sugden, D. (1985). *Movement skill development.* New York: Macmillan Publishing Company.

Kilburn, T. (1984). *An analysis of factors involved in cerebral palsied spastic children's stereognostic functioning.* Unpublished Masters Report, University of London Institute of Education.

Kopp, C. B., & Shaperman, J. (1973). Cognitive development in the absence of object manipulation during infancy. *Developmental Psychology, 9,* 430.

Kugler, P. N., Kelso, J. A. S., & Turvey, M. T. (1982). On the control and co-ordination of naturally developing systems. In J. A. S. Kelso & J. E. Clarke (Eds.), *The development of movement control and co-ordination.* New York: Wiley.

Laszlo, J. I., & Bairstow, P. J. (1985). *Perceptual motor behaviour. developmental assessment and therapy.* Eastbourne: Holt Saunders.

Lee, D. N., & Aronson, E. (1974). Visual proprioceptive control of standing in human infants. *Perception and Psychophysics, 15,* 529–532.

Lewis, V. A., & Bryant, P. E. (1982). Touch and vision in normal and Down's syndrome babies. *Perception, 11,* 691–701.

Lipsitt, L. P. (1971). Infant learning the blooming buzzing confusion. In M. E. Meyer (Ed.), *Second western symposium on learning: Early learning.* Bellingham: Western Washington State College.

Lipsitt, L. P., & Kaye, H. (1965). Changes in neonatal response to optimising and non-optimising sucking stimulation. *Psychonomic Science, 2,* 221–222.

Lydic, J. S., & Steele, C. (1979). Assessment of the quality of sitting and gait problems in children with Down's syndrome. *Physical Therapy, 59,* 1489–1494.

Meltzoff, A. N., & Moore, M. K. (1983). The origins of imitation in infancy: Paradigm, phenomena and theories. In L. P. Lipsitt & C. K. Rovee-Collier (Eds.), *Advances in infancy research* (Vol. 2). Norwood: Ablex Publishing Company.

McClenaghan, B. A., & Gallahue, D. L. (1978). *Fundamental movement: A developmental and remedial approach.* Philadelphia: W. B. Saunders.

McGraw, M. B. (1945). *The neuromuscular maturation of the human infant.* New York: Hafner.

Last printed 1934, then in 1945. Reprinted 1963 with a new introduction. 1945 edition is most frequently quoted.

Molnar, G. E. (1978). Analysis of motor disorder in retarded infants and young children. *American Journal of Mental Deficiency, 83*, 213–222.

Molnar, G. E., & Gordon, S. V. (1976). Cerebral Palsy: Predictive value of selected clinical signs for early prognostication of motor function. *Archives of Physical Medicine and Rehabilitation, 57*, 153–158.

Nashner, L. M. (1977). Fixed patterns of rapid postural responses among leg muscles during stance. *Experimental Brain Research, 30*, 13–24.

Nashner, L. M., Shumway-Cook, A., & Marin, O. (1983). Stance posture control in select groups of children with cerebral palsy: Deficits in sensory organisation and muscular co-ordination. *Experimental Brain Research, 49*, 393–409.

Nashner, L. M., & Woollacott, M. (1979). The organisation of rapid postural adjustments of standing humans: An experimental–conceptual model. In R. E. Talbot & D. R. Humphreys (Eds.), *Posture and movement*. New York: Raven Press.

Neligan, G., & Prudham, D. (1969). Norms for four standard developmental milestones by sex, social class and place in the family. *Developmental Medicine and Child Neurology, 11*, 413–442.

Neligan, G. E., & Prudham, D. (1969). Potential value for four early developmental milestones in screening children for increased risk for later retardation. *Developmental Medicine and Child Neurology, 11*, 423–431.

Nelson, K. B., & Ellenberg, J. H. (1978). Epidemiology in cerebral palsy. *Advances in Neurology, 19*, 421–435.

Nelson, K. B., & Ellenberg, J. H. (1982). Children who 'outgrew' Cerebral Palsy. *Pediatrics, 69*, 529–536.

O'Connor, N., & Hermelin, B. (1961). Visual and stereognostic recognition in normal children and mongol and non-mongol imbeciles. *Journal of Mental Deficiency Research, 5*, 63–66.

Paine, R. S. (1964). The evolution of infantile postural reflexes in the presence of chronic brain syndromes. *Developmental Medicine and Child Neurology, 6*, 345–361.

Parmalee, A., Fiske, C., & Wright, R. (1959). The development of ten children with blindness as a result of retrolental fibroplasia. *A. M. A. Journal of Diseases of Children, 98*, 198–220.

Peiper, A. (1963). *Cerebral function in infancy and childhood*. New York: Consultants Bureau.

Peters, M. (1984). Handwriting in left-handers. In D. H. Stott, F. A. Moyes, & S. E. Henderson (Eds.), *Diagnosis and remediation of handwriting*. Guelph: Brook Educational.

Prechtl, H. F. R. (1981). The study of neural development as a perspective of clinical problems. In K. J. Connolly & H. F. R. Prechtl (Eds.), *Maturation and development: Biological and psychological perspectives. Clinics in developmental medicine, No. 77/78*. London: S.I.M.P. with Heinemann; Philadelphia: Lippincott.

Rheingold, H. L. (1983). The social and socialising infant. In L. P. Lipsitt & C. K. Rovee-Collier (Eds.), *Advances in infancy research* (Vol. 2). Norwood: Ablex Publishing Company.

Roberton, M. A. (1977). Stability of stage categorisations across trials: Implications for the "stage theory" of overarm throw improvement. *Journal of Human Movement Studies, 3*, 49–59.

Roberton, M. A. (1982). Describing stages within and across motor tasks. In J. A. S. Kelso & J. E. Clarke (Eds.), *The development of movement control and co-ordination*. New York: Wiley.

Robson, P. (1970). Shuffling, hitching, scooting or sliding: Some observations in 30 otherwise normal children. *Developmental Medicine and Child Neurology, 12*, 608–617.

Robson, P., & McKeith, R. C. (1971). Shufflers with spastic diplegic cerebral palsy: A confusing clinical picture. *Developmental Medicine and Child Neurology, 13*, 651–659.

Sameroff, A. J., & Chandler, M. J. (1975). Reproductive risk and the continuum of caretaking casualty. In F. D. Horowitz, S. Hetherington, Scarr-Salapater & G. Siegel (Eds.), *Review of child development research*, (Vol. 4). Chicago: University of Chicago Press.

Scherzer, A. L., & Tscharnuter, I. (1982). *Early diagnosis and therapy in cerebral palsy: A primer on infant developmental problems.* New York: Dekker.

Seefeldt, J. D., & Haubenstricker, J. (1982). Patterns, phases or stages: An analytical model for the study of developmental movement. In J. A. S. Kelso & J. E. Clark (Eds.), *The development of movement control and co-ordination.* New York: Wiley.

Shik, M. L., & Orlovski, G. N. (1965). Co-ordination of the limbs during the running of the dog. *Biophysics, 10,* 1148–1159.

Shirley, M. M. (1931). The first two years: A study of twenty-five babies. *Vol. 1 Postural and Locomotor Development.* Minneapolis: University of Minnesota Press.

Shumway-Cook, A., & Woollacott, M. H. (1985). *The growth of stability: Postural control from a developmental perspective. Journal of Motor Behavior, 17,* 131–147.

Shumway-Cook, A., & Woollacott, M. H. (in press-b). *Dynamics of postural control in the child with Down's syndrome.*

Siqueland, E. R. (1969). *The development of instrumental exploratory behaviour during the first year of human life.* Paper presented at the meeting of the Society for Research in Child Development, Santa Monica, California.

Smith, S. L., Gossman, M. R., & Canan, B. C. (1982). Selected primitive reflexes in children with cerebral palsy. Consistency of response. *Physical Therapy, 62,* 1115–1120.

Statham, L., & Murray, M. P. (1971). Early walking patterns of normal children. *Clinical Orthopaedics and Related Research, 79,* 8–24.

Stott, L. H. & Ball, R. S. (1965). Infant and pre-school mental tests: Review and evaluation. *Monographs of the Society for Research in Child Development, 30,* No. 101.

Super, C. M. (1976). Environmental effects on motor development: The case of 'African Infant Precocity'. *Developmental Medicine and Child Neurology, 18,* 561–567.

Sutherland, D. H., Olshen, R., Cooper, L., Wyatt, M., Leach, J., Mubarak, J., & Schultz, P. (1981). The pathomechanics of gait in Duchenne muscular dystrophy. *Developmental Medicine and Child Neruology, 23,* 3–22.

Taft, L. T., & Cohen, H. J. (1967). Neonatal and infant reflexology. In J. Hellmuth (Ed.), *Exceptional infant, Vol. 1. The normal infant.* Seattle: Special Child Publications.

Thelen, E., Bradshaw, G., & Ward, J. A. (1981). Spontaneous kicking in month-old infants. Manifestations of a human central locomotor program. *Behavioural and Neural Biology, 17,* 237–257.

Thelen, E., & Fisher, D. M. (1982). Newborn stepping: An explanation for a disappearing reflex. *Developmental Psychology, 18,* 760–775.

Thelen, E., & Fisher, D. M. (1983). From spontaneous to instrumental behaviour: Kinematic analysis of movement changes during very early learning. *Child Development, 54,* 129–140.

Touwen, B. C. L. (1976). Neurological development in infancy. *Clinics in developmental medicine, No. 58.* London: S.I.M.P. with Heinemann; Philadelphia: Lippincott.

Touwen, B. C. L. (1978). Variability and stereotypy in normal and deviant development. In J. Apley (Ed.), *Care of the handicapped child. Clinics in developmental medicine, No. 67.* London: S.I.M.P. with Heinemann; Philadelphia: Lippincott.

Turvey, M. Y. (1977). Preliminaries to a theory of action with reference to vision. In R. Shaw & J. Bransford (Eds.), *Perceiving, acting and knowing.* Hillsdale, NJ: Lawrence Erlbaum.

Von Hofsten, C. (1980). Predictive reaching for moving objects by human infants. *Journal of Experimental Child Psychology, 30,* 369–382.

Von Hofsten, C. (1982). Eye-hand co-ordination in the newborn. *Developmental Psychology, 18,* 450–467.

Walk, R. D., & Pick, H. L. (1981). *Intersensory perception and sensory integration.* New York: Plenum Press.

Wickstrom, R. L. (1977). *Fundamental motor patterns* (2nd edition). Philadelphia: Lea and Febiger.

Wolfe, P. H. (1981). Normal variation in human maturation. In K. J. Connolly & H. F. R. Prechtl

(Eds.), *Maturation and development: Biological and psychological perspectives. Clinics in developmental medicine, No. 77/78.* London: S.I.M.P. with Heinemann; Philadelphia: Lippincott.

Wyke, B. (1975). The neurological basis of movement. In K. S. Holt (Ed.), *Movement and child development. Clinics in developmental medicine, No. 55.* London: S.I.M.P. with Heinemann; Philadelphia: Lippincott.

Zelazo, P. (1976). From reflexive to instrumental behaviour. In L. P. Lipsitt (Ed.), *Developmental psychology: The significance in infancy.* Hillsdale, NJ: Erlbaum.

Zelazo, P. R., Zelazo, N. A., & Kolb, S. (1972). Walking in the newborn. *Science, 176,* 314–315.

# PROBLEMS OF MOTOR DEVELOPMENT
## SOME PRACTICAL ISSUES

Sheila E. Henderson

## 'INTRODUCTION

In the previous chapter I reviewed some recent advances in the study of early motor development and tried to indicate the extent to which these have influenced our *understanding* of children whose motor development is atypical. Unfortunately, much of what was discussed remains in the realm of academic debate and has yet to have its effect on practice. The gap between theory and practice which causes distress in other aspects of the field of special education is similarly evident in the motor domain. It would be misleading to suggest, however, that all of the issues raised are sufficiently resolved to be of practical value. Clearly many are not. What I propose to do in this chapter, therefore, is to take

Advances in Special Education, Volume 5, pages 187–218.
Copyright © 1986 by JAI Press Inc.
All rights of reproduction in any form reserved.
ISBN: 0-89232-313-2

three topics of concern to all practitioners, illustrate the problems as they arise from a practical viewpoint, and, where possible, note the impact of recent research. I will deal with problems of description, definition and classification; assessment; and intervention.

# PROBLEMS OF DESCRIPTION, DEFINITION, AND CLASSIFICATION

The general question of how to classify handicapped children has been the subject of much debate on both sides of the Atlantic. As a method of generalization classification involves the grouping together of individuals with common attributes. Because the defining attributes can be described at different levels, different classification schemes emerge to serve different purposes, each being of practical import in its own right. One of the most intractable problems is that of reconciling the demands of different levels of classification (Alberman, 1984; Rutter, 1977). Alberman (1984) lists four different types of classification each one of which makes a vital contribution to our understanding of a particular impairment or constellation of impairments, and thus to the provision that is made for those affected. She notes that an *aetiological* classification (e.g., anoxia) is needed to help form hypotheses about causation and to direct possible preventive action; a *pathological* classification (e.g., cerebellar damage) is needed to help understand the nature of the defects in the condition; a *clinical* classification (e.g., ataxia) is necessary to help with prognosis and management in the individual case; and, a classification of *concomitants* which takes account of the impairments, disabilities and handicaps associated with the condition is needed to help plan services for the affected. Both Rutter (1977) and Alberman (1984) note that the more broadly acceptable a classification scheme is the greater its potential usefulness and the more possibilities it offers for collaboration between researchers and practitioners. Although attempts have been made to develop comprehensive methods of classification (e.g., World Health Organization, 1980), there have no large scale tests and their validity has not been demonstrated (Alberman, 1984).

The more specific problem of how to classify or categorize children in such a way that their educational needs are adequately met has also been the focus of much debate. Though major changes have occurred at the legislative level, problems of description and definition still exist. For example, though the medical model of handicap has received a great deal of criticism well-formulated alternatives do not yet exist (Yule, 1975). It is now widely recognized that an individual may be handicapped in one situation but not in another, in one role but not in another. Static notions of impairment have also been criticised. For example, the fact that some children who appear quite severely impaired at birth are later apparently normal is, in a sense, a nuisance for those whose job it is to estimate the incidence and prevalence of particular conditions. On the other hand, the fact that all children do not remain in the same state at all times is a much more accurate reflection of reality, and a fact that must be accommodated in classification schemes. In addition, failure to take sufficient account of social context is now widely acknowledged as a major deficiency in present systems.

With regard to the specific question of how to describe and classify movement problems in children, the issues raised in the previous chapter pointed to some of the difficulties which might be encountered. It is now time to discuss these systematically. Historically, there has been a tendency to consider atypical motor development in a number of quite separate arenas. For example, motor impairment is discussed as a primary deficit in cerebral palsy, as a secondary deficit accompanying blindness, as a concomitant of intellectual retardation, and as a specific deficit in the "clumsy child" syndrome. Whereas children with particular sensory deficits have often been judged to be sufficiently homogeneous to make general examination of their problems fruitful, discussion of children with motor problems has not been so regarded. This is partly because the definition and description of motor impairments in children has been undertaken almost exclusively by the medical profession, but it is also due to the fact that existing psychological accounts of motor development are as yet inadequate as models on which to base a classification.

In order to illustrate some of the difficulties to be overcome if a more unified description of motor problems in children is to be achieved, I propose to adopt in a very loose sense the medical approach as it now exists and point out its strengths and weaknesses from a psychoeducational point of view. It would be difficult at this stage to discuss blind or intellectually handicapped children in whom motor problems are fairly clearly secondary so the discussion will focus on children in whom motor problems qualify as a primary difficulty.

There are some initial differentiations that can be made which are medically, psychologically, and educationally useful, the most obvious being that between impairments which result from damage to the central nervous sytem (CNS) and those which do not. The difficulty of accurately describing problems of motor development in children is highly correlated with the extent to which the central nervous system can be shown to be implicated. In general terms, the reason for this is that damage to the developing brain is rarely focussed or localised in the way damage to the adult brain may occur. The implication of this is that motor impairment, when it occurs, is frequently accompanied by a wide variety of other problems. Such problems are, therefore, primary in the sense that they are part and parcel of the same disorder rather than the result of it.

Of those conditions known to have no CNS involvement, most are, relatively speaking, easy to diagnose and describe accurately (e.g., club foot, congenital hip dislocation, osteogenesis imperfecta, juvenile rheumatoid arthritis, scoliosis, etc.). Such disorders affect the physical conditions of the body and, therefore, may affect the child's motor development in a variety of ways. For example, the opportunity for total involvement in physical activity is often reduced. The acquisition of certain key skills such as walking may be delayed because it is medically undesirable, because the adaptation to the deformity is physically difficult for the child, or because his parents treat him more like a baby than they otherwise would. Such children, obviously have many difficulties to cope with, which frequently increase with age. As Reynell (1970) points out, however, any emotional disturbance or learning difficulties encountered by these children are secondary in origin, and may be easier to deal with than those encountered in other groups of children with motor impairments. However, such conditions account for a rather small proportion of children whose motor development deviates from normal. In the vast majority, the neuromotor system is believed to be affected (see below for further discussion of this point).

Within the group of children known to have suffered damage to the neuromotor system, two other distinctions are made which also have psychological and educational relevance. The first is between conditions resulting from damage to the brain and those involving parts of the neuromotor system below the brain. A range of disorders exist which involve the spinal cord (e.g., polio) the nerve fibres leading from the spinal cord to the muscles (e.g., infectious polyneuritis), the junction between the nerve fibre endings and the muscles (e.g., myasthenia gravis) the muscles themselves (e.g., metabolic myopathies) and even the tendons and supportive tissues connected to the muscles. The causes of these conditions are many and varied. Some are associated with other kinds of deficit (e.g., intellectual retardation) but others are quite specific and affect only the child's motor development. Thus, from an educational viewpoint understanding the origins of the condition can be useful. A second distinction which has some utility is that between progressive and nonprogressive conditions. The child with Duchenne muscular dystrophy presents different problems to the teacher or therapist than the child with arthritis or spina bifida.

So far, we have examined the broad distinction between CNS and non-CNS disorders, and within the general category of CNS disorders, the distinction between damage to the brain and to lower components of the neuromotor system as well as the distinction between progressive and nonprogressive forms. We can now examine the nonprogressive node in our decision tree. This we shall do with regard, first, to "cerebral palsy," and second, to "clumsiness." The decision to treat these topics in separate subsections requires some justification. That there is some overlap between cerebral palsy and clumsiness is beyond dispute. Continuities exist at two levels of description. It is widely accepted that a continuum of neurological damage underlies the motor impairment. Moreover, at the behavioural level, both putative syndromes exhibit great heterogeneity with considerable overlap of the symptom sets. This is true of the motor difficulties and of the various patterns of concomitant intellectual and emotional difficulties. For example, impairment of balance may be present in both syndromes, though in cerebral palsy its incidence and its severity are much greater. Again, in the nonmotor domain, underneath the statistical association between motor and intellectual impairment lies enormous variability of individual cases. Thus, one may encounter bright cerebral palsied children and dull clumsy children. My reasons for nevertheless treating the two topics separately, are primarily expository. I intend to use cerebral palsy to illustrate the problems encountered in trying to describe the neuromotor deficits and their behavioral consequence, and clumsiness to illustrate the difficulties produced by trying to circumscribe deficits or impairments which have no inherent boundaries.

## Cerebral Palsy

One of the most commonly quoted definitions of cerebral palsy is that of Bax (1964), "a nonprogressive disorder of movement and posture due to a defect or lesion of the immature brain." This is a deceptively simple definition. A fundamental problem is that cerebral palsy is not a single disease entity but a miscellany of clinical conditions with various causes. Although the use of the singular form obscures it, cerebral palsy has for a very long time been described as a collection of motor disorders (e.g., Freud, 1897; Little, 1862). There are only two characteristics which are generally acknowledged as common to all forms: the nonprogressive nature, and the presumed time of damage to the brain. The nature of the movement disorder, however, can take various forms, affect different parts of the body and range in severity from mild to profoundly debilitating. By itself, therefore, the label "cerebral palsy" conveys a very limited amount of information about an individual child.

There would, of course, be little difficulty if individual syndromes within the general condition could be reliably defined, but this is where the picture is most complicated. Broadly speaking, there are three diagnostic categories which are subsumed under the heading "cerebral palsy"—spasticity, athetosis (or dystonia), and ataxia. However, each of these subdivides in turn and it is common to find children who cannot be clearly classified because they exhibit more than one kind of impairment. Although one characteristic might predominate, spastic children may exhibit athetoid movements and athetoid children may suffer spasticity. Topographic distribution and severity are equally difficult to specify, due, in part, to the lack of reliable, objective assessment instruments. It is not uncommon to find a child classified by one pediatrician as diplegic and by another as quadruplegic. After all, diplegia can be taken to imply not that the upper limbs are completely unaffected but only that they are *less* affected than the lower limbs. These difficulties are well summarised by Alberman (1984). In a study of 21 cases of cerebral palsy, the diagnosis made by six clinicians had been compared. Only 40% agreed on the type of motor handicap (e.g., spastic, ataxic). A mere 50% agreed on the topographical distribution (e.g., hemiplegia, diplegia) and there was 60% agreement on the severity (e.g., mild, moderate, severe).

It is generally believed that early identification of children with handicapping conditions is a good thing, the assumption being that it leads to more effective intervention. However, early identification and classification of cerebral palsied children is particularly difficult (Robson, 1983). To begin with there are problems confined to the first year or so of life. Sometimes children who are extremely ill at birth show signs of neurological impairment which disappear quite quickly. These may manifest themselves in the motor domain. The major problem, however, is the extent to which the clinical picture can change *within* the motor domain. That is, changes in muscle tone are well documented, involuntary movements may emerge after months or even years, and severity often changes radically. Thus, it is almost impossible to make a firm diagnosis in the first year of life, and this leads to practical problems for parents, paediatricians, and administrators.

Problems of classification are not restricted to the first year of life, however. Some children with cerebral palsy change in diagnostic classification over time. This may mean a change from one cerebral palsy subgroup to another, or it may mean change from cerebral palsy to some other category altogether. Recall our discussion of cases of "transient" cerebral palsy in the previous chapter. Furthermore, Paneth and Kiely (1984) point to the fact that there are often mild cases not reported in the first few years who would be diagnosable by neurological examination. To further complicate the problem, injury to the brain in older children, caused, for instance, by abuse or a road accident, may create a clinical picture identical to that identifiable early in life. Some authors call this post-natal cerebral palsy, others do not. If we take as an example the case of the administrator whose job it is to allocate resources for the treatment and education of handicapped children, it should be obvious that the lack of clarity surrounding children with movement problems of this nature presents a considerable problem.

From the point of view of professionals who are directly responsible for the care of such children, there are still other complications. Though it has long been acknowledged that the same impairment in two individuals may have vastly different consequences for how they live their lives, a clear distinction between impairments and their functional consequences has not until relatively recently been formally drawn. A recent attempt to distinguish between an impairment, a disability, and a handicap is made in the World Health Organizations' International Classification of Diseases (WHO, 1980). These distinctions have received a considerable amount of attention (e.g., Hogg & Mittler, 1983) and are reflected in the formulation of laws concerning the establishment of the needs of children with problems of various types (in the United States, Public Law 94-142; in the United Kingdom, the 1981 Act). In order to characterize in any detail the way that a particular child copes with the impairment he or she has suffered, cognizance must be taken of the whole range of the child's strengths and weaknesses. In the case of cerebral palsy, this makes description very complex, indeed. Sensory and perceptual deficiencies are common, intellectual impairment occurs in a large proportion of cases, speech and language difficulties are often present, and emotional disturbance is not uncommon (see Robinson, 1973; Rutter, Graham, & Yule, 1970). Even without the assessment of social context any judgement of the cerebral palsied child's competence is extremely difficult.

In the course of this discussion we have moved from a consideration of the specific problem of how best to define and classify the variety of motor problems that are presently subsumed under the heading of cerebral palsy to the more general question of how best to encompass all the other deficiencies which so frequently occur alongside the motor impairment. One might well be inclined to ask whether something might be gained from abandoning the term cerebral palsy altogether. However, the weight of present medical opinion seems to favour its retention as a way of distinguishing children in whom the motor disorder is primary, and to use the collective form cerebral palsies to denote the heterogeneity of subgroups. (Alberman, 1984). Closely tied to the question of "who is cerebral palsied?" is the question of what to do for the children so defined. The label cerebral palsy can be reasonably reliably assigned but little has yet been achieved. What remains to be formulated can be subsumed under two headings: (a) the need for a more adequate description of the child's motor problems; and (b) the need for an adequate description of the resources which the child can bring to bear upon the solution of these motor problems.

*Clumsiness, Motor Delay, Developmental Apraxia, M.B.D?*

We have seen that systematic classification of impairment resulting from known damage to the neuromotor system (i.e., cerebral palsy) is fraught with problems of various kinds. These problems become even more severe when we attempt a taxonomy of movement problems which have no clear organic base and which are generally diffuse. I refer, of course, to clumsiness, motor delay, and the like. In the preschool period it is especially difficult to decide whether a particular child's problems are simply caused by lack of experience, timidity in new situations, or a genuine difficulty emerging in the face of more challenging motor problems to be solved.

At the heart of the difficulty of finding a way to classify movement problems which have no clear aetiology lies an appalling confusion in terminology. Words such as *"agnosia"* and *"apraxia"* are used alongside words like *"motor delay"* *"motor* (perceptuo-motor) *impairment,"* or just *"clumsiness."* The words *"clumsy"* or *"uncoordinated"* frequently appear in lists of symptoms which are said to define certain syndromes such as "the hyperactive child," "minimal cerebral dysfunction" and "L.D." Indeed, "the clumsy child syndrome" has been considered as a syndrome in its own right. Also, the concept of "minimal cerebral palsy" has been used to indicate that motor impairments vary along a continuum of severity. It may seem but a short step from the empirical notion of a continuum of severity to the conceptual notion of a continuum of neurological damage and this step is often unwittingly taken in debate. Whereas, the broader label, "minimal cerebral dysfunction" has been applied on the basis of a wide range of behavioral indicators, "minimal cerebral palsy" is usually confined to the realm of motor indicators. In neither case, of course, is the label of much clinical utility. The nature of the motor problem is not clearly defined in any way, nor are we any further forward in documenting the child's strengths and weaknesses in other areas of competence.

In addition to the fact that the identification of a clear motor syndrome, defined in terms of the co-occurence of "symptoms" has so far eluded us, there is also a problem in the formulation of the "symptoms" themselves. At present, the descriptive terms used represent numerous levels of analysis, diverse theoretical positions, and a great number of degrees of precision, e.g., finger agnosia, mixed laterality, tactile defensiveness, hyperactivity, awkwardness, inability to hop, poor body image, lack of spatial awareness, and so on. All appear in the literature as "symptoms" of clumsiness. It is not that these different phrases or words have no basis in reality. There are, indeed, children who find learning the difference between right and left difficult, who cannot sit still, and who cannot hop or catch a ball. The problem is that the motley nature of these symptoms does not offer much encouragement to the view that a theoretically cohesive account can be derived.

Yet another difficulty centres on the question of distinguishing abnormality from delay. At present there are two alternative approaches to the problem. The first is concerned with the existence of neurological evidence of pathology and was discussed in the previous chapter. The second, of more relevance here, is psychometric in nature. Essentially the rationale for this approach depends on the characteristics of the low end of ability scales; that is, that the proportion of poorly performing individuals is higher than one would expect if one assumes that such characteristics are normally distributed. Both intelligence and reading attainment scores have been shown to exhibit such characteristics (Rutter & Yule, 1977). The argument that is then made is that the secondary hump in the distribution results from the presence of individuals who are abnormal in addition to those bottom of the pile on a distribution basis. This argument has most frequently been mounted with respect to cognitive abilities but might equally be applied to motor abilities. Two points seem relevant. First, this interpretation is more useful as a basis for the general assertion that such and such a pathological condition exists than for the decision about whether some particular child suffers pathology or delay. Second, it is difficult to find some independent criteria of pathology which allow a test of the internal logic of the argument with its presuppositions about normal distribution. From a practical point of view, this is an important issue, as the way the problem is perceived influences the way it is dealt with. Acceptance of the notion that the child is likely to grow out of his/her difficulties leads easily to the view that nothing need be done about it.

Before concluding this part of the discussion, it is important to make explicit what has so far remained implicit. Movement problems in children manifest themselves in different ways and probably have a variety of different causes. Furthermore, children who experience motor problems in no sense form a homogeneous group. Much time has been wasted attempting to circumscribe patterns of behaviour in such a way that they form a clearly definable syndrome X, which can be distinguished from syndrome Y. However, the problem of how to deal with heterogeneity remains. The questions are: How, without postulating syndromes and the attendant diagnostic rules for mapping children into syndromes, can one achieve a more parsimonious description of impairment than is involved in simply inventorying each child's particular difficulties? Again without postulating syndromes, can one make pragmatic decisions about what sort of treatment program is likely to be fruitful for a particular child.

# ASSESSMENT

It is against this background that we move on to the question of assessment. There are three general points which will serve to set the scene for the more specific discussion to follow. First, the heterogeneity of children with atypical motor development implies the need to take account of multiple aspects of the child's development including cognitive and social competence. In this context, it is useful to take note of the current debate on the limitations of existing tests of cognitive competence in young children (e.g., Gaussen, 1984; Yang, 1979; Zelazo, 1982). Children with impaired motor functioning are particularly vulnerable to inaccurate assessment because they often lack the means to display their cognitive ability either motorically or verbally. The second point is simply to draw attention to the special problems one faces in testing preschool children and infants. These have been dealt with at length elsewhere and will be taken as understood here (see e.g., Paget & Bracken, 1983). Finally, it is important to be aware that assessment instruments cannot be evaluated in absolute terms but only in relation to particular objectives (Berger, 1977; Johnson, 1982). It is not my intention here to evaluate individual instruments in terms of their appropriateness as screening or diagnostic instruments. Rather, I will attend to the nature of their content and the contribution they make to our understanding of children's motor competence.

*Ways of Assessing Motor Performance in Preschool Children*

There are a number of ways of giving structure to a description of the tests available for the preschool child. Two approaches have simplicity in their favor: age (used by Connolly, 1984) and severity of handicap (used in Paget & Bracken, 1983). Taking either dimension, the available instruments fall quite naturally into neat groups. For our purposes, however, an approach currently favored by physical education specialists seems a more appropriate starting point. Various reviews exist which draw a distinction between what are called "product-oriented" and "process-oriented" tests (e.g., Gallahue, 1982; Williams, 1983). Product-oriented tests may be regarded as descriptive or opaquely behavioral in nature. They focus on what the child can or cannot do, without reference to underlying mechanisms. What is meant by process-oriented is rather less clear, however. For some, the term characterizes assessment of the means whereby an action is performed, such as the pattern of movements involved in throwing. For others, it describes instruments which purport to be diagnostic in that they afford inferences about the state of the underlying machinery. The problem with the product-process classification, however the classes are defined, is that it fails to distinguish between the nature of the items in a test and the interpretation placed upon the scores. In fact, if we compare the content of tests which claim to be "diagnostic" with those labelled as "descriptive" there is often little difference between them. Therefore, in this discussion the focus is on the nature of the component items rather than on the stated function of the test. To do this, I have adopted the convenient fiction that tests are entirely homogeneous with respect to the nature of their items. Broadly speaking, currently used instruments viewed in this way seem to fall into three classes. In the first group, the tests are concerned with action at a functional level. Those in the second group are concerned with the description of the movements comprising an action. The third group is made up of the neurodevelopmental tests which aim to provide an index of the integrity of the nervous system. Many items in these tests do not involve *voluntary* movement.

## Functional Tests

Many tests exist which contain items requiring the subject to perform a voluntary motor act (catch a ball, drink from a cup). The nature of the tests varies considerably. They range from tapping a finger as fast as possible to completing a form board or walking along a line or finding a way through a maze. Very loosely, a distinction can be drawn between two types of test which contain such items. On the one hand, there are tests which have their origin in what Kopp (1979) called the cataloguing phase of research in motor development. The authors of these instruments regard the items as representative "samples" of motor attainment. The composite score thus provides an index of motor ability in general terms. On the other hand, there are tests which are purportedly more diagnostic in nature. On these tests failure on the selected items is seen as indicative of various disordered underlying states.

Unfortunately, the distinction between these two groups of tests has become associated with the continuum between perceptual and motor performance. "Diagnostic" tests seem to be more heavily weighted with items at the "perceptual" end of the continuum whereas the more straightforward attainment tests are more saturated with items at the "motor" end. At a simple level, the different tests are associated with different professions and therefore, reflect different interests. However, there are also more fundamental differences in theoretical perspective.

Let us consider first the more conservative tests which seek to provide indices of motor attainment in young children. These have been recently reviewed by Wade and Davis (1982) and Davis (1984). Like their predecessors, the general developmental scales of the forties (e.g., Bayley, 1935; Cattell, 1940; Gesell & Armatruda 1941), most of these instruments are based on the maturational model of development and use age norms as the yardstick against which achievement is assessed. On individual items, success is measured either as "can do—cannot do" in absolute terms (e.g., sits, stands alone) or in terms of quantitative measures of performance (e.g., how far, how fast). Composite scores are derived in various ways but nearly always result in a statement of the child's competence with respect to his peers of the same chronological age.

In general form the instruments range from simple checklists (e.g., Keogh & Sugden, 1978) to fully standardised tests for which equipment and procedures are specified (e.g., Bruininks, 1978; McCarthy, 1972). Though they differ in content, decisions about what aspects of functioning to include are often not given theoretical rationale (Davis, 1984; Gallahue, 1982). They also differ considerably in their stated aims although in practice these differences are sometimes ignored. Some have been designed as screening tests, such as the Denver Developmental Screening Test (Frankenburg & Dodds, 1967), while others provide normative data on the whole range of ability (e.g., Bruininks, 1978).

At the lower age levels in particular, there is overlap between the tests focusing exclusively on *motor* development and the general developmental schedules. However, there is a difficulty with using the general developmental scales as measures of motor development. Whereas the items in the "motor" tests are at least grouped according to assumed components of "motor" ability (e.g., locomotor skills, throwing skills), those in the general developmental schedules are often grouped on nonmotor criteria. This is because Gesell and others were less interested in motor development per se than they were in the use of motor performance as a means of providing "a window to the mind." Though some schedules do make provision for the derivation of a "motor" quotient that is separate from the "mental" quotient, there may be many items which require a similar degree of motor coordination in both sections, as well as in specific subsections, such as the "personal-social" component (Gesell & Armatruda, 1941; Griffiths, 1954). Davis (1984) is critical of motor and general schedules alike because they are predicated upon the assumption that a general faculty labeled "motor ability" exists. The issues are similar to current arguments about the concept of cognitive abilities. With regard to the psychometric properties of these instruments, Wade and Davis (1982) conclude that many are inadequate. Predictive validity is a major issue and few good follow-up studies of children are available.

Within their recognized limitations, developmental tests serve as a useful starting point from which to document a child's strengths and weaknesses. Clearly they are open to the criticisms launched against any formal test for young children. For example, a young child's ability to demonstrate his maximum level of motor competence is related to his sensitivity to unfamiliar surroundings, to unfamiliar adults, to the proximity of lunch time. A second problem centers on the discriminative power of the items. In order to capture the entire range of performance within a normal population (the usual standardization population for these tests) the "grain" of the test has to be so coarse that items may not detect changes in impaired children which, while small compared to the spectrum of performance across individuals, may be highly significant as a measure of therapeutic outcome. A related difficulty is that there are children who cannot begin to perform the tasks contained in these tests. That is, the item content is not appropriate for the more severely handicapped. In this case the question of content relevance also arises. For the severely disabled child, whether intellectually impaired or not, the achievement of physical independence is a primary concern. Thus, practical motor competencies (whether the child can go to the toilet alone or dress himself), need to be assessed. There are several checklists and scales devised to fill this gap but few have been well standardised. Different approaches to assessment have also been proposed for such children, such as applied behavioural analysis (see Gerken, 1983). While the use of less formal methods of assessment may be useful in day to day practice, the lack of suitable, reliable instruments which span the entire range of motor competence make evaluation of intervention programs much more difficult. Finally, what these tests do not do, of course, is tell us anything about why the child fails to perform adequately on the set tasks.

*Diagnostic tests.*   Now we turn to the so-called "diagnostic" tests which contain more items at the perceptual end of the alarmingly vague perceptuo-motor continuum. In the 1960s there was a proliferation of such tests, among the most notable being the Developmental Test of Visual Perception (Frostig, 1963), the Purdue Perceptual Motor Survey (Roach & Kephart, 1966) and the South California Sensory Integration Tests (Ayres, 1972a). They differ in content from those described above in that they contain a miscellany of items some of which require only perceptual analysis (e.g., distinguishing figure from ground) and others which require a substantial degree of motor control (e.g., completing a paper and pencil maze test). The component items of these tests were designed to measure factors like body image, "tactile defensiveness," or directionality, all rather global concepts that rest on largely intuitive definition. The fact that it is often difficult to find an agreed definition of a notion like "body image" or that no well-documented accounts of the development of these abilities exist seem to have been discounted. For the authors of these tests, "perceptuo-motor ability" seems to have played the role of a hypothetical construct causally mediating between behavioural development and the integrity of the nervous system. In addition, causal links were assumed to exist between whatever deficits particular authors believed their test to be measuring and failure in academic attainment. Although many of these tests are still widely used, their psychometric properties, their theoretical underpinning, and the programs of therapy which accompany them have borne a great deal of criticism (Cratty, 1981; Kavale & Mattson 1983; Keogh, 1978, for reviews). They are particularly vulnerable because they are so predicated on theories which are often shown to be either untenable or untestable.

## Approaches to Describing the Pattern or Form in Movement

Countless methods have been used to describe the form of voluntary movement. To a large extent these reflect the particular interests of the observer. They range from attempts to produce a descriptive written notation to sophisticated measures having their origin in the physical sciences. For example, physiotherapists have used dance notation as a means of keeping a continuous record of patient's progress in walking (Horton & McGuiness, 1975). Computer analysis has been used to produce biomechanical measures from which the recovery of movement in stroke patients was monitored (Lough, Wing, Fraser, & Jenning, 1984). At present, the more sophisticated of these approaches are seldom used with children under the age of 6, but with the explosion of new technology, they become more and more feasible additions to our traditional armory of assessment procedures. It is useful, therefore, to consider them alongside those which are currently more frequently used with preschool children.

We will begin with a consideration of a group of instruments which require that an observer watch a child moving, then match the observation made against a verbal description. Though the research on which these instruments is based began as long ago as 1930, it is only recently that such observation has been incorporated into formally constructed assessment instruments (e.g., McClenaghan & Gallahue, 1978; Williams & Breihan, 1979). The basic format of these instruments is quite similar. Most take the form of checklists which contain a series of statements describing how the required movement task was performed. There are essentially two sources of variation, the item content and the nature of the descriptive statements. As far as item content is concerned, what varies is the number of skills to be observed and the extent to which the mode of presentation to the child is specified. For example, McClenaghan and Gallahue (1978) provide information on 5 gross motor skills, whereas Williams and Breiham (1979) deal with 16. It is interesting to note that more instruments focus on gross motor than on fine motor performance. (Perhaps this is a reflection of the fact that they are constructed by physical educators). Yet, there are excellent studies of the development of fine motor control (e.g., Elliott & Connolly, 1984) which may provide useful assessment data. Nearly all authors of such checklists specify that each task must be observed more than once; some specify the observation conditions precisely and others leave the conditions to the discretion of the observer. Most have the advantage of flexibility, although as Davis (1984) points out, the way an action is performed changes according to the environmental demands. For example, throwing for distance or for accuracy will result in differences in some of the movement parameters.

Turning now to the nature of the statements which describe the movements comprising each action, we find substantial differences. These are the key features of the instruments and it is their degree of precision which, partially at least, dictates the success or failure of the approach. To date relatively little work has been done on questions of reliability or validity (Wade & Davis, 1982). Whereas some instruments or checklists are explicitly based on "stage theory" in motor development, others focus on the description of deviance from an "efficient" motor pattern. Whatever the basis of organization, however, a varying number of verbal descriptions must be matched against an observed performance. Inevitably, problems of observer competence and performance variability arise. These have many parallels in the evolution of observational schedules in other areas of development and their solution simply requires careful research.

Wade and Davis (1982) have suggested, too, that these instruments may not be suitable for severely physically handicapped children. Thus, children who have suffered obvious damage to the neuromotor system and whose patterns of movement are often bizarre even when they do run, throw or catch are almost impossible to describe in the terms contained in the checklist. What is really meant, therefore, is that the instruments are sensitive to "immaturity" as opposed to deviance.

We now move from attempts to describe the pattern in movement verbally to attempts to produce quantitative measures of the spatial, temporal and force characteristics of movement. Such techniques are uncommon for two reasons. They require expensive equipment and produce complex data which are not easy to translate into a form which the ordinary practitioner can interpret. However, complete packages which simplify the process of making decisions about what constitutes noteworthy deviation from normality are becoming available. In specialist clinics biomechanical analysis has been used for a long time (e.g., Holt, 1966) and consistently yields valuable information which adds to what can be gleaned from simple observation. Consider, for example, the gait of a hemiplegic child. From simply listening to the uneven footfall, we can tell that unequal weight is being put on each leg. To be able to measure precisely the differences can help to establish whether undue stress is being put on a particular joint (e.g., the hip) and what course of action should be taken to alleviate the problem.

Taking together all forms of assessment which focus on the pattern of movement, there is no doubt that in practical terms they add a great deal to what we learn from the "functional" tests described above. The gathering of qualitative data about movement pattern should allow a more informative analysis of what a particular child's treatment program might contain. Moreover, there may be a seminal effect whereby the existence of qualitative data may provoke refinements of diagnostic and therapeutic ideas. There is a possible parallel to be made here with recent developments in intelligence testing where cognitive psychologists have taken an experimental and theoretical interest in the nature of the cognitive processes which underlie performance on test items. This procedure acts to counterbalance the blindly empirical psychometric tradition in which test items merely served as inscrutable measures along which performance could be scaled. In the motor domain there is clearly a need to apply similar principles to the analysis of "how" a task is performed. Describing the pattern in movement is clearly one component, but there is room for others which focus more specifically on other elements of the task. Though some centres make use of experimental techniques in the assessment of children's problems this is still relatively rare.

*Neurodevelopmental Tests*

Finally, the assessment of specific neurophysiological processes has been stimulated by the view that early diagnosis of abnormality in neurological functioning, accompanied by immediate intervention, can minimize problems experienced at older ages. Early diagnosis, of course, presupposes the existence of a reliable examination of the state of the integrity of the nervous system. Theoretically, diagnostic techniques should take into account the specific properties of the nervous system at different points in development and should be based upon what is known about the underlying mechanisms. In this regard, there is a fairly clear distinction to be made between the tests designed for use in early infancy, and those designed for older children. The increasing sophistication of infant tests allows us to specify different signs indicative of abnormality in a premature infant and a full-term infant (Dubowitz & Dubowitz, 1981). In contrast, the tests for older children are much less precise, especially those designed to detect "minor neurological dysfunction." The latter contain a mixture of so-called hard signs and soft signs plus a variety of items testing psychological attributes; unfortunately, many of these seem no more likely to relate to the integrity of the child's nervous system than does hair length.

While the distinction between the tests used on infants and those on older children is superficially between age bands, underneath lies a concern with different degrees of impairment. What is of primary concern in the assessment of infants who are either ill, premature, or "at risk" in some way or other, is the detection of signs which indicate clear abnormality. Given the complexity of the infant nervous system and its capacity for recovery, this is difficult enough. In older children, the task of the paediatric neurologist is less clearly defined and it is here that the contribution of the neurodevelopmental examination is often challenged. To be sure, there are some specific problems which only the medically trained professional can deal with. For example, children with certain neurological conditions may change dramatically in some way, suddenly having seizures or outbursts of temper. Detection of a degenerative neurological disease in its early stages is often done on the basis of a medical history and the physician's intelligent piecing together of minor signs which might otherwise be ignored as just "clumsiness." It is when we come to the question of whether minor degrees of neurological dysfunction can be detected in children with behavior problems or learning difficulties that the controversy begins. What constitutes minor neurological dysfunction, whether there are recognizable behavior patterns associated with inferred neurological syndromes, what practical significance such information has, and many other questions, are often the focus of acrimonious debate.

Whatever the uncertainties that surround them, tests which are aimed at the assessment of the state of the developing nervous system play a significant role in the assessment of the child with known or suspected *motor* problems. For simplicity, they are described below under two headings (a) Neonatal and Infant Tests, (b) Tests for Children Three Years Upwards. Note that although these test batteries contain a broad spectrum of items related to other "systems" (e.g., the auditory system), I will only describe those components which are aimed at an evaluation of the motor system.

*Neonatal and infant tests.* As these tests have been reviewed extensively elsewhere (e.g., Parmalee, Kopp, & Sigman, 1976) they will be dealt with only very briefly here. There are three basic components in all of the neurological assessment instruments, the evaluation of posture, of tone, and of various reflexes (or "reactions"). The evaluation of posture and tone occur simultaneously as they are intimately related to each other. For example, the infant with low tone adopts a frog-like posture when put down on his back. One of the earliest authors to draw attention to the importance of assessing tone was André Thomas (e.g., André Thomas & Ajuriaguerra, 1949). He identified three aspects of tone which should be included if a comprehensive view is to be obtained: (a) Active tone evident during voluntary movement; (b) Tone detected when joints are moved passively; and (c) the amount of resistance encountered when distal parts of the limbs are freely swung. There have been no radical changes in the assessment of tone since then. Although it can probably be assessed quite reliably by experienced clinicians there is still no means of quantifying it. In addition to aspects of posture directly related to tone, factors like asymmetry are also noted at the same time.

The assessment of reflex behavior is a much more complex affair. There are many possibilities to choose from and the basis of selection often seems fairly arbitrary. Borrowing a phrase from Connolly (1984) the early neurodevelopmental tests might be described as "atheoretical collages." Starting in the early 1960s, there have been several attempts to improve on the way reflexes are assessed (e.g., Capute, Palmer, Shapiro, Wachtel, Ross, & Accardo, 1984). Fiorentino, 1973; Milani-Comparetti & Gidoni, 1967a, 1967b). What characterises all of the improved schedules is that they no longer rely on "presence-absence" decisions. Rather they attempt to provide more refined ratings of the strength or weakness of the response. Moreover, there are also attempts to apply standard "psychometric" criteria to the measurement scales. Studies of test-retest and inter-tests reliability of the judgements are now beginning to emerge.

One of the most fundamental changes in these instruments arose out of the recognition that the infant was not just a passive recipient of the stimuli which impinged upon him during an examination. Writers such as Prechtl (e.g., Prechtl & Beintema, 1964) and Graham (e.g., Graham, 1956) were particularly influential in insisting that measures of tone or reflex behavior could only be usefully interpreted in conjunction with an evaluation of the infants' "state" at the time of testing. For example, Prechtl recorded the striking way in which an infants' responses changed according to its degree of wakefulness and subsequently attempted to define the optimal conditions for the elicitation of particular responses.

At the same time, there have been attempts to take more account of what the infant could "offer" voluntarily as opposed to what was elicited from him. By far the best known instrument which attempts this kind of analysis is the Brazelton Scale (Brazelton, 1973, 1984). Brazelton states quite explicitly that the examination he has produced should be viewed as an interaction between the tests and the child, the tester's role being to provide the best possible conditions for the child to demonstrate competence.

Change in response to theory is more clearly evident in the neurodevelopmental schedules than it is the functional tests discussed earlier. Yet, there are some who believe that there is a long way to go before the assessment of the infant yields a true picture of his competence (e.g., Gaussen Stratton, 1985). There is also debate about the relative contribution of instruments more heavily weighted with classical neurological items and those more biased towards "behavioral" responses. In Prechtl's opinion (Prechtl, 1977) scales like the Brazelton are not sensitive enough to detect abnormal neurological conditions, but are good complements to the more traditional neurological assessment. Brazelton, on the other hand, claims that the classic neurological examination *only* detects major neurological abnormalities and misses minor dysfunction identifiable with his own scale. Whatever view one holds on the relative merits of these tests, some facts are indisputable. First, highly reliable diagnoses can be made only in the most severe cases of neurological abnormality. Second, even that judgement is only valid for a short period of time. It is extraordinarily difficult to predict which child will remain impaired, which will recover, and which might become more impaired with time. Dubowitz and Dubowitz (1981) state quite baldly "We doubt whether any neurological examination, past, present or future, will be predictive in the long term. . . ."

*Testing children 3 years upwards.* By age 3, the child with severe damage to the neuromotor system will have been identified and should by then have received a considerable amount of assistance. However, there are other children in whom problems of motor control do not manifest themselves until much later. A small proportion of these are children who have accidents or suffer degenerative disorders of the neuromotor system. A larger number, however, belong to that nebulous class of children described by parent or teacher as "clumsy." Their motor difficulties may manifest themselves in isolation or as part of a constellation of symptoms including speech problems, emotional difficulties, distractibility, and so on. Not surprisingly, neurologists have attempted to assess the state of the nervous system in such children pursuing hypotheses of minimal forms of damage. This exercise has proved enormously contentious. When neurologists have succeeded in excluding frank pathology, any further speculation about the possibility of minimal damage is likely to be academic in the pejorative sense of indulging theory while lacking practical import.

One of the major difficulties lies in the variable nature of the instruments pediatric neurologists use to test the integrity of the nervous system in the older child. In some, the content extends well beyond anything which could reasonably be justified as assessing neurological functioning. In contrast, one of the most clearly articulated theoretical positions from which a test of the more focused kind has been constructed is that of Touwen and his colleagues (Touwen and Kalverboer, 1973; Touwen, 1979). Touwen and Kalverboer (1973) outlined the essential features of a test of the state of the nervous system in the older child, and in 1979 Touwen formally published his test. The criteria that were used for item choice were (a) items should be age-specific; (b) the techniques of recording should be standardised; (c) behavioural state should be standardised; (d) the results should be quantifiable; and (e) the sequence of item administration should be standardized. These criteria are clearly recognizable as being similar to those applied in infant testing. Unfortunately, the extent to which the criteria have been met, however, is not well documented. No reliaibility data has been published on the rating scales nor has the validity of the so-called optimality scores been demonstrated. One very fruitful line of research which has incorporated this test, however, is that of Kalverboer (1975), who explored in detail the relationship between performance on Touwen's battery and behavior in a free-field setting.

A problem which is common to many of these instruments is that scores from many different kinds of items are simply pooled into a single score. This is particularly true of the items which are described as soft signs. "Soft" apparently means different things to different people. In an attempt to clarify the position, Rutter (1978) subdivided so-called soft (or minor) signs into three groups. The first group consists of indications of developmental delay in functions such as speech, motor coordination, or perception. The second group includes those signs which may be due to either neurological or nonneurological causes. Nystagmus and strabismus both fall into this category. The third group of soft signs consists of slight abnormalities which are difficult to detect. These are often minor examples of classical signs such as *slight* asymmetry, *marginal* hypotonia or hypertonia, or *slightly* abnormal reflexes. The softness of these signs resides in the demonstrated unreliability of judgements concerning their presence. Evidently, the notion of soft signs is not a very satisfactory one and the pooling of scores given on such items can only be misleading.

In an attempt to evaluate the contribution of this kind of test, Rutter (1978) make two points. The first concerns the difference between testing groups vs individuals. He points out that there are statistical associations between scores on these tests and the presence or absence of brain damage and so it is reasonable to use them for research purposes. In the individual case, however, they are an unsatisfactory guide to the presence of brain damage. The second point he makes justifies their continued use in clinical practice. He notes that although the concept of soft signs of brain damage is equivocal, the items are often of value as reflections of current functioning (e.g., in perception, speech etc.).

## Overview of Available Instruments

The variety of instruments designed to assess motor behaviour even in the preschool years reflects the complexity of the neuromotor apparatus and the supporting systems which interact with it. For almost every level of analysis, a corresponding assessment procedure can be found, ranging from the qualitative evaluation of muscle tone to the quantification of the speed at which a complex action can be performed. The tests also vary in their degree of specificity, some being very focused, others covering a broad range of performance. What is singularly lacking, however, is a comprehensive instrument with a sound theoretical rationale which cuts across levels and permits us to evaluate systematically the relationships between them. As in every other domain, theorists are grappling with the problem of how best to conceptualise complex interactive processes but the effects of their efforts are not yet evident in the field of assessment.

We have considered a range of tests which are designed for different purposes so it is rather difficult to draw any conclusions about them in general terms. However, it might be said that an overall evaluation would bear a close resemblance to recent critiques of instruments currently used in the assessment of cognitive abilities in atypical infants and young children (e.g., Johnson, 1982). In general terms, the more atypical the child, the less useful most existing tests become, and, the nearer one gets to the point in the assessment process when intervention must be planned and executed, the more problematic they become.

In sum, for administrative purposes it can be cautiously concluded that the psychometrically sound instruments are as satisfactory as their counterparts in other domains. We can reliably identify children at the severe end of the continuum but we commit too many errors when subtle problems are at issue. Similarly, within the realm of intervention criticisms fall most heavily on the failure of the tests to register small improvements which take place over an extended period of time. Another problem which is particularly acute in the motor domain is the relationship between levels of measurement. Clinically, we are all aware that there is no one-to-one relationship between change measured by a physiotherapist, say, and that noted by the classroom teacher. Yet, empirically we know very little about the variables which intervene to affect these relationships. This problem becomes ever more frustrating when we ask about the most appropriate remedial strategies, the most appropriate outcome variables to measure, what constitutes effective intervention and so on.

## INTERVENTION

There are innumerable reasons why young children fail to acquire adequate motor competence. Many of the conditions which affect the neuromotor system are rare but among the more common there is enough variation so that no single approach to intervention is likely to be universally appropriate. When a child has a degenerative condition, for example, therapists must seek the best approach to maintaining the child's acquired competence for as long as possible. Such a problem is totally different from that presented by the child who arrives in school, unable to perform the skills expected of him because he has lived at the top of a high-rise apartment building, and has been ignored by an inadequate caretaker. These two examples represent the extreme polarities on a number of dimensions. In the first instance the problem has a clear focus, whereas in the second the problem is one of general social disadvantage and all its facets. In the first case, we have damage to the neuromotor system which, in the absence of a new scientific discovery, will progressively inhibit the child's movement; In the second it is likely that the child is medically normal. There is not space here to deal separately with the problem raised by each group of children. I shall, therefore, focus on some of the issues which arise with regard to children who exhibit signs suggestive of nonprogressive damage to the motor component of the central nervous system.

At the heart of any discussion about what can be done to help children with atypical motor behavior lies one crucial but intractable question: To what extent can the developing motor system recover from damage? and can this recovery process be aided by therapeutic intervention? Among the subsidiary questions which flow from this one are: if intervention can be shown to be effective is one approach better than another? Cutting across methodology, is it true that intervention is more effective if it is begun earlier rather than later? Are different forms of therapy effective with different types of children? Is there an optimal duration or frequency for formal intervention sessions? Does the effect of intervention generalize across the motor domain and/or extend to other domains? What are the long-term effects of intervention? It will probably come as no surprise to the reader that we are not close to answering these basic questions, despite their apparent priority in the applied field. Before proceeding to review the empirical work that does exist, it might be useful to start with a consideration of some conceptual issues.

## Issues of Intervention

In the area of motor impairment the improvement of motor competence has nearly always been the responsibility of the paramedical professions. As an overriding objective all approaches aim to help the child *function* as independently as possible. How that should be achieved, however, is what differentiates therapists from psychologists or educationists. Many of the therapies have their origins in techniques used with adult patients who loose normal function, as a result of a stroke for example. It took some time before therapists working with children accommodated to the idea that on top of everything else that might be wrong with a child's neuromotor machinery, there was also a problem of learning. Most therapists took a "bottom-up" approach to the problem. Starting from the position that the neuromotor system is hierarchically organized with cortical control as the pinnacle, it was argued that a logical place to start treatment was at the lower levels. It was assumed that by improving the functioning of lower level mechanisms, voluntary motor control was facilitated and would simply emerge. Though this view has been modified considerably in recent years, it is still true to say that the tendency to treat the child as a passive recipient of appropriate handling rather than an active participant still predominates in many therapies.

Robinson (1982) suggests that the "bottom up" approach puts educators and therapists in conflict. Taking a broader psychological perspective, she proposes four principles which should guide us in the design of intervention programs: (a) that active participation in an activity by an infant is preferable to passive participation; (b) that self selection of an activity or material by the infant is preferable to selecting activities or materials for the infant; (c) that the function that a behavior serves (e.g., locomotion) is more important to eventual development than the form of the particular behaviour (e.g., crawling versus walking); and (d) that the infant should have experience acting directly upon the environment as a foundation for use of others as intermediaries where necessary. This perspective, argues for a "top-down" approach to intervention, giving priority to the encouragement of voluntary effort and helping the child to "find his own solution" to the control problem. Obviously, there are practical difficulties with the implementation of this approach. For example, there are limitations in the extent to which a tiny baby or profoundly intellectually handicapped child can be induced to participate actively in the attempt to improve his motor control. What is a more difficult issue, however, is that physiotherapists argue against this approach on the grounds that the child's developmental progress in the motor domain may be impeded because abnormal reflex patterns are allowed to persist or because deformities develop as a result of the use of abnormal patterns of movement. Unfortunately, we have no empirical data which helps us to adjudicate between these two positions and, as with all complex problems, it seems probable that the question is one of the balance between active and passive elements of the intervention rather than an "either–or" question. Consistent with the changes in recent views of development in general, however, one is intuitively inclined to the view that the better strategy is to focus on maximizing voluntary effort.

## Overview of Alternative Therapies

Let us now consider the alternative forms of therapy which are currently popular. It would be misleading to give the impression that their content is similar or that the perspective on how the child is viewed in the enterprise is identical. There are quite radical differences between them, yet not a single good study exists which compares one approach with another. Space limitations preclude detailed outlines of different methods but it is important to draw attention to some of the factors which may prove important in specifying the most fruitful approaches.

A crude distinction can be drawn between approaches which systematically attend to sensory input and others which do not. For example, Ayres (1968, 1972b) places heavy emphasis on tactile and vestibular stimulation whereas Vojta (1984) does not. Working directly on the abnormal reflexes is of major concern in some approaches (e.g., Bobath & Bobath, 1984; Vojta, 1984) and tends to go hand in hand with attempts to produce a basic repertoire of normal patterns of movement. In contrast, conductive education (Cotton, 1965, 1970; Peto, 1955) is more concerned with functional achievement than with how actions are performed. Another difference resides in the target population for which the various therapies are designed, although in practice such differences are often blurred. Although originally Doman and Delecato's approach was aimed at profoundly handicapped children, we find examples of applications encouraging poor readers to indulge in crawling activities. At least one method of therapy was designed specifically for the cerebral palsied population (i.e., Bobath, 1967; Bobath & Bobath, 1984) and it is only recently that it has been tried on Down Syndrome and other mentally retarded children.

What separates the various therapies most clearly one from the other is the theoretical rationale. These range from bizarre to plausible, and from clearly explicated to loosely "eclectic." Of those that are clearly explicated most have been shown to be untenable (e.g., Ayres, 1972b; Delecato, 1964). Other postulate change which is not yet measurable. Until we develop techniques which enable us to measure neurological change directly we will be unable to test notions about what interventions are actually achieving. However, it is important not to be distracted by the theoretical backgrounds of the various therapies. In the ultimate analysis it is behavioral outcome that matters, and if a particular approach can be shown to be effective then we may begin to concern ourselves with what exactly is happening.

Finally, I wish to draw attention to a characteristic which differentiates one therapy from all the others. For a variety of reasons it has been our wont to treat the handicapped child differently from normal children with respect to overall development. The handicapped child is often treated as a composite of motor, speech, emotional, and educational problems, each requiring separate intervention from an army of therapists, psychologists, and teachers. Though all are well intentioned, this approach can have unfortunate consequences in that it produces an adult-oriented and often confused child. One approach avoids these arbitrary distinctions. Called Conductive Education and developed in Hungary by Peto (1955), it is an educational approach which starts from the position that the various strands of a child's development are inseparable and that motor problems, like all other problems, are basically problems of learning. Within the motor domain, emphasis is on helping the child to achieve voluntary control over his own impaired neuromotor machinery with only the minimum of physical assistance from the "conductor" (a highly trained teacher-therapist). Obviously influenced by the Russian literature on motor and language development (e.g., Bernstein, 1967; Luria, 1961; Vygotsky, 1962) the regulation of movement by speech is a fundamental component of the system. Several descriptions of this approach exist (e.g., Cotton, 1975; Hari & Tillemans, 1984) but sadly it still lacks proper evaluation.

## Efficacy of Approaches

Turning now to the empirical work on the efficacy of intervention, it will be assumed that readers are aware of the enormous methodological problems which are encountered by any worker in the field. These have been discussed in detail elsewhere (Stedman, 1977; Bricker & Sheehan, 1981). Without implying lack of competence it might be useful to note that the therapy professions have only recently begun to ask questions about their own effectiveness and still rely heavily on "clinical" evidence. A recent volume on the management of motor disorders of children with cerebral palsy edited by Scrutton (1984) contains no more than a handful of references to evaluative studies, an unthinkable situation in a volume produced by psychologists on any other childhood disorder.

In view of the fact that physiotherapy is costly and time-consuming it is alarming that there are so few evaluative studies. In 1973, Wright and Nicholson reviewed the literature dating from 1940–71, finding only 16 papers which dealt with the efficacy of physiotherapy. Though some of these studies included adequate numbers of children, none had a control group. Wright and Nicholson

(1973) undertook their own evaluative study in which 47 children under 6 were studied over a period of up to a year. The children who received therapy were treated by the Bobath method. Comparisons between the treated and untreated children were made on both functional achievement (e.g., head control) and on the state of reflexes. No significant differences between groups were obtained. This study evoked strong reactions from committed professionals (see Letters, D.M.C.N., 1973). Though the failure to document frequency of treatment and the administration of other forms of therapy at the same time are legitimate criticisms of the Wright and Nicholson study, these authors are not alone in drawing the conclusion that variables other than therapy are responsible for any improvements observed (e.g., Scherzer, Mike, & Ilson, 1976).

More recently there have been one or two studies which have addressed more specific questions and which have reported findings which were slightly more positive. Harris (1981) investigated the effects of Bobath's neurodevelopmental therapy on a group of young Down syndrome infants. She found that the specific objectives she had set for the treatment group were achieved to a significantly higher degree than in the control group, but that there was no carry over to the activities measured on the Bayley (1969) or Peabody Scales. Harris notes the need for an instrument which is sensitive enough to measure the kinds of improvements she observed clinically in muscle tone and postural control and suggests that this might be one reason for the failure to demonstrate any generalizing effect of the intervention. However, another possibility that must be considered is that the gulf between the neurodevelopmental objectives and the actions contained in the Bayley Scales may be too wide. Programmes may need to combine functional objectives and neurodevelopmental objectives in a coherent and systematic way. In a recent statement on their approach Bobath and Bobath (1984) provide an interesting account of their realization that it was necessary to "program" the link between movement and function. Unfortunately the extent to which they themselves are now successful in so doing has not been demonstrated empirically.

With regard to the question of generalization there are two other studies of interest, both of which are sobering in their outcome. In 1975 Levitt reported an observational study in which she compared the performance of a group of children she treated as a physiotherapist in a clinical setting and in an adventure playground. Levitt observed that *only* skills which a child could perform competently indoors were those exhibited outdoors. No new skills were acquired and those which the child was barely able to perform were rarely seen. In the other study, Hogg (1981) taught three Down syndrome preschoolers a manipulative skill. Generalization to different types of material in the teaching setting was demonstrated but spontaneous generalization to a free play setting was slight. A fundamental question arises from these two studies and it concerns the extent to which skills must be taught to handicapped children before they become part of the day-to-day repertoire. In the normal child there is no noticeable hiatus between a child learning and "using" a skill—they are part of the same process. For the impaired child, however, there seems to be a "Catch 22" situation. Because skill learning is such a long and arduous process the handicapped child needs more "practice" than his normal peer, in both formal and informal settings. Yet, most caretakers bemoan the fact that handicapped children do not spontaneously play and do not appear to "practice" skills they are formally taught. One is reminded here of the importance that Bruner (1973) assigns to the role of play in skill acquisition. In the behaviour modification literature, the problems of transfer and generalization have received much attention (e.g., Stokes & Baer, 1977). Yet in the motor domain therapists have so far done little more than note the difficulty.

## The Timing of Intervention

There is a belief among therapists that the earlier a child can be treated the better. Kanda, Yuge, Yamori, Suzuki and Fukase (1984) present some evidence in support of this view. Eight children whose treatment began before 9 months of age were compared with 21 children who began between 9 months and 3 years. Although the children treated early were more severe cases, they began to walk 8 months earlier than the late treated group and walked more steadily with a more normal gait pattern. The treatment method used was that advocated by Vojta (1984). Cunningham (1979) also provides data on the question of timing but in his study, Down syndrome children who were in the delayed treatment group caught up with the early group.

A study which addresses a number of issues of both practical and theoretical interest is that of Jenkins and Sell (1984). The participants were 45 children, aged 3–15, all motorically delayed but ambulatory. The pupils were stratified according to their scores on comprehensive assessment instrument and randomly assigned to one of three conditions—therapy 1 day each week for 15 weeks, therapy 3 days per week for 15 weeks, and no therapy. The therapy provided combined Ayres' and Bobath and Bobath's approach. In general terms the treatment groups progressed significantly more than the control group on a measure of gross motor performance and marginally more on a measure of fine motor performance. A rating of postural control failed to detect effects attributable to therapy. There were no differences between the groups receiving therapy once per week or 3 times per week. Jenkins et al. then attempted to identify which children benefited most from therapy, finding that there was a tendency for the more delayed children to do better than the less delayed. When "overflow" effects of therapy into other domains was examined no significant findings emerged. Although small and short term, this is an exemplary study which asks the right sort of questions and presents the right kinds of analysis. As Jenkins and Sell themselves conclude, what they have done is provide good bases for replication and derivative studies.

*Examples of Other Approaches*

There are two other approaches to traditional methods of physiotherapy which have recently received considerable attention. Though both are aimed directly at the improvement of motor function, they differ radically from each other. The first, the use of biofeedback, has been tried and tested in other domains; the second, the use of vestibular stimulation, is relatively new. Biofeedback is not really universally appropriate at present but has been used when an intractable problem, such as poor head control, is blocking further progress. A brief description of the methodology might be helpful. In this procedure, the child's head is fitted with a kind of helmet which gives positive, immediate, and accurate information on the angle of tilt of the head. When the head is within a predetermined angle from the midline, feedback, such as music, is switched on. When the head is allowed to fall outside this angle information is given as to the kind of "error" committed. Impressive improvements in control have been reported during biofeedback sessions (Woolridge & Russell, 1976) but the extent to which changes during therapy transfer to daily life situations seems rather limited (Catanese & Sanford, 1984).

Though vestibular stimulation has been a component of the armoury of many physical and occupational therapists for some time, its use in isolation is a recent innovation. For example, it is one component of Ayres (1968, 1972) approach which initially was used with mildly handicapped children exhibiting a variety of learning difficulties. Used in isolation it has been administered to much more severely handicapped children, including non ambulatory cerebral-palsied and Down syndrome preschoolers. (e.g., Chee, Kreutzberg, & Clark, 1978; Kantner, Clark, Allen & Chase, 1976; Sellick & Over, 1980). Vestibular stimulation is achieved by spinning the child in such a way that the semi-circular canals which comprise the vestibular system are affected. First, the child is spun in the upright position, then lying on the side and so on. In controlled studies the speed and amount of rotation is equated across conditions. The spinning movement is always brought to an abrupt halt in order to induce post-rotatory nystagmus, the amount of which varies from one individual to another and as a result of treatment. The means whereby changes resulting from vestibular stimulation might induce changes in motor function is far from clear but substantial improvements have been claimed (e.g., Chee et al., 1978; Kantner et al., 1976).

In a study which was very similar in design to that of Chee et al. (1978), however, Sellick and Over (1980) found no evidence of effects. It is impossible to establish any clear basis for the discrepancy between these two sets of results but Sellick and Over (1980) make some suggestions. For example, they note that the tests they used were sensitive enough to measure improvement in the control as well as treatment group whereas those used by Chee et al. were not. They also point to the difficulty of producing matched pairs of children for assignment to experimental groups and note that Chee et al. do not provide information on their subjects in terms of age, type of motor impairment, and so on. In a review of the literature on this topic Ottenbacher (1982) cites several studies which report positive results (e.g., Ottenbacher, Short & Watson, 1981) and others a negative outcome (e.g., Rogos, 1977). The method is simple and requires little effort on the part of therapist or child. It would be advantageous to conclude that it works. Unfortunately, we must reserve judgement. Many of these studies are methodologically flawed and as Sellick and Over (1980) point out, none has explored the long-term effects of the approach.

The most optimistic interpretation of the data available so far on the efficacy of physiotherapy in its various forms is that it is equivocal. On balance there are probably more negative than positive findings. An optimist might be encouraged by the fact that many of the studies are methodologically flawed, thus, take the view that properly designed studies would yield more positive outcomes. The pessimist on the other hand is more likely to be influenced by the fact that theoretical foundations of these approaches are often unknown and/or unsound, and that no lasting effects have yet been demonstrated. Clearly there is need for more research on this topic.

*Intervention as Interaction*

To conclude this discussion we must consider the context in which most of these studies have been undertaken. Interactional models of development do not predict optimal amounts of change with the sorts of intervention we have dis cussed so far. It is important to analyse specific effects of intervention, but it is probably necessary to test these in the context of a broader program. Hanson (1982) includes four important aspects of an intervention program conceptualized within an interactional model:

1. provision of treatment and direct skill training to accelerate the rate of acquisition of developmental milestones, which may result in a modification of parent expectations and thereby offer a more hopeful prognosis;
2. facilitation of the infant's active engagement with the environment which would serve to provide the child with increased learning opportunities and the caregiver with feedback about the infants capabilities;
3. assisting caregivers in coping and/or adjusting to the child's atypical behavior or special needs through direct training or counselling; and,
4. aiding parents in working with the myriad of agencies they have to interact with.

Taking Hanson's perspective, the outcomes of intervention must be recorded in ever increasing generality. Bricker, Bailey, and Bruder, (1984) suggest including child changes, changes in reciprocal interactions between caregiver and child, and changes in societal values. Bricker, et al. (1984) present a comprehensive review of studies which have attempted to take a broader perspective on intervention, reporting both positive (e.g., Hayden & Haring, 1976) and negative findings (Piper & Pless, 1980). Despite inconsistencies, studies of generalisability lead us to a better understanding of what can reasonably be expected given our present knowledge of handicapping conditions. In addition to the practical implications they also provide us with a means of studying the complex interactions between a handicapped child and his caretakers. However, from the point of view of those involved with children with motor impairment, a word of caution must be added. One can mount a cogent argument in favour of concentrating on cognitive and social competence but it should always be recognized that vital components of these depend upon motor competence.

## ACKNOWLEDGEMENTS

The work for these chapters was partially supported by a generous endowment from the Spastics Society of Britain to the Institute of Education. I am grateful to Philip Bairstow, Jack Keogh, David Sugden and in particular Pam Smith for their constructive criticism of earlier drafts of the manuscript. Without the patience, encouragement and helpful comments of Leslie Henderson and Barbara Keogh, completion of this lengthy statement would have been impossible. Thanks to Doreen Ward for typing the manuscripts.

## REFERENCES

André T., & de Ajuriaguerra, J. (1949). *Etude semiologique due tonus musculaire*. Paris: Editions Medicales Flammarion.

Alberman, E. (1984). Describing the cerebral palsies: Methods of Classifying and Counting. In F. Stanley & E. Alberman (Eds.), *The epidemiology of the cerebral palsies*. Oxford: S.I.M.P. with Blackwell Scientific Publications Ltd. Philadelphia: J. B. Lippincott Co.

Ayres, A. J. (1968). *Sensory integrative processes and neuropsychological learning disabilities*. In J. Hellmuth (Ed.) Learning Disorders, Vol. 3. Seattle: Special Child Publications.

Ayres, A. J. (1972a). *Southern California sensory integration tests*. Los Angeles: Western Psychological Services.

Ayres, A. J. (1972)b. *Sensory integration and learning disorders*. Los Angeles: Western Psychological Services.

Bax, M. C. O. (1964). Terminology and classification of cerebral palsy. *Developmental Medicine and Child Neurology, 6*, 295–307.

Bayley, N. (1935). The development of motor abilities during the first three years. *Monograph for the Society for Research in Child Development, 1*, 1–26.

Bayley, N. (1969). *Bayley scales of infant development*. New York: Psychological Corporation.

Berger, M. (1977). Psychological testing. In M. Rutter & L. Hersov (Eds.), *Child psychiatry: Modern Approaches*. Oxford: Blackwell Scientific.

Bernstein, N. A. (1967). The co-ordination of movements. Oxford: Pergamon Press.

Bobath, B. (1967). The very early treatment of cerebral palsy. *Developmental Medicine and Child Neurology, 9*, 373–390.

Bobath, K., & Bobath, B. (1984). The neuro-developmental treatment. In D. Scrutton (Ed.), *Management of the motor disorders of children with cerebral palsy. Clinics in developmental medicine No. 90*. London: S.I.M.P. with Blackwell. Philadelphia: Lippincott.

Brazelton, T. B. (1973). *Neonatal behavioural scale. Clinics in developmental medicine No. 50*. London: S.I.M.P. with Heinemann. Philadelphia: Lipincott.

Brazelton, T. B. (1984). *Neonatal behavioural assessment scale. Clinics in developmental medicine No. 88*. London: S.I.M.P. with Blackwell. Philadelphia: Lipincott.

Bricker, D., Bailey, E., & Bruder, M. B. (1984). The efficacy of early intervention and the handicapped infant: A wise or wasted resource. In M. Wolraich & D. K. Routh (Eds.) *Advances in developmental and behavioral pediatrics. Vol. 5*. Greenwich, CT: JAI Press.

Bricker, D., & Sheehan, R. (1981). Effectiveness of an early intervention program as indexed by child change. *Journal of the Division of Early Childhood, 4,* 11–27.

Bruininks, R. H. (1978). *Bruininks–Oseretsky test of motor proficiency.* Minnesota: American Guidance Service.

Bruner, J. S. (1974). Nature and uses of immaturity. In K. Connolly & J. S. Bruner, (Eds.), *The growth of competence.* London: Academic Press.

Capute, A. J., Palmer, F. B., Shapiro, B. K., Wachtel, R. C., Ross, A., & Accardo, P. J. (1984). Primitive reflex profile: A quantitation of primitive reflexes in infancy. *Developmental Medicine and Child Neurology, 26,* 375–383.

Catanese, A. A., & Sanford, D. A. (1984). Head-position training through biofeedback—Proschetic or cure? *Developmental Medicine and Child Neurology, 26,* 369–374.

Cattell, P. (1940). *The measurement of intelligence of infants and young children.* New York: Psychological Corporation.

Chee, F. K. W., Kreutzberg, J. R., & Clark, D. L. (1978). Semi-circular canal stimulation in cerebral palsied children. *Physical Therapy, 58,* 1071–1075.

Connolly, K. J. (1984). The assessment of motor performance in children. In J. Brozek & B. Schurch. (Eds.), *Malnutrition and behaviour. Critical assessment of key issues.* Lausanne, Switzerland: Nestle Foundation.

Cotton, E. (1965). The institute for movement therapy and school for conductors, Budespest, Hungary. *Development Medicine and Child Neurology, 17,* 437–446.

Cotton, E. (1970). Integration of treatment and education in cerebral palsy. *Physiotherapy, 56,* 143–147.

Cotton, E. (1975). *Conductive education and cerebral palsy.* London: The Spastics Society.

Cratty, B. K. (1981). Sensory-motor and perceptual-motor theories and practices: An overview and evaluation. In R. D. Walk & H. L. Pick (Eds.), *Intersensory perception and sensory integration.* New York: Plenum Press.

Cunningham, C. C. (1979). *Aspects of early development in Down's syndrome infants.* Unpublished doctoral dissertation University of Manchester, England.

Davis, W. E. (1984). Motor ability assessment of populations with handicapping conditions: Challenging Basic Assumptions. *Adapted Physical Activity Quarterly, 1,* 125–140.

Delecato, C. H. (1964). *The diagnosis and treatment of speech and reading problems.* Springfield, IL: Charles C. Thomas.

Doman, G. (1974). *What to do about your brain-injured child.* London: Cape.

Dubowitz, L., & Dubowitz, V. (1981). *The neurological assessment of the preterm and fullterm newborn infant. Clinics in developmental medicine.* London: S.I.M.P. with Heinemann. Philadelphia: Lippincott.

Fiorentino, M. R. (1973). *Reflex testing methods for evaluating C.N.S. development (2nd Ed). Springfield, IL: C. C. Thomas.*

Frankenburg, W. K., & Dodds, J. B. (1967). The Denver developmental screening test. *Journal of Pediatrics, 71,* 181–191.

Freud, S. (1897). Infantile cerebrallahunnung Nothnagel's specielle Pathologie und Therapie, 9, Vol. 12. Vienna: A. Holder.

Frostig, M. (1963). *Developmental test of visual perception.* Palo Alto, CA: Consulting Psychologists' Press.

Gallahue, D. L. (1982). *Understanding motor development in children.* New York: Wiley.

Gaussen, T. (1984). Developmental milestones or conceptual millstones? Some practical and theoretical limitations in infant assessment procedures. *Child: Care, Health and Development, 10,* 99–115.

Gaussen, T., & Stratton, P. (1985). Beyond the milestone model: A systems framework for alternative infant assessment procedures. *Child: Care, Health and Development, 11,* 131–150.

Gerken, K. C. (1983). Assessment of pre-school children with severe handicaps. In K. D. Paget & B. A. Bracken (Eds.), *The psychoeducational assessment of preschool children.* New York: Grune & Stratton.

Gesell, A., & Armatruda, C. S. (1941). *Developmental diagnosis*. New York: Harper.

Graham, F. K. (1956). Behavioural differences between normal and traumatised newborns 1. The test procedures. *Psychological Monographs, 70*, 17–23.

Griffiths, R. (1954). *The abilities of babies*. London: University of London Press.

Hanson, M. J. (1982). Issues in designing intervention approaches from developmental theory and research. In D. B. Bricker (Ed.), *Intervention with at-risk and handicapped infants: From research to application*. Baltimore: University Park Press.

Hari, M., & Tillemans, T. (1984). Conductive education. In D. Scrutton (Ed.), *Management of the motor disorders of children with cerebral palsy. Clinics in developmental medicine No. 90* London: S.I.M.P. with Blackwell. Philadelphia: Lippincott.

Harris, S. R. (1981). Effects of neurodevelopmental therapy on improving motor performance in Down syndrome infants. *Developmental Medicine and Child Neurology, 23*, 477–483.

Hayden, A., & Haring, N. (1976). Early intervention for high risk infants and young children: Programs for Down's syndrome children. In T. D. Ijossem (Ed.), *Intervention strategies for high risk infants and young children*. Baltimore, MD: University Park Press.

Hogg, J. (1981). Learning, using and generalising manipulative skills in a preschool classroom by non-handicapped and Down syndrome children. *Educational Psychology, 1*, 319–339.

Hogg, J., & Mittler, P. J. (1983). Aspects of competence in mentally handicapped people. In J. Hogg & P. J. Mittler (Eds.), *Advances in mental handicap research*. London: J. M. Wiley & Sons Ltd.

Holt, K. S. (1966). Facts and fallacies about neuromuscular function in cerebral palsy as revealed by electromyography. *Developmental Medicine and Child Neurology, 8*, 255–268.

Horton, M., & McGuiness, J. (1975). Movement notations and the recording of normal and abnormal movements. In K. S. Holt (Ed.), *Movement and child development. Clinics in developmental medicine, No. 55*. London: S.I.M.P. with Heinemann. Philadelphia: Lippincott.

Jenkins, J. R., & Sells, C. J. (1984). Physical and occupational therapy: Effects related to treatment, frequency, and motor delay. *Journal of Learning Disabilities, 17*, 89–95.

Johnson, N. M. (1982). Assessment paradigms and atypical infants: An interventionist's perspective. In D. D. Bricker (Ed.), *Intervention with at risk and handicapped infants. From research to application*. Baltimore: University Park Press.

Kalverboer, A. F. (1975). *A neuro-behavioural study in preschool children. Clinics in developmental medicine, 54*. London in S.I.M.P. with Heinemann. Philadelphia: Lippincott.

Kanda, T., Yuge, M., Yamori, Y., Suzuki, J., & Fukase, H. (1984). Early Physiotherapy and the treatment of spastic diplegia. *Developmental Medicine and Child Neurology, 26*, 438–444.

Kantner, R. M., Clark, D. L., Allen, L. C., & Chase, M. F. (1976). Effects of vestibular stimulation on nystagmus response and motor performance in the developmentally delayed infant. *Physical Therapy, 56*, 414–420.

Kavale, K., & Mattson, D. (1983). One jumped off the balance beam. *Meta-Analysis of Perceptual-Motor Training, 16*, 165–17?.

Keogh, B. K. (1978). Non cognitive aspects of learning disabilities: Another look at perceptual-motor approaches to assessment and remediation. In L. Oettinger (Ed.), *The psychologist, the school and the child with M.B.D./L.D.* New York: Grune & Stratton.

Kopp, C. P. (1979). Perspectives on infant motor system development. In M. Bornstein & W. Kessen (Eds.), *Psychological development from infancy*. Hillsdale, NJ: Erlbaum.

Levitt, S. (1975). A study of gross motor skills of cerebral palsied children in an adventure playground for handicapped children, Child: Care, Health and Development *1*, 29–43.

Little, W. J. (1862). On the incidence of abnormal parturition, difficult labour, premature birth and asphyxia neonatorum on the mental and physical condition of the child, especially in relation to deformities. *Transactions of the Obstetrical Society of London, 3*, 293–344.

Lough, S., Wing, A. M., Fraser, C., & Jenner, J. R. (1984). Measurement of recovery of function in the hemiparetic upper limb following stroke: A preliminary report. *Human Movement Science, 3*, 247–257.

Luria, A. R. (1961). *The role of speech in the regulation of normal and abnormal behaviour.* Oxford: Pergamon Press.

McCarthy, D. (1972). *McCarthy scales of children's abilities.* New York: The Psychological Corporation.

McClenaghan, B. A., & Gallahue, D. C. (1978). *Fundamental movement. A developmental and remedial approach.* Philadelphia: W. B. Saunders.

Milani-Comparetti, A., & Gidoni, E. (1967a). Pattern analysis of motor development and its disorders. *Developmental Medicine and Child Neurology, 9,* 625–630.

Milani-Comparetti, A., & Gidoni, E. (1967b). Routine developmental examination in normal and retarded children. *Developmental Medicine and Child Neurology, 9,* 631–638.

Neuhauser, G. (1975). Methods of assessing and recording motor skills and movement patterns. *Developmental Medicine and Child Neurology, 17,* 369–386.

Ottenbacher, K. (1982). Developmental implications of clinically applied vestibular stimulation. *A Review in Physical Therapy, 63,* 338–342.

Ottenbacher, K., Short, M. A., & Watson, P. J. (1981). The effect of a controlled program of clinically applied vestibular stimulation on the neuromotor development of children with severe developmental delay. *Physical and Occupational Therapy in Pediatrics, 1,* 1–11.

Paget, K. D., & Bracken, B. A. (1983). *The psycho-educational assessment of preschool children.* New York: Grune and Stratton.

Paneth, N., & Kiely, J. (1984). The frequency of cerebral palsy: A review of population studies in industrialised nations since 1950. In F. Stanley & E. Alberman (Eds.), *The epidemiology of the cerebral palsies. Clinics in developmental medicine No. 87.* Oxford: S.I.M.P. with Blackwell Scientific Publication Ltd. Philadelphia: Lipincott.

Parmelee, A. H., Kopp, C. B., & Sigman, M. (1976). Selection of developmental assessment techniques for infants at risk. *Merrill Palmer Quarterly, 22,* 177–199.

Peto, A. (1955). Konduktiv mozgasterapia mint gyogypedagogia. *Gyogypedagogia, 1,* 15–21.

Piper, M., & Pless, I. (1980). Early intervention for infants with Down syndrome: A controlled trial. *Pediatrics, 65,* 463–468.

Prechtl, H., & Beintema, D. (1964). *The neurological examination of the fullterm newborn infant. Clinics in developmental medicine, 12.* London: S.I.M.P. with Heinemann, Philadelphia: Lippincott.

Prechtl, H. (1977). *The neurological examination of the fullterm newborn infant (2nd edition) Clinics in developmental medicine, 63.* London: S.I.M.P. with Heinemann Medical; Philadelphia: Lippincott.

Reynell, J. (1970). Children with physical handicaps. In P. J. Mittler (Ed.), *The psychological assessment of mental and physical handicaps.* London: Tavistock Publications with Methuen and Co. Ltd.

Roach, E. G., & Kephart, N. C. (1966). *The Purdue perceptual-motor survey.* Columbus, OH: Charles D. Merrill.

Robinson, C. C. (1982). Questions regarding the effects of neuromotor problems on sensorimotor development. In D. D. Bricker (Ed.), *Intervention with at-risk and handicapped infants. From research to application.* Baltimore: University Park Press.

Robinson, R. D. (1973). The frequency of other handicaps in children with cerebral palsy. *Developmental Medicine and Child Neurology, 15,* 305–312.

Robson, P. (1983). *Motor screening.* Paper presented at Spastics Society Meeting on Screening Procedures in Child Health Clinics. Cambridge, England.

Rogos, R. (1977). *Clinically applied vestibular stimulation and motor performance in children with cerebral palsy.* Unpublished thesis, Ohio State University.

Rutter, M. (1977). Classification. In M. Rutter & L. Hersov (Eds.), *Child psychiatry: Modern approaches.* Oxford: Blackwell Scientific.

Rutter, M. (1978). Brain damage syndromes in childhood: Concepts and findings. In S. Chess & A. Thomas (Eds.), *Annual Progress—Child Psychiatry and Child Development.*

Rutter, M., Graham, P., & Yule, W. (1970). A neuropsychiatric study in childhood. *Clinics in developmental medicine No. 35–36*. London S.I.M.P. with Heinemann. Philadelphia: Lipincott.

Rutter, M., & Yule, W. (1977). Reading difficulties. In M. Rutter & L. Hersov. *Child psychiatry: Modern approaches*. London: Blackwell Scientific.

Scherzer, A. L., Mike, V., & Ilson, J. (1976). Physical therapy as a determinant of change in cerebral palsied infants. *Pediatrics, 58*, 47–52.

Scrutton, D. (Ed.). (1984). *Management of the motor disorders of children with cerebral palsy. Clinics in developmental medicine, No. 90*. London: S.I.M.P. with Blackwell; Philadelphia: Lippincott.

Sellick, K. J., & Over, R. (1980). Effects of vestibular stimulation on motor development of cerebral palsied children. *Developmental Medicine and Child Neurology, 22*, 476–483.

Stedman, D. (1977). Important considerations in the review and evaluation of educational intervention programs. In P. Mittler (Ed) Research to Practice in Mental Retardation. Vol. 1. Care and Intervention. Baltimore, MD: University Park Press.

Stokes, T. F., & Baer, D. M. (1977). An implicit technology of generalisation. *Journal of Applied Behaviour Analysis, 10*, 349–367.

Touwen, B. C. L. (1976). Neurological Development in Infancy. Clinics in Developmental Medicine, No. 58. London S.I.M.P. with Heinemann; Philadelphia: Lippincott.

Touwen, B. C. L., & Kalverboer, A. F. (1973). Neurologic and behavioral assessment of children with "minimal brain dysfunction." In S. Walzer & P. Wolff (Eds.), *Minimal cerebral dysfunction in children:* Seminars in psychiatry. New York and London: Grune and Stratton.

Touwen, B. C. L. (1979). *Examination of the child with minor neurological dysfunction*. Clinics in developmental medicine No. 71. London: S.I.M.P. with Heinemann; Philadelphia: Lippincott.

Vojta, V. (1984). The basic elements of treatment according to Vojta. In D. Scrutton (Ed.), *Management of the motor disorders of children with cerebral palsy. Clinics in developmental medicine No. 10*. London: S.I.M.P. with Blackwell. Philadelphia: Lippincott.

Vygotsky, L. S. (1962). *Thought and language*. Cambridge, MA: M.I.T. Press.

Wade, M. G., & Davis, W. E. (1982). Motor skill development in young children: Current views on assessment and programming. In L. G. Katz (Ed.), *Current topics in early childhood education* (Vol. 4). Norwood, NJ: Ablex Publishing Co.

Weeks, Z. R. & Ewer-Jones, B. (1983). Assessment of Perceptual-motor and fine motor functioning in K. D. Paget and B. A. Bracken. (Eds.) *The Psychoeducational Assessment of Preschool children*. New York: Grune & Stratton.

Williams, H. G. (1983). Assessment of gross motor functioning. In K. D. Paget & B. A. Bracken (Eds.), *The psycho-educational assessment of pre-school children*. New York: Grune and Stratton.

Williams, H., & Breihan, S. (1979). *Motor control tasks for young children*. Unpublished paper, University of Toledo.

Woolridge, C. P., & Russell, G. (1976). Head position training with the cerebral palsied child: An application of biofeedback techniques. *Archives of Physical Rehabilitation, 57*, 407–414.

World Health Organization. (1980). *International classification of impairments, disabilities and Handicap*. Geneva: W.H.O.

Wright, T., & Nicholson, J. (1973). Physiotherapy for the spastic child: An evaluation. *Developmental Medicine and Child Neurology, 15*, 146–163.

Yang, R. K. (1979). Early Infant assessment: An overview. In J. D. Osofsky (Ed.), *Handbook of infant development*. New York: Wiley.

Yule, W. (1975). Psychological and medical concepts. In K. Wedell (Ed.), *Orientations in special education*. London: Wiley.

Zelazo, P. R. (1982). Alternative assessment procedures for handicapped infants and toddlers. In D. B. Bricker (Ed.), *Intervention with at risk and handicapped infants. From Research to application*. Baltimore: University Park Press.

# THE DEVELOPMENTALLY DELAYED CHILD WITHIN THE FAMILY CONTEXT

Pamela Winton

## INTRODUCTION

In the not so distant past it would have been unlikely for a book on the developmentally delayed child to have had a chapter devoted to the family. The inclusion of a family chapter as part of the *Advances in Special Education* series is a reflection of the current importance being placed upon understanding and intervening with families. While parents, particularly mothers, have been subjects of study and intervention in the past, the focus on the family as a whole is a relatively new phenomenon within the field. Unlike the intervention with exceptional children in which special educators have developed considerable expertise within clearly defined and empirically documented conceptual frameworks, in-

Advances in Special Education, Volume 5, pages 219–255.
Copyright © 1986 by JAI Press Inc.
ISBN: 0-89232-313-2

tervention with families is an area in which there are few theories and models to guide practice. In a sense we are like the blind men in the elephant analogy, grappling to understand a complex and multifaceted creature whose nature remains hidden unless the relationships among the various parts are understood. As we wrestle with this problem we have looked to other fields, such as sociology and psychiatry, which have traditionally examined family issues, asking different questions and using different research methodologies than those usually used by special educators. As with any shift in direction, there have been apprehensions and uncertainties as how to proceed. However, there are many potential benefits of assimilating knowledge about families developed over the years by other disciplines. The challenge for us now is to generate from theory working models which can guide intervention with families.

The purpose in this chapter is to bring together information which might further that goal. The first section will provide an historical overview of the attitudes toward and treatment of families of developmentally delayed children by special educators. This look at the changing trends in the way families have been approached provides a useful backdrop in understanding new directions. The second section will provide a description of certain concepts, drawn from several models and theories of family functioning, which are current influences on many special educators who deal with family issues. The final section will focus on unresolved and vexing problems inherent in making the translation from theories of family functioning to practical and workable intervention programs with families of developmentally delayed children.

## HISTORICAL OVERVIEW OF TREATMENT OF DEVELOPMENTALLY DELAYED CHILDREN WITHIN THE FAMILY CONTEXT

During this century there have been dramatic shifts in professionals' expectations of and attitudes toward families of developmentally delayed children. Institutionalization of children was a prevailing approach to treatment during the first half of this century. Physicians routinely made this recommendation to parents shortly after birth, based upon the belief that this was best for child and famiily. For families who did not institutionalize their child, there was little support available to help them provide care or education. The child who was moderately or severely delayed was most often excluded from public school. The child who was mildly delayed was likely to be considered a misfit or lazy. The major form of intervention offered to families was counseling, and a professional goal for parents was often "acceptance" of their child's handicap.

During the 1950s and 60s several factors combined to promote the home care of developmentally delayed children. One was theoretical support and research evidence demonstrating the importance of the environment in shaping developmental outcome. The work of Hebb (1949), Skinner (1953), Hunt (1961), Bloom (1964) and Deutsch and Brown (1964) contributed to the "super-environmentalism" notion which became the intellectual orientation of the time (Clarke & Clarke, 1976). Evidence that developmentally delayed children could learn if provided with a stimulating environment gave parent advocacy groups such as the National Association for Retarded Citizens the information they needed to demand publicly supported special education and community services for handicapped children and a greater voice for parents in decisions about the treatment of their children.

Another phenomenon during this period was the growing Civil Rights Movement. One of the outgrowths of this movement, in combination with "super-environmentalism," was the development of early intervention programs for the poor. Headstart, which was the largest of these programs, had goals which went beyond cognitive gains for children and included family and institutional change (MIDCO, 1972). Federal regulations (PL 89–794) required parent participation not only as a learner and teacher but also as a paid employee and decision-maker.

Two assumptions undergirded the emphasis placed upon parent involvement in Headstart. One was based upon the premise that lower-class parents were in need of remediation and corrective experiences (Gordon, 1970) so that their families could become part of the "mainstream of society" (Hunt, 1971). From this perspective parents were treated as "learners" with middle-class professionals deciding the content of what should be learned. The other assumption was based upon the premise that political and institutional barriers perpetuated poverty and the high risk status of low-income children. From this perspective parents needed opportunities to increase advocacy and decision-making power in order to bring about institutional change. These assumptions crept into early intervention programs for biologically handicapped children. The importance of parent involvement was underscored when reviews of early intervention program effectiveness suggested that parental involvement was associated with successful child outcomes (Bronfenbrenner, 1974).

Another trend in the 1960s, paralleling the growth of special education programs and early intervention for the disadvantaged, was the normalization/deinstitutionalization movement. This sudden shift in policy which replaced "the conventions of care" (Rhodes, 1977) from institutions to communities inspired a completely different focus on the treatment of and services for the handicapped. Essentially the responsibilities for care and education were back onto the parents' shoulders. In addition, families became major socialization agents, responsible for integrating the developmentally delayed child into the neighborhood and the community. Early intervention for this group, as an offshoot of this trend (Wiegerink & Posante, 1977) became an attempt to make these tasks easier for parents.

The culmination of the trend toward involving parents was the passage of PL 94–142 (The Education for All Handicapped Children Act of 1975), in which parents' new and expanded roles were clearly stated. An analysis of the policy assumptions underlying the law (Turnbull & Turnbull, 1982) suggested that parents were expected to function in two major roles: as educational decision-makers and as learners; the goal was to make them better teachers of their child. Within this framework, the primary beneficiary of the parents' involvement was presumed to be the child.

This brief overview of the evolution of the professional view of families of developmentally delayed children makes it clear that tremendous changes have taken place in a relatively short time . . . short enough so that one parent described herself as experiencing "jet lag" in an attempt to assimilate the changes (Avis, 1984). In contrast to the earlier approach of being told by professionals to institutionalize and forget about the handicapped child, beginning with the 1970s parents have been expected to acquire a myriad of skills in order to successfully enhance their child's development (Karnes & Teska, 1980). Many of these skills are educational.

In a sense, legislative and policy assumptions underlying parent involvement have promoted the idea of the parent as an assistant special educator. This approach to parents is in many respects in keeping with the traditions of the field. Special educators have traditionally focused upon enhancing child progress; therefore, the child-oriented focus to parent involvement is not unusual. Special educators have developed expertise in teacher training; therefore, extending training models for use with parents is not illogical. The sharing of educational decision-making with parents is less traditional, although later in this chapter it is suggested that shared decision-making has not become a reality. The point to be made here, however, is that the basic direction in which the field has moved in regard to families of developmentally delayed children can be seen as a logical extension of the expertise and traditions of the field interacting with political and social trends.

## Criticism of the Current Approach to Families

While the benefits of the changes described (e.g., early intervention programs and legislation explicating the rights of handicapped children and their families) are clear, questions have been raised about the implications of parent involvement policy, as represented by the provisions of the law, for families. A review of the available data by Turnbull and Winton (1984) on the extent and outcome of parent involvement in educational decision-making suggests a discrepancy between the intent of policy and actual practice. Instead of the active decision-making role suggested by policy, the research reviewed indicated that parents were more likely to play a passive role. Perhaps the most surprising findings were that parents were generally satisfied with their roles as planning team members, regardless of their level of involvement. This research suggests that not all parents may be interested in an active decision-making role.

Further, while numerous studies have demonstrated that parents can learn to become effective teachers of their young developmentally delayed child (see Bailey & Simeonsson, 1984, for a recent review), there are some data suggesting possible negative results from parents being involved in a teaching role. A series of studies carried out at the University of Washington (Kogan & Tyler, 1973; Kogan, Tyler, & Turner, 1974) indicated that involving mothers in conducting physical therapy with their young handicapped children was accompanied by a decrease in the warmth and affection they displayed toward their child. The preliminary results of a mother-child interaction study with a population of developmentally delayed children reported by Mash (1984) indicated that these mothers exhibited high levels of control during both play and task situations with their children. Since their controlling behavior did not appear to be organized around the behavior of their child, Mash speculated that the results reflected the adoption of a teaching role by the parents which spilled over into play situations. In a review by Wright, Granger, and Sameroff (1984), the caution was raised that the emphasis on parents as teachers may have drawbacks for both the child and the family. Problems mentioned included the parents' feeling judged and evaluated in their teaching role, becoming more controlling and directive in their interactions with their child, and generally working harder and playing less with their child. These are possible explanations for the high parent attrition rate in parent involvement programs found by Stile, Cole, and Garner (1979). The irony of this situation is that parents may already be feeling pressured to work with their delayed child.

A mother participating in an interview study by Winton and Turnbull (1981) shared her feelings about the differences she felt in her parental responsibilities toward her nonhandicapped son as compared to her handicapped son:

> You take a lot for granted and tend to take things easier when there's no problem, but I think you always are going to feel more pressure if your little one is handicapped . . . there's no way around it. When you get a little one that doesn't do anything until you're the catalyst, it almost becomes an obsession because you feel like he'll be sitting there, and you know that either you could sew or you could get him to learn his ''k'' sound. (p. 14)

This study suggested that many mothers desire a break from the task of teaching their developmentally delayed child. Rather than seeking training in how to teach their child, many mothers hope that experts can take over that job so that they can have time for playing and relaxing with their child. Another mother in the interview study made this comment in regard to her parent role:

> I work full-time. When I get home in the afternoon, I'm tired and I have to fix dinner. Sally has been in a situation all day where she's had someone telling her she has to work on this and that. I don't feel like she's ready for more education at night. I think it's time for fun and enjoying Mommy for awhile. (Winton, Turnbull, & Blacher, 1984, p. 6)

These quotes illustrate the multiplicity of roles that parents play, in addition to the education role most often emphasized by intervention programs.

One way of conceptualizing the family is as a social system with a set of roles for individual family members which ensure that various tasks are performed effectively (Goldenberg & Goldenberg, 1980; Rollins & Galligan, 1978). These tasks can be defined as the functions of the family system. As many as nine family functions, serving both individual and family needs, have been identified in the literature (Turnbull, Summers, & Brotherson, 1984). The recognition that education is only one of these nine family functions makes the exclusive focus on parents as teachers seem narrow. The interview data provided by Winton et al. (1984), in combination with reports of clinical observations and anecdotal experiences, force a careful consideration of the current assumptions about parent involvement (Doernberg, 1978; Foster, Berger, & McLean, 1981; Kaiser & Hayden, 1984; Turnbull & Turnbull, 1982). This is not to say that parent involvement has been proven to be a bad idea. It does say that certain prevailing assumptions regarding parent involvement (e.g., "more is better," "what is good for the child is good for the family," and "all parents desire and benefit from active teaching and decision-making roles") require reexamination. There is an increasing awareness of the need to individualize parent involvement opportunities in much the same way that special educators have individualized teaching approaches for developmentally delayed children.

*New Directions*

From the growing body of professional literature questioning the current policy focus on parent involvement, there have emerged a set of alternative assumptions which are redirecting thinking and shaping new directions. One assumption is that parenting a developmentally delayed child is a persistent and ever-changing source of stress which affects the entire family (Bernheimer, Young, & Winton, 1983; Korn, Chess, & Fernandez, 1978; Turnbull & Turnbull, 1982). Acceptance of this assumption has meant reinterpreting certain parent behaviors. For example, "shopping for a diagnosis" has been described in the literature as indicating inadequate parental acceptance of the child's handicap (Anderson, 1971). However, data reported by Bernheimer, Young, and Winton (1983) indicated that mothers of developmentally delayed children, as compared to mothers of Down syndrome children, were often not given a specific diagnosis for their child's problem. Consequently, these mothers were more likely to seek additional opinions, an activity which the authors concluded was logical given the absence of a clear-cut diagnosis. Another example is the challenge to the long-held notion that parents' reactions to a handicapped child can be explained as a series of phases, culminating in a final state of acceptance of their child's handicap. When the stresses associated with parenting a developmentally delayed child are seen as persistent and ever-changing, the reality of a parent reaching a static state of "acceptance" seems unlikely.

The second assumption, which is a logical extension of the first, is that intervention efforts with parents should be broader in focus. Instead of being exclusively child-oriented in terms of goals and outcomes, interventions should involve helping families cope with the stresses (unique to their own situation) associated with having a developmentally delayed family member. This assumption has been accompanied by new demands upon special educators. Expertise in working with children, developed over the years, becomes inadequate when faced with the task of understanding and developing programs for entire families. The notions of "family-focused interventions" and "persistent and ever-changing stress" have led special educators to look to other disciplines for models and conceptual frameworks to guide research and intervention. Family systems theories, developed primarily by psychiatrists (Minuchin, 1974), are now being incorporated and referenced in the special education literature. Models of family functioning and family adaptation (Hill, 1949; McCubbin & Patterson, 1983) which take into account change over time are being recognized for their contribution by special educators dealing with family issues.

Although momentum is still gathering for the idea of broadening the focus of research and intervention efforts with families, many of the ideas appeared in the educational literature 10 years ago. In the 1970s Bronfenbrenner (1976, 1977) described a model of human development in which he urged researchers to consider the ecological context within which an individual develops and which mediates an individual's behaviors. Bronfenbrenner conceptualized the individual as residing within a nested arrangement of structures, each contained within the next and each influencing the other in an interdependent fashion. His model included recognition of developmental transitions and life cycle events; and underscored the importance of examining the individual's definition of the phenomenon being studied. Both of these points are increasingly being described in the special education literature as fundamental to both research and interventions with families.

The next section of this chapter is devoted to a descripion of six concepts which are current influences on special educators attempting to develop family focused research studies and interventions. The concepts are organized in a typological arrangement not unlike Bronfenbrenner's (1976, 1977). In Bronfenbrenner's model, like most of the models of family functioning or adaptation adapted for use by special educators, functioning is conceptualized in terms of mutual interactions between internal and external variables. The modified model presented in Figure 1 includes the following three concepts in the first circle: interrelatedness of family members, family structure, and family life cycle. These are internal or intra-family variables considered to be important in assessing impact. The second circle consists of the immediate social environment, including formal (i.e., neighbors, friends) and formal (i.e., professionals) sup-

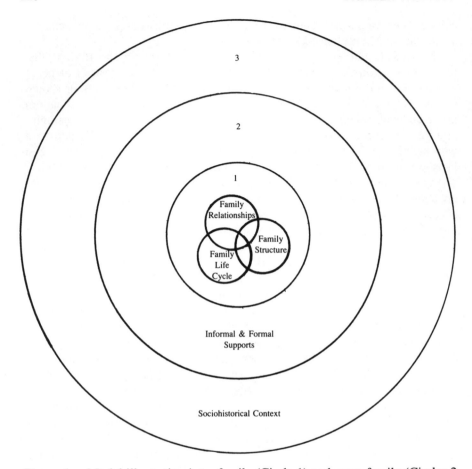

*Figure 1.* Model illustrating intra-family (Circle 1) and extra-family (Circles 2 & 3) variables important in assessing impact of developmentally delayed child on the family.

ports within the community. The third circle consists of the sociological, cultural, and political institutions which shape in a more general way the environment in which families reside. The second and third circles represent the external or extra-family variables influencing impact. Included in the discussion of each concept is a brief description of implications for intervention.

# CONCEPTS DRAWN FROM MODELS OF FAMILY FUNCTIONING

*Concepts Dealing with Internal Variables*

The internal or intra-family variables gaining attention as important factors having impact on families include some which have traditionally been studied by special educators; such as, SES level, religious affiliations, severity of child's handicap, and parent-child interaction. Others, such as family life cycle and perceptions of events, have only recently been considered by those assessing impact. The following three concepts as shown in Circle 1 in Figure 1 will be discussed in this section: the interrelatedness of family members, family structures, and the family life cycle.

*Interrelatedness of family members.* Using family systems theory (Minuchin, 1974) as a conceptual framework, special educators have begun to look at families as being composed of sub-systems which have reciprocal effects on one another (Stoneman & Brody, 1984; Turnbull et al., 1984). What affects one person in the family also affects the others. Change in any part of the system requires readjustment of the system as a whole and by individual family members.

The bulk of the research on "interrelatedness of family members" with a developmentally delayed child has focused on mother-child interaction. This area of research has received considerable attention, a compelling reason being the evidence that child abuse is disproportionate in the instance of developmentally delayed children (Frodi, 1981). Extensive reviews of the mother-child interaction literature are available elsewhere (Walters & Stinnett, 1971), but certain essential contributions should be noted here. One is Bell's (1968) reinterpretation of the "direction of effects," in which recognition was accorded to the important role that child characteristics play in the development of caregiver's attitudes and behaviors. This landmark article redirected and broadened the focus of much research, necessitating the development of more sophisticated methodologies for dealing with reciprocal rather than unidirectional interactions. In terms of developmentally delayed children, there has been increased attention paid to examining how various characteristics of delayed children (i.e., delayed social skills, impaired communication, limited mobility, and temperament) affect parent-child social interactions and the development of maternal attachment.

Another shift in the design of parent-child studies has been brought about by conceptual and empirical evidence calling for a broadening of research efforts beyond the mother-child dyad. The idea of reciprocity of influence has been enlarged to include the entire family system. There is evidence which demonstrates that conclusions drawn about the family as a whole from data from one individual or small segment of the family can be misleading. For instance, Gumz and Gubrium (1972) examined the concern of 50 parents of young mentally retarded children and found that mothers and fathers have different concerns. A more comprehensive study by Olson, McCubbin, Barnes, Larsen, Muxen, and Wilson (1983), conducted with 1000 families, identified a discrepancy between husbands, wives, and adolescent children in how they described their family. The authors concluded that "one should assume disagreement and a lack of congruence among family members rather than assume that one is dealing with an integrated and highly congruent group of individuals" (p. 235)

Other data have also demonstrated the importance of taking into account the interrelationships among family members. For example, Mash (1984) reported evidence indicating that mothers of young problem children appeared to be more stressed when fathers viewed the child in a negative light. Stoneman, Brody, and Abbott (1983) examined mother-father-child interactions in both dyadic (mother-child and father-child) and triadic (mother-father-child) family contexts. The observations of fathers in the triadic situation, in which mothers were also present, suggested that fathers were less involved and less interactive with their child than were mothers; however, the dyadic observations revealed few differences in mother-child and father-child interactions. The point was made by Stoneman and Brody (1984) that conclusions drawn from data collected in only one situation would have been misleading. The methodological difficulties of conducting research which takes into account the multiple interactions with families continue to challenge researchers. As Mash (1984) stated in regard to conceptualizing the family as an interactive system, "there is little doubt that our ability to conceptualize system complexity currently exceeds the measurement operations and research strategies we possess for studying it" (p. 68).

*Implications for intervention.* There are many gaps in our knowledge as we attempt to incorporate the concept of interrelatedness of family members into intervention efforts. For instance, what are the specific effects on fathers, siblings, and extended family members in cases where they are excluded from intervention? What type of direct intervention for them is most beneficial? While these questions cannot be answered from existing research, it is safe to say that we know enough to recognize the importance of being sensitive to the indirect effects on the family when engaging in typical intervention approaches focused only upon mother-child dyads. As noted by Doernberg (1978), based upon her clinical experiences, there may be more net losses than gains for the family when the mother's energies are disproportionately invested in the handicapped child.

In terms of siblings there are also many unanswered questions. Recent reviews of the literature (Gabel, McDowell, & Cerreto, 1983; Simeonsson & McHale, 1981; Simeonsson & Bailey, 1983; Skrtic, Summers, Brotherson, & Turnbull, 1984) have indicated that sibling reactions to a handicapped child in the family do not conform to a consistent pattern. Some siblings seem to have positive reactions, including increased feelings of family cohesiveness, more empathy for people with problems, greater understanding of problems faced by the handicapped, and more rewarding religious participation. Other siblings experience negative effects, including dealing with additional family financial strains, explaining the handicap to friends, having additional work responsibilities at home, and fearing that they may parent a handicapped child. A common theme in the recent reviews is the importance of conducting research and intervention efforts with siblings within a family context. Equally important is the need to individualize intervention with siblings according to numerous mediating variables (e.g., the sibling's existing role within the family). For instance, although Simeonsson and Bailey (1983) cite evidence that siblings can operate successfully as a teacher and tutor of handicapped children, they caution against an automatic adoption and promotion of this type of intervention activity without consideration of other factors, including siblings' preferences. Research indicating that some siblings already perceive themselves as having greater caretaking responsibilities than children whose siblings are nonhandicapped suggests that additional teaching responsibilities for siblings will not benefit all families.

The importance of including extended family members, such as grandparents, in intervention efforts also has received recent attention in the literature (Gabel & Kotsch, 1981; Gabel et al., 1983). Certainly there are sociological and demographic data to support the notion that grandparents may play a significant role in their adult children and grandchildren's lives. Hoffman & Manis (1978) reported that findings from a national sample of married couples indicated that contacts with relatives increase during the early stages of parenting (defined as being up to age 12 of the oldest child). Caplan (1978) reported that the modal family in urban America is still an extended one, in spite of popular discussion about the dissolution of extended family ties. Seventy to 80% of the older persons studied had personal contacts with at least one child within the previous week. Changes in the nature of the grandparent-grandchild relationship may have occurred over time, however. Neugarten (1976) reported that today's grandparents, who are likely to be more healthy and active than their counterparts in previous generations (Caplan, 1976), more often established an informal and playful relationship with their grandchild, emphasizing mutual satisfaction, as opposed to establishing themselves as formal authority figures. For grandparents who follow the "fun-seeking" pattern of grandparenting described by Neugarten, the disappointment of having a grandchild slow in developing social and play skills may be even more acute.

Exactly how grandparents react to a handicapped grandchild, how their reactions affect the nuclear family of the handicapped child, and what kinds of intervention might mediate impact are all unknowns. Figley (1983) has described a "secondary catastrophic stress reaction," meaning that being a member of a family and caring deeply about its members makes one emotionally vulnerable to the catastrophes which impact them. Gabel et al. (1983) suggested that grandparents may have strong, disruptive emotional reactions which diminish their capacity to be supportive to the child's parents. In some instances, as this quote indicates, grandparents may become an additional source of stress:

> I dreaded my mother-in-law's visits. Even though Lisa clearly had Down syndrome, her grandmother refused to believe anything was wrong. She constantly was asking if we had gotten another opinion, because she thought all of the previous doctors were wrong. She also continually asked if I were spending enough time with Lisa, as if this might be the cause of her problems. After a weekend of that, I was a wreck. (Winton, Turnbull, & Blacher, 1984, p. 38)

A study by McAndrews (1976) suggested that in many cases parents do perceive adverse changes in their relationships with grandparents following the birth of a physically handicapped child. Whether or not this change is temporary, and whether such changes occur following the birth of a normal child, are matters for speculation. However, there is enough information available to conclude that consideration of the needs, perceptions, and potential contributions, both negative and positive, of grandparents should be included in the design of intervention. Doing so increases the likelihood that a more complete picture of family needs will emerge.

There are some models or demonstration projects which have been heavily influenced by the concept of the interrelatedness of family members. For example, the Parent-Child Reciprocity Project at the Frank Porter Graham Child Development Center is based on research and clinical evidence documenting how the delay or absence of certain skills in young children may delay or prevent the development of reciprocity between mothers and delayed children. This intervention project with families, through a series of carefully edited videotapes of the child over time, attempts to demonstrate progress and change so subtle that it may not be readily apparent to parents. The overall goal of the project is to help families develop skill at "reading" cues elicited by their child and to recognize their child's developmental progress, progress which may be so slow by normal standards that it otherwise would not be evident. The project is ongoing and has yet to be evaluated, but is one example of how studies sensitive to the mutual and reciprocal affects of parent-child interaction have influenced intervention. A second example is the work of Foster and Berger (1979), who described two model demonstration programs for families of young handicapped children based on concepts from the work of Minuchin, Rosman, and Baker (1978) with psychosomatic problems. Using case histories to illustrate how theory has guided practice, Foster and Berger point out that in many instances the content of the tasks assigned to families did not change; however, the dyad selected to implement the task was altered. Intervention focused on family relationship patterns that were not considered to be adaptive. Other examples of intervention influenced by research related to family interactions are innovative medical practices (see Kaiser & Hayden, 1984, for a recent review) designed to facilitate early bonding in the case of high risk newborns and parents.

## Family Structure

Another way of looking at internal or intra-family variables that affect the impact of a developmentally delayed child on the family is to consider the concept of family structure. This conceptualization differs from "family structure" as used in the family therapy literature, but is one which has been adopted by some special educators. Summers, Brotherson, and Turnbull (in press) have defined family structure as consisting of the descriptive characteristics of the family that shape the way the family interacts with each other and with the world at large over time. They have looked at family structure as consisting of 3 major categories: *family membership characteristics,* including individual characteristics of family members and family size and type; *cultural style,* including socioeconomic status, ethnicity, religion, and geographic location; and *ideological style,* including beliefs, values, and coping styles. Rather than provide a complete review of the literature on structural variations and families of handicapped children (see Turnbull et al., 1984, for review), this section will highlight those findings that have particular relevance for intervention with families of young developmentally delayed children.

*Membership characteristics.* Membership characteristics include characteristics of individual family members and characteristics of the family as a whole. The majority of the research in this area has focused on the relationship between parent stress or parent attitudes and individual characteristics of the handicapped child, such as type and severity of handicap or temperament. Considering first the characteristics of the handicapped child, the conclusion that can be drawn from the research on type and severity of handicap is that impact on the family is mixed. A severely handicapped child is more likely to require extensive caretaking which has been shown to be associated with greater stress for parents (Beckman-Bell, 1980). However, mild handicaps may be harder to diagnose. Thus, families are more likely to have to search for a diagnosis, will be more uncertain about prognosis, may have a more difficult time knowing that services are appropriate for their child, and may have more difficulty getting their child accepted into programs for handicapped children (Bernheimer et al., 1983).

Holroyd and McArthur (1976) found that parents of autistic children experienced more stress than did parents of Down syndrome children. Because autistic children may appear normal at times, despite their frequent episodes of bizarre and disruptive behavior, and because of the history of confusion over the etiology of autism (see Bristol & Shopler, 1984, for review), it is possible that the ambiguity surrounding this disorder in part contributes to parent stress. In a discussion of chronic illness and family stress, Patterson and McCubbin (1983) concluded that ambiguity around cause of problem, prognosis, best treatment, long range plans for child's care, and expense outlay all contributed to the risk of family stress by increasing the chance for disagreements in how to best deal with the problem.

The assessment of temperament or behavioral characteristics such as social orientation, reactivity, and attention span is a recent method of describing handicapped young children and has been used as a way of documenting the characteristics of the child as they are perceived by parents. The increased interest in temperament has been generated in part by the longitudinal research of Thomas, Chess, and Birch (1968), who found that the three personality clusters of the "difficult," the "slow to warm up" and the "easy" child had predictive utility. These clusters have continued to be used by researchers. A study by Huntington and Simeonsson (1985) with developmentally delayed young children examined the correlation of child temperament scores with observational ratings of parent-child interaction. The results indicated that mothers of "easy" children received the highest mother-child ratings in terms of amount, quality, appropriateness, and general impression of interaction; the mothers of the "slow to warm up" children received the lowest ratings. The authors concluded that it may be the ambiguous behavior of the "slow to warm up" child that makes interactions difficult for parents (see also the chapter by Marcovitch and Nesker Simmons, this volume). Overall, this information suggests that a simple assessment of type and level of handicap may be inadequate for understanding the impact of the developmentally delayed child on the family. More subtle child characteristics, such as ambiguity surrounding cause, prognosis, and behaviors, as well as behavioral style may be salient for families and worthy of more attention from professionals.

Considering characteristics of the family, little attention has been paid to the relationship between family type and size and the family's reactions to a developmentally delayed child. Any discussion of type and size of family should emphasize the expanded possibilities for variation which exist in modern society. A large number of young children live in single-parent homes (Pearce & McAdoo, 1984), and many of these children may experience a reconstituted family if their primary caretaking parent remarries. The stresses associated with single parenting and blending families when remarriage takes place, combined with the stresses of parenting a handicapped child, have not been studied; however, research with single parent families suggest that certain problems may be exacerbated by the combination of a single parent and a handicapped child. As example, Hogan, Buehler, and Robinson (1983) found that some single-parent families had problems in estimating the future level of available resources because amount, sources, and control over resource use are not always certain.

Given the varieties of family types, it is important to define who constitutes a "family member" when conducting research and intervention. For example, Bristol (1983) found that in many single-parent families the father was involved in child care responsibilities, even though he was not a member of the household. In many black low-income families, males who recognize their paternity even though they may never marry their child's mother, often take on certain responsibilities for their child; in many cases, the responsibilities are shared by the father's entire kin network (Stack, 1975).

Another situation in which family membership may be unclear is in the case of "boundary ambiguity," a phenomenon described by Boss and Greenberg (1984) in which a family member's presence or absence in the household is not acknowledged in the family. For instance, family members may emotionally cut themselves off from an alcoholic family member who is physically present, or may continue to behave as though a deceased or absent family member is present. Chronic illnesses, which often are themselves ambiguous in their prognosis, will more likely result in "boundary ambiguity" than will predictable or treatable illnesses, according to Boss and Greenberg (1984). They made the point that the ultimate indicator of who is in and who is out of the family is based upon the family's perception of its structure. This information suggests the necessity of conducting a more careful assessment of family characteristics than that usually provided in standardized demographic data forms.

*Cultural style.*   Cultural style has been defined as the background or heritage that gives a family a sense of belonging or identity. It is usually described as containing four major components: ethnicity, religion, socioeconomic status and geographic location (Turnbull et al., 1983). The relationship of socioeconomic status and the presence of a developmentally delayed family member has received considerable attention, the research suggesting that SES levels may make a difference in impact of handicap on family. Farber (1960) described differences in the responses of low and middle SES families to the birth of a handicapped child, based upon an extensive survey of a large number of families. According to his analysis, lower SES families experienced the problems associated with the handicapped child in terms of actual caretaking and financial demands. Middle SES families experienced the impact of the handicapped child in terms of a "tragic crisis" in which their dreams and aspirations for their child's achievement and future were shattered. Marion (1981) has suggested that for middle-class families the birth of a handicapped child punctures the "American dream" of their child having a better life than they did. An interview study of 404 rural, poor families by Dunlap (1979) substantiated Farber's analysis of the responses of low SES families. The types of problems identified by families in his study had to do with physical and financial demands; their needs were for services, such as financial assistance, day care, babysitting, and homemaker services which would give the family relief. It is likely that lower income families may be less able than middle or upper SES families to alleviate the stress accompanying increased physical and time demands upon the family. Two strategies identified by Rollins and Galligan (1978) for reducing "role strain," the situation that exists when there is an escalation in the demands placed upon parents, are: role delegation (delegating jobs to others, such as hired employees); and, role integration (engaging in one activity which serves two functions, such as eating out with the family as a means of fulfilling physical and recreational needs). Clearly, having a young handicapped child may hinder a family's ability to use these strategies, but having limited financial resources in addition will further limit opportunities of this sort.

The question of direction of effects in terms of family SES and the impact of the handicapped child is one about which there is little information (Crnic, Friedrich, & Greenberg, 1983). The information that does exist suggests that the presence of a handicapped child may, in fact, affect SES levels. Watson and Midlarsky (1979) indicated the working mothers of retarded children were twice as likely as mothers of nonretarded children to work part-time rather than full-time. Finding appropriate day care or babysitters is a problem identifed by mothers of handicapped children (Dunlap, 1979; Watson & Midlarsky, 1979) which could affect a mother's ability to contribute to the family's income. Thus, the relationship between family SES and a handicapped family member may be reciprocal, not unidirectional.

Another variable which has been found by some researchers to influence family reaction to stress in general and to a handicapped child specifically is religion. In a nationwide survey of 1000 families, a predominant number of whom were Lutheran church members, Olson, McCubbin et al. (1983) identified "seeking spiritual support" as the most important coping strategy used by families. Olson and his associates hypothesized that this strategy may decrease social ambiguity by acting as a reference point for norms and expectations that guide the family in stressful situations. In early studies with handicapped populations (Farber, 1959; Zuk, Miller, Bantram, & Kling, 1961) it was found that Catholics tended to be more accepting than non-Catholics of a retarded child. It is interesting to note that recent studies (Briston & Schopler, 1984; Turnbull, Brotherson, & Summers, in press) have suggested that it is religious beliefs, as opposed to specific affiliations with religious institutions, which are important factors in coping with a handicapped child. This information is of importance because demographic forms are more likely to identify affiliations as opposed to beliefs. The latter may require interview or other more extensive assessment techniques.

*Ideological style.* Increasingly those interested in family issues have described the importance of broadening research methods so that a fuller understanding of parents' perceptions, values, and beliefs are taken into account. These can be defined under the more general heading of ideological style. One of the propositions in Bronfenbrenner's (1976) ecological model of human development was that a researcher must assess each participant's definition of the situation. He described this as the requirement for "phenomenological validity." Hetherington (1984) stated that "perceptions of behavior may be more important than the behavior itself" (p. 16), and went on to elaborate that "parents and children (should be) seen as feeling, interpreting, evaluating, remembering, anticipating individuals with histories, futures, belief systems, family myths, and values that shape their behavior and responses to stress" (p. 17). Olson et al. (1983) considered a family's perceptions of a problem to be important enough to include a measure of perceptual coping strategies in their study of family adaptation to stress. The two types of strategies that they identified were *passive appraisal* (the family's ability to define the stressor event as something that will "go away" or take care of itself) and *reframing* (the family's ability to identify selectively which events can be altered and which ones are beyond control, those being redefined in a way that makes them easier to live with).

A fairly unique approach to examining ideological style has been employed by Sameroff and his associates, as reported in a review article by Wright et al (1984). Sameroff et al. theorized that parents develop more or less complex theories of child development that reflect their ability to cope with child rearing and that parents with more sophisticated conceptions of development are able to deal more effectively with the problems presented by a handicapped child. A study by Granger cited in Wright et al. (1983) examined the relationship between maternal understanding of child development and stress in mothers of young handicapped children; the amount of social support was found to be an important intervening variable. The lack of a sophisticated understanding of child development was not a source of stress unless mothers were confronted with interventionists and support systems with conflicting (more sophisticated) beliefs.

*Implications for intervention.*    From this brief review, it is clear that differences among families in terms of the various components of the broader concept of family structure are associated with differences among families in terms of family needs. Families of more severely handicapped children may need help with physical caretaking demands and respite care. Families of mildly developmentally delayed children may need help in dealing with issues associated with the ambiguity of their child's handicap, such as, interpreting conflicting opinions on diagnosis, prognosis, and decisions about appropriate intervention programs. Lower SES families may require more physical and financial assistance, while middle class families may need more social/emotional support in dealing with shattered aspirations for their child. Existing evidence suggests that cultural factors may affect a family's definition and interpretation of intervention efforts. Shapiro (1983) described values held by Mexican-American families which were shown to interfere with the successful implementation of an intervention program; Stack's research (1975) indicating that low-income, urban black families may be distrustful of representatives of social agencies has relevance for interventionists. Interventionists must also consider that more subtle characteristics of families, such as their definition of ''family membership'' and their ideological style, may substantially affect their reactions to intervention. Taken as a whole, these findings suggest that various structural characteristics of families should be considered when designing family focused intervention. In addition, they point up limitations of relying exclusively on standardized family assessment measures. Information on many of the characteristics discussed in this section may depend on alternative assessment measures, such as interviews and observations. The difficulties in conducting accurate and in-depth family assessments will be discussed in the final section of this paper.

## Family Developmental Transitions

The third concept receiving considerable attention from special educators interested in family issues is the recognition that families, like individuals, go through developmental phases. These phases have been described in various ways (e.g., family passages, family developmental tasks, family life events or family transitions). For instance, Olson et al. (1983) applied the following seven broad stages to their study of family systems across the life cycle: couple, child bearing (families with preschoolers), school age, adolescence, post-parental, and aging. In contrast, Bronfenbrenner's (1976) ecological model of human development includes an extensive list of transition events such as bringing a new baby home from the hospital, getting a new teacher, losing a job, and so on, all of which entail change in the family system. In spite of the differences in how theorists describe family developmental stages, there appear to be certain central themes which are important when considering families of developmentally delayed children.

Developmental transitions disrupt established family routines and patterns, and this change from a familiar to an unknown state is accompanied by anxiety and a certain degree of stress (Haley, 1973; Hansen & Johnson, 1979). Even if the transition event appears to affect only one family member, the impact will reverberate throughout the entire family system (Bronfenbrenner, 1976; McCubbin & Patterson, 1983). It is through reorganization and the creation of new routines that the family returns to a state of relative stability. This adaptation can be thought of as requiring change *within* the family, that is, renegotiation of roles and functions to deal with modifications in level and type of demands placed upon individual family members; and, change *between* the family and external organizations, such as schools, hospitals, and job places. Boss and Greenberg (1984) described developmental transitions as particularly stressful to families because they often entail redefinition of family boundaries; members come (as in birth) or go (as in death) or the family adapts to external organizations whose representatives may develop significant relationships with the family.

As interest in family transitions has grown, researchers have begun to try to document the nature and content of different developmental stages and the processes by which families cope with transition events associated with each stage. In their nationwide survey Olson et al. (1983) identified specific stressors, resources, and coping strategies associated with families in each of seven stages of the family life cycle. An important finding that emerged from their study was that stressors and resources used by families varied by stage of the family life cycle. Of particular relevance to this chapter are the data suggesting that the major stressors identified by families with preschoolers related to financial, business, and intra-family strains (i.e., increases in the amount of "outside activities" in which children were involved and increases in the number of tasks which did not get done). Olson's data substantiated Rollins and Galligan's (1978) theoretical position that family roles accumulation (or number of activities expected to be performed by family members) is greatest when dependent children are in the home, a time when housekeeping, caregiving, and financial demands are high. According to Rollins and Galligan, when the accumulation of roles is too great, role strain ensues. The child-bearing families in Olson's study who appeared to experience low amounts of stress were those that had high levels of family accord and who felt good about financial management, family communication, and relationships with family and friends. It is conceivable that these characteristics enabled families to successfully engage in role integration and role delegation, two of the strategies identified by Rollins and Galligan as alleviating role strain. The ways in which families of young handicapped children differ from a general population of families in terms of coping strategies is not known. However, the literature indicates that families of handicapped children experience additional stressor events with which they must cope.

Transition events associated with family developmental phases have been described in terms of being either normative or expected (i.e., birth, adolescence), or nonnormative or unexpected (i.e., divorce, debilitating disease, or birth of a handicapped child) (Hetherington, 1984; McCubbin & Patterson, 1983; Neugarten, 1976; Wikler, 1981). The nonnormative events are considered to be stressful to families for a number of reasons. When expected life events occur, families can draw upon the wisdom of society for support and guidance in how to deal with the associated stress. As McCubbin and Figley (1983) stated, there is "comfort in sharing" and it is relatively easy to find others who are willing to share their experiences in coping with an adolescent or in dealing with the birth of a new baby. In the case of unexpected life events, there are no clear guidelines as to how to proceed for families or for their support systems. Using the specific example of birth of a handicapped child, friends of the family are often at a loss as to whether to express congratulations or condolences. In addition, because of the nature of the child's developmental delays, many normative transition events are "off schedule," and additional transitions associated with the delays add to the stress. Wikler (1981) identified 10 critical events for families of developmentally delayed children, some relating to "missed" developmental milestones and some relating to the disability itself. Turnbull et al. (1984) hypothesized 42 potential stressor events associated with Olson et al.'s (1983) seven phases of family development.

*Implications for intervention.* The concept of family development has overall significance for intervention in that it illustrates the dynamic and changing nature of family stresses, needs, and coping strategies. In terms of the family of a developmentally delayed young child, the following particular stressor events (Turnbull et al., 1984; Wikler, 1981), in addition to the stressors identified by Olson et al. (1983), are likely: (a) obtaining a diagnosis or additional diagnostic information about the child's condition; (b) informing siblings, extended family, and friends of child's condition; (c) making initial emotional adjustments to the child and to this information; (d) experiencing "missed" developmental milestones, such as child's walking and talking; (e) experiencing younger sibling surpassing developmentally delayed child in terms of skill development; (f) dealing with behavior and health problems related to child's delays; (g) dealing with a large number of health and educational specialists; (h) locating and deciding upon the most appropriate intervention programs.

Sensitivity on the part of interventionists to these potential events and how they might affect the family roles, family structures, family relationships and needs would broaden the focus of intervention considerably. Of particular relevance for interventionists might be the transition of the developmentally delayed child into and out of early intervention programs. Research by Klein and Ross (1958) suggests that families of normally developing young children experience certain anxieties about the kindergarten transition. They worry about their child's ability to adjust to the new situation, feel a sense of loss associated with their child's entering school, experience value conflicts (i.e., school values and home values differed), and experience tension in regard to the adjustment to sharing authority with their child's teacher. Other evidence suggests that families of developmentally delayed children may experience additional adjustment problems relating to the child's handicapping condition when the child moves from one program to another (Winton, Turnbull, & Blacher, 1984). Locating an appropriate program may in itself be stressful for several reasons. It is at the preschool level that many families are first confronted with the issue of mainstreaming. Trying to clarify their personal ideology in regard to mainstreaming as a prerequisite to deciding upon an intervention program may be stressful for some families. If parents do decide that a mainstreamed program would be best for their child, they are then confronted with the challenge of finding one. With the exception of Headstart, publicly supported mainstream preschool programs are limited. In most communities there is no central clearinghouse where parents can find out about mainstreamed programs (public or private) that are receptive to serving handicapped children. One mother made this comment about the search for a preschool program:

> I am aware of the tremendous struggles that families in this sophisticated and liberal community have in finding help for their impaired children. Often excellent programs exist, but parents and professionals are unaware of them. To a great extent this is because there is a lack of coordinated services, a lack of publicity about services that exist, and uncertain funding—a program may be here today and gone tomorrow. I am appalled by the lack of knowledge about programs that I see among professionals who counsel parents. To take our own example, even though our child was diagnosed soon after birth as (1) cerebral palsied, (2) retarded, (3) functionally blind, and (4) hydrocephalic, we were never directed by the follow-up clinic staff, the pediatrician, numerous psychologists, our ophthalmologist, or the neurosurgeon to any program that could help our son. (Winton, Turnbull, & Blacher, 1984)

Research by Becker, Bender, and Kawabe (1980) validated this mother's perceptions. Their data indicated that services are often available, but there is not an adequate communication system between professionals and agencies and parents. The outcome for families is that they often must engage in the search for an appropriate program on their own. If a child's diagnosis is unclear, then parents may have an even more difficult time deciding upon and locating an appropriate program. Bernheimer et al. (1983) concluded from their research with parents of young developmentally delayed children that the delayed child without a clear diagnosis, as compared to the child with Down syndrome, often does not have a "label" to match the categorical programs that exist. Furthermore, ambiguity surrounding the child's problem can mean that parents find themselves functioning in the role of seeking services without having the information necessary to know what kind of services they should be seeking.

In addition to the difficulties of deciding upon and locating an appropriate preschool program, families of developmentally delayed children may have other problems adjusting to the transition. Families who have children entering a specialized program serving only handicapped children may experience initial anxiety over seeing their child among a large number of handicapped children, especially if the handicaps represented differ from their own child's handicap (Winton, 1981). Families choosing a mainstreamed placement for their child may have anxieties about their child's acceptance by peers, their family's acceptance by other families, and the teacher's willingness and ability to deal with their child's special needs (Turnbull & Winton, 1984).

There are several ways that interventionists can help families as they undergo the transition into and out of programs. They can establish a clearinghouse with updated information on programs and services available within the community. In addition, professionals might establish a volunteer network of parents who have recently been through the decision-making process. Providing intervention services directly related to the process of deciding upon an educational placement is another avenue of help. For example, at the University of Kansas, Fowler and her associates have developed and are implementing a transition program for families of young handicapped children in which they assist families in identifying and evaluating program alternatives within the community, the goal being to help the family determine the best match to intervention program. This project has yet to be evaluated but offers promise as a model for how interventionists can assist during family transition events.

## Concepts Dealing with External Variables

The external variables generally considered to be important in assessing impact of the developmentally delayed child on the family can be divided into two components. One component includes the broader social environment of the family or what Bronfenbrenner (1976) called the "exosystem." It is shown by Circle 2 in Figure 1. This system is comprised of formal (i.e., schools, agencies, service providers) and informal (i.e., neighbors, friends) associations and resources which may provide support to families. The other component shown by Circle 3 in Figure 1 represents the cultural, political, and legal systems which shape in a more general way the environment in which families reside. This component has been labeled in various discussions as the "macrosystem"

(Bronfenbrenner, 1976), the "sociohistorical context" (Turnbull & Winton, 1984), or an "historical cohort effect" (Hetherington, 1983).

*Informal and formal supports.* Caplan (1976) defined support systems as "continuing social aggregates (namely, continuing interactions with another individual, a network, a group or an organization, that provides individuals with opportunities for feedback about themselves and for validation of their expectations about others, which may offset deficiencies in their communications within the larger community context)" (p. 19). According to Caplan, support systems may provide help in the following three ways: (a) by helping an individual mobilize his psychological resources and master his emotional burdens; (b) by sharing his tasks; and, (c) by providing him/her with extra supplies of money, tools, and guidance to improve handling of the situation. An important assumption underlying informal networks, according to Olson et al. (1983), is that they are reciprocal. In other words, individuals are more likely to ask for support if they know that they can provide help to someone else at a later date.

Families are most likely to call upon support networks during times of stress (Olson et al., 1983). Particularly helpful resources for dealing with stress are "sources of guidance" or help from others who have been through similar experiences (McCubbin & Figley, 1983). Not only can these persons share their experiences, but they might also function as role models if the stress involves a role transition. Suelzle and Keenan (1981) used the term "anticipatory socialization" to describe contact that allows identification with persons already functioning in the role into which a person is moving.

Because giving birth to a developmentally delayed child is not a normative stressor event, the traditional informal support networks may not be available for families. Friends, neighbors, and co-workers are not likely to have had relevant experiences with developmentally delayed children to share with families. They may be struggling themselves with how to relate to the child and unable to perform the identified support tasks of "validating the families' experiences," "sharing tasks," and "providing guidance." Anecdotal evidence suggests that families of developmentally delayed children often find themselves in the reverse role—rather than receiving support, they may be putting their friends at ease by explaining the handicap, reassuring them that their reactions are understandable, and basically trying to ease their anxiety. This can be difficult, if not impossible, for parents and families struggling with these issues themselves. Research corroborates the anecdotal evidence that families of developmentally delayed children may not feel support from the community. A study by McAndrew (1976) indicated that families found adverse changes in friendships after the birth of a physically handicapped child. Watson and Midlarsky (1979) found mothers of mentally retarded children were more likely than mothers of nonretarded children to believe that the average person had negative opinions about the mentally retarded.

The implication of this information is that families of delayed children may have difficulty in using both formal and informal resources to help deal with stress. In the general population Olson et al. (1983) found that families only turn to formal supports when informal resources are exhausted. Yet, the extent to which professionals and specialists who comprise the formal support network provide parents with relief from stress is unclear. Suelzle and Keenan (1981) noted a drawback to the use of formal support: it represents an unequal-status contact. There is little likelihood of engaging in a reciprocal or mutually helpful relationship: the family will always be on the receiving end of the support exchange. Anecdotal evidence has suggested that the formal support network is at times "uncoordinated, uninformed about the complete range of resources available and unable to supplement diagnosis with specific advice about parenting a retarded child" (Suelzle & Keenan, 1981, p. 268). On the other hand, there is evidence that parents who have participated in specific intervention programs have gained knowledge and skill. However, whether or not intervention programs have affected parental adjustment, enhanced coping skills, or alleviated stress is not known because measures of this type have rarely been used (Baker, 1984). In a review of 16 intervention studies focusing on families Bailey and Simeonsson (1983) found that measures of parent satisfaction were the closest approximation to any type of measure of coping or adjustment. While satisfaction is important, they noted, it requires a leap in inference to equate satisfaction with stress reduction.

A study by Granger, cited by Wright et al. (1984), suggested that the relationship between level of stress and level of support from intervention may be a complex one mediated by maternal understanding of child development. Social support provided by intervention programs primarily reduced anxiety for mothers with a sophisticated understanding of child development; in contrast, mothers with less sophisticated understandings expressed more anxiety as they experienced greater social support. The explanation offered for this finding was that social support provided the less sophisticated mother with alternative perspectives and new information which challenged her existing views and led to confusion and anxiety. In other words, there may be certain trade-offs between the advantages and disadvantages of social support for some mothers. While the complex nature of the interactions are unclear, studies of this kind demonstrate the importance of assessing a multitude of variables in deciding upon an appropriate intervention for families.

*Implications for intervention.* A theme that has been repeated throughout this chapter is the need for interventionists to take into account many aspects of a family's situation; this would include their perceptions of formal and informal support systems and resultant needs in those areas. In addition, intervention outreach efforts need to include the general population. Although Handicapped Awareness programs (Schnitzler & Rappaport, 1983) and materials (Simpson,

1983) have been developed and disseminated in certain localities to promote acceptance of handicapped individuals, families apparently perceive the need for greater efforts in this direction. The results of a survey by Suelzle and Keenan (1981) could be interpreted as suggesting that progress is being made in the general level of societal support to families. In their study of 330 families, divided into four stages of the life cycle according to age of handicapped child, they found that parents of younger children used more services and support networks and were more supportive of mainstreaming than were families of older children. Since families of children in the oldest group had not experienced the guarantees for services provided by PL 94–142 throughout their children's lives, one could assume the differences reflected improved services and greater community acceptance. However, these results could also be interpreted as a reflection of lower levels of support and services currently available for older, as compared to younger handicapped children, parental "burn-out," or increased awareness of their child's limitations. The cross-sectional design of the study makes interpretation difficult, but it does emphasize several points: parents' needs for support vary across the life cycle, and the availability of informal and formal support may vary according to the age of the child. These data also emphasize the importance of considering the impact of political and societal trends on families of developmentally delayed children.

## Sociohistorical Context

The historical overview at the beginning of this chapter provided a look at the families of developmentally delayed children within the context of the changing political and legal climate which culminated in the passage of PL 94–142. As pointed out in that section, the 1960s and 1970s were a time of increasing acceptance of cultural pluralism and of the rights of minorities to a place in society. The implementation of social programs and the passage of legislation reflective of these beliefs brought about significant changes for families. The benefits in terms of increased services and clearly stated rights were also accompanied by greater responsibilities and demands upon families. Overall, however, the events of that time period must be viewed as positive and promising. This mother's recount of what it was like before state and federal laws were passed guaranteeing education for handicapped children make that clear:

> [Parents spent] years running their own day care centers, begging for about-to-be-torn-down buildings from cities and counties, [holding] raffles and cake sales, [fighting] ever higher tuition costs, and [having] no transportation except car pools. This was the educational system for handicapped children of school age. Parents went through all of the hardships above, and more, and all for programs that were constantly running on a shoestring, about to go under, about to be evicted, and quite often not much more than a kind of group babysitting anyway. For many years this was considered good enough for children who were demonstrating daily that they did have the ability to learn. (Isbell, 1983, p. 76)

Less promising for the handicapped and other minorities are the political and societal directions being taken in this decade. Society, as reflected by the popularly elected administration, is less supportive of social programs. This attitude has been attributed partially to concern over ever-increasing federal budget deficits, but also seems to be part of a general shift in values and individual goals. The results of research contrasting the future goals of college students in 1970 with students in 1980 demonstrated this change. In 1970 goals related to contributing to a just society; in 1980 they related to achieving financial success. The lure of the so-called "Yuppie" (young, urban, professional) lifestyle, and the emphasis in popular publications on satisfying one's "own needs" suggests a lessening commitment to ideals conducive to providing opportunities for minorities. Thus far, threats to dismantle special education legislation and regulations have been met by strong opposition from parents and advocacy groups. The pressure on parents to maintain a vigilant and advocacy-oriented stance is one characteristic of the 1980s. To what extent the 1980s will actually bring about significant changes in level of services and support to the handicapped remains to be seen.

*Implications for practice.* Perhaps the greatest pressure during this decade, given the concerns over budget deficits and domestic budget cutting, will be on interventionists to document the cost effectiveness of services for families. On one hand, this calls for carefully designed studies with large samples and standardized measures. On the other hand, what has been emphasized in this chapter is the need to provide individualized services for families, an approach which does not lend itself to traditional research methodologies.

## Models of Family Functioning

The description of the array of internal and external variables related to family functioning covered in this section was useful in conveying the complexity of understanding the developmentally delayed child within the family context. However, what is lacking is an overriding framework for organizing the concepts so they can be put to practical use. If one accepts the premises presented earlier that parenting a developmentally delayed child is a source of persistent, ever-changing stress which affects the entire family, and that intervention efforts should focus on helping families cope with stress, then one must ask how to organize these variables for study. Are there models which predict family adaptation or coping and which can answer the questions of why some families are able to adapt successfully to crises and others are not? Of particular interest are instances in which family and stressor events appear similar, yet coping and adaptation are markedly different.

Models and theories (Farber, 1960; Hill, 1958; McCubbin & Patterson, 1983; Shapiro, 1983) have been developed or used to examine directly how families cope with the stresses associated with parenting chronically ill and developmentally delayed children. One such model is Hill's (1958) ABCX Model and McCubbin and Patterson's (1983) Double ABCX extension of Hill's model. In these models, a family's vulnerability to crisis depends on the interaction of the stressor event (A factor) with existing resources (B factor) and with family perception (C factor). McCubbin and Patterson extended the original model to include:

1. Pile-up (Aa), which they define as the multiple demands and hardships associated with the major stressor event. Pile-up includes: intra-family strains (i.e., increased caretaking, change in roles); overextension of time and energy in the family's efforts at coping; and, ambiguity around cause, prognosis, and best treatment.
2. Existing and new resources (bB), "the psychological, social, interpersonal and material characteristics of individual family members (e.g., ability to earn an income), of the family unit (e.g., flexibility, organization), and the community (e.g., medical services, support groups), which are used to meet family demands and needs" (Patterson & McCubbin, 1983, p. 29).
3. Coping strategies (BC), strategies which consist of a set of interactions *within* the family and transactions *between* the family and the community to manage stress.

These models have been used by special educators as a conceptual framework for describing research data on the impact of preschool mainstreaming on families (Winton, in press); and, as a framework for conducting research with families of autistic children (Bristol, 1984). Bristol's research is particularly significant in that she was able to demonstrate the effectiveness of the Double ABCX model in predicting healthy adaptation in families. Her results showed that family adaptation was more closely related to resources and beliefs than to the severity of the child's handicap. Bristol (1984) made the point that these results were encouraging to the extent that family resources and beliefs, as compared to severity of handicap, were more likely to be affected by carefully planned intervention. The next step for professionals is to generate a comprehensive family-focused intervention model.

# ISSUES IN TRANSLATING THEORIES AND MODELS TO PRACTICE

If one accepts that an ultimate goal for special educators is the development and implementation of improved services, then the translation from models to practice is an important one. However, there are certain issues which need to be addressed and resolved before the translation to practice can be realized fully.

## Issues Related to Assessment

As mentioned earlier in this chapter, a criticism of the current approach to parent involvement in intervention programs is that accurate and systematic assessments of family needs rarely occur. A central theme has been the importance of such assessment so that a family-focused intervention plan can be developed and implemented. Unfortunately, there are no agreed-upon methods or procedures for accurately assessing family needs. In fact, there is considerable controversy over the value of different methods which might be used.

*Self-report measures.* An increasing number of self-report measures yield information useful for family assessment (e.g., Maternal Social Support Index—Pascoe, Loda, Jeffries, & Earp, 1981; Parental Stress Index—Abidin, 1983; The Definition Scale—Bristol & Devellis, 1980). However, the value of self-report measures, in general, has been challenged on numerous grounds. Stoneman and Brody (1984) reviewed the data illustrating discrepancies between behaviors reported by family members and actual family interactions. They also pointed out that self-report measures often are developed without regard to psychometric precision. To complicate the matter further, even psychometrically adequate self-report measures have been criticized by those who argue that the gain in precision from using a standardized measure may be lost because the questions asked are irrelevant or limited (Glaser & Strass, 1967; Wilson, 1977). The questions and response choices in self-report measures are decided upon by researchers; respondents are not allowed to share their own unique perspectives. Critics, thus, argue that this approach may lead to selective data and lack of sensitivity to respondents' beliefs.

*Indepth interviews.* Another technique for gathering information useful in family assessment is the personal or focused interview. An example is the interview format advocated by Merton, Fiske, and Kendall (1946) and used by a number of authors (Denzin, 1970; Gorden, 1969; Selltiz, Jahoda, Deutsch, & Cook, 1965). In essence, the technique calls for the interviewer to identify in advance what specific aspects of an experience s(he) wishes to have the respondents cover; thus, certain types of information are required of all subjects. In addition, the interviewer employs an interview guide with a list of objectives and suggested questions in order to obtain this information. However, the interviewer has considerable latitude within the framework of the interview guide and may redefine the order of questioning to fit the characteristics of each interview situation.

This type of approach is derived from the phenomenological tradition, which emphasizes the importance of assessing an individual's definition of the event under study. This type of interview offers the following advantages over the standardized self-report measure: (a) information gained is shaped by what the respondents feel to be important and relevant issues rather than by categories provided by professionals; (b) the approach is more open to "unanticipated" perspectives unique to each family's situation; (c) respondents feel listened to and "valued" as persons whose perspectives are worth knowing. The approach is not without disadvantages, which include: (a) respondents may misinterpret questions unless care is taken in using language and symbols familiar to respondent; (b) respondents may give either socially desirable responses or may not be motivated to give relevant information; (c) interviewers may bias what respondents say; (d) large amounts of qualitative information are difficult to transform into discrete units for analysis and for practical use. Guidelines, strategies and techniques for dealing with the first three disadvantages are provided in several sources (Barber, 1973; Gorden, 1969; Hyman, 1954; Phillips, 1971; Selltiz et al., 1965). The fourth item, having to do with data management and analysis, is one for which there are few clearcut guidelines. Winton and Turnbull (1981) developed procedures for coding focused interviews for research purposes, but procedures for using the focused interview as a needs assessment device are generally not available.

*Direct observations.* A third means of gathering family assessment information is observation of the interactions of family members. The rationale behind this approach is that it provides the most direct method for identifying patterns of interaction, including those in need of change or reinforcement. As mentioned earlier in this chapter, research interest in observational study of parent-child interactions has been high, and attempts are being made by many researchers to include a larger number of family members. Several observational coding schemes have been developed (Bakeman & Brown, 1977; Farran, Kasari, & Jay, 1983; Kogan & Tyler, 1973) which have potential application for development of intervention strategies. This approach, however, like the others described, is not without drawbacks. The assumption that parent-child observations, even if conducted over time, accurately provide significant information about the parent-child relationship must be questioned. Mash (1984) demonstrated that family members' regulated their behavior while being observed, thus distorting data. An important mitigating variable in collecting observational data is the context in which the observations are being made. What behaviors, which family members, and where to observe are all factors which must be considered. The approach is also time-consuming, expensive, and possibly intrusive for family members, especially if done in the home. The effect of being observed on different families and individuals within families is another unknown which is likely to affect results.

The disadvantages and advantages of each of the three strategies described clearly point out the need for multi-method family assessment approaches. Yet even a broadened approach raises questions. What combination of measures should be used? What range of variables should be included? To what extent will intervention be able to respond adequately to broadly defined needs? The family-focused intervention programs mentioned thus far in the chapter, that is, the transition programs (Fowler & associates), the life planning programs (Turnbull & associates), and structural family intervention programs (Foster & Berger) have each focused on one particular aspect of a family's needs (life planning, transitions) or on one particular theoretical framework pertaining to a single aspect of family functioning (Minuchin's definition of family structure). It is clearly more expedient to limit assessment to those areas of need in which interventionists feel they have existing expertise and resources to help families.

It is possible that a broader model of family functioning, such as Hill's ABCX Crisis Model (1959), may provide a framework for assessing families which would allow families to define a wide range of stressor events or needs. Such information might be the basis for a broad-based intervention effort, using different approaches and strategies to meet different needs. The relationship between needs assessment and evaluation makes this an important question for interventionists and leads to the next issue in this discussion—how to translate information from needs assessment measures into clearly stated and agreed-upon goals which can then be evaluated.

## Issues Related to Setting and Evaluating Goals

The idea of an "individualized family plan" or set of family-focused goals (Karnes & Zehrbach, 1975; Turnbull & Turnbull, 1982) is one that makes good sense. However, the absence of a tried and accepted model for putting the family plan idea into practice leads to a number of unresolved issues. A basic question is: Who should determine family goals and means of implementation . . . family? professionals? a collaboration between the two? Research by Cadman, Goldsmith, and Bashim (1984) indicated that parents and professionals have different opinions and priorities about goals for the handicapped child. This information suggests that parents and professionals may sometimes be working toward different ends. Bailey and Simeonsson (1984) made the point that whenever professionals set goals for children or for families they make certain judgments about what is "right" or "best" for those individuals. Such value judgments are often without empirical base. For example, a family may feel that their child is better off at home than in a center-based intervention program. Professionals may feel that the child would benefit more from the services available at the intervention program. Should enrollment in intervention be a priority goal for that family? The data are not clear. Granger's data (as cited in Wright et al., 1984) showed that high involvement types of intervention programs may increase stress for certain families. At the same time, there is accumulating evidence that early intervention is effective for many children. Clearly, guidelines and empirical support are needed for structuring professional-parent collaboration around family goal-setting.

Closely related to issues about needs assessment and goal setting is, of course, evaluation of outcome. The same concerns about choice of measures apply here; and once again, if a broadly based family-focused approach is taken, then multiple outcome measures are warranted. An alternative to the types of measures described earlier (i.e., self-report, interview, and direct observation) is the application of Goal Attainment Scaling for assessment and evaluation of family goals. Goal Attainment Scaling was originally developed as a means of making mental health therapy subject to measurement (Kiresuk & Lund, 1976). It has since been used for evaluating individualized goals for handicapped children (Simeonsson, Huntington, & Short, 1982); its application to evaluating family goals has been proposed recently by Bailey (1983). Although at this point there are not enough clinical data to test the feasibility of this idea, the direction is in keeping with an individualized focus for family intervention and may offer a method of evaluating diverse goals in a standardized and consistent fashion.

## Issues Related to Implementation of Family-focused Intervention

The concepts, new directions and unresolved issues relating to family-focused intervention presented in this chapter represent a radical departure from the traditionally child-focused approach for which most interventionists have been trained and in which they have developed expertise. Because the success of any program depends upon the skill of those implementing it, the ultimate direction of family-focused intervention efforts is likely to rest in the hands of interventionists and those who train them. An underlying set of assumptions in this chapter has been that an optimally functioning family is a critical component for a child's development; and, therefore, intervention programs should focus on enhancing family functioning. It may be unrealistic to expect that interventionists accept this assumption. Certainly, the training traditionally provided in special education programs has not prepared interventionists with the theoretical knowledge or practical skills to deal with families in the ways suggested by this chapter. Furthermore, using parents as unpaid staff has been described as a cost-effective way of intervening with young developmentally delayed children (Ora, 1973) without recognition that the approach may be detrimental to overall family functions. A major change in intervention perspective is required if families are to define their needs apart from and unrelated to the program's needs. We are only at the beginning stages of translating the family-focused intervention idea into practical applications. Such a change in focus will no doubt require inservice and preservice training in areas such as family systems theory, group dynamics, family assessment, and communications skills.

# SUMMARY

Changes in the way families of developmentally delayed children have been viewed by professionals have been dramatic and certainly hold the promise for more sophisticated intervention efforts. However, the final section of this chapter highlights what is perhaps the biggest dilemma faced by professionals attempting to bridge the gap between theory and practice: How to evaluate program effectiveness by isolating variables which demonstrate causality while at the same time responding to the clinical need to broaden goals and to include variables which are difficult to operationalize. Family research is complex. Lamb (1978) suggests more interdisciplinary research which combines sociologists' abilities to formulate useful questions about families with developmental psychologists' proven sophistication at addressing questions. Yando and Zigler (1984) caution against letting the current emphasis on family systems theory take precedence over the continued need for researchers to focus on specific outcomes at specific points in time. Perhaps the most important guiding principle in conducting research or designing intervention with families is to be able to direct one's focus to certain aspects of the system, while at the same time making sure to acknowledge what parts of the system are being ignored and why. In this way the complexities of the system are recognized but do not become overwhelming obstacles to moving in the directions outlined.

# REFERENCES

Abidin, R. (1983). *Parenting Stress Index.* Unpublished measure.

Anderson, K. (1971). The "shopping" behavior of parents of mentally retarded children: The professional person's role. *Mental Retardation, 9,* 3–5.

Avis, D. (1984). Deinstitutionalization jet lag. In A. Turnbull & R. Turnbull (Eds.), *Parents speak out: Then and now* (2nd ed.) (pp. 185–191). Columbus, OH: Charles Merrill.

Bailey, D., & Simeonsson, R. (1984). Critical issues underlying research and intervention with families of young handicapped children. *Journal of the Division for Early Childhood, 9,* 38–48.

Bailey, D., & Simeonsson, R. (1983, March). *Design issues in family impact evaluations.* Paper presented at the Conference on Evaluating Early Intervention, Nashville, TN: Vanderbilt University.

Bakeman, R., & Brown, J. (1977). Behavioral dialogues: An approach to the assessment of mother-infant interaction. *Child Development, 48,* 195–203.

Baker, B. (1984). Intervention with families with young, severely handicapped children. In J. Blacher (Ed.), *Severely handicapped children and their families: Research in review* (pp. 319–375). New York: Academic Press.

Barber, T. (1973). Pitfalls in research: Nine investigators and experimenter effects. In R. Travers (Ed.), *Second handbook of research on teaching* (pp. 382–404). Chicago: Rand McNally & Co.

Becker, L., Bender, N., & Kawabe, K. (1980). Exceptional parents: A survey of programs, services and needs. *Academic Therapy, 15,* 523–538.

Beckman-Bell, P. (1980). *Characteristics of handicapped infants: A study of the relationship between child characteristics and stress as reported by mothers.* Unpublished doctoral dissertation, University of North Carolina.

Bell, R. (1968). A reinterpretation of the direction of effects in studies of socialization. *Psychological Review, 75,* 81–95.

Bernheimer, L., Young, M., & Winton, P. (1983). Stress over time: Parents with handicapped children. *Journal of Developmental and Behavioral Pediatrics, 14* (3), 177–181.

Berger, N., & Fowlkes, M. (1980). Family Intervention Project: A family network model for serving young handicapped children. *Young Children, 35* (4), 22–32.

Bloom, B. (1964). *Stability and change in human characteristics.* New York: John Wiley.

Boss, P., & Greenberg, J. (1984). Family boundary ambiguity: A new variable in family stress theory. *Family Process, 23,* 535–546.

Bristol, M., & Devellis, R. (1980). *The definition scale: The subjective meaning of having a handicapped child.* Unpublished assessment instrument, University of North Carolina at Chapel Hill.

Bristol, M., & Shopler, E. (1984). A developmental perspective on stress and coping in families of autistic children. In J. Blacher (Ed.), *Severely handicapped children and their families: Research in review* (pp. 91–141). New York: Academic Press.

Bristol, M. (1983, December). *Issues in the assessment of single parent families.* Paper presented at Handicapped Children Early Education Program Meeting, Washington, DC.

Bristol, M. (1984, October). *Families of developmentally disabled children: Healthy adaptation and the Double ABCX Model.* Paper presented at the Family Systems and Health Pre-Conference Workshop, National Council on Family Relations, San Francisco, California.

Bronfenbrenner, U. (1974). Is early intervention effective? In M. Guttentag and E. Struening (Eds.), *Handbook of evaluation and research* (pp. 519–603). Beverly Hills: Sage Publications.

Bronfenbrenner, U. (1976). The experimental ecology of education. *Educational Researcher, 5,* 5–15.

Bronfenbrenner, U. (1977). Toward an experimental ecology of human development. *American Psychologist, 32,* 513–531.

Cadman, D., Goldsmith, C., & Bashim, P. (1984). Values, preferences and decisions in the care of children with developmental disabilities. *Developmental and Behavioral Pediatrics, 5* (2), 60–64.

Caplan, G., (1976). The family as a support system. In G. Caplan & M. Killilea (Eds.), *Support systems and mutual help: Multidisciplinary explorations* (pp. 19–36). New York: Grune & Stratton.

Clarke, A., & Clarke, A. (1976). *Early experience: Myth and evidence.* New York: The Free Press.

Crnic, K., Fredrich, W., & Greenberg, M. (1983). Adaptation of families with mentally retarded children: A model of stress, coping and family ecology. *American Journal of Mental Deficiency, 88,* 125–138.

Denzin, N. (1970). *The research act: A theoretical introduction to sociological methods.* Chicago: Aldine Publishing Co.

Deutsch, M., & Brown, B. (1964). Social influences in negro-white intelligence differences. *Journal of Social Issues, 20,* 24–35.

Doernberg, N. (1978). Some negative effects on family integrations of health and educational services for young handicapped children. *Rehabilitation Literature, 39,* 107–110.

Dunlap, W. (1979). How do parents of handicapped children view their needs? *Journal of Division of Early Childhood, 1,* 1–10.

Farber, B. (1959). Effects of a severely mentally retarded child on family integration. *Monographs of the Society for Research in Child Development,* No. 71.

Farber, B. (1960). Family organization and crises: Maintenance of integration in families with a severely mentally retarded child. *Monographs of the Society for Research in Child Development*, No. 25.

Farran, D., Kasari, C., Jay, S. (1984). *Parent-child interaction scale*. Unpublished measure. University of North Carolina at Chapel Hill.

Figley, C. (1983). Catastrophes: An overview of family reactions. In C. Figley & H. McCubbin (Eds.), *Stress and the family: Vol. 11. Coping with catastrophe* (pp. 3–20). New York: Bruner/Mazel.

Foster, M., & Berger, M. (1979). Structural family therapy: Application in programs for preschool handicapped children. *Journal of the Division for Early Childhood, 1*, 52–58.

Foster, M., Berger, M., & McLean, M. (1981). Rethinking a good idea: A reassessment of parent involvement. *Topics in Early Childhood Special Education, 1*, 55–65.

Frodi, A. (1981). Contribution of infant characteristics to child abuse. *American Journal of Mental Deficiency, 85*, 341–349.

Gabel, H., & Kotsch, L. (1981). Extended families and young handicapped children. *Topics in Early Childhood Special Education, 1* (3), 29–36.

Gabel, H., McDowell, J., & Cerreto, M. (1983). Family adaptation to the handicapped infant. In G. Garwood & R. Fewell (Eds.), *Education handicapped infants* (pp. 455–493). Rockville, MD: Aspen.

Glaser, B., & Strauss, A. (1967). *Discovery of grounded theory*. Chicago: Aldene.

Goldenberg, I., & Goldenberg, H. (1980). Family therapy: An overview. Monterey, CA: Brooks/Cole Publishing Co.

Gorden, R. (1969). *Interviewing: Strategies, techniques and tactics*. Homewood, IL: Dorsey Press.

Gordon, I. (1970). *Parent involvement in compensatory education*. Champaign, IL: Illinois Press.

Gumz, E., & Gubrium, J., (1972). Comparative parental perceptions of a mentally retarded child. *American Journal of Mental Deficiency, 77*, 175–180.

Haley, J. (1973). *Uncommon therapy*. New York: Horton.

Hansen, & Johnson (1979). Rethinking family stress theory: Definitinal aspects. In W. Burr, R. Hill, F. Hye, & I. Reiss (Eds.), *Contemporary theories about the family. Vol. 1. Research-based theories* (pp. 582–603). New York: The Free Press.

Heatherington, M. (1984). Stress and coping children and families. In A. Doyle, D. Gold, & S. Moskowitz (Eds.), *Children in families with stress* (pp. 7–33). San Francisco: Jossey-Bess.

Hebb, D. (1949). *The organization of behavior*. London: Chapman & Hall.

Hill, R. (1949). *Families under stress: Adjustment to the crises of war, separation and reunion*. New York: Harper.

Hill, R. (1958). Social stresses on the family. *Social Casework, 39*, 139–150.

Hoffman, L., & Manis, J. (1978). Influences of children on marital interaction and parental satisfactions and dissatisfactions. In R. Lerner & G. Spanier (Eds.), *Child influences on marital and family interaction: A life-span perspective* (pp. 165–212). New York: Academic Press.

Hogan, M., Buehler, C., & Robinson, B. (1983). Single parenting: Transitioning alone. In H. McCubbin & C. Figley (Eds.), *Stress and the family: Vol. 1. Coping with normative transitions* (pp. 116–132). New York: Bruner/Mazel.

Holroyd, J., & McArthur, D. (1976). Mental retardation and stress on the parents: A contrast between Down's syndrome and childhood autism. *American Journal of Mental Deficiency, 80*, 431–436.

Hunt, J. (1961). *Intelligence and experience*. New York: Ronald Press.

Hunt, J. (1971). Parent and child centers. *American Journal of Orthopsychiatry, 41*, 13–37.

Huntington, G., & Simeonsson, R. (1985). *Temperament characteristics of infants and toddlers with Down syndrome*. Unpublished manuscript, University of North Carolina at Chapel Hill.

Hyman, H. (1954). *Interviewing in social research*. Chicago: University of Chicago Press.

Isbell, L. (1983). Your child, education, the law and how to stand up to it all. In T. Dougan, L.

Isbell, & P. Vyas (Eds.), *We have been there: A guidebook for parents of people with mental retardation* (pp. 75–82). Nashville, TN: Abingdon Press.

Kaiser, C., & Hayden, A. (1984). Clinical research and policy issues in parenting severely handicapped infants. In J. Blacher (Ed.), *Severely handicapped young children and their families: Research in review* (pp. 275–317). New York: Academic Press.

Karnes, M., & Tesca, J. (1980). Toward successful parent involvement in programs for handicapped children. In J. Gallagher (Ed.), *New Directions for exceptional children: Parents and families of handicapped children* (Vol. 41), (pp. 85–111). San Francisco: Jossey-Bass, Inc.

Karnes, M., & Zehrbach, R. (1975). Matching families and services. *Exceptional Children, May,* 545–549.

Kiresuk, T., & Lund, S. (1975). Process and outcome measurement using Goal Attainment Scaling. In J. Zusman & C. Wurster (Eds.), *Program evaluation: Alcohol, drug abuse, and mental health services* (pp. 213–228), Lexington, MA: D.C. Heath and Co.

Klein, D., & Ross, A. (1958). Kindergarten entry: A study of role transition. In M. Krugman (Ed.), *Orthopsychiatry and the school* (pp. 60–69). New York: American Orthopsychiatric Association.

Kogan, K., & Tyler, N. (1973). Mother-child interaction in young physically handicapped children. *American Journal of Mental Deficiency, 77,* 492–497.

Kogan, K., Tyler, N., & Turner, P. (1974). The process of interpersonal adaptation between mothers and their cerebral palsied children. *Developmental Medicine and Child Neurology, 16,* 518–527.

Korn, S., Chess, S., & Fernandez, P. (1978). The impact of children's physical handicaps on marital quality and family interaction. In R. M. Lerner & G. B. Spanier (Eds.), *Child influences on marital and family interaction.* New York: Academic Press.

Lamb, M. (1976). *The role of the father in child development.* New York: John Wiley & Sons.

Lamb, M. (1977). Father-infant and mother-infant interaction in the first year of life. *Child Development, 48,* 167–181.

Lamb, M. (1978). Influence of the child on marital quality and family interaction during the prenatal, perinatal, and infancy periods. In R. Lerner & G. Spanier (Eds.), *Child influences on marital and family interaction: A life-span perspective* (pp. 137–163). New York: Academic Press.

McCubbin, H., & Figley, C. (1983). Budging normative and catastrophic family stress. In H. McCubbin & C. Figley (Eds.), *Stress and the family Vol. 1. Coping with normative transitions* (pp. 218–228). New York: Bruner/Mazel.

McCubbin, H., & Patterson, J. (1983). The family stress process: The double ABCX model of family adjustment and adaptation. In H. McCubbin, M. Sussman, & J. Patterson (Eds.), *Advances and developments in family stress, theory and research.* New York: Haworth.

McCubbin, H., & Patterson, J. (1983). Family transitions: Adaptation to stress. In H. McCubbin & C. Figley (Eds.), *Stress and the family: Vol. 1. Coping with normative transitions* (pp. 5–25). New York: Bruner/Mazel.

Marion, R. (1981). *Educators, parents and exceptional children.* Rockville, MD: Aspen.

Mash, E. (1984). Families with problem children. In A. Doyle, D. Gold, & D. Moskowitz (Eds.), *Children in families with stress* (pp. 65–84). San Francisco: Jossey-Bass.

Merton, R., Fiske, M., & Kendall, P. (1946). *The focused interview: A manual of problems and procedures.* Glencoe, IL: The Free Press.

MIDCO Educational Associates. (1972). *Investigation of the effects of parent participation in Head Start.* Washington, D.C.: Project Head Start, Office of Child Development, U.S. Department of Health, Education and Welfare.

Minuchin, S. (1974). *Families and family therapy.* Cambridge, MA: Harvard University Press.

Minuchin, S., Rosman, B., & Baker, L. (1978). *Psychosomatic families.* Cambridge, MA: Harvard University Press.

Moroney, R. (1981). Public social policy: Impact on families with handicapped children. In J. L. Paul (Ed.), *Understanding and working with parents of children with special needs* (pp. 180–204). New York: Holt, Rinehart & Winston.

Neugarten, B. (1976). Adaptation and the life cycle. *The Counseling Psychologist, 6*, 16–20.

Olson, D., McCubbin, H., Barnes, H., Larsen, H., Muxen, M., & Wilson, M. (1983). *Families: What makes them work.* Beverly Hills: Sage Publications.

Olson, D., Russell, C., & Sprenkle, D. (1983). Circumplex model of marital and family systems: v1. Theoretical update. *Family Process, 22*, 69–83.

Ora, J. (1973). Involvement and training of parent and citizen workers in early education for the handicapped. In M. Karnes (Ed.), *Not all little red wagons are red* (pp. 66–77). Reston, VA: Council of Exceptional Children.

Pascoe, J., Loda, F., Jeffries, V., & Earp, J. (1981). The association between mothers' social support and provision of stimulation to their children. *Developmental and Behavioral Pediatrics, 2*, 15–19.

Patterson, J., & McCubbin, H. (1983). Chronic illness: Family stress and coping. In C. Figley & H. McCubbin (Eds.), *Stress and the family: Vol. 11. Coping with catastrophe* (pp. 21–37). New York: Bruner/Mazel.

Pearce, D., & McAdoo, H. (1984). Women and children: Alone and in poverty. In R. G. Genovese (Ed.), *Families and change: Social needs and public policy* (pp. 161–176). New York: Praeger Publishers.

Phillips, B. (1971). *Social research: Strategy and tactics* (2nd Ed.). New York: Macmillan.

Rhodes, W. (1977). The transformation of caregiving: A proposal. In J. Paul, D. Stedman, & G. Neufield (Eds.), *Deinstitutionalization* (pp. 80–93). Syracuse, NY: Syracuse University Press.

Rollins, B., & Galligan, R. (1978). The developing child and marital satisfaction of parents. In R. Lerner & G. Spanier (Eds.), *Child influences on marital and family interaction: A life-span perspective* (pp. 71–102). New York: Academic Press.

Schnitzler, C., & Rappaport, K. (1983, April). *More alike than different: An activities book for handicapped awareness.* (Available from New Jersey State Department of Education, 225 West State Street, Trenton, NJ 08625).

Selltiz, C., Johoda, M., Deutsch, M., & Cook, S. (1965). *Research methods in social relations.* New York: Holt, Rinehart & Winston.

Shapiro, J. (1983). Family reactions and coping with physically ill or handicapped children. *Soc. Sci. Med., 17*, 913–931.

Simeonsson, R., & Bailey, D. (1983, September). *Siblings of handicapped children.* Paper presented at NICHHD Conference on Research on Families, Quail Roost, NC.

Simeonsson, R., Huntington, G., & Short, R. (1982). Individual differences and goals: An approach to the evaluation of child progress. *Topics in Early Childhood Special Education, 1* (4), 71–80.

Simeonsson, R., & McHale, S. (1981). Review: Research on handicapped children: Sibling relationships. *Child: Care, Health & Development, 7*, 153–171.

Simpson, R. (1983, July). *Mainstreaming Curricula: Vols. 1-5.* (Available from the Severely Handicapped Integration Project, Department of Special Education, University of Kansas Medical Center, Kansas City, MO 66103).

Skinner, B. (1983). *Science and behavior.* New York: MacMillan Publishing Co.

Skrtic, Summers, J. Brotherson, M., & Turnbull, A. (1984). Severely handicapped children and their brothers and sisters. In J. Blacher (Ed.), *Severely handicapped young children and their families: Research in review* (pp. 215–246). New York: Academic Press.

Stack, C. (1975). *All our kin.* New York: Harper.

Stile, S., Cole, J., & Garner, A. (1979). Maximizing parental involvement in programs for exceptional children: Strategies for education and related service personnel. *Journal of the Division for Early Childhood, 1*, 68–82.

Stoneman, Z., Brody, G., & Abbott, D. (1983). In-home observations of young Down syndrome children with their mothers and fathers. *American Journal of Mental Deficiency, 6,* 591–600.

Stoneman, Z., & Brody, G. (1984). Research with families of severely handicapped children: Theoretical and methodological considerations. In J. Blacher (Ed.), *Severely handicapped young children and their families: Research in review* (pp. 179–214). Orlando, FL.: Academic Press.

Suelzle, M., & Keenan, V. (1981). Changes in family support networks over the life cycle of mentally retarded persons. *American Journal of Mental Deficiency, 86,* 267–274.

Summers, J., Brotherson, M., & Turnbull, A. (in press). The impact of handicapped children on families: Implications for educators. In E. Lynch & R. Lewis (Eds.), *Introduction to special education,* Glenview, IL: Scott-Foresman & Co.

Thomas, A., Chess, S., & Birch, H. (1968). *Temperament and behavior disorders in children.* New York: New York University Press.

Tseng, W., & McDermott, J. (1979). Trixial family classifications: A proposal. *Journal of American Academy of Child Psychiatry, 18* (1), 22–43.

Turnbull, A., Brotherson, M., & Summers, J. (in press). The impact of deinstitutionalization on families: A family systems approach. In R. Bruinicks (Ed.), *Living and learning in the least restrictive environment (pp. 26–52). Baltimore, MD: Paul H. Brookes Publishing Co.*

Turnbull, H., & Turnbull, A. (1982). Parent involvement: A critique. *Mental Retardation, 20* (3), 115–122.

Turnbull, A., & Winton, P. (1984). Parent involvement policy and practice: Current research and implications for families with young, severely handicapped children. In J. Blacher (Ed.), *Severely handicapped young children and their families: Research in review* (pp. 377–397). New York: Academic Press.

Walters, J., & Stinnett, N. (1977). Parent-child relationships: A decade review of research. *Journal of Marriage and the Family, 33,* 70–111.

Watson, R., & Midlarsky, E. (1979). Reactions of mothers with mentally retarded children: A social perspective. *Psychological Reports, 45,* 309–310.

Wiegerink R., & Posante, R. (1977). Consumerism. In J. Paul, D. Stedman, & G. Neufield (Eds.), *Deinstitutionalization* (pp. 63–79). Syracuse, NY: Syracuse University Press.

Wikler, L. (1981). Chronic stresses of families of mentally retarded children. *Family Relations, 30,* 281–288.

Wilson, S. (1977). The use of ethnographic techniques in educational research. *Review of Educational Research, 47,* 245–265.

Winton, P. (in press). The consequences of mainstreaming for families of young handicapped children. In J. Meisel (Ed.), *Mainstreamed handicapped children: Outcomes, controversies and new directions.* Hillsdale, NJ: Erlbaum Associates.

Winton, P. (1981). Descriptive study of parents' perspectives of preschool services: Mainstreamed and specialized. *Dissertation Abstracts International, 42,* 3562A. (University Microfilms No. 42-08).

Winton, P., & Turnbull, A. (1981). Parent involvement as viewed by parents of preschool handicapped children. *Topics in Early Childhood Special Education, 1* (3), 11–19.

Winton, P., Turnbull, A., & Blacher, J. (1984). *Selecting a preschool: A guide for parents of handicapped children.* Austin, TX: Pro-Ed.

Wright, J., Granger, R., & Sameroff, A. (1984). Parental acceptance and developmental handicap. In J. Blacher (Ed.), *Severely handicapped young children and their families: Research in review* (pp. 51–90). New York: Academic Press.

Yando, R., & Zigler, E. (1984). Severely handicapped children and their families: A synthesis. In J. Blacher (Ed.), *Severely handicapped Children and their families: Research in review* (pp. 401–416). New York: Academic Press.

Yogman, M. (1982). Observations on the father-infant relationship. In S. Cath, A. Gurwitt, & J. Ross (Eds.), *Father and Child: Developmental and clinical perspectives* (pp. 101–122). Boston: Little, Brown & Co.

Zuk, G., Miller, R., Bantram, J., & Kling, F. (1961). Maternal acceptance of retarded children: A questionnaire study of attitudes and religious background. *Child Development, 32,* 525–540.

# EDUCATIONAL IMPLICATIONS OF DEVELOPMENTAL PROBLEMS IN THE PRESCHOOL YEARS

Jeanne M. McCarthy

## INTRODUCTION

Developmental problems in infancy and the preschool years frequently lead the child and the family into the complex network of educational services available for young handicapped or at-risk children within a community. Such services may be provided from the time of first suspicion of the existence of a problem to the time when the child would normally be expected to enter the regular school program. Such services may be available through a vast array of delivery systems which vary from state to state; they frequently include programs operated through federal, state, and locally funded services under the aegis of Departments of Maternal and Child Health, Education, Mental Health, and such De-

Advances in Special Education, Volume 5, pages 257–273.
Copyright © 1986 by JAI Press Inc.
All rights of reproduction in any form reserved.
ISBN: 0-89232-313-2

partment of Human Service programs as Head Start or Developmental Disabilities.

The myriad of services in both the public and private sectors available to serve the educational needs of infants and toddlers with developmental problems has evolved over a relatively brief period of time. Growth has been facilitated in large measure by advances in neonatology, special education, and public concern for the handicapped reflected in Congressional passage of The Handicapped Children's Early Education Act in 1970. As each program of service has developed, whether as a part of a national initiative, a state commitment, or in response to the plight of one family with a handicapped child, it has become increasingly clear that decisions regarding the delivery of services to preschool handicapped children involve a great many specific and nonspecific variables of which the decision-makers may be unaware. These include such obvious factors as the identified needs of the children, the demographics of the population, the resources available through community, state, and federal laws governing the education of handicapped children, the awareness and commitment of the community, budgetary considerations, and so on. In 1962, Jay Hirsch conceptualized some of the factors involved in the educational process (see Figure 1). In 1984, Kirk and Chalfant extended this concept with a paradigm which is useful in defining some of the variables involved in the education of young handicapped children. They have conceptualized the major contributing factors in underachievement as being divided into two major types: extrinsic and intrinsic. Intrinsic factors include all of the individual child factors included as "psychological disorders" in assessing handicapped children. "Extrinsic conditions refer to contributing factors in the environment" (p. 7).

In this chapter another level of variables is explored, that is, the conceptual level of thinking upon which specific programmatic decisions may be based. This analysis is predicated upon the assumption that a conceptual frame of reference exists in the heads of policy framers and decision makers. The conceptual frame of reference may vary from sophisticated philosophical and theoretical approaches to prejudices, beliefs, and attitudes drawn from familial or cultural folklore or mores, often totally unsupported by facts or data. These complex systems of beliefs may exist at conscious or subconscious levels, and frequently determine decisions and action. Some of these may approximate systems of values which guide the decisions of individuals. It is important to note that the surface structure upon which decisions appear to be made about the delivery of services to preschool handicapped children is not addressed in this chapter. Rather the focus is on the deep structure, or the "gut level" basis of decision making.

## THE POWER OF BELIEF SYSTEMS

Why are any of us convinced that early intervention can make real, long-lasting changes in the lives of young children and their families? Certainly not because

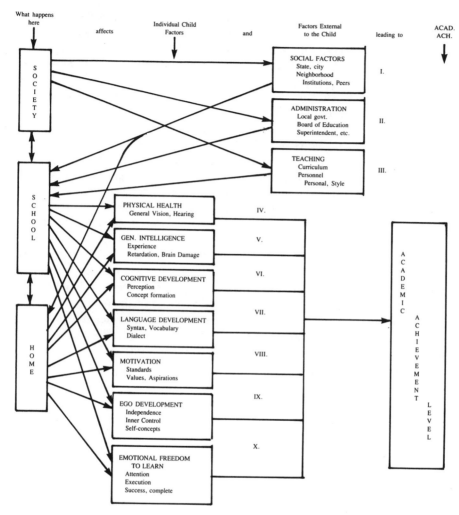

*Figure 1.*   Some dimensions of academic achievement

our research base is so convincing! Efficacy studies have raised more questions than they have answered. Since the early work of Skeels and Skodak with infants in the Iowa orphanage (1939) and the preschool study of Kirk (1958), data have been available to support the intuitive commitment of many special educators to the importance of early intervention (see Lazar and Darlington monograph, 1982, for a detailed review of 12 programs. These results have been expanded by the Consortium for Longitudinal Studies in the 1983 book *As the Twig is Bent. . . . Lasting Effects of Preschool Programs*). Yet, there is conflicting evidence in the Westinghouse Report (1969) and in Bronfenbrenner's Report on

Longitudinal Evaluations of Preschool Programs (1974). In recent research efforts, the Early Intervention Research Institute at Utah State University (Casto, in press) utilized a meta-analysis to reanalyze 75 earlier studies of the efficacy of early intervention with young handicapped children, finding for the most part nonsignificant effects of intervention. However, the findings have had little effect on the deeply held beliefs of the environmentalists and developmentalists in our midst. Apparently our decisions are influenced by our belief systems as well as by data.

Another example of the power of our belief systems comes out of a recent follow-up study of all newly funded preschool programs in the State of Arizona (McCarthy & Daley, 1985). A survey of the local education agencies that did *not* submit proposals for funding indicated that one third of the decisions were made because of philosophical beliefs about whether preschool special education services should be delivered by the public schools. "Concern about the appropriateness of the preschool special education function for public schools may be the strongest and most persistent barrier to participation of these districts, at least short term" (p. 3). This belief continues to guide the decision-making process, in spite of the mandate of P.L. 94-142, the successful experience of hundreds of other school districts, and the avowed good intentions of the decision-makers. Sherlock Holmes' concern with "the dogs that didn't bark," reiterated by Daniel Patrick Moynihan in discussing Lyndon Johnson's War on Poverty, has helped to focus on these elements of the decision-making process that are seldom considered as significant in shaping the preschool programs serving children with developmental problems.

It is the intent in this chapter to explore the major issues which impact on the delivery of services to these children. An attempt will be made to explore both members of the sets of opposed assumptions that currently form the axioms of the disciplines serving preschool handicapped children. By exploring some of the polarized premises current in the field, referred to by Holton (1973) as "themata," it may be possible to sharpen our awareness of some of the conceptual issues underlying choices about services made by policy makers and decision makers at all levels.

## MAJOR THEMATA IN DELIVERY OF SERVICES

The major themata impacting the delivery of educational services center around at least five major clusters.

1. *The concepts involved in the nature-nurture controversy, i.e., the role of experience in infancy.* Is the legacy of biological determinism alive and well in the hearts of policy-makers? Is the social prejudice engendered by hereditarians more pervasive than the beliefs of the environmentalists?

2.  *The concept of the educability of intelligence.* Is intellectual development predetermined and fixed by heredity? How do the infant and the environment interact in the achievement of competence?

3.  *The concept of resiliency in psychological development.* Do the experiences of infancy have a prolonged effect on the child? Are the effects of early experience not malleable to change? Or, are the effects of early experience reversible under optimum environmental conditions?

4.  *The perception of society and the family of the reasons why they have a handicapped child.* Did God especially designate this family because of special strengths or special needs? Or, did God send the handicapped child as punishment for evil, as retribution for the sins of the parents?

5.  *The concept of responsible agent for the 0-5 range of handicapped infants and toddlers.* Should one agency at the federal, state, and local levels be designated to provide educational services for the 0-5 range? Or, should Maternal and Child Health be responsible for 0-3, and Education take over at 3? How can the roles of Health, Mental Health, Human Services, and Education agencies function most effectively in meeting the educational needs of preschool handicapped children and their families?

# THE NATURE-NURTURE CONTROVERSY REVISITED

Although philosophical and psychological speculation about the effects of the environment and experience on development has been ongoing for at least 2,000 years, recent research and reanalysis of earlier findings suggest a need to reexamine the issue. Beliefs about the role of early experience in shaping the behavior of the infant or young child with developmental problems are critical to the delivery of educational services to these children. Such beliefs are frequently rooted in brief encounters with information which may have been called into question by the professional community, or which has been superseded by technological advances in research and theory. Those who make decisions about services (i.e., legislators, administrators, school boards, educators, parents, etc.) seldom have the opportunity to keep abreast of this critical issue. Thus, it is imperative that leaders in the field of special education pay a return visit to the nature-nurture controversy in an effort to collate strands of thinking that are emerging from widely divergent arenas of research.

Some of the excitement has been captured in the new breed of scientists concerned with the biological basis of human learning. These are now known as behavioral biologists, neuropsychopharmacologists, behavioral neurophysiologists, neurobiologists, cellular biochemists, human psychobiologists, evolutionary biologists, social biologists, and so on. Their research is on the biological basis of human learning and nonlearning. One side of this issue has been strongly supported by such biological determinists as Cyril Burt (1959, 1972), H. J.

Eysenck (1971), Arthur Jensen (1969), Thurstone (1947), and others. The issue has been explored in depth by Stephen J. Gould (1981) in his book "This Mismeasure of Man." This fascinating exploration of the concept that differences in people arise from genetic inheritance has focused on the current resurgence of biological determinism and presents a sizeable bibliography in support of this position. Gould describes the principal theme of one side of this issue as holding "that shared behavioral norms, and the social and economic differences between human groups—primarily races, classes, and sexes—arise from inherited, inborn distinctions" (p. 20). The issue of biological potentiality versus biological determinism is clearly presented, with issues that need to be incorporated into the thinking of those responsible for serving young children.

The opposing view has been summarized by Bronfenbrenner (1972) in his review of studies which concern the interplay of biological factors, human interaction, social structures, and cultural forces in shaping the individual. In response to the question, "Is 80% of intelligence genetically determined?" he responded, "Thus, our analysis has brought us to a paradoxical conclusion: An inquiry into the heritability of inborn capacities has shed new light on the power and potential of the environment to bring about the fuller realization of genetic possibilities" (p. 126).

The ecological approach to the study of the brain explicated by Roger Walsh in his book *Towards an Ecology of Brain* (1981) synopsizes much work on the study of environment and brain ongoing in such varied research areas as ecology, sensory psychophysics, general systems theory, perception, and so on. Walsh has commented on the present state of knowledge of the impact of the environment on the developing organism: "If we remember that is is less than a quarter of a century since the brain was widely assumed to be immutable, then we are left to wonder just how large its responses can be and what the limits of plasticity truly are" (p. 153). His emphasis on the role of environmental stimuli in ameliorating brain damage is summarized in his statement: "Similarly, environmental sensory influences on the damaged brain have been almost completely ignored in the past, but we continue to ignore them at our own risk" (p. 115). The scholar concerned with the nature-nurture themata would do well to review Walsh's thinking about environmental effects on the total brain-behavior-body system, with emphasis on the brain.

Similarly, the educational implications of recent brain research described by Robert Sylvester, Jeanne Chall, M. C. Wittrock, Leslie A. Hart, and others in *Educational Leadership,* the Journal of the Association for Supervision and Curriculum Development (1981) is worthy of review. Sylvester's discussion of the educational implications of Epstein's 1978 work on spurts in brain growth, that is, the development of axon/dendrite extensions and the formation of the myelin sheath around the axons, is of particular relevance to this themata. Two of these periods of rapid brain growth occur in the preschool years. Some of

Sylvester's discussion needs to be included in the development of philosophy and policy about the role played by the environment in modifying outcomes for young children with developmental delays. A realistic resolution to this issue has been proposed by the geneticist Theodosius Dobzhansky (1950) who said:

> The geneticist is constantly forced to remind his colleagues, especially those in the social sciences, that what is inherited is not this or that particular phenotypic trait or character but a genotypic potentiality for an organism's developmental response to its environment. Given a certain genotype and a certain sequence of environmental situations, the development follows a certain path. The carriers of other genetic endowments in the same environmental sequence might well develop differently. But, also, a given genotype might well develop phenotypically along different paths in different environments. In most abbreviated terms, the observed phenotypic variance has both a genetic and an environmental component. . . . What we inherit thus is the mode of response to the environment. (p. 19–23)

# THE CONCEPT OF THE EDUCABILITY OF INTELLIGENCE

The concept of the educability of intelligence includes and extends the concepts discussed in the first thema, but specifies in more detail several sub-themata unique to the concept of intellectual development. Hunt (1980) has described many of these as "fictions, widely held, that pass for theory in developmental psychology" (p. 55):

a. The environment as a threshold;
b. Educability as heritability, not as a range of reaction;
c. The limited role of experience in language acquisition;
d. The unity of behavioral development reflected in simultaneous development of the major domains of development.

Alfred Binet, in his 1911 treatise Les Idées Modernes sur les énfants made a profound contribution to one view of this theme when he said:

> After the evil, the remedy; after exposing mental defects of all kinds, let us pass on to their treatment. . . . If nothing is done, if we do not actively and effectively intervene, we will continue to lose time. . . .
> I regret that I have often found a prejudice against the educability of intelligence. . . . Some modern philosophies seem to have given their moral support to these deplorable verdicts by asserting that the intelligence of an individual is a fixed quantity which cannot be augmented. We must protest and react against this brutal pessimism. We shall try to demonstrate that it has no foundation.
> Now if we consider that intelligence is not a single function, indivisible and of a particular essence, but that it is formed by the union of all the little functions of discrimination, observation, retention, etc., whose plasticity and extensiblity have been determined, it will

appear undeniable that the same law governs the ensemble and its elements, and that consequently anyone's intelligence is susceptible to being developed; with practice, training, and above all, with method, one arrives at augmenting one's attention, memory, and judgment, and in becoming literally more intelligent than before; that improvement will continue until one reaches one's limit. (p. 200–202).

Although Binet's commitment to the importance of the role of early education of "defective" children was supported by the work of Montessori, Seguin, Itard, and others, little influence was felt in psychological or educational centers in the United States. It was not until the late 1930s that one side of this thema began to emerge with the early work of Skeels and Dye (1939), Skodak (1939), Hebb (1949), and Kirk (1958). Hunt (1961), in his book *Intelligence and Experience,* succeeded in weaving Piagetian concepts into a format palatable to diverse segments of the psychological community; he also documented the critical importance of environmental stimulation on the developing intellect of the infant. Cognition, thought by some to have been buried by behaviorism, began to regain credibility, and support for the concept of the educability of intelligence began to accumulate.

Hunt, after an exhaustive examination of the various domains of the life sciences including animal behavior, ontogenesis, pathological phenomena, genetics, and experimental psychology, moved from a belief that "intellectual development was essentially predetermined and fixed by heredity" (p. 2) to a new view of intellectual development. "According to this view, an infant's effort to make sense out of his perceptual encounters . . . leads him to strategies of information processing and skills in coping which build one upon another" (p. 3).

Operating within the frame of reference that the influence of the environment is only indirect, Hunt documented a substantial case for his statement that "it is the experience of functioning rather than the environment per se that controls, along with genetic endowment, the course and rate of development, and the ultimate level of achieved competence" (p. 65). Based on his intensive review of the literature and findings from research on the developmental outcomes of variations in child-rearing conditions, Hunt modified his view of specific theoretical formulations prevalent in current developmental psychology. Thus, he proposed his "fictions."

The first of Hunt's fictions addresses the concept of a threshold of environmental adequacy. According to some bio-determinists, such a threshold significantly reduces or increases the effects of environmental variations on intelligence. After presenting detailed data on infants raised in varying environments, Hunt concludes that "it is not the environment, but the functioning of an organism that influences the course and rate of its development. . . . Similarly, the competencies and motivational systems that an infant develops are not the product of his environment, but rather of his adaptive functioning.. . . Thus, it is the experience of functioning rather than the environment per se that controls along with genetic endowment, the course and rate of development, and the ultimate level of achieved competence. Excellence of genetic endowment does not in itself guarantee either rapid development or high-level competence'' p. 65).

The second fiction concerns estimations of educability based on traditional indirect assessments of ''heritability.'' After reviewing works published since Galton's early study of 1883, Hunt concluded that such approaches ''are not only dubious and indirect but also basically irrelevant indices of educability'' (p. 66). He then reintroduced a concept of ''range of reaction'' proposed by the geneticist Richard Woltereck in 1909 (see Dunn, 1965, p. 95ff.) As explicated most recently by Dobzhansky (1950), direct measurement of the variation in any phenotypic characteristic (developmental landmark) that a given genotype can produce in response to variations in life experiences would produce a range of possible changes. The concept of ''range of reaction'' offers the decision-maker a viable option to the either/or dichotomy addressed in this thema (p. 22).

The third of Hunt's fictions addresses the nativistic approach to language acquisition spawned by Chomsky's theorizing about an innate language acquisition device (LAD). Hunt has countered this interpretation with a Piagetian view. That is, that the sensorimotor roots of language are to be found in object construction and vocal imitation, with stress on the intrinsic motivation involved in evoking vocal interaction with adults through vocal initiations. Of importance to this discussion is the interactive relationship between the infant and the care-giver, with the care-giver providing experiences that prove effective in fostering the acquisition of language. The recent work of the Carolina Institute for Research in Early Education of the Handicapped (CIREEH) on infant-caretaker interaction appears to support this interpretation (Ramey, 1984).

The fourth fiction involves the Gesellian concept that maturation proceeds at the same pace along all dimensions, emphasizing the unity of the organism. Using data from infants reared in varying environments, Hunt builds a case for independence of rates of development along different dimensions, noting varying rates with different kinds of experience. This point of view has important implications for assessment as well as for early intervention. Rather than averaging across areas of development as is done in most measures of intelligence or developmental estimates, Hunt argues for independent assessments of the rates of development along separate areas of function. Such differentiation would allow matching of specific methods of intervention.

## Practical Implications of this Thema

The concepts involved in this issue have practical implications for the delivery of services to preschool handicapped children. If the policy-maker, decision-maker, administrator, or parent believes that intellectual development is fixed by heredity, efforts to enrich environmental encounters of the young child would be minimal or nonexistent. If support for Jensen's (1969, p. 60) view that "above this threshold, environmental variations cause relatively small differences in intelligence" is part of the decision-maker's philosophy, services to many preschool children would be reduced, even negated. If the correlational approach to the heritability question is inculcated into administrative thinking, efforts to vary the environment of the at-risk young child would be difficult to support. If Chomsky's notion of an innate Language Acquisition Device were to be viewed as the explanation for delayed language, the current emphasis on parent-training to foster language acquisition would find little justification. If behavioral development/maturation is viewed in Gesellian terms, intra-individual differences in children resulting from different kinds of experiences would not be addressed in a program of environmental stimulation.

Conversely, the decision-maker who is convinced of the other side of this issue, that is, the educability of intelligence, the impact of rearing practices on cognitive development, the importance of the child's functioning on the course and rate of development, and the significance of specific intra-individual developmental delays, will support early and extensive programs for young handicapped children. Such decision-makers will seek interventions that provide experiences which foster psychological development.

From a practical perspective, however, the administrator, parent, or teacher will find a bewildering array of curricular and instructional materials from which to select. These range from the recommendations for a systematic program of "mental orthopedics" made by Binet in 1909 (which offers a challenge to the teacher three-quarters of a century later), to the plethora of materials emerging from publishers primarily as the result of the infusion of federal and state dollars into programs for preschool handicapped children.

It is interesting to note that the 7th Annual Report to Congress on the Implementation of the Education of the Handicapped Act (1985) reports that all 50 states, Guam, and the Bureau of Indian Affairs provided services to 243,087 preschool children ages 3–5 under P.L. 94–142 during the 1983-1984 school years. A study of the approaches to curricula reported by the model demonstration centers funded by the U.S. Office of Education under the Handicapped Children's Early Education Program (1983) indicates that the largest percentage of programs (37%) used a diagnostic-prescriptive approach; the second largest (10%) were based on a behavioral approach, with smaller numbers reporting the use of Piagetian, Montessori, experiential/traditional, or other approaches. While there is a lack of consensus, all approaches appear to have some merit. Those with a cognitive emphasis are particularly interesting within the context of this chapter.

Underlying many of these curricular approaches are the cognitively oriented research-based formulations of J. McV. Hunt (1980), Samuel A. Kirk (1968), and Burton White (1975). Hunt conceptualized suggestions for practice based on Piagetian theory and the epigenesis of intrinsic motivation. His principles are applicable to the development of infants and toddlers as well as children in the preconceptual phase. The Ordinal Scales of Psychological Development (Uzgiris & Hunt, 1975) provide a hierarchy of cognitive skills which have been incorporated into such curricular programs as High Scope (Weikhart, Rogers, Adcock, & McClelland, 1971), ABACUS (McCarthy, Lund, & Bos, 1985), and others.

Kirk's work with the Illinois Test of Psycholinguistic Abilities, based on the psycholinguistic formulation of Osgood (1954), is evident in such programmed materials as the GOAL Kits developed by Merle Karnes (1972), the Peabody Language Development Kits developed by Dunn, Smith, and others (1967), and the MWM program (1975) developed by Minskoff, Wiseman, and Minskoff. White (1975), based on 17 years of research on the development of competence during the first three years of life, formulated principles of child-rearing useful in helping parents to foster the development of cognitive and language competence. These principles have not resulted in a formal curriculum for infants, but have impacted parent-training programs.

Other cognitively oriented curriculums include Lillie's Carolina Curriculum (1975) based on Thurstone's (1947) Primary Mental Abilities, and Feuerstein's instrumental enrichment (1980) program of cognitive modifiability. The latter was developed by Feuerstein to correct deficient cognitive functions of socioculturally disadvantaged adolescents and appears to have curricular potential for the *prevention* of deficient cognitive functions in preschool children.

The selection of a curriculum to implement the concepts considered important by decision makers should be the logical consequence of the process of examining the issue of the educability of intelligence. The cohesiveness of philosophy and practice should be evident both in *what* children are being taught and *how* they are being taught.

# THE CONCEPT OF RESILIENCY IN PSYCHOLOGICAL DEVELOPMENT

Critical to efforts to intervene in the lives of infants and toddlers with developmental problems is the belief that positive change will result for the child and the family. Unless we believe that early intervention can ameliorate the effects of infantile deprivation or physical or psychological trauma, the efforts expended by teachers, parents, child-care workers, and other professionals would be an unnecessary waste of time, effort, emotion, and money. The question of the irreversibility of effects induced by early experience has been explored in depth by Clarke and Clarke in their book *Early Experience: Myth and Evidence* (1976). The Clarks have presented data on both sides of this question, quoting the works of Freud (1949), Hebb (1949), Bowlby (1951), Rutter (1972), and Morgan (1975), as well as those of Kirk (1958), Bronfenbrenner (1974), Kagan and Moss

(1962), Piaget (1952), and others. Two prevalent points of view are documented in the literature. The first holds that experiences in infancy make a permanent impression on the young child, an impression that has a continuous influence throughout life. The second holds that the infant is much more resilient than earlier assumed, and that the effects of early deleterious experience can be reversed under optimum circumstances. Clarke and Clarke propose a "reformulation; this should not be interpreted literally as a counter-balance . . . but rather as an attempt to achieve a balanced view" (p. 269). They have concluded that: "a child's future is far from wholly shaped in the 'formative years' of early childhood. Rather, human development is a slow process of genetic and environmental interactions with sensitivities (rather than critical periods) for different processes at different times" (p. 24).

A clear understanding of this issue (critical period or life span perspective) is imperative if those involved in making decisions about programs for young children are to be convinced of the importance of environmental changes. By reviewing the dates of publication of much of the research supporting the concept of irreversibility of early experiences, it becomes clear that many decision-makers have been exposed to the side of the themata which argues that certain events during the first year produce irreversible consequences in children. There has been less exposure to the side of the themata which emphasizes the resiliency of the human infant and the powerful ameliorative influence of time and environmental change. Such a perspective, currently gaining support, has major implications for the continuity of services over time.


# THE PERCEPTIONS OF SOCIETY AND THE FAMILY OF THE REASONS WHY THEY HAVE A HANDICAPPED CHILD

Closely related to the concept of services to the family in societal context are the concepts proposed by sociologist Bernard Farber (1985) in an essay entitled *Families with Mentally Retarded Members: An Agenda for Research—1985– 2000*. Drawing heavily upon Emil Durkheim's (1915) and Vogt's (1951) representation of cults, Farber has proposed applying the religious-cult paradigm to the study of families with retarded offspring. The concepts proposed by Farber appear to offer another dimension in analyzing the conceptual bases for decision making about services to young children with developmental problems. The most obvious analogy relates to parents, but the perceptions of the reasons for the existence of handicaps may form the unconscious bias behind the decisions of policy-makers as well. Using such a paradigm, Farber postulates that the kind of cultish form followed by families is related to their stance on the relative power of God (or conventional society) as opposed to the power of mental retardation to intervene in their lives. In Farber's view, the reaction of parents of retarded offspring appears to sort into four groups or subcults:

1.   The family-management subcult, in which society is regarded as orderly and predictable, and management of the retarded member becomes a focal point of family life. This subcult is characterized as making effective use of legal, medical, and educational services, viewing mainstreaming as a right of the retarded, and being closely bound to the social structure. Significant others chosen would be persons who represent the social structure—physicians, administrators, priests, rabbis, ministers.

2.   The parallel structures subcult, in which the order in society is viewed as being threatened by the existence of handicapped members and compartmentalization is seen as an appropriate solution to management of the retarded. Such a view of the relative power of God (or social order) and mental retardation may involve a duplication of mainstream institutions such as special classes, special social services, special athletic competitions, and special living arrangements like half-way houses. Persons conforming to the cult of parallelism may attempt to separate the lives of the retarded from the normal. Significant others are then chosen from within the mental retardation community.

3.   The subcult of communal action, in which God (or society) is seen as powerless to meet the challenges of mental retardation, with parents seeking participation in support groups and significant others drawn from proponents of unorthodox procedures, gurus, or charismatic leaders opposed to conventional ways of facing the problem of delayed development.

4.   The residual group made up of those who withdraw from the conventional social structures as well as those established by the mental retardation cult and pursue idiosyncratic solutions to their situations.

The cult paradigm, related to the perception of the power of God or conventional social order and the reification of mental retardation as a force of evil, is unique in its application to the involvement of families of young handicapped children. Such a concept, however, draws support from the responses of many parents who ask, "Why me?" "Why did this happen to us?" The resolutions to these questions may include the belief that God specially designated this family because of special strengths or special needs. Another resolution may include the belief on the part of the parents and society that God sent the handicapped child as punishment for evil, as retribution for the sins of the parents or members of the extended family.

The approach to these questions may vary among members of many formal religions, presenting another side to this themata. The responses of parents as well as decision-makers may reflect conscious or unconscious attitudes buried deeply in personal religions or philosophical beliefs. As with other beliefs already discussed, they may be powerful influences on practical decisions about care and intervention.

# THE CONCEPT OF RESPONSIBLE AGENT
# FOR THE 0–5 RANGE OF
# HANDICAPPED INFANTS AND TODDLERS

Wiegerink and Bartel (1981) have described the essence of this themata in the introduction to *Early Childhood Services for the Eighties,* "despite the fact that the 1960s and 1970s could be called the awakening of understanding of early childhood services for handicapped children and their families, these services are in a state of uncoordinated disarray" (p. 1). This disarray is attributed to five factors:

1. Lack of commitment to develop coordinated comprehensive service pathways;
2. Lack of coordination in federal legislative and state agency jurisdictions;
3. Disincentives in P.L. 94–142 to serve preschool children, causing eight states to raise mandatory school ages;
4. Deleterious consequences of short-term funding of demonstration and model projects;
5. Overestimates of incidence rates of handicapping conditions in the 0-8 age range.

Wiegerink and Bartel's state of the art review of the issues and primary barriers to more effective coordination and delivery of service led them to conclude that "no agency is assigned leadership responsibility for young children, especially for infants, and there was no consensus as to which agency should have this role" (p. 6).

In order to thoroughly understand the importance of this themata to the development of comprehensive statewide services to the 0-5 age range, it would be necessary to assimilate the entire series of topical papers on developmental disabilities entitled "DD Themes and Issues" published as part of the National Review of Child Development Services by the Frank Porter Graham Center. Much of the difficulty comes from the fact that states have a minimum of 10 federal/state programs offering services to young handicapped children (Wiegerink & Bartel, 1981), with little coordination or communication among them. Some states are involved in 25 major federal programs serving young DD children.

One side of this themata is represented by those who suggest a lead agency for ages birth to 3, and a lead agency for ages 3 through 6. The most frequently mentioned coordinating agency for the 0-3 group appears to be Maternal and Child Health, with responsibility for the 3-6 group assigned to Education. Wiegerink and Bartel (1981) nominate Headstart to coordinate interagency responsibilities at the federal level. They would also delegate to Developmental Disabilities a role as an "unbiased evaluator of what the best lead agency or agencies in each state could be" (p. 3).

A slightly different approach to the resolution of this issue has been taken by Barbara Smith in her Policy Options paper for the Council for Exceptional Children (1980). After analyzing current state policy related to providing early intervention services for very young exceptional children and their families, Smith discusses a variety of policy options that may facilitate resolution of identified constraints.

Another resolution to this issue is presented by those who would assign primary responsibility for the education of the 0-8 group to the Department of Education, primary responsibility for medical services to the Department of Health, and primary responsibility for related service and welfare needs to Human Services and Developmental Disabilities. The complex solutions to the problems which now exist in every state suggest that simplistic solutions accomplished by administrative fiat would be doomed to failure.

The policy options approach taken by Smith appears to hold promise if applied differentially in state and local situations. This themata presents knotty problems to be addressed by decision-makers as they attempt to provide coordinated pathways to services for parents of young handicapped children.

## SUMMARY

The bases upon which decisions are made about the delivery of services to preschool handicapped children and their families are frequently confounded by concepts deeply buried in the minds of the decision-makers, whether they be legislators, administrators, teachers, or parents. Several of these themata have been explored in this chapter, in the hope that the serious reader will be motivated to pursue these concepts in depth and to construct a data-based personal philosophy, well documented, and at the level of conscious awareness. Other similar concepts which need similar investigation include the efficacy of early intervention, the focus of service, the inclusion of at-risk children who may not be diagnosed as handicapped, the integration/segregation issue, as well as issues surrounding home based versus center based programs, half-day versus full-day programs, and issues involved in the training of personnel to serve the full range of preschool handicapped children. The exciting challenges in the field of preschool programming lie in the pursuit of progress in seeking answers to these issues.

## REFERENCES

Bandura, A. (1969). Social-learning theory of identification processes. In D. A. Goslin (Ed.), *Handbook of socialization theory and research*. New York: Rand McNally.

Binet, A. (1911). L'Education de l'intelligence. Translated from Les Idées modernes sur les enfants. Chapter V, Part III. In S. A. Kirk F. E. Lord (Eds.), *Exceptional children: Educational resources and perspectives* (pp. 141–161). Boston: Houghton Mifflin Co.

Bowlby, J. (1969). *Maternal care and mental health.* Geneva: World Health Organization.

Bronfenbrenner, U. (Ed.). (1972). *Influences on human development.* Hinsdale, IL: The Dryden Press, Inc.

Bronfenbrenner, U. (1974). *A report on longitudinal evaluations of preschool programs, Vol. 1. Is early intervention effective?* Washington, DC: Department of Health, Education and Welfare, Publication No. (OHD) 74–25.

Burt, C. (1959). Class differences in general intelligence: III. *British Journal of Statistical Psychology, 12,* 15–33.

Burt, C. (1972). The inheritance of general intelligence. *American Psychology, 27,* 175–190.

Casto, G. (in press). The efficacy of early intervention programs for handicapped children: A meta-analysis. *Exceptional Children.*

Chall, J. (1981). Educational implications of recent brain research. In *Educational Leadership. Association for Supervision and Curriculum Development.*

Clarke, A. M., & Clarke, A. D. B. (1976). *Early experience: Myth and evidence.* London: Open Books Publishing Limited.

Consortium for Longitudinal Studies. (1983). *As the twig is bent. . . . Lasting effects of preschool programs.* Hillsdale, NJ: Lawrence Erlbaum.

Dobzhansky, T. (1962). *Mankind evolving.* New Haven: Yale University Press.

Durkheim, E. (1915). *Elementary forms of religious life.*

Epstein, H. (1978). Growth spurts during brain development: Implications for educational policy. In J. Chall (Ed.), *Education and the brain.* Chicago: National Society for the Study of Education.

Eysenck, H. (1971). *The IQ argument. Race, intelligence and education.* New York: Library Press.

Farber, B. (1985). *Families with mentally retarded members: An agenda for research—1985–2000.* Unpublished paper, Arizona State University, Tempe, AZ.

Fuerstein, R. (1980). *Instrumental enrichment.* Baltimore: University Park Press.

Freud, S. (1949). *An outline of psychoanalysis.* J. Strachey (Trans.). London: Hogarthe Press.

Galton, F. (1980). Inquiries into the human faculty and its development. In Plomin, DeFries, & McLearn (Eds.), *Behavioral genetics: A primer* (p. 27, 1980). San Francisco: W. H. Freeman (Original work published in 1883).

Gould, S. J. (1981). *The mismeasure of man.* New York: W. W. Norton & Co.

Hart, L. A. (1981). Educational implications of recent brain research. In Educational Leadership. Association for Supervision and Curriculum Development.

Hebb, D. O. (1949). *The organization of behavior.* New York: John Wiley.

Holton, G. (1973). *Thematic origins of scientific thought.* Cambridge: Harvard University Press.

Hunt, J. McV. (1961). *Intelligence and experience.* New York: Ronald Press.

Hunt, J. McV. (1980). *Early psychological development and experience* (Vol. X). Clark University Press.

Itard, J. M. G. (1932). *The wild boy of Aveyron.* (Translated from the French by G. Humphrey and M. Humphrey). New York: Appleton-Century-Crofts.

Jensen, A. R. (1969). How much can we boost I.Q. and scholastic achievement? *Harvard Educational Review, 39,* 1–123.

Kagan, J., & Moss, H. A. (1962). *Birth to maturity.* NY: John Wiley.

Karnes, M. (1972). *GOAL: Language development.* Springfield, MA: Milton Bradley.

Kirk, S. A. (1958). *Early education of the mentally retarded.* Urbana, IL: University of Illinois Press.

Kirk, S. A., & Chalfant, J. C. (1984). *Academic and developmental learning disabilities.* Denver: Love Publishing Co.

Lillie, D. (1975). *Early childhood education: An individualized approach to developmental instruction.* Chicago: Science Research Associates.

McCarthy, J., & Daley, J. M. (1985). *Young children with handicaps: Arizona's most precious renewable natural resource*. Phoenix, AZ: Governor's Council on Developmental Disabilities.

McCarthy, J., Lund, K., Bos, C. (1985). *Arizona basic assessment criterion utilization system*. Denver: Love Publishing Co.

Minskoff, G., Wiseman, D., & Minskoff, E. (1972). *The MWM program for developing language abilities*. Ridgefield, NJ: Educational Performance Associates.

Morgan, P. (1975). *Child care: Sense and fable*. London: Temple Smith.

Osgood, C. E. (1954). Psycholinguistics: A survey of theory and research problems. *Journal of Abnormal Social Psychology, 49,* Part 2, Supplement.

Piaget, J. (1952). *The origins of intelligence in children*. New York: International Universities Press.

Ramey, C. T., Ferran, D. C., & Campbell, F. A. (1979). Early intervention: From research to practice. In B. L. Darby and M. J. May (Eds.), *Infant assessment: Issues and applications* (pp. 215–232). Seattle: Western States Technical Assistance Resource.

Rutter, M. (1972). *Maternal deprivation reassessed*. Harmondsworth: Penguin.

Seguin, E. (1866). *Idiocy: Its treatment by the psychological method* (reprinted 1907). New York: Teachers College Press.

Sinnott, E. W., Dunn, L. C., & Dobzhansky, T. G. (1958). Principles of genetics. N.Y.: McGraw-Hill.

Skeels, H. M., & Dye, H. B. (1939). A study of the effects of differential stimulation on mentally retarded children. *Proceedings of the American Association on Mental Deficiency, 44,* 114–136.

Skodak, M. (1939). Children in foster homes: A study of mental development. *University of Iowa Studies in Child Welfare, 15,* No. 4.

Smith, B. J. (1980). *Policy options related to the provision of appropriate early intervention services for very young exceptional children and their families*. Unpublished manuscript. Reston, VA: Council for Exceptional Children.

Sylvester, R. (1981). Educational implications of recent brain research. In *Educational leadership. Association for supervisors and curriculum development*.

Thurstone, L. L. (1947). *Multiple factor analysis*. Chicago: University of Chicago Press.

Uzgiris, I., & Hunt, J. McV. (1975). *Assessment in infancy: Ordinal scales of psychological development*. Urbana: University of Illinois Press.

Voigt, I. C. (1957).

Walsh, R. (1981). *Towards an ecology of brain*. Jamaica, NY: Spectrum Publications.

Weikart, D. P., Rogers, L., Adcock, C., & McClelland, D. (1971). *The cognitively oriented curriculum: A framework for preschool teachers*. Urbana: University of Illinois.

Westinghouse Learning Corporation. (1969). *The impact of Head Start: An evaluation of the Head Start experience on children's cognitive and affective development*. Westinghouse Learning Corporation, Ohio University.

Wiegerink, R., & Bartel, J. M. (1981). *Early childhood services in the 80's*. Prepared for the National Review of Child Development Project. Chapel Hill: Frank Porter Graham Child Development Center, University of North Carolina.

Wittrock, M. C. (1981). Educational implications of recent brain research. In *Educational Leadership. Association for Supervisors and Curriculum Development*.

# OVERVIEW

## Barbara K. Keogh

Authors in this volume have addressed a number of different problems of development in the preschool years. Their perspectives vary somewhat according to individual interests and expertise, and according to the particular problem under consideration. Despite these differences in emphases and perspectives, however, there are some striking commonalities and consistencies which deserve discussion as they point toward greater understanding of developmental problems in the early years. The consistencies also underscore important areas to consider when planning and implementing services for young handicapped children.

Two important and related points, regardless of the nature of the disability or risk conditions, had to do with multiple influences and with transactional effects. Sameroff's (1975) transactional model has clearly had a major impact on how problems in development are conceptualized; the model has changed our perspectives about treatment and prognosis. Within the framework of a transactional model development is obviously not a linear, monotonic function; and, biological predispositions and maturational forces do not provide a full explanation or description of development or of problems in development. The rate and degree

Advances in Special Education, Volume 5, pages 275–278.
Copyright © 1986 by JAI Press Inc.
All rights of reproduction in any form reserved.
ISBN: 0-89232-313-2

of development of children with various kinds of handicaps, thus, are not just matters of child conditions. Understanding handicapped children's development of necessity requires consideration of contributions which are not exclusively child-locussed, but rather which take into account the powerful and continuing interactions between child and environment. The importance of non-child variables on children "at risk" has been well illustrated by Sameroff and Chandler (1975). Authors in the present volume provide further evidence for the notion of transactional effects, and the volume as a whole argues for the necessity of such a model in the study and treatment of handicapped children.

While the transactional model has proved to be an important influence on our thinking, it also presents a number of problems for researchers and clinicians who work with young handicapped children. Inherent in the model is the assumption that many factors contribute to growth. Some may be facilitating, others may be disruptive, some may have a negative impact. From a research perspective understanding the development of handicapped children requires consideration of many influences. Thus, research designs and analytic approaches must necessarily be modified to include many variables. Univariate research designs, while reasonably direct and manageable, do not incorporate the range of influences which affect development. It should not surprise us, then, that univariate approaches shed relatively little light on the nature of development of children with handicaps. Research carried out within a transactional framework by definition must be concerned with an increasingly large number of child and extra-child variables. The clinical corollary is that treatment and intervention must also be directed at a range of possible influences. Short term, child-focussed treatment programs may be useful in teaching particular skills but treatment programs aimed at broader developmental changes must include a range of individual and setting considerations. The broadening of intervention to be consistent with the notion of multiple transactions places an additional, albeit positive, burden on clinicians.

Fundamental to the transactional model is recognition that change produces change in an ongoing sequence. Thus, the handicapped child and family we study today will likely not be the same child and family we study at another time period. The point has been touched upon by a number of authors in this volume. Two illustrations will suffice. The impact of a handicapped child's mastery of simple self-help skills changes his relationship to his parents, allowing them to devote their energies and time to other aspects of his development. Changes in his experiences and interactions in turn may lead to improved mastery behavior. Less positively, a handicapped child's language delay may lead to parental discouragement and withdrawal, thus further limiting the child's opportunities for language interaction and delaying his communication skills. Because children influence parents and parents influence children we must expect changes over time. From a research perspective this means multiple data collection points. From a clinical perspective it means multiple and continuing services. The stable family which is doing well in one time period may be a fragmented and disturbed family in another time period. Assessing and understanding the long term consequences of handicapping conditions from a transactional perspective presents challenging problems to researchers and clinicians alike. At the same time, such an approach increases enormously our insights into the nature of development of handicapped young children, a point well argued by authors in this volume.

Another and closely related point of commality had to do with the caution with which authors approached questions of prediction of long term consequences of handicapping conditions. Whether the focus was on language, affective-behavioral, social, motor, or cognitive problems, the complexity of prediction of outcome based on child condition alone was underscored in the materials in the present volume. The continuum of *biological* casualty and the continuum of *care taking* casualty are interactive, and both contribute to handicapped children's development. Given the complexities of these contributions and the still unspecified nature of their interactions and transactions, it is not surprising that prediction is limited. Whether in Kuai, Canada, Britain, or the continental United States, prediction of outcomes for individual children is still "iffy." As evidenced in the content of this volume, our predictions for groups of risk children have become more accurate. Yet, the course of progress for individual children is still less certain.

Material in this volume also underscored the difficulties in measuring important variables in the developmental equation. For the most part, standardized assessment techniques provide only gross estimates of developmental status and they are sorely limited as means of documenting change. Further, they tend to be focussed on a relatively narrow array of child characteristics. We lack refined measures of a host of motor, affective, motivational, social, and attitudinal variables, and we have only gross techniques for describing families, homes, schools, or treatments. It is not surprising, then, that our efforts to understand family-child or child-family-school transactions are limited. Recognition of the limitations of well used developmental assessment techniques does not negate their clinical usefulness nor their value in describing groups of handicapped children. However, their limitations become apparent when we attempt to document and understand the functional interactions and transactions between child and parent, or between family and clinician. It may be necessary to develop techniques which allow accumulation of more broadly based data in order to capture the ongoing nature of these interactions. Despite the functional usefulness of current assessment methods, it is clear that measurement is still a major issue in the study of developmental problems in the early years.

A final point of agreement among authors deserves brief discussion as it may set a tone for the future. A number of difficulties and problems in carrying out research or in working directly with young handicapped children and their families have been discussed. Yet, there is throughout this volume a sense of progress and of optimism. The last 2 decades have yielded a number of major theoretical

and practical advances. Early identification and intervention techniques have improved, and legislative and legal protections have become more comprehensive. We know more about medical preventive techniques and we are increasingly sensitive to the effects of social and economic status on the developmental progress of young handicapped or at risk children. Our theoretical notions about development, especially the development of handicapped children, are more complex but more powerful. Although there is a great deal to be done, on a scientific level we have at least some reasons to be optimistic. However, the impact of greater understanding on families and children will be felt only if we are willing to implement our knowledge. Whether or not our optimism is warranted will likely depend more upon policy makers and advocates than upon researchers and clinicians. As noted over 15 years ago by Sarason and Doris (1969), "Facts and theories never lead to social action programs—it is only when expert knowledge interacts with a meaningful value system that programs involving social action occur" (p. 252).

# REFERENCES

Sameroff, A. J. (1975). Early influences on development: Fact or fancy? *Merrill-Palmer Quarterly, 20,* 270–301.

Sameroff, A. J., & Chandler, J. J. (1975). Reproductive risk and the continuum of caretaking casualty. In F. D. Horowitz, E. M. Hetherington, S. Scarr-Salapatek, & G. Siegel (Eds.), *Review of child development research* (Vol 4). Chicago, IL: University of Chicago Press.

Sarason, S. B., & Doris, J. A. (1969). *Psychological problems in mental deficiency* (4th ed). New York: Harper & Row.

# INDEX

# Research Annuals and Monographs in Series
## in the
# BEHAVIORAL SCIENCES

**Research Annuals**

**Advances in Adolescent Mental Health**
Edited by Ronald, A. Feldman and Arlene R. Stiffman, *Center for Adolescent Mental Health, Washington University*

**Advances in Behavioral Assessment of Children and Families**
Edited by Ron Prinz, *Department of Psychology, University of South Carolina*

**Advances in Behavioral Medicine**
Edited by Edward S. Katkin, *Department of Psychology, State University of New York at Buffalo* and Stephen B. Manuck, *Department of Psychology, University of Pittsburgh*

**Advances in Business Marketing**
Edited by Arch G. Woodside, *College of Business Administration, University of South Carolina*

**Advances in Descriptive Psychology**
Edited by Keith E. Davis, *Department of Psychology, University of South Carolina* and Thomas O. Mitchell, *Department of Psychology, Southern Illinois University*

**Advances in Developmental and Behavioral Pediatrics**
Edited by Mark Wolraich, *Department of Pediatrics, University of Iowa* and Donald K. Routh, *Department of Psychology, University of Iowa*

**Advances in Early Education and Day Care**
Edited by Sally J. Kilmer, *Department of Home Economics, Bowling Green State University*

**Advances in Family Intervention, Assessment and Theory**
Edited by John P. Vincent, *Department of Psychology, University of Houston*

**Advances in Health Education and Promotion**
Edited by William B. Ward, *School of Public Health, University of South Carolina*

**Advances in Human Psychopharmacology**
Edited by Graham D. Burrows, *Department of Psychiatry, University of Melbourne* and John S. Werry, *Department of Psychiatry, University of Auckland*

**Advances in Law and Child Development**
Edited by Robert L. Sprague, *Institute for Child Behavior and Development, University of Illinois*

**Advances in Learning and Behavioral Disabilities**
Edited by Kenneth D. Gadow, *Office of Special Education, State University of New York, Stony Brook*

**Advances in Marketing and Public Policy**
Edited by Paul N. Bloom, *Department of Marketing, University of Maryland*

**Advances in Mental Retardation and Developmental Disabilities**
Edited by Stephen E. Breuning, Director of Psychological Services and Behavioral Treatment Polk Center, Johnny L. Matson, *Department of Learning and Development, Northern Illinois University,* and Rowland P. Barrett, *Section on Psychiatry and Human Behavior, Brown University Program in Medicine*

**Advances in Motivation and Achievement**
Edited by Martin L. Maehr, *Institute for Child Behavior and Development, University of Illinois*

**Advances in Nonprofit Marketing**
Edited by Russell W. Belk, *Department of Marketing, University of Utah*

**Advances in Psychophysiology**
Edited by Patrick K. Ackles, *Institute for the Study of Developmental Disabilities, University of Illinois at Chicago,* Richard Jennings, *Western Psychiatric Institute and Clinic, University of Pittsburgh School of Medicine* and Michael G.H. Coles, *Department of Psychology, University of Illinois*

**Advances in Reading/Language Research**
  Edited by Barbara Hutson, *College of Education, Virginia Polytechnic Institute and State University*

**Advances in Special Education**
  Edited by Barbara K. Keogh, *Graduate School of Education, University of California at Los Angeles*

**Advances in Substance Abuse**
  Edited by Nancy K. Mello, *Alcohol and Drug Abuse Research Center, Harvard Medical School McLean Hospital*

**Annals of Child Development**
  Edited by Grover J. Whitehurst, *Department of Psychology, State University of New York at Stony Brook*

**Annual Review of Psychopathology**
  Edited by Peter A. Magaro, *Department of Psychology, The Ohio State University*

**Perspectives in Personality: Theory, Measurement and Interpersonal Dynamics**
  Edited by Robert Hogan and Warren H. Jones, *Department of Psychology, University of Tulsa*

**Research in Community and Mental Health**
  Edited by James R. Greenley, *Department of Psychiatry, University of Wisconsin Medical School*

**Research in Consumer Behavior**
  Edited by Jagdish N. Sheth, *School of Business, University of Southern California*

**Research in Marketing**
  Edited by Jagdish N. Sheth, *School of Business, University of Southern California*

**Research in Organizational Behavior**
  Edited by Barry M. Staw, *School of Business Administration, University of California, Berkeley* and L.L. Cummings, *J.L. Kellogg Graduate School of Management, Northwestern University*

**Research in Personnel and Human Resources Management**
  Edited by Kendrith M. Rowland, *Department of Business Administration, University of Illinois* and Gerald R. Ferris, *Department of Management, Texas A & M University*


**Monographs in Series**


**Contemporary Studies in Applied Behavioral Science**
  Series Editor: Louis A. Zurcher, *School of Social Work, University of Texas at Austin*

**Handbook in Behavioral Economics**
  Edited by Stanley Kaish and Benny Gilad, *Department of Economics, Rutgers University*

**Monographs in Organizational Behavior and Industrial Relations**
  Edited by Samual B. Bacharach, *Department of Organizational Behavior, New York State School of Industrial and Labor Relations, Cornell University*


*Please inquire for detailed brochure on each series*

 **JAI PRESS INC., 36 Sherwood Place. P.O. Box 1678
Greenwich, Connecticut 06836**
**Telephone: 203-661-7602          Cable Address: JAIPUBL**